Contents

Adobe® Premiere® Elements 2

Steve Grisetti
Chuck Engels

in a Snap

SAMS
Teach
Yourself

Sams Publishing, 800 East 96th Street, Indianapolis, Indiana 46240 USA

Adobe® Premiere® Elements 2 In a Snap

International Standard Book Number: 0-672-32853-4

Library of Congress Catalog Card Number: 2005929747

Printed in the United States of America

First Printing: December 2005

08   07   06   05   4   3   2   1

Trademarks

Warning and Disclaimer

Bulk Sales

Sams Publishing offers excellent discounts on this book when ordered in quantity for bulk purchases or special sales. For more information, please contact

> **U.S. Corporate and Government Sales**
> **1-800-382-3419**
> corpsales@pearsontechgroup.com

For sales outside of the U.S., please contact

> **International Sales**
> international@pearsoned.com

Acquisitions Editor
Linda Bump Harrison

Development Editor
Alice Martina Smith

Managing Editor
Charlotte Clapp

Project Editor
Tonya Simpson

Production Editor
Heather Wilkins

Indexer
Ken Johnson

Proofreader
Lisa Wilson

Technical Editor
Douglas Dixon

Publishing Coordinator
Vanessa Evans

Multimedia Developer
Dan Scherf

Interior Designer
Gary Adair

Cover Designer
Gary Adair

Page Layout
Bronkella Publishing

About the Authors

 Steve Grisetti earned a master's degree in writing for television and film from Ohio University. He has taught college-level courses in television and video production and adult education classes on Photoshop and principles of design. Steve spent nearly 10 years in the Los Angeles–based entertainment industry, working on the sets and in the production offices of several large television and film companies. He is currently employed as a graphic designer in the marketing and communications department of a Milwaukee-based investment firm. He also serves as host on Adobe's official Premiere Elements Support Forum (http://www.adobeforums.com/cgi-bin/webx?14@@.3bb574e6).

 **Chuck Engels** graduated from Trans American School of Broadcasting in Wausau, Wisconsin. He worked in the radio industry for five years and studied theater and film at the University of Minnesota. Chuck has spent the past 18 years in the transportation industry, in management, and in software development. He currently lives near Atlanta, Georgia, with his wife and three children. He is a senior programmer and analyst in the software development department for an Atlanta-based freight transportation company. Chuck is also involved in the media department for a 10,000-member church, and is an active member and regular contributor to the Adobe Premiere Elements User Forum. Chuck also hosts a website where users can share their videos, tips, and tricks (http://www.chuckengels.com/PremierVideo).

Dedications

As a veteran of several nonlinear editing systems, I have been a big supporter of this amazing program since discovering it shortly after its release. You'll find me regularly on the Premiere Elements's peer-to-peer users' forum, where it's been my privilege to share my experience, learn from others, and above all, enjoy the friendship and inspiration of my fellow video makers. I dedicate this book to them, as well as to dear Jeanne, who has so patiently lent her much-appreciated support throughout the writing of this book, and to the amazing Sarah, who made me believe a little girl could fly.
—*Steve Grisetti*

This book is dedicated to my God and Savior; my wife, Criss; and my children, Heather, Britt, and Josh. Without your love, support, and sacrifice, none of this would have been possible. I humbly thank you all.
—*Chuck Engels*

Acknowledgments

In any major undertaking, there are many people who knowingly or unknowingly play big roles. The following people have played their parts well and to them I am truly thankful: Linda Harrison, for her help and support through this entire process. Alice Martina Smith, Tonya Simpson, Heather Wilkins, and Douglas Dixon, for giving us such great advice and timely help; you all helped make this book the best. The Media Department at Trinity Chapel, especially Tres, Rich, Hector, and Pastor Randy; you have inspired me more than you will ever know. To my bosses and co-workers, who have bent over backward to give me the time to write this book; a special thanks to Glenn, Keith, Greg, and Dan. To everyone who prayed for me; your prayers were answered, and I thank you. All of my fellow Premiere Elements forum members are as much a part of this book as I am. And finally, to Steve Grisetti, a man I truly respect and admire. He has helped me in more ways than he will ever know, and I consider it an honor to be his co-author.

—Chuck Engels

Likewise, I've enjoyed the privilege of working with the ever-patient Linda Harrison as well as the entire development team at Sams Publishing. Thank you for making us look great! And Chuck, my partner and my friend, it's been a pleasure sharing this adventure with you.

—Steve Grisetti

We Want to Hear from You!

As the reader of this book, *you* are our most important critic and commentator. We value your opinion and want to know what we're doing right, what we could do better, what areas you'd like to see us publish in, and any other words of wisdom you're willing to pass our way.

You can email or write me directly to let me know what you did or didn't like about this book—as well as what we can do to make our books stronger.

Please note that I cannot help you with technical problems related to the topic of this book, and that due to the high volume of mail I receive, I might not be able to reply to every message.

When you write, please be sure to include this book's title and author as well as your name and phone or email address. I will carefully review your comments and share them with the author and editors who worked on the book.

E-mail: graphics@samspublishing.com

Mail: Mark Taber
Associate Publisher
Sams Publishing
800 East 96th Street
Indianapolis, IN 46240 USA

Reader Services

For more information about this book or another Sams Publishing title, visit our website at **www.samspublishing.com**. Type the ISBN (excluding hyphens) or the title of a book in the **Search** field to find the page you're looking for.

Bonus Content on the Web

Visit **www.samspublishing.com/title/0672328534**, register your book, and download additional information to enhance your Premiere Elements experience:

- Guide to setting preferences
- Description of available transitions and effects
- Sample videos illustrating effects taught in this book

✔ Start Here

It really is pretty amazing when you think about how far video technology has come in such a short time. Just a little more than 20 years ago, broadcast professionals were editing analog video using what was essentially a mechanical controller between two VCRs. (And, before that, editors were literally cutting and splicing tape—a primitive age best forgotten.) The innovation of computer-based, nonlinear digital editing has not only changed the way video is assembled, it has changed our entire concept of the editing process.

Nonlinear editing takes a process that was once stressful, time-consuming, and expensive, and turns it into something that is intuitive, simple, and above all, easily revisable. There's more freedom to be creative, to try new things, to experiment, and to play.

Before Premiere Elements, most video-editing software aimed at consumers was designed with an easy-to-use interface as its priority. Adobe, however, took a different tack. Using as its base its top-of-the-line prosumer video-editing software, Premiere Pro, Adobe stripped back a few higher-end and professional features (features you will probably never miss), made many of the features more user-friendly, and produced an application that combines both a relatively simple, intuitive interface with the power and customizable features of a professional editing package. A product that's easy to learn—and yet capable of going as deep as the user dares to dig.

But dig a little deeper and you'll find even more. And more. In fact, every time you think you've discovered everything this program can do, you round a corner and find even more features, more things to customize, and more tricks, tweaks, and new applications. Premiere Elements can take you as far as you dare to go with your videos.

And that's the good news.

The bad news, though, is now that you are armed with Premiere Elements 2.0 and this book, you're never again going to have an excuse for creating a less-than-dazzling video. No more shoot-and-play home movies. No more boring family vacation videos.

Such is the responsibility that comes with a master's knowledge.

What Is Nonlinear Editing?

Throughout most of the past half century, video editing was done using a linear system. In other words, if you had a scene at the beginning of a videotape and you wanted to cut from it to a scene at the end of a videotape, you had to locate and dub the first scene onto a master tape, then *physically wind the tape* to the other end, locate the next scene and then dub it onto the master. It took a lot of time and effort and, as whenever such logistics are challenging, it stifled, at least to some small degree, the creative process.

Nonlinear editing, which professionals began to incorporate into their workflow in the late 1980s, is about having an easier and more efficient way to access, juggle, and trim video clips. With nonlinear editing, rather than your video clips being stored in a linear format (such as on a videotape), scenes or clips are stored in an easily accessible catalog or bin where they can be quickly grabbed in any order, thrown together, cut, trimmed, rearranged, and reassembled. Your project can then be easily previewed, test-driven, undone, redone, revised, tweaked, and massaged until it is precisely the movie you want to make—and all with little more effort than editing text in a word processor.

▶ KEY TERM

Nonlinear editing—A computer-based video-editing system in which collected media can be easily assembled, trimmed, and re-ordered indefinitely.

This innovation gives you total creative freedom to experiment, to dream, to pull together in seconds what used to take minutes or hours—and then to throw it all away and try it again without even working up a sweat. That's total creative freedom, unhindered by any logistics.

And there's another advantage to nonlinear editing: The process is *nondestructive*. Simply put, this means that no matter what or how much you cut, trim, or manipulate your video project, the original clips remain unaltered. You can safely experiment with dozens of clips and effects assemblages, knowing that nothing you do will affect the original footage. The original clips remain fresh and unchanged, ready to be re-used or reassembled into the next draft. Nothing is risked, nothing that's done can't be undone. It's like sketching with a pencil attached to the world's most efficient eraser!

► **NOTE**

In addition to the nondestructive nature of the nonlinear editing process, Premiere Elements offers the option to Undo (**Ctrl+Z**) all the way back to the most recent opening of your project. You can also jump back to certain points in your work by locating these points in the **History** panel.

A Few Key Premiere Elements Terms You Ought to Know

Before you begin to explore this program, several key features and terms, some unique to or uniquely used by Premiere Elements 2.0, crop up regularly. You'll definitely want to be clear on their definitions before you move forward:

The Media Panel
Folders   Clips

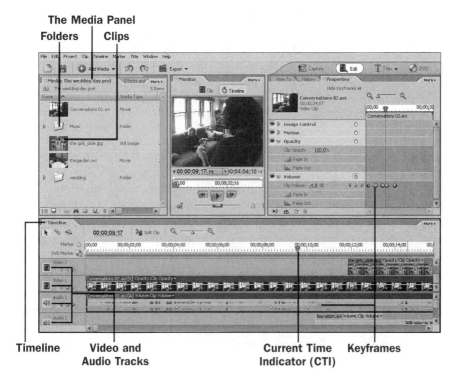

Timeline   Video and   Current Time   Keyframes
**   Audio Tracks   Indicator (CTI)**

- *Timeline*—This is where it all happens. The **Timeline** is the set of video and audio tracks where your clips assemble to become your video project. It's where you paint your masterpiece of sounds and images in time. Premiere Elements offers one of the most versatile timelines available at this level of software with the potential for a virtually unlimited number of video and audio tracks. (See **29 About the Timeline and Video Layers**.)

  The vertical hairline that moves along the **Timeline** and indicates what part of the project is currently being viewed in the **Monitor** panel is called the current time indicator, or *CTI* for short.

▶ KEY TERMS

Timeline—The linear panel in which audio and video clips are assembled to create a video project.

CTI—The current time indicator is the vertical hairline that indicates your frame position on the **Timeline** (also known as the *playhead*).

- *Clip*—Although this word usually refers to a segment of video footage, Premiere Elements also uses the word to describe audio, photos, graphics, and other media you use in your video project. The reason for using *clips* as a universal term for your media is that, as far as your **Timeline** is concerned, all media is handled the same way. All clips—all media added to the **Timeline**— can be trimmed, sliced, effected, and transitioned into and out of.

▶ KEY TERM

Clip—Any graphic, still, audio, or video segment placed on the **Timeline** in a video project.

- *Folders*—Folders are one of the most useful and under-used features of the **Media** panel (the panel to which all your clips are added when you import them into your project and from which you drag clips to the **Timeline**) and a feature Adobe has been incorporating into virtually all its products. What do you do when you've captured dozens of clips for your project and you're going crazy sifting through them all every time you want to locate one for a scene you're building? Add a folder to the **Media** panel. In fact, add several folders. Even add folders within folders. Name them. Drag your clips into them. When every set of clips is neatly categorized, you're just a few clicks away from any clip you want. (See **16 Create and Use Media Folders**.)

▶ KEY TERM

Folders—A sorting system used in the **Media** panel (similar to Windows Explorer's folder system) in which clips can be stored in collections and subcollections for easy access and categorization.

- *Scrubbing*—This term is used to describe the process of moving the CTI back and forth across the **Timeline** to locate a scene or to test a cut, transition, or effect. Premiere Elements offers a variety of ways to do this at a variety of speeds, including keyboard shortcuts and mouse controls. Scrubbing is something you'll be doing countless times as you build your project, and you'll very quickly be operating the controls without even thinking about it. But the important thing for now is that when someone mentions scrubbing you know what he is talking about.

▶ KEY TERM

Scrubbing—Manually moving the CTI back and forth along the **Timeline** to locate a specific clip or frame or to test a transition. Watch the video in the **Monitor** panel as you scrub on the **Timeline**.

- **Video tracks**—Think of your video tracks as a stack of clips. Most of the time, you'll only see the clip on the top of the stack. But if you resize the top clip or make portions of it transparent, the clip below shows. Resize or reshape many layers or add transparency to them, and you can see down through several layers of video clips at the same time. You can add a virtually unlimited number of video and/or audio tracks to your Premiere Elements project. When you start seeing how useful tracks can be, you'll wonder how you ever edited without them. (See **30** **Add, Delete, and Size Tracks**.)

- *Keyframing*—A key tool in Premiere Elements that, once mastered, will give you an amazing amount of control over virtually every other feature and effect in the program. The principle of keyframes is basically this: You indicate the frames on your **Timeline** in which you want an effect to occur or a position or effect to change; Premiere Elements automatically creates the movement, effect, or animation transitioning between these frames. Keyframing shows up in many of this book's tasks. After you develop an understanding of how the process works, you'll find a universe of ways to customize your effects, animation, and transitions with them. (See **67** **About Keyframing**.)

▶ KEY TERM

Keyframing—The method used by Premiere Elements (as well as Premiere Pro and After Effects) for creating motion paths and transitioning effects. Points representing precise settings for effects or positions are placed on the **Timeline**, and the program automatically creates a movement or transition between those points.

- *Rendering*—In common video-editing use, this term refers to the process of converting nonvideo clips (such as photos) or clips that have had **Transitions** or effects applied to them into frames of video. But there's another definition of this term that comes up regularly. As you add nonvideo media (such as photos and graphics) to your **Timeline**, you'll notice a red line appearing on the **Timeline** above the clips. The red line indicates that this segment of your timeline has not yet been hard rendered. So how does this affect your life? Well, when you first play back a still or clip that's been effected or keyframed (or a transition that has been added between two not-yet-rendered clips), you might be a little disappointed with the preview. That's because Premiere Elements is desperately trying to create these changed frames on the fly—and depending on how intensely you've affected the clips and how powerful your computer is, the result can look rather ragged and choppy. Rendering this segment creates a temporary file to which the program can refer that displays a much clearer preview of what your final output will look like. This type of hard rendering is easy. Just press the **Enter** key and watch as the red line turns green. Of course, if you change the effect or transition, you'll need to re-render the segment. Rendering usually takes only a few seconds. When it's done, you are able to see exactly what this portion of your video will look like when you're finished. (See **43** **About Rendering the Timeline.**)

▶ **KEY TERM**

Rendering—The process in which Premiere Elements creates video frames from stills or transitioned or effected video clips.

Getting to Know Premiere Elements 2.0

If you're a veteran of Premiere Elements 1.0, you'll find much of version 2.0 very familiar. Ergonomic enhancements have been added to the workspaces to make your workflow more efficient, but if you've mastered 1.0, you'll likely feel right at home with 2.0. And as you dig a bit deeper, you'll start to appreciate just how improved and how powerful this program has become.

For one thing, Premiere Elements 2.0 is much more tolerant of non-DV-AVI files, especially MPEGs. In fact, not only can you use the Adobe **Media Downloader** to load files from MPEG sources, including DVD camcorders attached via USB, but this new feature also brings photos and video clips in directly from digital still cameras, rips VOB files (the audio, video, and menu files on DVDs) from non–copy-protected DVDs, and even grabs photos and video from most picture phones. (See **14** **Add Media with the Adobe Media Downloader.**)

Granted, every unusual file type brings with it some potential liability. Premiere Elements is, after all, built around a DV-AVI workflow, the PC-based file format produced when digital video is imported using FireWire. But in version 2.0, any issues with non-DV-AVI files will be few and far between. And that's a major development.

Other new features, including version 2.0's greatly enhanced DVD workspace, are detailed in the next section.

If you're moving to Premiere Elements 2.0 from another PC-based video-editing software, you might at first be intimidated by the program's interface. It's not as immediately accessible as say, Pinnacle's Studio or Ulead's VideoStudio. And if you've never edited on a computer before, you might be completely lost at first. On the other hand, the interface isn't nearly as complicated as it appears on first pass, and most of the controls are fairly intuitive to operate after you learn where to look for them.

Premiere Elements is, in essence, a slightly scaled-down version of its big brother, Premiere Pro, long the standard for PC-based prosumer editing software. In fact, it maintains a remarkable number of Pro's features (just as Photoshop Elements maintains a remarkable number of Photoshop's features). But that doesn't mean that these features are complicated or hard to use. After you learn a few basic principles (which this book is designed to provide), you'll feel right at home here. And when you realize how much you can do with this program and how many ways you can customize your effects, we're betting you'll never look back.

New Features in Version 2.0

Premiere Elements 2.0 offers a variety of new features, including some very nice aesthetic and ergonomic improvements:

- All clips added to the **Timeline** offer convenient controls for adjusting image quality, position, opacity, and volume control. In addition, one-click switches have been included so clips can easily be rotated in 90° increments and video and audio fades can be instantly added.

- As an enhancement to its Add Media function, Premiere Elements 2.0 now includes the Adobe **Media Downloader**, a feature for adding files directly from scanners, digital cameras, and a variety of devices attached by USB, including DVD camcorders and picture phones. The Adobe **Media Downloader** can also rip video files directly from non–copy-protected DVDs.

- In addition to FireWire capture, Premiere Elements 2.0 also includes support for capture from camcorders that use the new USB Video Class 1.0 standard.

One of the biggest improvements in version 2.0 is its enhanced DVD authoring capabilities. Some new menu templates have been added and all templates now offer the ability to change fonts and change positions of the menu controls. Adobe has also added the ability to include a customized still or looping video background and an audio track to your menu screens. Although you still can't create DVD menus from scratch in Premiere Elements, this feature does exist in Premiere Elements's companion software, Photoshop Elements 4.0, and these new

Photoshop Elements–created templates are automatically added to the Premiere Elements DVD menu library.

Starting Premiere Elements 2.0

When you first launch Premiere Elements, you will find yourself at the *splash screen*. As you can see, this screen offers three main options: **New Project**, **Open Project**, and **Capture Video**. On the right side of the screen, at the very top, are two other icons, **Tutorials** and **Setup**.

This is the splash screen; it is your starting point whenever you open Premiere Elements.

Use the **New Project** option to start a brand new project. You are asked to name your project before going to the Premiere Elements workspace. Use the **Open Project** option to open an existing project. When you click this icon on the splash screen, the **Browse** dialog box opens so you can select the project you want to open. The **Capture Video** option takes you right to the **Capture** window, ready to capture (import) video. See Chapter 3, "Get the Picture: Capturing Video," for further instructions.

▶ NOTES

Premiere Elements project files end in **.prel**. When looking for existing project files, look for files with the **.prel** extension.

Premiere Elements Version 1 users beware: If you open a version 1 project and save it in version 2, you will not be able to open that project in version 1 again. To preserve the version 1 file, open it and choose **File**, **Save As** to save the file as a version 2 file, leaving the version 1 file unaltered.

When you click the **Tutorials** icon, you are taken into the Premiere Elements workspace and the **Tutorial** project opens. This is a short project, complete with Help, that introduces you to many of the concepts involved in creating a movie. The **Setup** window allows you to set the format for your projects: NTSC or PAL, Standard or Widescreen. (Get to this screen by clicking the **Setup** icon in the upper-right corner of the splash screen.) This is where you select a default format for your first and future projects. By selecting the **New Preset** button, you can change some of the settings and create your own customized preset format, making that the default for your projects. Click **New Project** to begin.

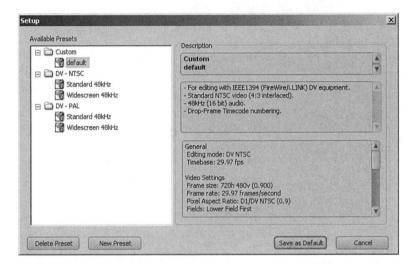

This is the splash screen's **Setup** window; you can select NTSC (the television system primarily used in North America and Japan) or PAL (the television system used in most of Europe) settings for your projects.

Using the Four Main Workspaces

To access the main work area, click the **New Project** icon on the splash screen. Premiere Elements has four main workspaces: **Edit**, **Capture**, **Titles**, and **DVD**, only one of which can be open at any time. When the **Edit** window is showing, there are several panels that also appear.

The **Edit** window is broken up into parts called panels.

▶ **NOTE**

The panels can be added, removed, moved, resized, and rearranged to suit your needs and workflow. To learn how to do this, take a look at **2** Customize Your Workspaces.

✔ Start Here

Taskbar Monitor Panel Workspace Tabs

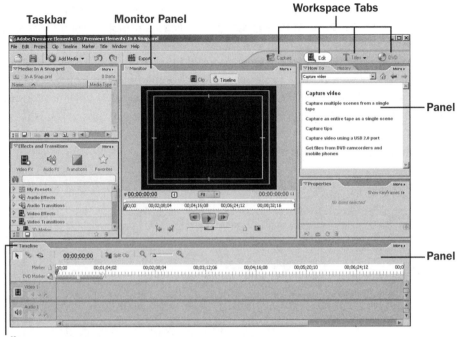

Panel

Panel

Timeline
Panel

Welcome to the Premiere Elements Edit window!

The panels located in each workspace all have context menus. These menus are activated by right-clicking in a blank area of the panel. These context menus give you quick access to many other options and features.

At the top-right of each panel is a small **More** button. The **More** button drops down a list of various options and settings, much like the panel's context menus. The **More** menus are specific to the particular panel they are on. If you are looking for a particular option or setting for a panel, check the panel's **More** button menu; chances are that you will find it there. Information about the individual **More** menus are covered in tasks that make use of that particular panel.

The Edit Workspace

The **Edit** workspace is where you will spend most of your time in Premiere Elements. The **Edit** workspace is where you put brush to canvas and create your video masterpieces. It includes the following panels:

- The **Media** panel is where your video clips, images, titles, and audio files are stored. You can add media to the panel using the **Add Media** button in the taskbar. For more information on adding media, see **14** **Add Media with the Adobe Media Downloader**. The **Media** panel is explained in detail in **13** **About the Media Panel**.

- The **Effects and Transitions** panel is where you select from the hundreds of effects and transitions available to you in Premiere Elements. You can customize most of these effects to suit your needs for each project, making the number virtually limitless. To learn more about effects and transitions, see **44 About Transitions**, **58 About Preset Effects**, and **74 About Advanced Effects**.

- Across the entire bottom of the **Edit** window is the **Timeline** panel. This is where your movie in progress is. You can drag and drop images, clips, titles, and audio from the **Media** panel to the **Timeline**; you can also capture video directly to the **Timeline**. This is where you make cuts and edits, add effects and transitions, and piece your movie together. To learn more about the **Timeline**, see Chapter 6, "Editing on the Timeline."

- In the very center of the screen is the **Monitor** panel. In this panel you can view a clip that's in the **Media** panel (but not yet on the **Timeline**), view the **Timeline**, set in and out points, and create customized effects. To learn more, see **11 View Captured Clips** and **20 Navigate the Monitor Panel**.

- At the top right of the **Edit** workspace are the **How To** and **History** panels. These panels, by default, are nested one over the other. The **How To** panel contains tips and help about Premiere Elements. It has a drop-down menu from which you can select the type of task with which you want help. The **History** panel is where the history of your project is kept. Every cut, effect, transition—everything you do—is kept in the **History** panel to provide a clear view of what you have added or removed, and in what order. The **History** panel, used with the **Undo** and **Redo** functions, is a powerful tool, as described later in this chapter.

▶ NOTE

Any panel can be nested with other panels. To learn more about nesting panels, see **3 Nest Your Panels to Save Desktop Space**.

- The **Properties** panel is where the fun begins. Most of the effects and transitions can be customized in some way, and the **Properties** panel is the place to perform your surgery. The **Properties** panel contains all the effects applied to a clip, with the ability to make modifications. To learn more about the **Properties** panel, see **68 About the Properties Panel**.

The Capture Workspace

To move from the **Edit** workspace to the **Capture** workspace, click the **Capture** tab at the top-right of any screen. The **Capture** workspace has one real purpose: To get video into your project. Whether from a digital camcorder, USB Video Standard 1.0 device, or DV Converter, this is where you go to get the picture. You can learn more about the **Capture** workspace in Chapter 3.

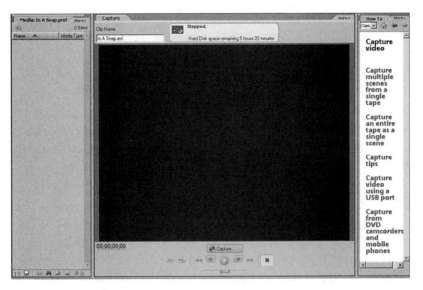

The **Capture** workspace.

The Title Workspace

To view the **Title** workspace, click the **Title** tab at the top-right of any screen. The **Title** workspace is where you create the stunning intros, rolling credits, and subtitles for your movie. Premiere Elements provides more than 280 titles in 10 categories from which you can choose. With the ability to customize the titles any way you want, including making a title from scratch, the list is endless.

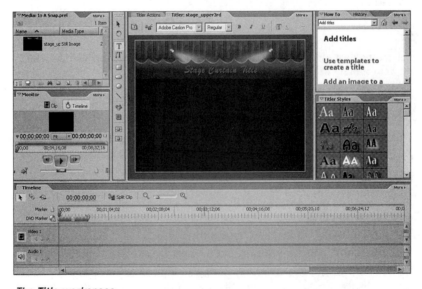

The **Title** workspace.

The center area of the **Title** workspace holds the **Titler** and **Titler Actions** panels. These panels are the workspace for building titles and credits. The options and customization is limited only by your own imagination. The **Titler toolbar**, along the left edge of the **Titler** and **Titler Actions** panels, gives you many options right at your fingertips.

You can give your titles style with the preset fonts provided in the **Titler Styles** panel. You can also customize the fonts or create your own using one of these presets as a template.

To learn more about titles and credits, see Chapter 13, "Adding Text, Creating Titles, Making Credits."

The DVD Workspace

The last main workspace is the **DVD** workspace. It is the final step in creating your movie. Whether you have created a five-minute slideshow or a two-hour epic film, you can burn it to a DVD from the **DVD** workspace. Single-layer and dual-layer DVD support allows you great functionality and a high-quality output no matter how long your video is (for best quality, try to keep your movies to one hour or less for a single-layer DVD, and to two hours or less for a dual-layer DVD).

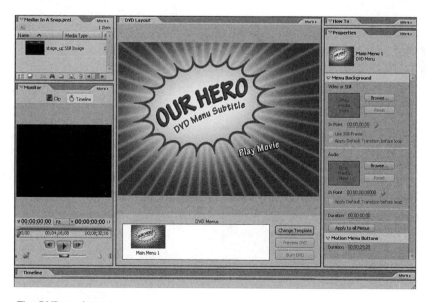

The **DVD** workspace.

From here, you will customize your DVD menu starting with one of the templates (there are more than 60 of them). Again, the ability to customize, add your own images, and change text leaves the possibilities limitless. When you are finished creating your DVD menu, you can burn your DVD movie!

In this workspace you also find the **DVD Layout** panel. This is where you add a DVD menu template, background images, sound, and motion menu buttons; select scenes and scene or chapter menus; and burn your DVD.

Setting Preferences

As is true for most other complex software, Premiere Elements has a litany of preferences you can set to optimize your work with the program. To access the **Preferences** window, choose **Edit**, **Preferences**, and then choose the category of preferences with which you want to work. If you don't know where to start, click the **General** category; you can easily access any category after the **Preferences** window is open by clicking the category name in the list on the left side of the **Preferences** window.

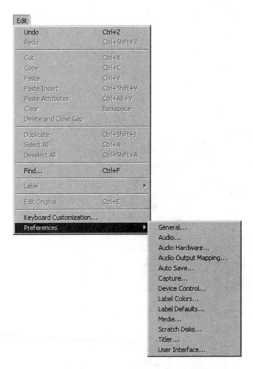

*Open the **Preferences** window and select a category by making a selection from the **Edit** menu.*

Using the History Panel

One of the great features in Premiere Elements is the **History** panel. This is where a complete history of your project is kept. As you add media, drop items on the **Timeline**, add effects, add transitions, and make edits, the **History** panel keeps track of all these activities. You can revert back to any point in time just by clicking on that point in the **History** panel. As you work through your project, keep an eye on the **History** panel to see that everything you do is recorded there. Whereas the **Undo** and **Redo** buttons on the taskbar take you forward or backward through the project history one step at a time, the **History** panel allows you to jump backward and forward in leaps. By clicking a history item early in the project, you can revert back to what everything looked like at that point; then you can jump forward in time again. You also have the ability to delete a history item and clear the history by right-clicking the **History** panel or by clicking the **More** button in the panel's title bar.

The **History** panel.

Understanding the DV-AVI Workflow

When working with Premiere Elements, as with any video-editing software, it's important to understand the difference between digital and analog video. In simple terms, it's the difference between a clock and a digital watch or between a record album and a CD.

In the old days (actually more like 10 years ago), consumer camcorders recorded video the way tape recorders record sound. Impulses of light and sound were translated into electronic pulses that were recorded magnetically onto a moving tape. Naturally, the quality of those pulses was limited by the camera's optics, the quality of the recording head, and the quality of tape. But the biggest liability was that every time a copy was made of the video, it was merely an analog attempt to reproduce an analog signal. With each copy, the quality of the recording diminished. Every generation of the video was a continually degraded approximation of the generation before.

Digital video was a major step forward for video quality. Rather than simply capturing electronic impulses of light and sound, digital video takes approximately

25 or 30 snapshots of more than 450,000 *pixels* of light and thousands of samplings of sound every second and records them not as electronic pulses but as binary code—exactly the same binary code your computer uses. The quality of this data is limited only by the camera's light and sound sensors. More importantly, when a copy is made, rather than simply approximating the original recording, the data itself is transferred from one source to another—meaning that each copy of the digital data is *identical* to the original recording!

▶ KEY TERMS

Digital video—Also called DV, it is video that records sound and motion as computer data, or chains of 1s and 0s.

Pixel—The basic building block of digital images. Although they seem to be painted with continuous color, digital images—on television, on your computer, or in your digital camera—are actually composed of tiny rectangles (pixels) of various settings of red, green, and blue color. In most cases, pixels are so small that they blend into a smooth flow of color. However, when an image is stretched beyond its intended resolution, or *over-rezzed*, the pixels become visible, and the image appears jagged or *pixelated*.

When transferred into your computer using an IEEE-1394 connection (commonly called *FireWire*) or *USB Video Class 1.0*, the video data stream from your digital camcorder remains virtually unchanged. The computer merely packages the digital video (DV) data into *DV-AVI* clips. You can edit those clips, cut them, and reassemble them. When you output the data back to your camcorder, it comes out in the same type of binary code stream as it went in. In other words, when working from a digital video camcorder and using a DV-AVI workflow, your camcorder and computer speak the same binary language (see **4** **About Video Capture**).

▶ KEY TERMS

FireWire—Initially a brand name for Apple's high-speed data connection, it has become universal shorthand for any OHCI-compliant IEEE-1394 connection. It is also the current standard for transferring digital video data from a camcorder to a computer and back again.

USB Video Class 1.0—A relatively new high-speed standard for transferring digital video from specially equipped camcorders to a computer over a USB 2.0 connection.

▶ NOTE

The two forms of digital video available on consumer camcorders are miniDV and Digital8. The differences are minor. They both use exactly the same method for coding and transferring the digital video information—and they both create identical DV-AVI data streams when connected to a computer. The only difference is in the media themselves. MiniDV uses a small cassette specifically designed to work in miniDV camcorders. Digital8 uses slightly cheaper 8mm videocassettes (Hi-8 tapes are recommended). Additionally, many Digital8 camcorders can also play 8mm and Hi-8 analog tapes, an advantage when it comes to transferring video from these tapes into a computer.

DV-AVI is the *lingua franca* of PC-based video editing. All video-editing applications speak it fluently, and it is the highly recommended format for transferring files between your camcorder and your computer and its editing program and back again.

Premiere Elements, like virtually all PC-based nonlinear editors, uses a *DV-AVI* workflow. That means that no matter what you put into it—photos, graphics, or other video file formats—Premiere Elements assimilates it as some form of DV-AVI (ultimately delivering the final product as a DV-AVI). This is one of the reasons Premiere Elements can sometimes find it challenging to work with *MPEGs*, QuickTime, Windows Media, and other video files.

▶ KEY TERMS

DV-AVI—A PC-based video file format, designated by the file extension **.avi**, but distinguished from other kinds of AVI files by its use of the near-lossless DV codec, or file compression system. Because of its perfect balance of size and quality, it is the preferred video format for PC-based video editors, as well as being the universal language that all PC-based video-editing software speaks.

MPEG—A video file format developed by the Motion Picture Experts Group, MPEGs use a temporal compression system, a system of compressing the file by re-using repeated elements from frame to frame, that produces very small files—although they are sometimes technically challenging to edit. Although Premiere Elements 2.0 can work with MPEGs, you should consider them to be chiefly a *delivery* format (the files you burn to your DVDs) and not the preferred format for editing.

A number of products are available that convert analog video into a digital file for your computer. Although Premiere Elements 2.0 is capable of handling a wide variety of video file types, it's always to your advantage to use a product that produces DV-AVI files. We recommend a few modestly priced pieces in **8** **Capture Analog Video**.

For more information on transferring your camcorder's video into your computer, see **4** **About Video Capture**. And for information on capturing video from DVD and MicroMV camcorders, as well as from unusual sources such as digital still cameras and picture phones, see **14** **Add Media with the Adobe Media Downloader**.

A Word About System Requirements

Although Premiere Elements will work on most computers sold in the past five years or so, it is definitely to your advantage to have a more powerful system. DV-AVI video files devour huge chunks of hard drive space (at a rate of about a gigabyte of space for every five minutes of video), and the process of capturing, manipulating, effecting, rendering, and outputting those files, particularly on longer projects, can be very processor- (and hard drive space) intensive.

Processors running at more than 1GHz will power the program, but to a limited degree. You might have to shut down background processes in your operating system to capture and output, and rendering larger files can take a frustratingly long time if you're using one of these slower processors. (See **12 About Troubleshooting Capture Problems.**)

Most processors running at more than 2GHz should run the program effectively, with 3+GHz Hyper Threading Pentium 4s and Athlon64 3000s and higher having more than adequate power to run all of the program's features. (Note that Premiere Elements works only with Athlons that use the SSE2 instruction set. A BIOS update might be required on some older machines, and pre-XP Athlon chips might not be able to run the program at all.)

Likewise, although 256MB of RAM is the minimum recommended by the program, at least 500MB is highly recommended and 1–2GB of RAM is ideal.

A large hard drive is also very important, not just because video files are huge but because Premiere Elements requires large amounts of free, contiguous hard drive space to write temp files and to use as *scratch disk* space. Maxing out a hard drive is something most people don't consider but, especially with larger projects, it happens more often than you'd expect. At least 60GB of *free* space is recommended for a typical project, although high-demand projects might require more. (See **124 About Troubleshooting DVD Output.**)

▶ KEY TERM

Scratch disk—An area of your hard drive in which Premiere Elements writes temporary files while rendering and encoding your project. Often the amount of scratch disk space needed to render and encode a project exceeds the size of the output file.

Although a second hard drive, one dedicated to your captured video and video temp files, is ideal (and is standard equipment for most professional editors), most desktop computers sold in the past year or two are more than capable of handling the video files and operating system on a single hard drive. However, if you experience data flow problems (such as dropped frames or interrupted capture or output), know that the installation of a second, video-dedicated hard drive often remedies the problem. (See **12 About Troubleshooting Capture Problems.**)

Finally, a nice, large monitor is definitely to your advantage when you're editing video. There's a lot going on onscreen, and you can greatly benefit from as much real estate as possible to allow for viewing all your timelines and having ready access to your tools and folders. Although a 17-inch monitor set to 1024×768 resolution will give you enough room to see everything, a 19-inch monitor with resolution settings at 1280×960 or higher allows you much more room to work. For the truly ambitious, Premiere Elements supports dual monitors so you can place your **Monitor** panel on one screen and your controls and tools on the other.

Whatever you choose, you'll find that you'll appreciate every pixel of screen space you can afford.

First Things Last

Remember that editing video is only one small part in the creation of a memorable and entertaining video production. You can do a lot of magic in post-production, but you'll be ahead of the game if you come to the desktop with a good supply of well-shot video footage from which to assemble your masterpiece.

Although it's beyond the scope of this book to teach you production as well as post-production techniques, there are a couple of key principles to keep in mind as you shoot your video. After all, you might spend weeks assembling your video in a variety of ways—but you'll only get one chance to capture that precious moment on tape. Make sure you get the material you need *now* so you'll be able to use it later.

Here are 10 tips, plus 1, for making great videos:

1. **Take control of light, white balance, and focus.**

   These settings are automatic on most camcorders, so we tend to neglect them. But you can only fix so much in post-production! If you can manually adjust these settings, definitely do. If not, do what you can to remedy the challenging lighting situations when you shoot (for example, don't shoot someone standing in front of a window and watch out for mixtures of fluorescent lighting and daylight). Professional cinematographers are masters of painting what you see on screen with light. Few things give life and dimension to a video or movie like a well-lit picture.

2. **Pay attention to sound.**

   Sound is another aspect of video we often neglect. I guess we tend to get comfortable with the way those microphones are so conveniently mounted on the top of our camcorders. But people tend to speak very softly, especially when they're on camera, and background sounds and crowd noise can render some important conversations pretty much unintelligible. If your camera can support an external microphone, definitely invest in a wireless lavaliere (a shotgun microphone with a very focused pick-up pattern) or, at the very least, a clip-on microphone with a long extension cord, and use it whenever the dialogue is important. You'll be amazed how much good sound presence adds to a well-shot video.

3. Don't shoot scenery.

Okay, *do* shoot scenery—but don't expect it to look good. Scenery looks great on film and even in photographs. But for some reason, it looks flat and dead on video. It doesn't seem to matter whether it's the Great Wall of China, the Grand Canyon, or Mount Kilimanjaro. Video just doesn't seem to capture landscapes well. (Even stranger is the fact that if you load a photo into Premiere Elements and pan-and-zoom around it, the effect is more powerful than shooting video of the actual scenery in the photo. It doesn't make sense, but try it and you'll see!)

If you *must* shoot scenery (and you usually must), try to interact with it or get your cast to interact with it or talk about it. Bring it to life. Don't just show scenery—show people in the scenery. Walk through it or drive around it to give it depth and dimension. Maybe even describe it in a voiceover. But scenery for scenery's sake just doesn't work. Trust us on this.

4. Establish every scene.

Give every scene context. Never shoot a wedding without getting a shot of the church from the outside. Never get a close-up without grabbing a few long shots of the room, too. Every moment has a context. Get as much footage as you can that tells your audience where it's happening, at what time of day, what the weather is like, who is present. Otherwise it all seems to be happening in some nameless limbo.

5. Get the necessary coverage.

This point is related to the previous point: Every great film director knows first and foremost how to get the coverage. Coverage is a Hollywood term for "way too much footage." Getting coverage means getting a good mix of long shots, close-ups, and reaction shots. Don't just show the event; show who was there watching it happen. Getting lots of footage of the bride and groom at a wedding, for instance, is vital—but so is getting shots of the guests, the tear in the father-of-the-bride's eye, the organist, the flower girl who can't seem to stand still, a reverse shot looking back at the church from the altar. Never sit still. Run around as much as you can. Catch your scene from every possible angle and at every possible distance, even if it means you're so busy shooting that you don't get to enjoy the event itself. When you sit down to edit you'll be grateful for the wealth of material you have to work with.

6. Find a story to tell.

Just as no scene happens without a context, neither does any event happen without its context. Footage of a birthday party for your 90-year-old grandmother is just a home movie. But make it a celebration of her 90 years of life, and it becomes a story! Look for the unique angle, the story behind the event. Gather old footage and photos. Interview people. Catch some candid footage. Think like a newspaper reporter. It's not enough to merely report the facts; look for the story behind the facts. Tell your audience why we're here and what's really special about these people at this place at this time, and you'll win their hearts and minds.

7. Learn to see what the camera sees.

This is what really separates the home movie maker from the true videographer. *Look through the viewfinder.* Teach yourself to see only what the camera sees (because, after all, that's all that's going to be captured on your tape). In film school, they call it *mise en scene*. It's everything that composes the shot. Consider every video clip you shoot as if it were a photograph. Consider what's in the background, what's in the foreground, how the subject fits into the shot, and how the picture is composed. Never just point and shoot. Think about the image that's ultimately going to end up on your tape.

8. Tell stories with pictures.

A video of someone telling a story is not a very interesting video, no matter how interesting a story they have to tell. Find ways to help him or her tell their story with pictures. Listen carefully to what's being said and then look for ways to bring it to life with pictures. If Dad is talking about his beloved old '55 Chevy, do your best to find an old home movie or a snapshot of Dad with that car. Find the images that can bring those words to life! Master the cutaway, the J-cut, and L-cut (described in **38** **Create an L-Cut or a J-Cut**). Make everything as visual as possible. Remember, movies move! The audio may tell us what's going on, after all, but it's the visuals that will leave the lasting impression.

9. Don't be afraid to speak directly to your audience.

For some reason, video reaches us on a more personal level than any other medium. Think about how much television programming features people talking directly to us. So don't be afraid to speak directly to your audience in your video. Have the people on camera address the camera directly. It adds a level of interactivity to your video. Narration is also a very effective way to draw your audience into your video and help them discover meanings in the images you're showing them. We enjoy watching people do things on video— but when someone in a video addresses the audience directly, we feel much more a part of the event we're watching.

10. Keep it moving.

Every shot has a lifespan. Learn to watch your videos objectively. Learn to recognize when a shot or scene has gone on too long and cut it or cut away from it. Keep it lively. Use more of that coverage you shot back in point 5. Cut from close-ups to long shots, from long shots to reaction shots. Most visuals shouldn't last more than a few seconds before we're on to the next. The continuous audio that plays as we cut around with the video shots will help keep it all together. Music can even offer you a beat to cut to. But keep it fast. Keep it interesting. Keep it fun.

11. Editing is about throwing away.

Learn to be ruthless when it comes to what you use and what you throw away. Cut everything that isn't necessary to tell your story—and then come back later and tighten it a little more. (Remember, this is a non-destructive process so, if you cut too much, you can easily put it back in later.) Better to have your audience complaining that you left them wanting more than to have them squirming in their seats, wondering when this over-long thing is going to wrap up.

And if your audience really insists on more, there's always that special features section on your DVD....

By all means, learn to watch television and movies more objectively. Notice how the pros make use of their media. Even those awful reality shows have an artistry to them. Notice how they establish a scene and create characters and conflicts. Watch how quickly they move from shot to shot. And certainly take note of the way they use sound, music, L-cuts, and J-cuts to unify sequences and to tell a story.

Premiere Elements gives you the tools to do the same things to similar effect.

Good luck, have fun, and happy moviemaking.

—Chuck and Steve

2

Getting to Know the Workspace

IN THIS CHAPTER:

1. Start a New Project
2. Customize Your Workspaces
3. Nest Your Panels to Save Desktop Space

Now that you have covered the need-to-know items in Chapter 1, "Start Here," it is time to get started on your first masterpiece. But, before you can get down to the business of creating your movie, you will need a little more help navigating through Premiere Elements.

---

1 **Start a New Project**

→ **SEE ALSO**

2 Customize Your Workspace
3 Nest Your Panels to Save Desktop Space
4 About Video Capture
14 Add Media with the Adobe Media Downloader

Chapter 1 provided enough information for you to start a video project. You might want to get together all the images and clips you will be using to create your video masterpiece. It never hurts to be organized. The more organized you are for a project, the more time you will have to spend on future projects (or other things). In this task, you'll learn how to start a new project in Premiere Elements and give it a name and storage location on your computer.

▶ TIPS

Put together a storyboard, just like the pros. You can download free storyboards and get tips on how to use them; just search for *storyboard* on the Internet. A storyboard is a panel, or series of panels, on which a set of sketches is consecutively arranged depicting the important changes of scene and action in a series of shots (as for a film, television show, or commercial).

Put together a list of images, video clips, and tapes to capture (and place them in their own folder on your computer, with a label such as Next Project). Add thoughts on transitions that you might like to use and what menu might look good for this project. The more you do on the front end, the easier it will be when you start putting your video project together in Premiere Elements.

1 Start Premiere Elements

Double-click the **Premiere Elements** shortcut icon on your desktop or go to the **Start** menu and choose **Premiere Elements**. Premiere Elements launches and the splash screen appears.

2 Select New Project

From the splash screen, click the **New Project** icon. The **New Project** dialog opens.

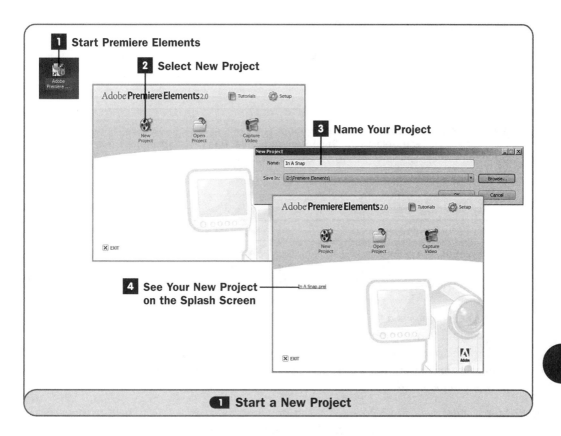

1 Start Premiere Elements

2 Select New Project

Adobe **Premiere Elements** 2.0

3 Name Your Project

4 See Your New Project
on the Splash Screen

3 Name Your Project

In the dialog box that appears, you can either enter a new name or leave the
default name **untitled**. You also want to specify an appropriate **Save In** location—this is where Premiere Elements will save the files for this project.

▶ **TIP**

Provide a project name that is descriptive and meaningful for your new project. If you
have a second internal hard drive or an external USB 2.0 drive, it is best to use it for
storing all your video and project files. If you can designate a second drive solely for
video, you will speed up the processes and make your life a whole lot easier. Whatever
drive you use, be sure to run the Windows Defragmentation utility on a regular basis.
Digital video production software of all kinds runs best on a clean, well-organized drive.

When you've provided a project name and specified a storage location, click
OK. The Premiere Elements workspace appears, with the new, blank project
loaded.

4 See Your New Project on the Splash Screen

The next time you visit the splash screen (when you launch Premiere Elements), your new project will appear in the list of recent projects.

▶ NOTE

If you've already launched Premiere Elements, you can still access your existing projects. From the main menu, select **File**, **Open Project** or **File**, **Open Recent Project**. You can also return to the splash screen by selecting **File, Close**.

---

2 Customize Your Workspaces

✔BEFORE YOU BEGIN	→ SEE ALSO
1 Start a New Project	3 Nest Your Panels to Save Desktop Space

---

Premiere Elements is a task-oriented tool. Many capabilities have been added to the program to allow users to create workspaces that suit their needs. At times, some of the panels and various screens can get in the way of getting the job done. For this reason, the workspaces in Premiere Elements can be changed to each user's requirements.

Many options exist to help you get and stay organized, as well as to help create a smooth workflow. Changing defaults, creating label colors, and shrinking panels can all help make Premiere Elements a versatile tool.

1 Adjust Interface Brightness

From the main menu, choose **Edit**, **Preferences**. When the **Preferences** dialog box opens, click the **User Interface (UI)** option at the bottom of the list on the left side to open the dialog box to the **User Interface** page. Drag the slider to set the darkness and brightness of the application's user interface. This setting does not affect the way video or any images appear on the screen; only the workspace windows and panels are affected by the changes you make here. You can also specify that you want Premiere Elements to use the Windows background color as its own background color. The best way to see what type of effect this has on your workspace is to change the settings and look at the difference. Moving the slider to the left darkens the UI; moving it to the right lightens the UI. You always have the option to return the UI to the default setting by clicking the **Default Brightness** button.

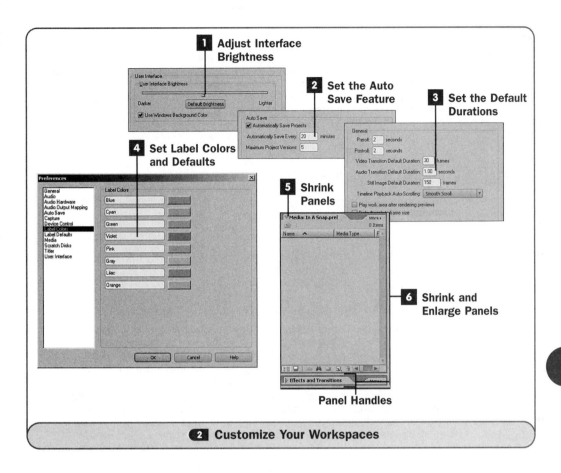

1 Adjust Interface Brightness

2 Set the Auto Save Feature

3 Set the Default Durations

4 Set Label Colors and Defaults

5 Shrink Panels

6 Shrink and Enlarge Panels

Panel Handles

2 Customize Your Workspaces

2 Set the Auto Save Feature

To get to the Auto Save settings, choose **Edit**, **Preferences**, **Auto Save** (if the **Preferences** dialog box is still open from step 1, click **Auto Save** in the list of categories on the left). You use the **Auto Save** feature to save copies of your project at regular intervals. This function saves you tons of time if something bad should ever happen to your computer while you're working on a project. To activate the **Auto Save** feature, check the **Automatically Save Projects** check box (it should already be checked by default). By default the **Automatically Save Every** field is set to **20** minutes and the **Maximum Project Versions** is set to **5**. Changes to these numbers take effect immediately. The **Auto Save** message pops up for a second or two at the set intervals. Because this message can be annoying when you're working on a project, make sure that the setting is low enough to save your work frequently, but not so short that you are constantly being interrupted by it.

▶ **NOTE**

The **Auto Save** feature is not activated until you save your project manually at least one time. After saving manually, the **Auto Save** feature kicks in and saves your project at the intervals set in the **Preferences** dialog box. The project versions are saved to the **Adobe Premiere Elements Auto Save** folder. The saved projects can be used to recover your project after a crash or to start your project over from a specific point. If you select five project versions (the default), five versions of each project are saved. These project files take up very little space, so for safety, more is better.

3 Set the Default Durations

Chances are you will want to change the duration of certain transitions or images at some point in your editing career. These durations can be changed easily under the **General** category in the **Preferences** dialog box. From the main menu at the top of your screen, select **Edit**, **Preferences**, **General** to open the **General Preferences** dialog box.

▶ **NOTE**

Changes to the duration settings are not applied to any items already on the **Timeline** in any project. If you already have all your images and transitions on the **Timeline** and decide the durations are too short or long, there are two options: You can change all the transition and image durations manually (see **24 Set Still Image Duration** and **44 About Transitions**). This can be quite a time-consuming procedure, as you can imagine. Alternatively, you can remove all the transitions and images from the **Timeline**, change the default durations in the **Preferences** dialog box, and then put the images and transitions back on the **Timeline**. This can also be quite time consuming. The best practice is to think ahead; make sure your defaults will work with your project before you start.

Video transitions, by default, are set to 30 frames because you are working with the NTSC format (that PAL format has a 25-frame transition default). Your video is captured at 30 frames per second, so a 30-frame transition lasts for a total of one second. If your transition is between two clips or images, one-half second would be over the first clip and another one-half second over the second clip. This might or might not work for your project at any given time. It is not difficult to change the duration of transitions manually if there are only a few.

▶ **TIP**

To change the duration of a single clip on the **Timeline**, drag either end of the clip to the right or left. Be careful if there is a clip on either side because dragging over the adjacent clip could overlay the video. If you *want* to overlay the video, just drag the edge of the clip over the adjacent clip and drop it there. If you *do not want* to overlay, press and hold the **Ctrl** key while dragging the clip to move the other clips over to make room for the current clip's new duration. You can use this technique to make clips longer or shorter.

But if you are going to add many images and many transitions, make sure that the default is set where you need it before adding items to the **Timeline**. When changing the duration, remember that you set the value in frames, 30 frames per second for NTSC, 25 frames per second for PAL.

Audio transitions, like video transitions, last for one second by default. Changes you make to the **Preferences** dialog box do not affect any audio files already on the **Timeline**. This setting is given in seconds of audio.

As you drag **still images** from the **Media** panel to the **Timeline**, Premiere Elements needs to determine how long that image will be displayed in your movie. By default, the still image duration is 150 frames. 150 frames divided by 30 frames per second equals a 5-second duration (for PAL, the default still image duration is 125 frames). Again, manually changing the duration of a few still images is not hard or time consuming; changing the duration for hundreds of images is. Think ahead before adding groups of stills to the **Timeline**; is the default duration going to be too long or short? For information about changing the duration of individual still images, see **24** **Set Still Image Duration**.

4 Set Label Colors and Defaults

Open the **Preferences** dialog box if it is not already open and click the **Label Colors** category on the left. This page of the dialog box shows the default label colors available. Click the button next to the color name to open a panel that enables you to choose a color. Then click in the box with the color name and change the name to best describe the color you just selected (you can type whatever you like in this text box). After you have chosen and named up to eight colors, it is time to apply them to the various available items.

Click **Label Defaults** in the category list on the left side of the **Preferences** dialog box to see a list of the items to which you can apply the colors you just selected: Folders, Timeline, Video, Audio, Movie (audio and video), Still, and Adobe Dynamic Link. For each of the items listed, choose a color from the drop-down list next to the item. Play around with assigning colors to the items until you have everything the way you like it, just like doing some interior designing. The colors visually separate one type of item from another when you are working on a project to help you achieve a well-organized project.

5 Shrink Panels

Sometimes the panels get in the way of the work you're doing on a project. By clicking the little blue triangle in the top-left corner of a panel, you can shrink, or collapse, the panel. Click the arrow again (it faces right when the panel is collapsed) to open the panel again.

6 Shrink and Enlarge Panels

In ❸ **Nest Your Panels to Save Desktop Space,** you learn to move the panels to make more room in the workspace. Here is another means of creating some extra room in the work area when you need it.

Click and hold on one of the panel sides to drag the panel up and down or right and left. Changing the size of the panel will be a big help when, for example, you need your **Monitor** panel to be a little larger.

---

3   Nest Your Panels to Save Desktop Space

✔ **BEFORE YOU BEGIN**

❶ Start a New Project
❷ Customize Your Workspaces

As you have seen, there are many panels, windows, dialog boxes, and workspaces. With all of that going on in one screen, it can be hard to keep track of where everything is. For this reason, Premiere Elements helps you create the perfect working environment, just for you. The panels can be moved anywhere on the screen. The panels can be nested in with other panels and can also be free floating. In this task, you see how easy it is to customize you own workspace according to your workflow needs.

▶ NOTE

After moving or nesting panels, the workspace remains that way until you either make another change or restore the workspace to its default. The panel arrangement remains as you left it even after closing and re-opening the program or opening another project.

1 Drag a Panel

Simply click the tab at the top of the panel and hold down the left mouse button to drag and drop the panel wherever you want it to be. As you drag the panel, notice that three-dimensional boxes appear to show you what space is available for your panel and what it would look like if it were dropped at that location. You can drop the panel in a whole new panel, or drop it in a panel that already contains other panels (this is where the space savings comes in). You can nest all the panels in one panel if you like—the possibilities are pretty much endless. It just depends on what is best for the way you work and what panels you tend to need most often, as well as what panels you don't use. Even the **Timeline** can be nested with other panels. Try moving a few panels to get a good idea of how the process works. Don't worry if things get a little messed up; at the end of this task, we will show you how to restore your workspace.

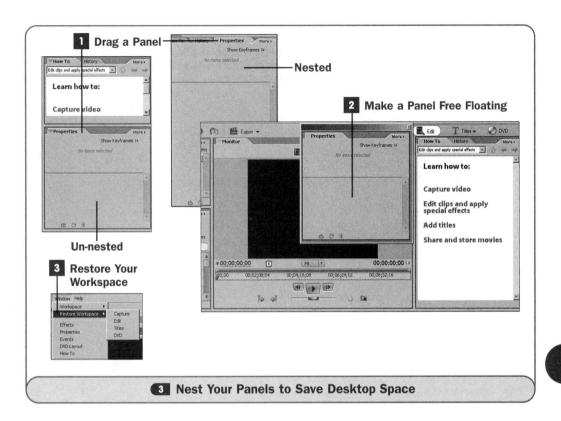

3 Nest Your Panels to Save Desktop Space

2 Make a Panel Free Floating

If you want to have a particular panel floating rather than in another panel, Premiere Elements allows you to do that also. Drag the panel, as described in step 1, to the top of your screen (the taskbar area) and drop it there. That's all there is to it. Now you have a free-floating panel you can move anywhere on the screen. Just be careful where you drop it, or you will nest it within another panel.

3 Restore Your Workspace

The ability to restore your workspace will come in handy on more than one occasion, I'm afraid. As you start moving things around, panels begin to hide themselves or end up in places other than where you want them. In that case, you can always restore the workspace to its default appearance. Choose **Window, Restore Workspace** and then click the workspace you want to restore (**Capture, Edit, Titles,** or **DVD**).

▶ **NOTE**

After you restore a workspace, it remains that way until you again make changes. Changes made to the workspace are not kept in the **History** panel, and there is no way to restore to a custom workspace; you can only restore a workspace to its default configuration.

In its seemingly unlimited ways to customize the application to your needs, Premiere Elements has gone all out with these types of features. Features that allow you to be in control of your own workspace and workflow are very important in the world of video editing, something that Adobe knows a lot about.

3

3

Get the Picture:
Capturing Video

IN THIS CHAPTER:

Before you can edit your video, you need to somehow get it into your computer—a process known as *capturing*. (There are means of getting media into your computer other than traditional capture, however. See **14 Add Media with the Adobe Media Downloader**.)

In this chapter, you'll see the ways Premiere Elements can turn the video in your camcorder into video files on your computer. And then you'll learn how to troubleshoot problems when things don't go quite as smoothly as they should.

4   About Video Capture

The word *capture* is the universally used, if not always entirely accurate, term used to describe the process by which video in your camera becomes editable video files on your computer.

▶ KEY TERM

Capture—The process by which video is transferred from a camcorder to a computer-based editing program and, if necessary, digitized in the process.

The physical mechanics of capturing video from your camcorder to your computer is similar, no matter what type of capture you're doing. It always involves streaming your video from your camcorder, down a cable or other connection, into your computer using some sort of capture software. But what type of camcorder, what type of cable connection, and even what types of computer files you ultimately end up with can vary tremendously.

Before you can begin editing your video with Premiere Elements, you need to get it into your computer.

To understand why different methods—and different types of hardware—are used in different situations, you need to first understand the difference between analog and digital video.

The word *analog* pretty much describes the world as it existed in the days before computers. The hands on clocks moved by way of a system of mechanical connections and kept time through the interactions of the gears, springs, and other internal machinery. (Sundials, likewise, used one type of movement—the Earth's rotation—to measure another movement—that of time.) Music was recorded by etching pulses into some surface as the sounds physically vibrated a stylus. And camcorders recorded light and sound as electronic impulses on magnetic tape.

▶ KEY TERM

Analog—Literally meaning a representation of something else, the word *analog* is used, for our purposes, to mean the recording of sound or images with traditional, non-computer-based means, such as a vinyl record album or a VHS videotape.

The *digital* revolution changed all that. Rather than sound or light being recorded as electronic pulses, computer-based transducers interpret thousands or hundreds of thousands of samplings of sound or light every second, recording them not mechanically but as digital code—as 1s and 0s—that reproduce the images and sounds as perfectly and as precisely as they were recorded, time after time and copy after copy.

▶ KEY TERM

Digital—The recording and processing of any information, including picture and sound, using mathematical measurement, as the way computers use chains of 1s and 0s to represent all data.

If *analog* is like a classic pocket watch, *digital* is like a precise chronometer, accurate to within microseconds, unfettered by the limitations of traditional mechanics. Right on the nose all the time, every time.

For those of us who love to edit video, there is another advantage to the advent of digital recording. Digital video (DV) camcorders and computers speak the same language. They both record and interpret data saved as 1s and 0s. When we bring our digital video into our computers for manipulation and editing, there's virtually no need to translate anything between them. What one puts out the other takes in, and vice versa.

For those using analog camcorders, computer-based video editing poses a bit more of a challenge, although not an insurmountable one. This is because, unlike digital video camcorders, analog camcorders record video with more "mechanical" methods. (Think of the difference between music recorded on an analog cassette tape and music recorded on a digital compact disc.) To translate analog video into something that your computer can work with, the analog video must be *digitized*, or converted into computer code. (See **8** **Capture Analog Video**.)

▶ KEY TERM

Digitizing—The process of converting analog information or video into computer files or digital information.

Digital video, on the other hand, includes systems introduced to consumers within the past 10 years or so, including the two formats favored by most PC-based video editors: MiniDV and Digital8.

▶ NOTE

Although their media is slightly different, MiniDV and Digital8 camcorders record identical types of digital data files. In fact, when you're capturing them, your computer can't tell the difference.

For consumer and prosumer editors who use programs such as Premiere Elements and Premiere Pro, the preferred method of transferring digital video into a computer is through an IEEE-1394 connection, commonly referred to as FireWire. In fact, when transferring files from MiniDV and Digital8 camcorders over FireWire, the word *capture* doesn't accurately apply. The data recorded by MiniDV and Digital8 camcorders remains unchanged as it passes over a FireWire connection, only the "envelope" the data travels in changes as clips of video data are saved in the computer as DV-AVIs. (See **5** **Capture Digital Video Using FireWire**.)

DV-AVIs are the preferred workflow for PC-based editing. They are by far the most efficient, trouble-free files you can use in Premiere Elements. Use them whenever possible, and you increase the odds of having a problem-free project.

▶ NOTE

Not all AVIs are created equal! The *DV* in *DV-AVI* refers to the codec or compression-decompression method used to squeeze the data into the file. The DV codec is favored by PC-based video editors because it is nearly lossless. But an AVI (a PC-based media format which stands for Audio Video Interweave) could be using any one of the dozens of codecs available, however, and unless you have that codec installed on your computer, these files will not play well with Premiere Elements.

In addition to those camcorders that connect to your computer using FireWire, a newer class of digital camcorders has recently come on the scene. These camcorders connect to computers through the recently developed USB Video Class 1.0.

These DV camcorders, however, should not be confused with DVD camcorders or MicroMV camcorders that connect to a computer using a traditional USB 1.0 cable. Because of the way DVD and MicroMV camcorders store their data (usually as MPEGs) and that they stream this video data at a much lower rate, their video files are captured with the **Media Downloader** rather than in Premiere Elements's standard **Capture** workspace. (For more information, see **14** **Add Media with the Adobe Media Downloader**.)

▶ **NOTE**

As an alternative to using the **Media Downloader**, video files from MicroMV and DVD camcorders can be captured with the same methods used to capture analog video. (See **8** **Capture Analog Video**.)

USB Video Class 1.0 is an extremely fast delivery system for streaming video data over a standard USB 2.0 connection, in some ways even superior to FireWire. And, while this system is new and still relatively rare, Premiere Elements 2.0 is capable of connecting to these camcorders and capturing the files with a method not unlike that used for traditional FireWire capture. (See **6** **Capture Digital Video Using USB**.)

▶ **NOTE**

Although DVD camcorders and MicroMV camcorders offer tremendous advantages in size and conveniences, these camcorders store their video files as MPEGs and offer no direct method for capturing these files as DV-AVIs. The best methods for transferring their video into Premiere Elements is either by means of the **Media Downloader** (See **14** Add Media with the Adobe Media Downloader) or by connecting them to the computer through a DV bridge system capable of capturing video as DV-AVIs (see **8** Capture Analog Video).

4

One method for capturing analog video is to use a passthrough, attaching your analog camcorder to your computer through a DV camcorder.

Although *transfer* might be a better term to describe the way DV is brought into a computer, *capture* is a fairly accurate term for the way analog video is brought into a computer. Because analog camcorders and digital computers store their video files as very different formats, some type of device is required to capture them, or convert these analog pulses into digital code, in order to transfer them into a computer. (See **8** **Capture Analog Video**).

Capturing any video to your computer is a processor-intensive activity. Current systems and computers sold in the past few years seem to be able to handle it effortlessly, but users of older computers can find it somewhat challenging. Regardless of how powerful your system is, some basic computer maintenance can always work to your benefit:

1 **Clean off the spyware regularly**—Spybot Search & Destroy, Ad-Aware, and Microsoft's AntiSpyware are all great, free tools for keeping the spyware and other dangerous malware files at bay. Load them all, keep them updated and, at least once a week, use them to get that junk off your computer. Not only is spyware annoying and potentially dangerous, it eats at your resources, diverting precious computer power and interrupting intensive processes such as capture and output.

2 **Keep your virus software up to date**—The last thing you want is some new bug running lose in your computer, possibly rendering all of your hard work unusable.

3 **Keep your system files in order**—Along with your weekly spyware cleaning, it's well worth using a program such as Norton Systemworks to check your operating system's integrity and clean out the unnecessary stuff that's accumulated in your registry. Doing so can help keep your computer running like new.

4 **Defragment your hard drive(s)**—Another nice step in your weekly maintenance schedule, defragging your drive or drives helps keep all your computer files neatly ordered. The more you do so, the more contiguous hard drive space you'll have when your system demands it. More than one user has found himself struggling with a video project that keeps crashing because there simply wasn't a large enough block of space for the program to write its temp files.

5 Capture Digital Video Using FireWire

✔ BEFORE YOU BEGIN	→ SEE ALSO
4 About Video Capture **7** Control Your DV Camcorder During Capture	**9** Capture Video or Audio Only **10** Capture to the Timeline or Media Panel **11** View Captured Clips **12** About Troubleshooting Capture Problems

Initially an Apple brand name, the word *FireWire* has become standard shorthand for an OHCI-Compliant IEEE-1394 high-speed data connection. (Sony calls their IEEE-1394 port iLink.)

FireWire connections are fast and, what's more, they're consistently fast. In fact, when it comes to capturing, outputting, or otherwise exchanging data between your camcorder and your computer, there's almost no substitute (with the possible exception of the new USB video standard).

Capturing video into your computer and outputting data from your computer to your camcorder are two of the most processor-intensive tasks a computer can do, and you need a fast, consistent, uninterrupted data flow or it's not going to work.

This is why an IEEE-1394 cable and port is the preferred method for getting digital video, or DV, from your camcorder and back again. (In fact, even when digitizing analog video with a piece of third-party software, FireWire is the preferred method for connecting the digitizer to the computer. (See **8** **Capture Analog Video**.)

1 Connect Your Camcorder

All MiniDV and Digital8 camcorders have a FireWire connection, even if an IEEE-1394 cable wasn't included with the camcorder when you bought it.

Although the risk of a surge damaging your equipment is low, it's best to turn off your camcorder when you connect the cable between your camcorder and your computer. After the two devices are connected, however, set your camcorder to the VTR mode. Windows registers the connection, usually with a sound effect. A connection icon also appears in the lower-right corner of your Windows taskbar. (See **12** **About Troubleshooting Capture Problems**.)

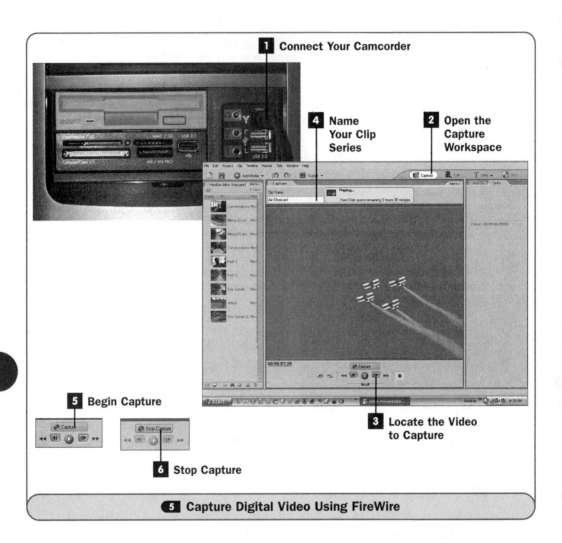

1 Connect Your Camcorder

4 Name Your Clip Series

2 Open the Capture Workspace

5 Begin Capture

6 Stop Capture

3 Locate the Video to Capture

5 Capture Digital Video Using FireWire

▶ NOTES

If your computer doesn't have a FireWire port and you plan to do any serious video editing, particularly with digital video, a FireWire card is one of the best investments you can make. Virtually any OHCI-Compliant IEEE-1394 card will work. Some even come with a free FireWire cable.

A display at the top of the **Capture Monitor** panel estimates how much room you have to store captured video on your hard drive. It's important to note, however, that it's impossible to fill a hard drive. When free space on your drive gets pretty low, you probably won't be able to continue to capture video.

▶ TIP

Windows might not be able to detect a connected camcorder unless the camcorder is also connected with an AC adaptor to a power source.

2 Open the Capture Workspace

Often, simply connecting your camcorder automatically opens the **Capture** workspace. Otherwise, clicking the **Capture** button in the upper-right corner of any Premiere Elements workspace will open it.

3 Locate the Video to Capture

By using Premiere Elements' playback and shuttle controls to operate your camcorder (see **7** **Control Your DV Camcorder During Capture**), locate a scene on your videotape you want to capture to your computer. Pause the video where you want to begin capture.

▶ TIP

Ideally, capturing video, as well as outputting video back to your camcorder, is a simple process. However, occasionally it doesn't go as smoothly as it should. If you're having problems, such as dropped frames or interruptions, or you simply can't get Premiere Elements to connect to your camcorder, see 12 About Troubleshooting Capture Problems.

4 Name Your Clip Series

In the **Clip Name** space at the upper-left corner of the **Monitor** panel, drag to select the name (which defaults to the name of your video project) and give it a name.

As Premiere Elements breaks this captured sequence into short clips, these clips are automatically given the names you specify here followed by a numerical sequence beginning with **01**, then **02**, and so on.

▶ NOTE

By default, Premiere Elements breaks your captured video into clips, based on points at which your camcorder was started and stopped when you initially shot your video. If you'd like to turn off (or on) this feature, click the More button in the Monitor panel and uncheck (or check) the Scene Detect option.

5 Begin Capture

Above the playback controls at the bottom center of the **Capture** workspace is the **Capture** button. Click the **Capture** button while your video is paused, and capture begins as your video plays in the **Monitor**.

It's also possible to simply click the **Capture** button while your camcorder video is playing. However, the capture process takes a few seconds to start up, and you might miss a key moment. To ensure that your capture is beginning where you want it to begin, it's best to always begin your capture from the video's paused state.

6 Stop Capture

Click the **Stop Capture** button when you want your capture to stop. Your camcorder returns to pause mode and your clip or clips are automatically added to the **Media** panel. To review your captured clips, see **11** **View Captured Clips**.

For custom captures, see **9** **Capture Video or Audio Only** and **10** **Capture to the Timeline or Media Panel**.

---

6 Capture Digital Video Using USB

✔ BEFORE YOU BEGIN	→ SEE ALSO
4 About Video Capture	**9** Capture Video or Audio Only
7 Control Your DV Camcorder During Capture	**10** Capture to the Timeline or Media Panel
	11 View Captured Clips
	12 About Troubleshooting Capture Problems

Several models in a newer class of DV camcorders are capable of transferring digital video to your computer by way of the recently developed USB Video Class 1.0, an extremely fast delivery system for streaming data over a USB 2.0 connection. A powerful new feature of Premiere Elements 2.0 is its capability to connect to these camcorders and then capture their video files at least as effectively as it can capture over FireWire.

It's important to note, however, that the Premiere Elements USB capture system is designed to work only with this still relatively rare class of camcorder. Other USB-connected devices, including MicroMV and DVD camcorders, digital still cameras, picture phones, or other non-DV media should load their files using Premiere Elements's **Media Downloader**. (See **14** **Add Media with the Adobe Media Downloader**.)

▶ NOTE

Your Windows XP operating system must include Service Pack 2 in order to interface with a USB Video Class device.

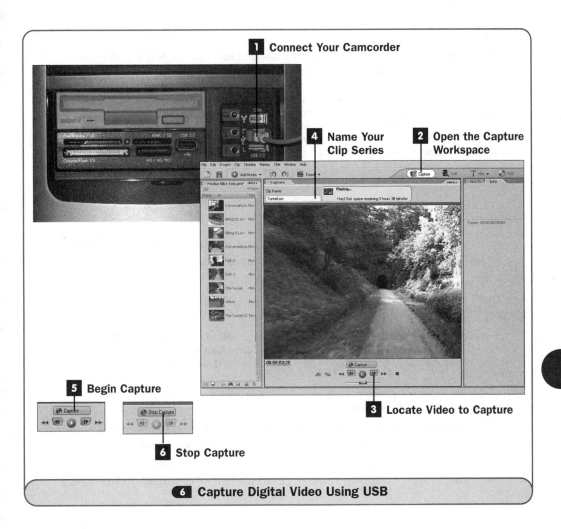

1 Connect Your Camcorder

4 Name Your Clip Series

2 Open the Capture Workspace

5 Begin Capture

6 Stop Capture

3 Locate Video to Capture

6 Capture Digital Video Using USB

1 Connect Your Camcorder

Although the risk of a surge damaging your equipment is low, it's best to turn off your camcorder when you connect the cable between your camcorder and your computer. After the two devices are connected, turn on your camcorder and put it in VTR mode. Windows registers the connection, usually with a sound effect. A connection icon also appears in the lower-right corner of your Windows taskbar.

▶ **TIPS**

Windows might not be able to recognize a connected camcorder unless it is also connected with an AC adaptor to a power source.

Premiere Elements should recognize your USB Video Class 1.0 camcorder after a connection has been made. However, if Premiere Elements does not recognize your camcorder, click the **More** button in the upper-right corner of the **Capture Monitor** panel, select **Device Control** and, from the **Devices** drop-down list, select **USB Video Class 1.0**. It might also be helpful to click on the **Options** button on this screen and specify the driver for your model of camcorder. (See **12** About Troubleshooting Capture Problems.)

2 Open the Capture Workspace

Often, simply connecting your camcorder automatically opens the **Capture** workspace. Otherwise, click the **Capture** button in the upper-right corner of any Premiere Elements workspace to open it.

▶ **NOTE**

No preview image appears in the **Monitor** panel until you play your first clip of video. After playback has begun, the clip continues to be displayed, even while in the pause mode. When you stop the camcorder, the **Monitor** again displays black.

3 Locate Video to Capture

By using the playback and shuttle controls at the bottom center of the **Capture** workspace to operate your camcorder (see **7** Control Your DV Camcorder During Capture), locate a scene on your videotape that you want to capture to your computer. Pause your video where you want to begin capture.

▶ **TIP**

Ideally, capturing video and outputting video back to your camcorder is a simple process. However, occasionally it doesn't go as smoothly as it should. If you're having problems, such as dropped frames or interruptions, or you simply can't get Premiere Elements to connect to your camcorder, see **12** About Troubleshooting Capture Problems.

4 Name Your Clip Series

In the **Clip Name** window at the upper-left of the **Monitor** panel, drag to select the name (which defaults to the name of your video project) and then type the name you'd like to give this clip.

As your footage is captured, your clips are automatically named with the name you supply here as well as a sequential number, as in **My Movie 01**, **My Movie 02**, and so on.

5 Begin Capture

Click the **Capture** button just above the playback controls while your video is paused; capture begins as your playback is displayed in the **Monitor** panel.

It's also possible to begin capture by simply clicking the **Capture** button while your video is playing. However, the capture process takes a second or two to start up, and you might miss a key moment. To ensure that your capture begins where you want it to begin, it's best to always start your capture from the video's paused state.

6 Stop Capture

Click the **Stop Capture** button when you want your capture to stop. Your camcorder goes to pause mode and your clip or clips are automatically added to the **Media** panel. To review your captured clips, see **11** **View Captured Clips**. For custom captures, see **9** **Capture Video or Audio Only** and **10** **Capture to the Timeline or Media Panel**.

---

7 **Control Your DV Camcorder During Capture**

✔ BEFORE YOU BEGIN	→ SEE ALSO
4 About Video Capture	**9** Capture Video or Audio Only
5 Capture Digital Video Using FireWire	**10** Capture to the Timeline or Media Panel
6 Capture Digital Video Using USB	**11** View Captured Clips
	12 About Troubleshooting Capture Problems

7

After you've connected your camcorder to your computer and Premiere Elements using a FireWire or USB Video Class 1.0 connection, you can operate the camcorder using the controls in the **Capture** workspace.

1 Open the Capture Workspace

Your **Capture** workspace might open automatically when you connect your camcorder. (See **12** **About Troubleshooting Capture Problems**.) Otherwise, you can jump to it by clicking the **Capture** button in the upper-right corner of any Premiere Elements workspace.

If your camcorder is properly connected to the program, this condition is indicated in the status bar at the top of the **Monitor** panel. The status bar also estimates how much capture time is left on your hard drive.

7

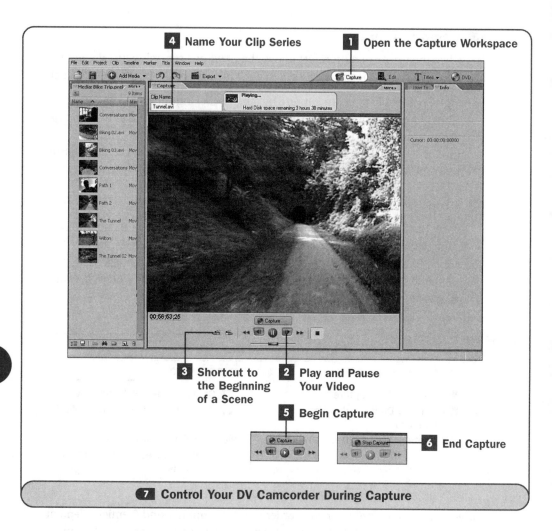

4 **Name Your Clip Series**

1 **Open the Capture Workspace**

3 **Shortcut to the Beginning of a Scene**

2 **Play and Pause Your Video**

5 **Begin Capture**

6 **End Capture**

7 **Control Your DV Camcorder During Capture**

No preview image appears in the **Monitor** panel until you play your first clip of video. After you play your first clip, the digital time code on the lower-left of the **Monitor** panel tracks along with your camcorder's time code.

The basic playback controls are intuitive and exactly like those in the **Edit** workspace's **Monitor** panel except that here they control your *camcorder* rather than your **Timeline** playback. The slider below the playback controls can be used to shuttle through your video at various speeds, depending on how far to the left or right you drag it.

2 **Play and Pause Your Video**

Click the **Play** button to start playback on your camcorder and display the video in the **Monitor**. During playback, the **Play** button becomes a **Pause** button.

When you pause the video, the **Monitor** continues to display the paused video until you click the **Stop** button or jump to a new workspace.

3 Shortcut to the Beginning of a Scene

To the left of the playback controls are two shortcut buttons. Click the shortcut button on the left to shuttle your camcorder to the beginning of the current scene on your video.

Likewise, click the second shortcut button to shuttle your camcorder to the beginning of the next scene.

4 Name Your Clip Series

Type the name you'd like to give your clip series in the space in the upper-left corner of the **Monitor** panel (which, by default, is the name of your video project).

As your footage is captured, your clips are named using the name you type here as well as a sequential number, as in **My Movie 01**, **My Movie 02**, and so on.

5 Begin Capture

To begin capture, click the **Capture** button.

It's always best to start a capture from the paused tape position because it takes a second or two for the capture to kick in. Clicking the **Capture** button while the tape is moving can mean missing a key moment in your clip. Starting your capture from the paused state ensures that the capture begins at the exact point in the tape where you want it to begin.

6 End Capture

To end capture, click the **Stop Capture** button. Your camcorder automatically shifts back into pause mode as the capture footage is added to your **Media** panel.

Playback automatically stops if you jump to another workspace. When you leave the **Capture** workspace or view your clips, be sure to disconnect or turn off your camcorder (See **11** View Captured Clips.)

7

8   Capture Analog Video

✔ BEFORE YOU BEGIN	→ SEE ALSO
4 About Video Capture	9 Capture Video or Audio Only
	10 Capture to the Timeline or Media Panel
	11 View Captured Clips
	12 About Troubleshooting Capture Problems
	14 Add Media with the Adobe Media Downloader

Analog video includes most of the video systems consumers have been using for the past couple of decades: VHS, VHS-C, 8 millimeter, Hi-8, and S-VHS.

Capturing analog video can present some unique challenges. Chief among them is that fact that, because computers must store files in digital code to be able to work with them, the video information from an analog camcorder or VCR must be converted, or digitized, as it is streamed in to your computer. Whatever hardware device or set-up you choose to use to capture your video, it is best to do your capturing with Premiere Elements over a FireWire connection.

Although you don't necessarily need a compatible driver to connect a digitizing device, or *DV bridge*, to your computer, Premiere Elements 2.0 comes loaded with drivers for most digitizing devices capable of converting your analog video to DV-AVIs, the preferred digital file format for editing on a PC. If you don't have a bridge but do own both a digital and an analog camcorder, this task offers an alternative method for analog capture, commonly called a *passthrough*.

▶ KEY TERMS

DV bridge—A hardware device that connects an analog camcorder to a computer for the purpose of converting the analog video stream into digital video files.

Passthrough—A method of digitizing analog video by connecting an analog camcorder to a computer through a digital camcorder.

▶ NOTES

Premiere Elements marries nicely with virtually all of the top brands of DV bridges, including many higher-end pieces that can cost more than the average home computer! When searching for a DV bridge, your priority should be to choose one that can convert your analog video files to DV-AVIs, the preferred file format for PC-based video editing.

The two most popular and affordable analog capture devices are the **ADS Pyro AV Link** and the **Canopus ADVC** series, both of which connect easily to your computer with a FireWire connection and produce excellent quality digital files.

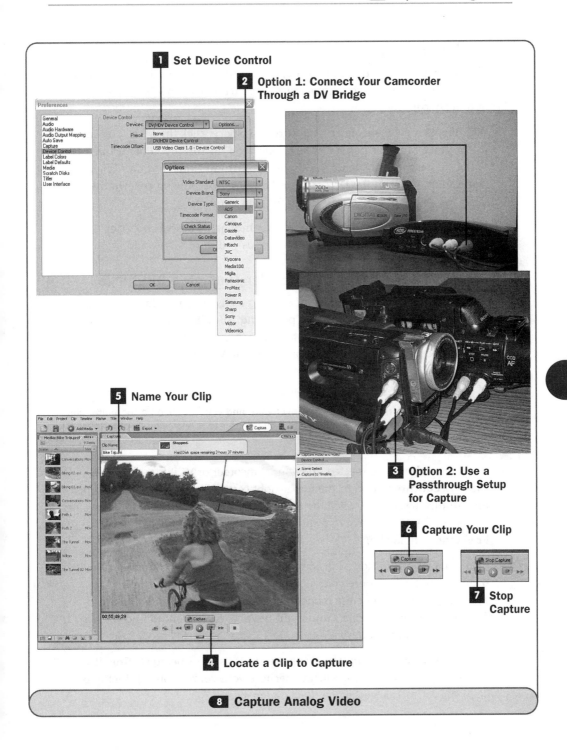

1 Set Device Control

2 Option 1: Connect Your Camcorder Through a DV Bridge

5 Name Your Clip

3 Option 2: Use a Passthrough Setup for Capture

6 Capture Your Clip

7 Stop Capture

4 Locate a Clip to Capture

8 Capture Analog Video

1 Set Device Control

The only real inconvenience in a properly set up analog capture is that you are not able to control your camcorder with Premiere Elements, as you can during DV capture.

With Premiere Elements in the **Capture** workspace, click the **More** button in the **Capture Monitor** panel and select **Device Control**. If you are using a DV bridge, as described in step 2, set **Device Control** to **None** and then click the **Option** button. From the **Device Brand** and **Device Type** drop-down lists, select the device driver you are using for your capture.

If you are using a DV camcorder as a passthrough as described in step 3, set up your DV connection and device control as you normally would.

2 Option 1: Connect Your Camcorder Through a DV Bridge

Premiere Elements 2.0 is capable of creating a custom connection with all major digitizing devices capable of producing DV-AVIs. These devices have standard *AV inputs* for connecting to your camcorder or VCR, and an output port that you can plug into your computer's FireWire port.

8

▶ KEY TERM

AV inputs—The usually red, white, and yellow (white and yellow only on a monaural unit) RCA-style jacks used for connecting an analog camcorder to a television or other playback device.

After the cabling is connected and your camcorder or VCR is powered on, click the **Capture** button in the upper-right corner of any workspace to open the **Capture** workspace. Click the **More** button in the **Capture Monitor** panel and select **Device Control** to display the **Device Control** page of the **Preferences** dialog box.

Click the **Options** button to display the **Options** dialog box; from the **Device Brand** drop-down, choose your digitizing device brand. From the **Device Type** drop-down, choose the model number, if possible, or one of the standard or alternative options. (You might have to experiment to find the best generic driver for your device.)

Click the **Check Status** button if your device is listed as being **Offline**. If your device is still listed as being **Offline**, recheck your connections and setup or go to **12** About Troubleshooting Capture Problems.

▶ **NOTE**

The **Scene Detect** feature in Premiere Elements is available only for DV capture using IEEE-1394 FireWire or USB Video Class 1.0. You can break your analog footage into clips based on content or timing, if you'd prefer, by using a third-party program called Scenalyzer (available at www.scenalyzer.com) to run your capture. Because the files captured using Scenalyzer are still DV-AVIs when the software is used with one of the digitizing methods recommended here, they can be easily imported and used in your Premiere Elements video project.

3 Option 2: Use a Passthrough Setup for Capture

A passthrough setup can be a very effective alternative to using a DV bridge to capture your analog video.

To set up a passthrough, connect your analog camcorder's AV inputs to the AV inputs of a DV camcorder connected to Premiere Elements by FireWire or USB Video Class 1.0. (See **5 Capture Digital Video Using FireWire** or **6 Capture Digital Video Using USB** for instructions on setting up your DV connection.)

Ensure that there is no tape in the DV camcorder and set it to VTR mode.

Your analog tape is played through the DV camcorder and across the cable connection to your computer, where Premiere Elements saves it as a DV-AVI. (You are not able, of course, to operate your camcorder with Premiere Elements's playback controls.)

Although this setup usually works quite effectively, every DV camcorder has its quirks, and you might have to do some additional setup, such as ensuring that your DV camcorder's AV inputs are set to receive the incoming signal. Also note that some DV camcorders allow for AV output but not AV input. Naturally, these camcorders are not capable of functioning as a passthrough.

4 Locate a Clip to Capture

Operating your analog camcorder with the camcorder's physical playback controls, locate the clip you want to capture.

5 Name Your Clip

Type the name you'd like to give your clip in the space in the upper-left corner of the **Monitor** panel. By default, your clip is given your project's name.

▶ **NOTE**

During analog capture, Premiere Elements will sometimes give you warnings of dropped frames or even abort your capture completely. This is because the program has become confused by the nonstandard connection. If you're receiving these warnings but your clips look fine on playback, you can turn off the warnings and the **Abort on Dropped Frames** option as explained in **12 About Troubleshooting Capture Problems**.

8

6 Capture Your Clip

Start your analog tape rolling at least five seconds before you want to begin capture and immediately click the **Capture** button in the **Monitor** panel. (It takes a few seconds for capture to kick in, so a little extra start-up time is better than too little.)

Your video should play in the **Monitor**, and the **Capture** button becomes a **Stop Capture** button.

7 Stop Capture

Click the **Stop Capture** button to stop your capture. Your new clip is added to the **Media** panel. To review your captured clips, see **11** **View Captured Clips**.

Stop your video playback with your camcorder's VTR controls or set up for your next clip capture.

---

9 Capture Video or Audio Only

✔ BEFORE YOU BEGIN	→ SEE ALSO
4 About Video Capture	**10** Capture to the Timeline or Media Panel
5 Capture Digital Video Using FireWire	**11** View Captured Clips
6 Capture Digital Video Using USB	**12** About Troubleshooting Capture Problems
7 Control Your DV Camcorder During Capture	
8 Capture Analog Video	

By default, Premiere Elements captures both audio and video from your camcorder. However, it can also be set up to capture video only (as when you want visuals without the sounds), or audio only (as when you plan to use a clip recorded on your camcorder as a narration track).

1 Open the Capture Workspace

Connect your camcorder as described in **5** **Capture Digital Video Using FireWire**, **6** **Capture Digital Video Using USB**, or **8** **Capture Analog Video**.

If connecting your camcorder did not automatically open the **Capture** workspace, click the **Capture** button in the upper-right corner of any workspace.

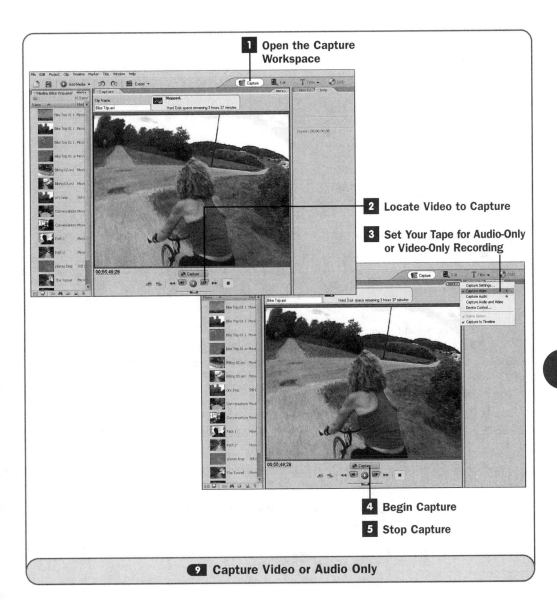

1 Open the Capture Workspace

2 Locate Video to Capture

3 Set Your Tape for Audio-Only or Video-Only Recording

4 Begin Capture

5 Stop Capture

9 Capture Video or Audio Only

2 Locate Video to Capture

By using the various playback and shuttle controls or your camcorder's VTR controls, locate the video clip you want to capture and pause your camcorder. (See **7** Control Your DV Camcorder During Capture.)

3 Set Your Tape for Audio-Only or Video-Only Recording

Click the **More** button in the **Monitor** panel and click to place the check mark next to either **Video Only** or **Audio Only**.

4 **Begin Capture**

Click the **Capture** button while your video is paused. If the **Device Control** for your camcorder is enabled (Premiere Elements turns this on for you if your camcorder is capable of supporting it), the camcorder's tape begins to play as capture begins. Otherwise, begin playback using your camcorder's physical controls.

5 **Stop Capture**

Click the **Stop Capture** button when you want your capture to stop. Your audio-only or video-only clip(s) are added to the **Media** panel.

To review your captured clips, see **11** **View Captured Clips**.

10 | **Capture to the Timeline or Media Panel**

✔ BEFORE YOU BEGIN	→ SEE ALSO
4 About Video Capture	**9** Capture Video or Audio Only
5 Capture Digital Video Using FireWire	**11** View Captured Clips
6 Capture Digital Video Using USB	**12** About Troubleshooting Capture Problems
7 Control Your DV Camcorder During Capture	
8 Capture Analog Video	

By default, Premiere Elements captures your video directly to your **Timeline**, a very convenient feature if you plan to simply capture, adjust your clips, and output.

However, many editors prefer to capture to the **Media** panel only, trimming and ordering their clips before assembling them on the **Timeline**.

Whatever your preference, you can easily change this default setting.

1 **Open the Capture Workspace**

To open the **Capture** workspace, click the **Capture** button in the upper-right corner of any workspace.

2 **Open Capture Preferences**

Click the **More** button in the **Capture Monitor** panel.

3 **Set Your Capture Option to Timeline**

Check or uncheck the **Capture to Timeline** option. Continue the process of capturing your audio or video, as described in the preceding tasks.

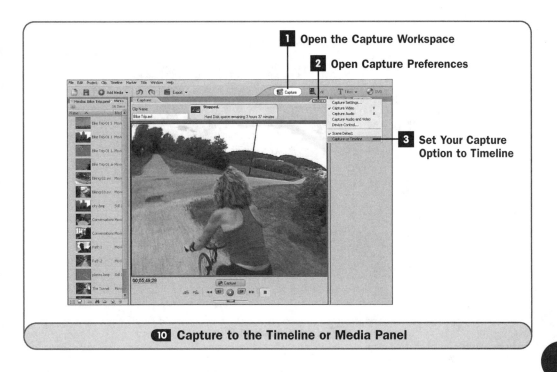

1 Open the Capture Workspace

2 Open Capture Preferences

3 Set Your Capture Option to Timeline

10 Capture to the Timeline or Media Panel

11 View Captured Clips

✔ BEFORE YOU BEGIN	→ SEE ALSO
4 About Video Capture	**7** Control Your DV Camcorder During Capture
5 Capture Digital Video Using FireWire	**9** Capture Video or Audio Only
6 Capture Digital Video Using USB	**10** Capture to the Timeline or Media Panel
8 Capture Analog Video	**12** About Troubleshooting Capture Problems

After you've captured your clips, you can view them right in your **Capture** workspace to ensure that your captures have been successful.

1 Disconnect Your Camcorder

Disconnect or simply turn off the camcorder. This might seem like a superfluous step but, because of the way Premiere Elements diverts resources during capture and output to tape, it can make a real difference in playback. If you leave your camcorder plugged in when you view your captured clips, the video playback often appears jumpy and uneven.

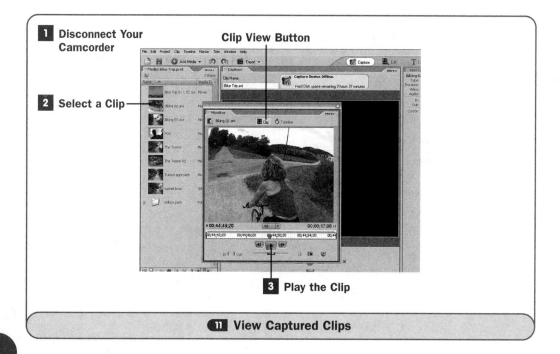

1 Disconnect Your Camcorder

Clip View Button

2 Select a Clip

3 Play the Clip

11 View Captured Clips

11

2 Select a Clip

While still in the **Capture** workspace, double-click the clip you want to review in the **Media** panel. This action opens the **Edit Monitor** panel. If your clip doesn't immediately appear in the **Monitor**, double-click it again or click the **Clip View** button at the top of the panel.

3 Play the Clip

Use the playback controls and the shuttle slider in the **Monitor** panel to play the selected clip in the **Edit Monitor** panel.

To keep your workspace from becoming cluttered, you can close the **Edit Monitor** panel.

12 About Troubleshooting Capture Problems

Capture is a vital part of a video editor's workflow. And there are few things as frustrating as not being able to start a project because you can't get your video into your computer.

Unfortunately, capture, along with its companion process of output to tape, is one of the processes most prone to technical challenges—some are related to the amount of power it demands and some are related to the way the operating system's drivers conflict or corrupt as they are affected by other programs installed on your computer.

If you're experiencing challenges connecting your camcorder to Premiere Elements or capturing to the program, here are some troubleshooting suggestions.

Your Camcorder Won't Connect to Windows

If a connection is being made between your camcorder and computer, you'll hear a tone or sound of some sort from your computer registering the connection. Your camcorder will also appear as an icon on the right side of the taskbar at the bottom of the screen. If your computer isn't registering your connection, a closer look at your system can yield some clues as to why not.

With your camcorder plugged in to your computer and turned on, right-click the **My Computer** icon on your desktop, select **Properties** from the context menu, click the **Hardware** tab at the top of the System Properties dialog box, and click the **Device Manager** button to open the **Device Manager** dialog box. Under the **Imaging Devices** category, you should see your camcorder listed.

The Windows Device Manager lists your camcorder.

If your device does not appear, you are not making a proper connection—quite possibly the result of a defective or improperly installed USB, USB Video Class 1.0 or IEEE-1394 (FireWire) device. If an unfamiliar driver name appears, your capture driver might have been overwritten or customized by another piece of capture software.

If you suspect that your drivers might be corrupted, there's an undocumented method for refreshing your drivers that, at the very least, won't do your computer or your operating system any harm. With your device connected and turned on, right-click on your device's listing in the **Imaging Devices** section of the **Device Manager** listing and select **Uninstall**. Your device listing temporarily disappears; a few moments later, Windows recognizes your device and installs fresh drivers for it. (If your camcorder or digitizing device came with a CD of its own driver software, be sure to install that software before refreshing your drivers. The hardware's website might provide even more recent driver updates.)

If you are connecting your computer and camcorder using FireWire, check under the listing for **IEEE-1394 Bus Host Controller** to ensure that it is listed as an **OHCI-Compliant IEEE-1394 Host Controller**. Only OHCI-compliant IEEE-1394 FireWire units can be guaranteed to work with Premiere Elements.

► **NOTES**

USB Video Class 1.0 connections require Windows XP with Service Pack 2.

Windows is only as good as the drivers it has in its library. Keep your drivers updated by installing any driver software that came with your camcorder or other digitizing device and regularly check the product's website for updates.

Your Camcorder Connects to Windows but Premiere Elements Doesn't Show It As Connected

Unfortunately, programs installed on your computer don't like to share. Video-editing programs are particularly greedy, each one vying for control over your video capture driver. If you have more than one video-editing program installed on your computer (particularly if you're running another version of Adobe Premiere), you might be experiencing a conflict.

In most cases, the most recently installed editing program takes control of the capture drivers. However, sometimes the simple act of opening another editing program transfers control of those drivers back to the other editing program.

► **NOTES**

Unlike most video-editing programs, Windows MovieMaker seems to freely share capture drivers with other editing programs and virtually never causes a programming conflict. In fact, a good test to find out whether Windows is connecting to your camcorder is to attempt to capture your video in MovieMaker.

Running a version of Adobe Premiere, especially an older version, on the same computer as you're running Premiere Elements has been known to cause capture problems. It's best to uninstall all but your current or preferred version of the software.

If this seems to be your situation, try re-installing Premiere Elements. You can also try re-installing Premiere Elements without uninstalling it, which will give you the option of running the repair utility. If this doesn't solve your problem, you might have to uninstall the conflicting program(s), refresh your drivers (as described in the preceding section), and re-install Premiere Elements as your only DV-AVI editing program.

It might also be worth your while to make sure that all is well in your **Device Manager**, as described in "Your Camcorder Won't Connect to Windows" earlier in this task. Also refer to the "You Can't Control Your Camcorder in Premiere Elements" section, later in this task.

Your Digitizing Device Doesn't Operate with Premiere Elements

Most third-party digitizing devices, particularly those sold to capture footage for export directly to DVDs, do not capture directly into Premiere Elements. These devices usually come with proprietary software and work ideally with that software. In most cases, the files (usually MPEGs) produced by these devices can then be imported into Premiere Elements using the **Media Downloader**.

However, only digitizing devices capable of saving video as DV-AVIs capture directly into Premiere Elements. (See **8** **Capture Analog Video**.)

On the other hand, many USB-connected digitizing devices work with the **Media Downloader**. (See **14** **Add Media with the Adobe Media Downloader**.)

To ensure your device is properly set up in Premiere Elements, see the following section.

You Can't Control Your Camcorder from Premiere Elements

Only camcorders connected directly to Premiere Elements by a FireWire or USB Video Class 1.0 connection can be controlled by the program.

If your camcorder is connected to Windows but you aren't making a proper connection with Premiere Elements, go to the **Capture** workspace (click the **Capture** button in the upper-right corner of any workspace) and, in the **Monitor** panel, click the **More** button and select **Device Control**.

Check the **Devices** drop-down menu to make sure that your connection method (**DV/HDV Device Control** or **USB Video Class 1.0 - Device Control**) is selected. If so, click the **Options** button to open the **Options** dialog box.

From the **Device Brand** drop-down list, choose your camcorder or digitizing device. If the specific brand is not listed, select **Generic**. Then open the **Device Type** drop-down list and, if available, choose the model number of your device. If you are using **Generic** or **Alternative** drivers, you might have to experiment with different settings from this second menu.

12

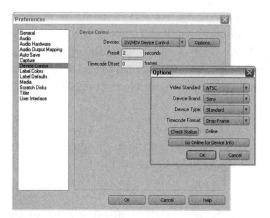

*Check the **Device Control** page of the Premiere Elements **Preferences** dialog box to make sure that the correct capture device is selected.*

If your device is turned on, Windows is registering it as being connected, but its status in this menu is still listed as **Offline**, click the **Check Status** button. If your device is still listed as being **Offline**, check to ensure that you have a proper connection as described in "Your Camcorder Won't Connect to Windows," earlier in this task.

12

Premiere Elements Doesn't Break Your Footage into Clips During Capture

Premiere Elements breaks your captured footage into clips based on points at which your camcorder was paused during recording. It is a time code–based process, and only works with DV that was captured using a FireWire or USB Video Class 1.0 connection.

*Capture options in the Premiere Elements **Preferences** dialog box.*

In the **Capture Monitor** panel, click the **More** button and ensure that the **Scene Detect** option is enabled.

Capture Continually Aborts

Your capture aborts for one of three reasons: The data flow cannot be sustained, a process has interrupted the data flow, or Premiere Elements believes you are dropping frames.

Your system might not be able to sustain the necessary data flow for video capture for a variety of reasons, all related to hardware. If your hard drive is too full (if it has less than 10–20GB of free space, for instance), the program has likely run out of space to write its relatively large video files. If this is the case, you might have to clear considerable data off your hard drive or add a larger drive for your captures. (See the "You Receive a Disk Full Error" section, later in this task.)

Processes interrupting your data flow can be more challenging. Most new computers can handle the intensive data flow required for video capture. However, computers operating at less than 2GHz or without enough RAM might find background processes and even spyware choking their captures. Some recommendations for streamlining this process are listed in **4** **About Video Capture**.

Your capture might also abort because of an indication of dropped frames. To override this, use the steps described in the following section.

Capture Continually Shows Dropped Frames Warning

Dropped frames can occur when a process or some other stoppage interrupts your capture. But you can also get a dropped frames warning when the program just can't quite figure out what's going on with your capture. These warnings are quite common when you're trying to capture analog video using a passthrough or DV bridge (See **8** **Capture Analog Video**). They don't always mean, however, that your captured video will be unusable.

Play back your captured video (see **11** **View Captured Clips**). If you find that the video is full of dropped frames and is unacceptable in terms of quality, you might want to turn off some background processes and/or increase your hardware resources (see **4** **About Video Capture**).

If you find that your captured video looks acceptable despite these warnings, you can turn off the dropped frame warning by clicking the **More** button in the **Capture Monitor** panel and selecting **Device Control**. In the **Preferences** dialog box that opens, click the **Capture** category in the list on the left side and disable both the **Abort Capture on Dropped Frames** and **Report Dropped Frames** options.

12

You Cannot Capture to an Internally Installed Second Hard Drive

A second drive, one dedicated to your video files, can greatly improve your performance, especially during capture and output to tape. But if you're continually finding your captures aborted or if your captured files look corrupted, your drive is likely set up improperly.

There is some debate about whether it is better to install your second hard drive as a slave channel with your C drive as the master, or whether you should install your second drive as the master on a second channel with your DVD burner as the slave. In our experience, either is acceptable and both should provide for an easy data flow during capture and output to tape.

Of greater importance is that your second drive is properly installed in your BIOS. In most cases in which capture to a second internal drive is problematic, an improper installation in the BIOS is the problem.

When you first boot up your computer, follow the instructions at your logo screen, before Windows starts up, to access your BIOS setup. (Usually you press the **Esc** or **F1** key.) If your drives are set up properly, you should see them listed as drives in this setup area. Otherwise, follow the necessary steps to set up your hardware. Remember that your hardware must be set up here—regardless of whether it is set up in your operating system—for it to function properly.

12

You Cannot Capture to an External Hard Drive

The challenges of capturing to an externally connected drive usually have to do with the limitations of the connection. An external drive that is connected to your computer with a FireWire connection might have problems maintaining the data flow of a video capture because it is sharing the line with your camcorder's incoming video data. This is definitely the case if you are using a router of some sort so you can have both devices attached to the same FireWire card at the same time. As a rule, it's not a good idea to have both your camcorder and an external drive attached to your computer by FireWire.

You might be able to capture your camcorder's video over a FireWire connection to an external drive connected to your computer by USB 2.0. A USB 1.0 connection for your external drive, however, is not able to handle the necessary throughput to accept video files as they are being captured.

You Receive a Disk Full Error

Although you might believe you still have room on your hard drive, it's technically impossible to literally fill a disk. Your operating system and other programs are continually writing temporary files to and reading temporary files from your disk. And huge files, such as video captures, often require large, contiguous blocks of space.

Try to keep at least 10–20GB of space available on your hard drive to ensure smooth operation of your system. (Encoding for DVD output can require much, much more. See **124** **About Troubleshooting DVD Output**.)

In short, the less free space you have on your hard drive, the more likely you are to run into processing errors. If you find the free space on your disk getting a bit lean, move or delete some of your files to make more room or install a larger hard drive. Giving your programs and your operating system lots of breathing room, especially when working with extremely large files, will definitely save you a lot of heartache in the long run.

12

4

Adding Media

IN THIS CHAPTER:

Being able to capture and edit your video is great; but what if you would like to add more? This chapter covers all the other types of media you can add to your project. It also discusses how to perform some simple edits on the front end, before your clips are actually on the **Timeline**.

You might want to add many file types to your movie. Sometimes you might find short clips on the Internet you would like to download and use.

▶ **WEB RESOURCE**
http://www.archive.org/details/prelinger
The Prelinger Archives have many videos that can be downloaded. Some of these date back to the early 1900s. Many of the clips are available in a number of formats and are in the public domain. This can be a fun place to search for clips that will add a special touch to your movie.

One creative way of enhancing your movie is to add still images along with the video. To do that, you have to import still image files from your hard drive. Whether the original source was from a digital camera, a scanner, or the Internet, you can add those still images to your movie. Another fun addition covered in this chapter is the Counting Leader (you know, the little countdown before the movie starts).

13

You will also learn how to extract video from a non-copy-protected DVD. This way, you can get clips from previous projects into new ones, even if you don't have the original files anymore. You can also download still images directly from your digital camera. So let's see what the **Media** panel is all about.

13 About the Media Panel

✔ **BEFORE YOU BEGIN**

1 Start a New Project
4 About Video Capture

You are on your way to becoming a video artist. If you were a painter, you would need tools to work with—paint, brushes, canvas—and the **Media** panel is where you keep the paint. The **Media** panel holds all the clips and images that may, and usually do, end up in your movie.

The figure shows the **Media** panel with two images: one is a captured video clip and the other is a title. The other features in the figure include

▶ **NOTE**
To learn about titles and how to create them, see 95 About Titles.

Play Button
  Poster View
    Preview Window

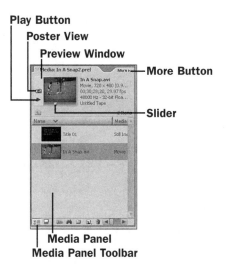

More Button

Slider

Media Panel
Media Panel Toolbar

*The **Media** panel holds all the clips and images that may be used in your movie.*

- **Preview window**—This is where you get an advanced look at your clips and images. Click a clip in the **Media** panel to view it in this preview window. To open the preview window, click the **More** button and choose **View, Preview Area**.

- **Poster view**—This little camera icon allows you to set the image you would like displayed as the thumbnail view in the **Media** panel. It can be any frame in the clip—just move the slider or play the clip until you come to the image you want and then click the **Poster View** button.

- **Play button**—This button, when clicked, plays the highlighted clip in the **Media** panel. After you click the **Play** button, it turns into a **Stop** button.

- **Media panel**—This is where all of the clips and images that you import are stored.

- **Media panel toolbar**—This toolbar holds a number of useful shortcuts. Each icon does the following (from left to right); **List View, Icon View, Create Slideshow, Find** (this enables you to search for media in the **Media** panel), **Create a New Folder, Add New Item,** and lastly, **Clear** (or **Delete**).

- **More button**—The **More** button, as always, leads to a list of many options from which to choose. Click the **More** button to open a menu with the options shown in the following figure.

13

The *More* button menu for the *Media* panel.

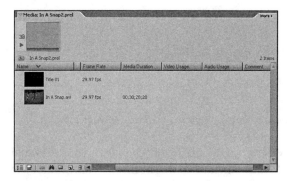

Drag the edge of the Media panel to expand it; notice the different columns.

13

By clicking the right mouse button on an empty space in the **Media** panel (such as in a blank spot in the **Media** bin), you open a context menu that provides additional options concerning the **Media** panel.

The *Media* panel context menu.

That concludes your tour and basic overview of what is available from this panel. In the following tasks, you will discover the individual functions performed in the **Media** panel and how to get media from various locations into your project.

14　Add Media with the Adobe Media Downloader

✔ BEFORE YOU BEGIN	→ SEE ALSO
🔢 About the Media Panel	🔢 About Troubleshooting Media Additions
	🔢 Make an Instant Slideshow

You can add media from a various number of sources: DVDs, images and video from your hard drive, images stored on removable drives, or images from a digital camera. Premiere Elements makes it very simple to add image and video files to your projects with the Adobe **Media Downloader** and the **Add Media** button.

1　Select Add Media from Files or Folders

Click the **Add Media** button in the taskbar and select **From Files or Folders**. The **Add Media** dialog box opens.

2　Browse for Media

In the **Add Media** dialog box, you can go browsing for images or video that you want to use in your project. From the **Look in** drop-down list, choose the drive or main folder in which you want to look for media.

3　Select Individual Media or an Entire Folder

To select multiple media files, press the **Ctrl** key and click the images you want to bring into your project. Alternatively, click to select an image, press the **Shift** key, and use the down-arrow key to select consecutive images. If you want to add all the images in a folder to the **Media** panel, just click to select the folder.

4　Add Media to the Media Panel

If you have selected a number of images inside a folder, click the **Open** button to add those images to the **Media** panel. If you selected an entire folder, click the **Add Folder** button.

▶ **NOTE**

After adding an audio file or a video file that contains audio, Premiere Elements performs a scan of the audio. At the bottom-right side of the screen you might see the message "Conforming audio" or "Generating peak file." This process is normal and is needed for Premiere Elements to play back the audio properly. Depending on the size of your file and the speed of your computer, this process can take anywhere from a few seconds to more than 10 minutes.

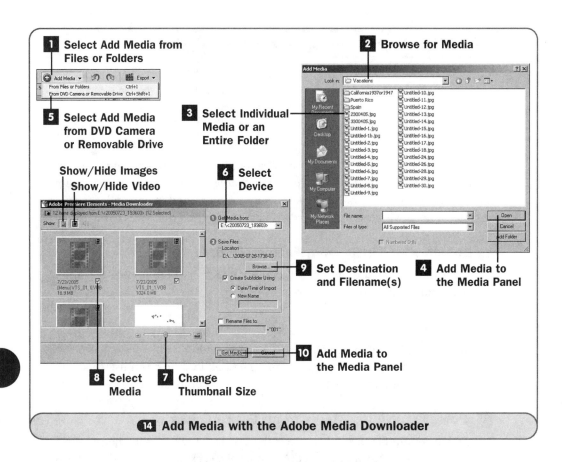

1 Select Add Media from Files or Folders

2 Browse for Media

5 Select Add Media from DVD Camera or Removable Drive

3 Select Individual Media or an Entire Folder

Show/Hide Images
Show/Hide Video

6 Select Device

9 Set Destination and Filename(s)

4 Add Media to the Media Panel

10 Add Media to the Media Panel

8 Select Media

7 Change Thumbnail Size

14 Add Media with the Adobe Media Downloader

5 Select Add Media from DVD Camera or Removable Drive

To add media that's located on a DVD, digital camera, or a removable drive, click the **Add Media** button and select **From DVD Camera or Removable Drive**. This command takes you to the **Adobe Media Downloader** dialog box.

6 Select Device

When the **Media Downloader** first opens, the center area, where the media is displayed, is empty. You see a message in that area that says, "Please select a device to get media."

The **Get media from** drop-down list at the top-right side of the screen is where you select the device from which you want to retrieve the media. If you have only one device (such as a digital camera) connected to your computer, that device is the only option in this list. If, however, you have multiple DVD drives and have inserted a DVD in each one, plus you have connected your digital camera, you can select any of these devices from the **Get media from** list.

The combo box displays the message "Select a Device;" click the down arrow and select the device that holds the media you want to add to the **Media** panel. After the device is selected, the images appear automatically in the **Media Downloader**'s importable files area.

7 Change Thumbnail Size

At the bottom center of the screen there is a slider. Move the slider to the right to make the images in the center part of the screen larger; move the slider to the left to make the images smaller.

▶ **NOTE**

The **Adobe Media Downloader** dialog box can be resized by dragging the sides of the dialog box in or out. The dialog box does have a minimum size, however, and will not let you make it smaller than that minimum.

8 Select Media

Each media item shown in the center of the box has a filename and check box. The filename tells you something about the file and its size. Click to place a check in the box under each file that you want to download into the **Media** panel for the current project. There are two buttons at the top of the **Media Downloader**: One is a small framed picture icon and is used to show or hide the images in the importable files area. The other is a small film icon that is used to show or hide the video in the importable files area.

14

9 Set Destination and Filename(s)

On the right side of the screen are various **Save Files** options for the destination and name of the files you are going to download. You can browse for a destination folder for the files. You can also have the **Media Downloader** create a subfolder for you with options of date/time and name. You can even give each file a name of your choice, followed by an incrementing number starting with 001 (such as **MyMediaFile001**, **MyMediaFile002**, and so on).

10 Add Media to the Media Panel

Now that you have selected the media files to be downloaded and specified where you want these files stored on your computer, click the **Get Media** button. The files are added to the **Media** panel and saved in the location you selected. The default location is **My Documents**, **My Videos**, **Adobe**, in a new subfolder named with the date and time.

▶ **NOTE**

Depending on the size of the file(s) and your computer speed, downloading media can take from several minutes to several hours.

---

15   Add Special Media Clips

✔ BEFORE YOU BEGIN	→ SEE ALSO
13 About the Media Panel	**34** Trim a Clip on the Timeline
	72 Control a Video Track's Opacity over Time
	93 Show Your Video Through a Shape or Text

Premiere Elements comes with four clips that will become quite valuable to you and your movies. The clips include Bars and Tone, Black Video, Color Matte, and a Universal Counting Leader.

14

1 Open the Context Menu and Choose New Item

Find an empty area in the **Media** panel and right-click it. This action brings up a context menu with various options; the third item down is **New Item**.

Move your mouse to highlight the **New Item** selection; another menu drops down. This submenu holds all the special media clip choices.

▶ **NOTE**

At the top of the **New Item** submenu, notice the **Title** option. To learn about titles and how to create them, see **95** About Titles.

2 Select Clip Option

From the **New Item** submenu, select the name of the clip you want to add to the **Media** panel (and eventually to the **Timeline** and your movie).

You might have seen something similar to a **Bars and Tone** clip come up on your television set from time to time. (This kind of clip is also known as a *test pattern* or *test screen*.) The special clip in the **New Item** submenu is called **Bars and Tone** because that is what you see and hear: There are colored bars that appear on the screen and a very audible tone to go along with it. To add the **Bars and Tone** clip to the **Media** panel, select that option.

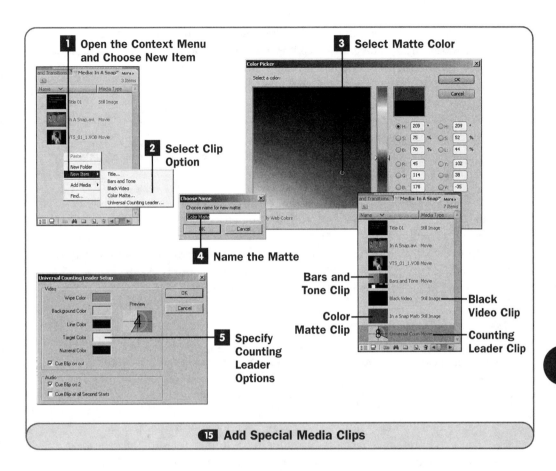

1 Open the Context Menu and Choose New Item

2 Select Clip Option

3 Select Matte Color

4 Name the Matte

5 Specify Counting Leader Options

Bars and Tone Clip

Color Matte Clip

Black Video Clip

Counting Leader Clip

15 Add Special Media Clips

15

▶ **TIP**

Use the **Bars and Tone** clip at the end of your movie to remind you when the movie ends. That way you will never have to wait and wonder if there is another clip coming up.

The **Black Video** clip is just what it says, a clip of nothing but black. To add the **Black Video** clip to the **Media** panel, select that menu option.

▶ **TIP**

The **Black Video** clip is great for separating clips and for using as a background for text-only titles. You will use this special clip in **101** Create a *Star Wars*-Style Credit Roll.

Another clip option is the **Color Matte**. Similar to the **Black Video** clip, the **Color Matte** clip allows you to choose from millions of colors. This is an excellent tool for adding color background to your slideshows along with many other uses. The **Color Matte** clip also gives you the ability to add a

White Video, which works well as a background for a title with black or dark-colored text. The **Color Matte** clip has many uses, and in time you will probably think of them all. If you select the **Color Matte** option, you will be taken to the **Color Picker** dialog box (continue with step 3).

▶ **TIP**

You can export the **Color Matte** clip, add a cutout to the matte in Photoshop Elements, and import the clip back into Premiere Elements. Then you can use the edited matte as an overlay for a title or intro clip.

The next clip option is the **Universal Counting Leader**. Leaders are used to mark the beginning of a roll of film. You sometimes see them at the start of a movie, counting down from 10 to 1 with a few beeps thrown in. Many people like to have the countdown at the beginning of their movies, and it is a very popular addition. Premiere Elements gives you one counting leader clip option, but many ways to enhance and customize it.

▶ **TIP**

Be sure to give your **Color Matte** a pertinent name. Use a name that will help remind you of its purpose, and where it will be used (such as **pink matte for baby video**).

15

3 Select Matte Color

In the **Color Picker** dialog box, choose a color for your matte. You can choose from millions of colors, or from a more limited selection of web-safe colors. Simply pick the color you want the matte to be and click **OK**.

4 Name the Matte

After you have chosen the color for your **Color Matte** clip and clicked the **OK** button, you are asked to name your matte. Simply type the new name for the matte in the text box and click **OK**. Your new **Color Matte** clip is added to the **Media** panel.

5 Specify Counting Leader Options

If you select the **Universal Counting Leader** option from the **New Item** submenu, the **Universal Counting Leader Setup** dialog box opens.

You can change the color of any object on the counting leader screen—from the target to the number and the wipe. To select a new color for that object, click the color box next to the object's name. The **Color Picker** appears, offering you a choice of millions of colors. Because you can select a different color for each of the objects (**Wipe Color, Background Color, Line Color, Target**

Color, and **Numeral Color**), the combinations are limitless. You can also set the audio cue blips—the little *blip* noises you hear during the countdown. The options are **Cue Blip on Out, Cue Blip on 2,** and **Cue Blip on all Second Starts**. The counting leader clip is a fun clip to play around with.

After you have set your sound options and colors for the counting leader, click the **OK** button to add the **Universal Counting Leader** clip to the **Media** panel.

16 Create and Use Media Folders

✔ BEFORE YOU BEGIN	→ SEE ALSO
13 About the Media Panel	**17** Sort the Media Panel by Different Characteristics
14 Add Media with the Adobe Media Downloader	

Something that will help you stay organized is the ability to add folders to the **Media** panel. You can name these folders anything you want, and they will hold any number of clips. You can expand and collapse the folders, saving space in the **Media** panel, and you can use the folders to organize your clips better. In **14** **Add Media with the Adobe Media Downloader**, you learned that it was possible to add an entire folder of images to the **Media** panel. When you do that, the folder appears in the **Media** panel with all its images contained within it. You also have the option of adding and naming an empty folder and dragging clips or images into it. You open and close the folders by clicking the little arrow to the left of the folder. This feature helps keep your **Media** panel nice and tidy—as well as making it a bit easier to find and keep track of things.

16

1 Click New Folder

At the bottom of the **Media** panel is a small folder icon. Click this icon to create a new folder in the **Media** panel.

2 Name Your New Folder

After the folder is created in the **Media** panel, you can give the new folder a name. Make sure to use a name that will clearly explain what is inside, such as a particular date or event (for example, **My Wedding** or **Heather 1995**). Press **Enter** after you have typed the name of the new folder.

▶ TIP

To rename an existing folder, simply click the folder name; when the text becomes editable, type the new name.

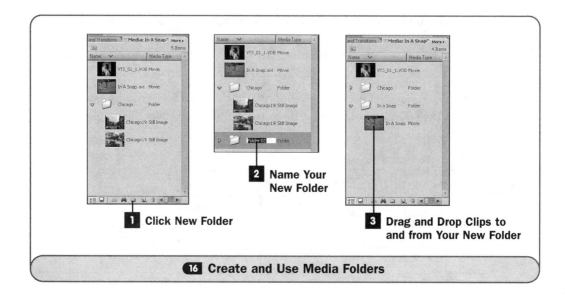

2 Name Your
New Folder

1 Click New Folder

3 Drag and Drop Clips to
and from Your New Folder

16 Create and Use Media Folders

3 **Drag and Drop Clips to and from Your New Folder**

After naming the folder, all there is left to do is drag your clips into it. You
can drag clips from other folders into the new folder, drag clips that exist in
the **Media** panel but not in a folder, or drag clips from Windows Explorer or
My Computer. You can move clips to and from folders as often as you like;
you also can add as many folders as you need. You can nest folders inside
each other (and even nest folders inside those nested folders). Just drag and
drop one folder onto another to make it a subfolder. Access the subfolders by
clicking the little arrow in front of the folder icon.

17 **Sort the Media Panel by Different Characteristics**

✔ **BEFORE YOU BEGIN**

13 About the Media Panel
16 Create and Use Media Folders

→ **SEE ALSO**

2 Customize Your Workspaces
3 Nest Your Panels to Save Desktop
Space

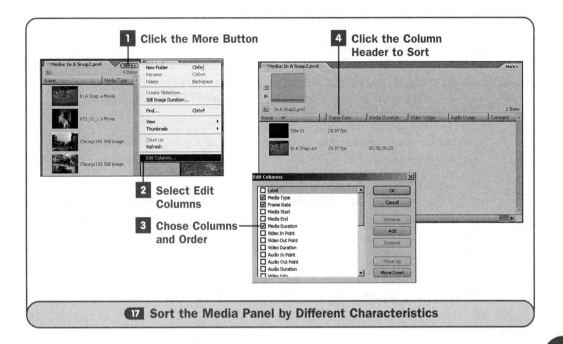

1 Click the More Button

4 Click the Column Header to Sort

2 Select Edit Columns

3 Chose Columns and Order

17 Sort the Media Panel by Different Characteristics

Another nice function in Premiere Elements is that you can sort the **Media** panel in many ways. This can help you find clips and information about the use of those clips in your project. The **Media** panel has columns of information for each clip. You can add a total of 28 columns to the panel, and you can sort your clips by any of the columns displayed. The information in some of the columns is quite handy, such as the **Comment**, **Description**, and **Log Note** columns. These columns allow you to add text to your clips' information, making it easier to remember why that clip is there in the first place. If you do any major projects, you can have hundreds of clips, titles, videos, stills, and so on. Keeping track of it all—and remembering the purpose for each clip—can be quite a chore. The **Media** panel can help make that chore a little less laborious.

1 Click the More Button

To open the **Edit Columns** dialog box that lists all the columns you can display in the **Media** panel, click the **More** button at the top-right side of the **Media** panel.

2 Select Edit Columns

From the **More** menu, select **Edit Columns** to display the **Edit Columns** dialog box.

3 **Chose Columns and Order**

In the **Edit Columns** dialog box, choose the columns you want to display in the **Media** panel. Although you can sort by any of the columns you display, the more columns you have, the more you will have to expand the **Media** panel to see them all. Simply check the box in front of the column name you want to display in the **Media** panel.

You can also move the columns up or down, add new ones, rename existing ones, and delete them.

Select a column that you want to move closer to the top of the list in the dialog box (and closer to the left edge of the **Media** panel). Click the **Move Up** button to move the selected column up one slot closer to the top of the list; keep clicking **Move Up** until the column is positioned where you want it in the list. Do the same with the **Move Down** button to move a column toward the bottom of the list in the dialog box (and farther from the left edge of the **Media** panel).

When you have finalized the order of the columns, click **OK**.

17

▶ **NOTE**

The columns you've selected in the **Edit Columns** dialog box appear in the **Media** panel from left to right. In the **Edit Columns** dialog box, the column at the top of the list is the first to appear on the left side of the **Media** panel; as you move down the list in the dialog box, the columns move right in the **Media** panel. (Just remember, top is left and bottom is right.) You want the most important columns to be at or near the top of the list in the **Edit Columns** dialog box.

4 **Click the Column Header to Sort**

Drag the edge of the **Media** panel out to the right, expanding it, to see the columns you chose to display. If there is not enough room for them all to appear on screen, a scroll bar appears at the bottom of the **Media** panel that you can use to scroll to all the columns. To sort your clips by the different column characteristics, click the column name, or header, at the top of the panel.

To type text in the **Comment**, **Description**, or **Log Note** column, click in the area below the column header and type the note or comment.

18 | **About Troubleshooting Media Additions**

✔ BEFORE YOU BEGIN	→ SEE ALSO
14 Add Media with the Adobe Media Downloader	**19** Trim Clips in the Media Panel **49** Control Interlacing and Field Options

In the attempt to add various types of files to your project, you might at times run into some problems.

Not only are there many types of files containing video, still images, and audio, you can put these files together using any number of software solutions. Take, for instance, still images; a digital image is just that, a digital image. When you compress it with software, it becomes a particular type of image, such as TIF, JPEG, or GIF. These types of files are only wrappers for the image itself. The wrappers tell your software how the images are compressed and how to uncompress them. The same goes for video and audio files.

File Types and Codecs

Still image file types are very common and widely used; therefore, you should not have any problem with the basic still image formats such as TIF, JPEG, PSD (Photoshop files), or GIF. These formats all work just fine in Premiere Elements.

Unlike their still-image counterparts, however, video and audio files are not so universally accepted. Video comes in a number of formats; MPEG1, MPEG2, MPEG4, MOV, AVI, DV-AVI, and WMV are the most common. For audio files, there are the WMA, WAV, and MP3 formats, among others. The one thing that is common between them all is that video is video and audio is audio. The names, or file types, are simply wrappers that the video or audio comes in. These wrappers are made by many software companies; some are industry standard and others are proprietary. The proprietary versions are generally made to work with that company's software and not with any other software. This is why we sometimes say that these types of files don't play well with Premiere Elements.

The software used to wrap your video and audio are called *codecs* (*compressor/ decompressor*). Codecs are also used to burn and play DVDs (in this instance, the word *codec* refers to *encoders/decoders*). All codecs work the same way: They instruct the software how to compress or decompress the file. Some codecs do not work well with various video-editing software programs. You sometimes find a file that opens and plays fine in one program but not in another. Premiere Elements is particularly choosy about what codecs it will and will not use. Some of the symptoms of bad files are video but no audio, no video or audio, only importing a small portion of the file, not being able to edit the file after importing it, and not being able to burn a DVD using that file.

Usually the problem appears right from the start—when the file cannot be imported at all. If you have a problem with particular file types, there are a few ways to deal with them.

18

▶ **NOTE**

Even though you can import various types of files into Premiere Elements, the program is designed specifically to edit DV-AVI files and does that best. Whenever possible, use DV-AVI formatted files.

Converting Files

Many programs can be used to convert video and audio files to different formats. Sometimes it is as simple as importing the file and then using the **Save As** command to save the file in the new file type. At any time, you can convert a file to either the MainConcept DV-AVI file type or the Microsoft DV-AVI file type (using a third-party conversion tool); you can then successfully bring those files into your project. One possible solution is to first import the file into Windows Movie Maker. From there, you can export the file as a Microsoft DV-AVI file. You can then import that converted file into Premiere Elements.

▶ **NOTE**

Microsoft DV-AVI and MainConcept DV-AVI are two separate proprietary codecs available for encoding/compressing or decoding/decompressing video files. Premiere Elements works best using video files contained in either of these two codecs.

18

▶ **WEB RESOURCE**

www.virtualdub.org/

Virtualdub is a free video-conversion program used by many professionals and hobbyists alike. Download a copy from this site.

http://sourceforge.net/projects/audacity/

Audacity is a free audio-conversion and editing tool. Download it from this site.

Some media files can be converted using programs already on your computer. Both Windows Movie Maker and Windows Media Player can convert some file types to others. To save yourself time and headaches, use DV-AVI files captured with Premiere Elements as often as possible.

Downloaded Music Files

For a small amount of money, you can download a song from a website today. During your video career, you will probably have the need to do that at some point, with the goal of using the audio file in your movie project. The problem is, when you download the file, you cannot use it in your project. The music files are licensed and have built-in security, making them unusable in their present state except in Media Player, Quicktime, or RealPlayer. There is a workaround for this that will get those songs into your project with little effort.

After downloading your song, simply use your CD-burning software to burn the song to a CD. Then rip the music back to your computer. That resulting file can be easily imported into your project.

▶ TIPS

When you rip the music file back to your hard drive, save the file as a WMA, MP3, WAV, or PCM file. These file formats work best with Premiere Elements. Windows Media Player 10 does an excellent job of burning and ripping—and best of all, it came free with your computer.

When you need to work with QuickTime files (MOV and certain MP3 files), you must have at least the free version of QuickTime 6 or later installed on your computer. You can also purchase a copy of QuickTime Pro and convert QuickTime files to other formats.

Peak File and Conforming Audio

When you see the messages "Generating peak file" or "Conforming audio" in the bottom-right of your screen, you might think there is a problem but there isn't. Whenever you import an audio file that was not captured by Premiere Elements, Premiere elements might generate a peak file or conform the audio on the imported audio file. The peak files hold information that Premiere Elements uses when playing the audio file on the **Timeline**. Conforming audio is changing the audio sample rate to match the rate specified in the project settings. Depending on the size of the original audio file and the speed of your computer, generating the peak file and conforming audio can take from 10 seconds to more than 10 minutes.

Interlaced and De-interlaced Video

When capturing video in either NTSC (at 30 frames per second) or PAL (at 25 frames per second), you are actually capturing fields at twice that rate. *Interlaced video* is what you view on a television set. A standard television set cannot display the captured frames consecutively, so it breaks the frames into fields and inter-laces the fields together. Therefore, you have really captured 60 frames for NTSC and 50 frames for PAL. The frames are split into odd fields and even fields, and then interlaced together to create the 30 or 25 frames needed for the display. In some cases this interlacing can cause problems, such as flickering.

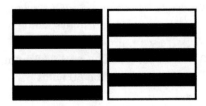

Interlaced video takes fields from one frame and combines them with fields from the next frame.

18

In the figure, you see that there are two frames. These frames are split into odd and even fields. The odd field is then combined, or interlaced, with the even field to create one single frame. The reason for this is that a long time ago in a land not so far away, when television was new and still in black and white, televisions were unable to refresh at high speeds. They were limited to 30 or 25 frames per second, potentially causing flickering on the screen. Interlacing solved this problem. When playing interlaced video on your computer, you will notice black bars at times. These interlacing artifacts occur mostly during high-motion scenes. These artifacts are not generally noticed on your television set, primarily because of resolution and refresh rates, but on your computer, with high resolutions and refresh rates, they become visible.

Contrary to the interlaced approach of the TV, your computer plays the full frames consecutively, or de-interlaced. This approach to playing video is also called *progressive scan*, one full frame at a time. To display the video properly on your computer, it might be necessary to de-interlace your interlaced video. In reverse, it might be necessary to interlace your de-interlaced video for display on your television.

▶ WEB RESOURCES

www.100fps.com/

www.answers.com/topic/deinterlacing

www.videoguys.com/dtvhome.html

There is a variety of information about progressive scan, or de-interlacing and interlacing on the World Wide Web; videoguys.com has a wide range of information on all aspects of digital video.

Besides visiting the websites listed above, do a Google search for *interlacing* or *de-interlacing*.

Most professional digital video editors not only have a computer monitor to watch the developing video on, they also have a television monitor hooked up to the computer as well. This dual-screen approach is especially handy for dealing with captured, analog video (although interlacing artifacts can also occur with digital video from your camcorder).

When a TV capture card or camcorder records video to be shown on a TV screen, it must interlace frames. Interlaced frames are what a TV screen displays, while a computer screen displays de-interlaced, or progressive scan, images. Therefore, even though we are working with speeds of 30 frames per second (in NTSC format; 25 frames per second in PAL), your camcorder is actually recording 60 fields per second (NTSC). Every other field is interlaced (combined) with the next field (60 interlaced fields adds up to 30 interlaced frames) to give you the picture you see on the TV screen. Your computer screen is happy with just the 30 uncombined frames, and displays that just fine.

▶ **NOTE**

An interlaced display alternates between drawing the even-numbered lines and the odd-numbered lines of each picture. In the PAL and NTSC standards, the lower (even) field is always drawn first.

19 Trim Clips in the Media Panel

✔ BEFORE YOU BEGIN	→ SEE ALSO
4 About Video Capture	**20** About the Monitor Panel
13 About the Media Panel	**34** Trim a Clip on the Timeline
14 Add Media with the Adobe Media Downloader	**37** Remove a Section of a Clip
18 About Troubleshooting Media Additions	**39** Remove Audio and Video from a Clip

You can perform some simple edits before moving your clips to the **Timeline**. The **Timeline** is where you do your precise editing—adding effects and transitions—on the way to your finished product. If you are like most videographers, you end up capturing more video than you can use in the final movie project. Sometimes you have no choice but to add an entire clip when all you want is a small piece of it. This task explains how to trim those clips down to just the size you need while the clip is still in the **Media** panel. One of the great things about Premiere Elements is that it is a nonlinear editing system, which means that any clips you happen to trim or cut into pieces actually remain intact. The process of editing the clips on the **Timeline** never harms the original file in any way. You can add that original file to other projects over and over—in its original state. All information about the clips and what has been done to edit them is stored in the Premiere Elements project files.

Even if you have already dropped the clip on the **Timeline**, you can extract a small piece to be used again, without having to drop the whole clip onto the **Timeline** a second time.

▶ **NOTE**

Before you begin this task, make sure that you have at least one video clip added to the **Media** panel.

19

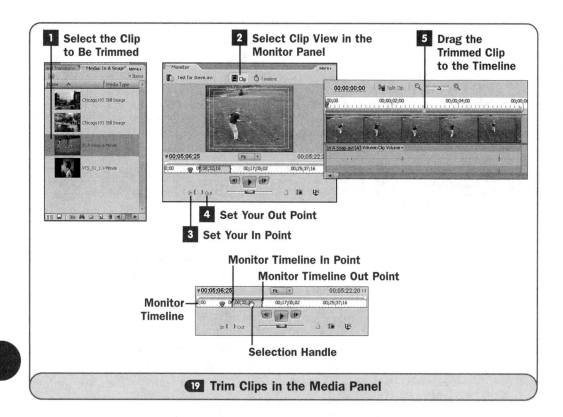

1 Select the Clip to Be Trimmed

2 Select Clip View in the Monitor Panel

5 Drag the Trimmed Clip to the Timeline

4 Set Your Out Point

3 Set Your In Point

Monitor Timeline In Point

Monitor Timeline Out Point

Monitor Timeline

Selection Handle

19   Trim Clips in the Media Panel

1 Select the Clip to Be Trimmed

Click the clip in the **Media** panel that you want to trim. This action high-lights the clip. Double-clicking the clip in the panel also works; the clip opens in the **Monitor** panel. You can also drag the clip to the **Monitor** panel and drop it there. (If you double-click or drag and drop the clip, continue with step 3.)

2 Select Clip View in the Monitor Panel

With your clip highlighted, click the **Clip View** button in the **Monitor** panel. This action opens the selected clip in the **Monitor**. If you double-clicked the clip in step 1, the clip should already be visible and the **Clip View** button already engaged.

3 Set Your In Point

First find the scene you want to add to your project. Use the shuttle and VCR controls or drag the CTI along the timeline in the **Monitor** panel to find the beginning of the scene you want to keep from the current clip. When you

have the beginning frame of your scene in the **Monitor,** click the **In** button
to set your *In point.* You have just marked the beginning point of your video
clip that will be added to the **Timeline** later.

▶ **TIP**

With Premiere Elements, you can choose to trim audio and video together, audio only, or
video only by clicking the **Audio/Video Toggle** button. See **20** About the Monitor Panel
for details.

▶ **NOTE**

The shuttle is a great tool and can show the video at fast or slow speeds in the **Monitor**
panel. The VCR controls can be used to play the video at normal speed; use the **Step**
Forward button to advance one frame at a time; use the **Step Back** button to reverse
through the video one frame at a time. These controls give you the ability to set precise
In and **Out** points. Your **In** and **Out** points can be as close together or as far apart as
you like.

4 Set Your Out Point

Just as you located the beginning of the scene to set the **In** point, use the controls to advance the video to find your ending or **Out** point. When you find
the place where you want the scene to end, click the **Out** button.

As you set your initial **In** and **Out** points, the selected area appears in the
Monitor Timeline. You can also grab the **In** and **Out** points on the **Monitor**
Timeline and drag to the right or left to set new **In** and **Out** points. You can
also grab the selection handle and drag all of the selected area right or left
along the **Monitor Timeline.**

5 Drag the Trimmed Clip to the Timeline

You have just created one small clip out of the larger clip. The **In** point you
set is the beginning and the **Out** point is the end of your new subclip. Click
the clip in the preview window (any area that shows your clip will do) in the
Monitor panel, drag it to the **Timeline,** and drop it there. Only the trimmed
section of the original video clip is now on the **Timeline.** The entire clip still
remains in the **Media** panel to be used again.

For example, you can go back to the **Monitor** panel and set new **In** and **Out**
points for the original video clip to create a different subclip. You can then
drag that new trimmed clip to the **Timeline** as well.

▶ **NOTE**

You can set only one **In** and one **Out** point each time you trim a clip.

---

20   About the Monitor Panel

✔ BEFORE YOU BEGIN	→ SEE ALSO
1 Start a New Project **4** About Video Capture **14** Add Media with the Adobe Media Downloader	**19** Trim Clips in the Media Panel **21** Grab a Still from Video

The **Monitor** panel is where all the action is. This is the where you view your clips. You can click to view the video from either the **Media** panel or the **Timeline**, but the video is displayed in the **Monitor**. You use the **Monitor** to view effects and transitions applied to your clips, trim your clips, and grab still images from your clips. This task takes you on a tour of the **Monitor** panel and all of its offerings.

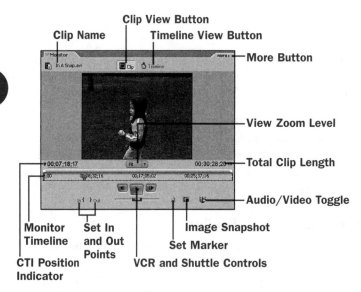

The **Monitor** panel offers many controls for viewing and working with your video clips.

There are many options to choose from in the **Monitor** panel:

- **The Timeline View button**—When the CTI is over a clip in the **Timeline**, click this button to display the **Timeline** clip in the **Monitor**.

- **The Clip View button**—This button displays a highlighted, or selected, clip from the **Media** panel in the **Monitor**.

- **View zoom level**—Select the zoom level of the clip shown in the **Monitor** from this drop-down list.

- **Clip name**—This is the name of the clip currently being displayed in the **Monitor**.

- **CTI position indicator**—This item shows the current time position of the CTI in the **Monitor** panel timeline. The time is shown in **Hours; Minutes; Seconds; Frames** format.

- **Monitor timeline**—The timeline for the current clip in the **Monitor**.

- **Set In and Out points**—Click these buttons to set **In** and **Out** points to trim clips in the **Media** panel (see **19** **Trim Clips in the Media Panel**).

- **VCR and shuttle controls**—Use the VCR and shuttle controls to move through the clip in the **Monitor**.

- **Set Marker**—Click this button to set an unnumbered timeline marker. For more information on the unnumbered timeline marker and its purpose, see **27** **Change Slides to the Beat of Music**.

- **Image Snapshot button**—Click this small camera icon to produce a still image of the current **Monitor** view.

- **Audio/Video toggle**—The **Audio/Video** toggle is visible if you have the **Monitor** in **Clip View** and a clip is highlighted in the **Media** panel. This button toggles between **Video and Audio**, **Video Only**, and **Audio Only** modes. When trimming clips in the **Media** panel, you can create a new clip. That clip can include video only, audio only, or video and audio combined. When this button is toggled to the Audio Only mode, you will see the audio waveform in the **Monitor** window. The icon switches from a film and speaker icon (Video and Audio), a film icon (Video Only), and a speaker icon (Audio Only) so you always know what you're trimming.

20

Take Video and Audio   **Take Video Only**   **Take Audio Only**

*The **Audio/Video** toggle in its three positions.*

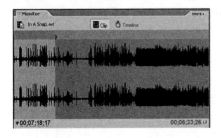

*When the **Audio/Video** toggle is in the **Audio Only** position, you see the audio waveform in the **Monitor**.*

- **Total clip length**—This shows the total length of the clip in the **Monitor** view in **Hours; Minutes; Seconds; Frames** format.

- **More button**—As do all panels, the **Monitor** panel has a **More** button in the top-right corner. Click this button to see the **Safe Margins** and **Playback Settings** options.

  Safe Margins is a very helpful tool and can be turned on and off from the **More** menu. It is best to keep safe margins turned on when you are using text or resizing clips. The safe margins are two boxes inside the **Monitor** view: The inside box is the safe margin for titles and other text and the outer box is the safe margin for actions or images. These margins let you know when you are out of the viewable area for a television screen. If your project is only going to be viewed on a computer, you can turn off or ignore the **Safe Margins** because the whole screen area is viewable on a computer monitor. Especially when working with titles, it's important to have the **Safe Margins** turned on so you can see whether all your titles will show on the TV screen.

**Title and Text   Action Safe
Safe Margin   Margin**

The Action and Title or Text safe margins.

  Choose the **Playback Settings** option from the **More** menu to display the **Playback Settings** dialog box. There are settings available for **Realtime Playback, Export Device, 24p Conversion,** and **Desktop Video Mode**.

- **Monitor panel context menus**—When you right-click in a blank area on the **Monitor** panel, a context menu appears. This menu provides additional options that can be useful as you work with Premiere Elements. You will be directed to use the context menu when appropriate in the upcoming tasks.

20

21 Grab a Still from Video

✔ BEFORE YOU BEGIN	→ SEE ALSO
4 About Video Capture	**23** Scale and Position a Still
14 Add Media with the Adobe Media Downloader	**116** Customize an Image as a Chapter Icon
19 Trim Clips in the Media Panel	**118** Customize a Menu with Any Background
20 About the Monitor Panel	

Eventually, you will look at captured video and decide it would be nice to grab a still image from the video footage. Sometimes you get a great shot with your camcorder and wish you would have used a camera. These great shots *can* be exported as still images with Premiere Elements in a few simple steps. The stills you capture from your video footage can be added to your project automatically and also saved to your hard drive.

► NOTE

The still is saved as an interlaced 720×480 pixel image in the format you select in step 4. The quality of video stills is a bit low for printing—although a 4"×6" photo print might be satisfactory. The resolution of the extracted still image also depends on the source of the clip (analog video from a VHS tape or video from a DV camcorder). If you want to print your still image, you might have to de-interlace it in Premiere Elements (as explained in **49** Control Interlacing and Field Options) or with photo-editing software such as Photoshop Elements. If you use the image in your project and burn it to a DVD, the interlaced image will look just fine when viewed on a TV screen. For computer viewing, just as with printing, the still image must be de-interlaced to get a clearer image.

1 Place a Clip in the Monitor View

Select the clip from which you want to grab the still image. You can select a clip from the **Media** panel or one from the **Timeline**. Select the clip and click the **Clip View** button at the top of the **Monitor**, or simply double-click the clip. The clip appears in the **Monitor** view. Scrub through the clip to locate that one frame that is a keeper by using the VCR and shuttle controls. When the image you want to grab appears in the **Monitor** view, continue with step 2.

2 Click the Export Frame Button

The image you see in the **Monitor** view is the image that will become your still. To grab this still, click the **Export Frame** button (the camera icon). The **Export Frame** dialog box appears.

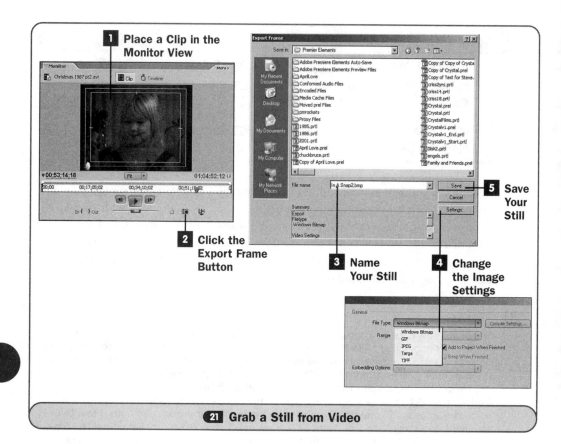

1 Place a Clip in the Monitor View

2 Click the Export Frame Button

3 Name Your Still

4 Change the Image Settings

5 Save Your Still

21 Grab a Still from Video

▶ **TIP**

Your video is a mass of frames; 30 frames per second to be exact. With 30 frames per second to choose from, there must be one that is "just right." Use the **Step Forward** and **Step Back** buttons in the VCR controls to move the clip one frame at a time until you find just the right one.

3 **Name Your Still**

Decide on a name for your clip and type it in the **File name** text box. You can also select the directory where you would like the image to be placed from the **Save in** drop-down list at the top of the dialog box.

4 **Change the Image Settings**

Click the **Settings** button to open the **Export Frame Settings** dialog box. From the **File Type** drop-down list, select the format in which you want to save the still image: **Windows Bitmap**, **GIF**, **JPEG**, **Targa**, or **TIFF**. Depending on your selection, other options become available.

▶ **TIP**

If you save your image as a GIF, you will have the option of a transparent background. However, many videographers choose the TIFF format because it has less compression and holds its quality better after editing and copying.

5 Save Your Still

After you have made any desired changes in the **Export Frame Settings** dialog box, click the **OK** button and click the **Save** button in the **Export Frame** dialog box. Now your still image is preserved on your hard drive for this project (and possibly for future projects) as well as being added to the **Media** panel for this project.

▶ **TIP**

Still images grabbed from video clips and used in your project make great backgrounds for titles and DVD menus.

21

5

Working with Stills and Graphics

IN THIS CHAPTER:

Chances are you'll regularly use still photos and graphics in your video projects. They're a great way to compliment your video footage and, when properly used, a still can be every bit as exciting and full of movement as a video clip. (See **69 Add Motion to a Still** and **70 Pan and Zoom Still Images a la Ken Burns** for ways to bring your still photos and graphics to life.)

Premiere Elements offers many features that help you make the most of your stills and graphics, including some powerful automatic features (see **26 Make an Instant Slideshow** and **27 Change Slides to the Beat of Music**).

Before you bring a photo or graphic into Premiere Elements, however, you'll need to make sure it's properly formatted and prepared. In **22 Prepare a Still for Video**, you learn how to ensure that the graphic or photo you put in looks great when you output it as video.

22   Prepare a Still for Video

✔ BEFORE YOU BEGIN	→ SEE ALSO
14 Add Media with the Adobe Media Downloader **21** Grab a Still from Video	**16** Create and Use Media Folders **23** Scale and Position a Still **24** Set a Still Image Duration **70** Pan and Zoom Still Images a la Ken Burns

22

Although they share many basic features, a digitized photo and digitized video are two very different media. Although Premiere Elements does its best to render your photo into a video format, an improperly prepared photo can often produce some unfortunate results in your project, and photos with unnecessarily high resolution can cause extremely long rendering times and even complete system lockups.

Premiere Elements accepts a wide variety of graphics file formats including TIFs, BMPs, JPGs, PNGs, GIFs, PDFs, EPSs, and even native Photoshop (PSD) and PhotoDeluxe (PDD) files. Your choice of graphic format will often be a matter of convenience. However, there are definite advantages (and disadvantages) to each format type.

There are two prime considerations when selecting a format for your graphic. First, consider the amount and type of compression the file format uses. JPEGs, for instance, are relatively small graphics files. However, they also use a compression system that, at higher levels, can actually change or even damage the details of your graphic. Whether the effect this type of compression has on your file is at an acceptable level and worth the trade-off for a smaller file depends on your personal feelings and how you plan to ultimately use this graphic.

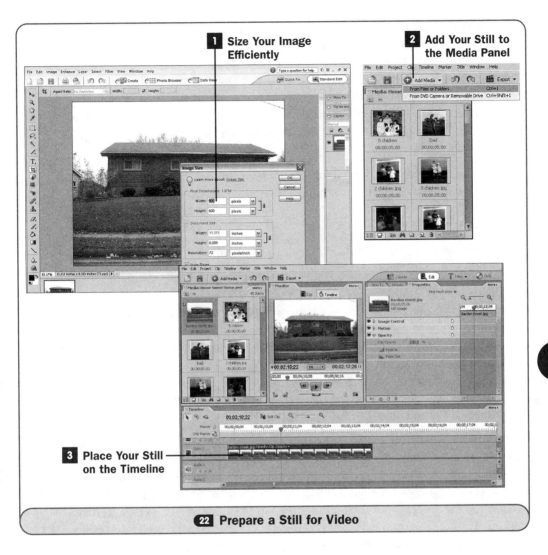

1 Size Your Image Efficiently

2 Add Your Still to the Media Panel

3 Place Your Still on the Timeline

22 Prepare a Still for Video

The second consideration in selecting the ideal format for your graphic has to do with the file's capability to carry an alpha channel. Alpha channels can be a powerful aspect of your graphics workflow, as you can see in **94** **Frame Your Video with an Image.**

Tagged Image Format (TIF or TIFF) files are one of the most commonly used image formats. Because they are relatively uncompressed, they are the preferred format of professional designers. A TIF can be opened, modified, and resaved indefinitely without any loss or damage to the image data (unlike more compressed file formats such as JPEGs), and they are far and away the most hardy digital image format in use today.

An added advantage of TIFs is that they can also save layers of images. This means that if you've created an image sized or shaped differently than your canvas in Photoshop Elements and you leave your background layer blank, your image is displayed in Premiere Elements with the transparent background carried as an alpha channel, displaying as transparent in Premiere Elements. (Technically, this is because Premiere Elements reads the transparent areas as an alpha channel. See **94** **Frame Your Video with an Image**.)

The *PSD* format is a native Photoshop file. PSD files can be imported into Premiere Elements with their alpha channels, or transparent areas, displayed as transparent. Additionally, Premiere Elements and Photoshop Elements are designed to work hand in hand; for a variety of reasons, PSD is an ideal format for bringing Photoshop and Photoshop Elements graphics into Premiere Elements.

Bitmap (BMP) is an older file format created by Microsoft in the early days of personal computers. Although BMPs are not the most efficient size-wise, they are a perfectly acceptable graphics format in which to save your video graphics.

Named for the Joint Photographic Experts Group, *JPGs* (also known as *JPEGs*) are perhaps the most common graphics format used by consumers. Most digital still cameras save their photos as JPEGs because the format allows for a high compression of the image data and a much smaller file size than TIFs. Unfortunately, the smaller file size comes with a price. Repeated saving of JPEGs, especially at higher compression levels, can damage the image data, resulting in corrupted pixels, particularly in the finer details of your photo and at color breaks.

In most cases, however, a first- or second-generation JPEG file is perfectly acceptable for your video—the exception being in situations in which the finer details of your graphic are going to be scrutinized (as when you're applying a major scaling effect), when you are planning to use the Chromakey effect on your photo, or you are applying a color substitution. Because JPEGs use a compression system that averages the color values of pixels near color breaks, any precise effect applied to a color might appear with ragged edges. In these cases, a TIF or BMP might be a better graphic format choice.

Portable Network Graphics (PNG, and pronounced *ping*) files were initially developed for the Internet. For Premiere Elements's needs, the chief advantage of this format is that it can be created with transparent areas that remain transparent when the image is placed in your video timeline.

The *Graphic Interchange Format (GIF)* was developed by CompuServe and is correctly pronounced *jiff*. This format was initially developed for the Internet and has advantages related to its color management properties that are relevant to web design. For Premiere Elements's needs, the chief advantage of this format is that it can be created with transparent areas that remain transparent when the image is placed in your video timeline.

The *Portable Document File (PDF)* format was created by Adobe, which has long promoted the format's use as a lightweight, universal way to transfer text and graphics files between programs.

Encapsulated Post Script (EPS) files are unique in that they are usually a vector rather than raster format. The difference between these two formats is that raster images are composed of blocks of pixels while vector images are defined by a series of outline points that designate fields of color (a square, for instance, is defined only by its four corners). The main advantage to using a vector graphic is that, unlike raster images, you do not need to worry about *resolution*. Because a vector image is defined by outline points rather than being painted with blocks of color, it can be scaled to any size without becoming pixilated. This advantage is somewhat nullified by the fact that after a vector EPS is added to the **Timeline** of your video, it becomes a piece of raster art by nature of the medium. Therefore, you still need to concern yourself with issues such as resolution and the dangers of over-scaling your image.

▶ NOTE
Although EPS files are presumed to be vector art, programs such as Photoshop can produce raster EPS files. Only EPS files created in a vector art program, such as Adobe Illustrator, will produce true vector EPS files.

▶ KEY TERM
Resolution—The pixel density of an image. Print images require a much higher resolution (200–300 pixels per inch) than onscreen images (about 72 pixels per inch), but too little resolution in any medium reveals the pixels that make up the image, making the picture look jagged.

❶ Size Your Image Efficiently
The primary issue for you to consider when working with any still image you plan to use in your video is the image's resolution. If you use a still image straight from your digital camera (today's 3.5 megapixel digital cameras produce images at 2048×1536 pixels, nearly 10 times the size of a video frame), the still file is too large to be handled efficiently by Premiere Elements. On the other hand, if the still image doesn't contain enough pixels, you won't be able to zoom in on or pan the image in the video project without the image becoming pixelated. See **70** **Pan and Zoom Still Images a la Ken Burns.**

Unlike most digital imagery, video is composed of non-square pixels. NTSC video (a frame made up of 720×480 pixels) uses pixels that are about 90% as wide as they are tall to produce standard 4:3 video and 120% wider than they are tall to produce a 16:9 widescreen video. The PAL system (a frame of

786×576 pixels) uses pixels that are 106% wider than they are tall for standard video and 142% wider than they are tall for widescreen. Fortunately, you won't need to reshape the pixels in your stills before placing them in your video. Premiere Elements converts standard, square-pixel images to their non-square pixel equivalents automatically.

▶ NOTES

Because a video frame is made up of non-square pixels and most digital images are made up of square pixels, the pixel dimensions for a full-screen image are different for stills and photos than they are for video. Here are approximate dimensions for full-screen graphics in each video system:

- NTSC's 720×480 non-square video pixel TV screen is approximately equal in size to a graphic that measures 720×535 square pixels.

- PAL's 786×576 non-square video pixel TV screen is approximately equal in size to a graphic that measures 835×576 square pixels.

Don't worry that your graphics are composed of square pixels and video is composed of non-square pixels. Premiere Elements renders your graphics to a full screen of video as long as you use the dimensions given here.

22

Should you work in widescreen video, the following dimensions will work for your graphics (oddly, for widescreen video, only the non-square pixel shapes change—they're much wider—the actual number of video pixels are the same as for standard video):

- NTSC's 720×480 non-square video pixel widescreen is approximately equal in size to a graphic that measures 865×480 square pixels.

- PAL's 786×576 non-square video pixel widescreen is approximately equal in size to a graphic that measures 1220×576 square pixels.

The goal is to find a balance between too much and too little resolution for your stills. Assume that you're going to load your photo into a standard NTSC 720×480 video and that you plan to zoom in to a spot about a fourth of the area of the image. (In other words, you're going to scale the image to four times the area of the screen.) What does the resolution of the original still image file have to be?

A 720×480 NTSC screen has an area of about 345,000 pixels. Four times that size is about 1,380,000 square pixels, or approximately 1440×960—about twice the width and twice the height.

Too much math? Don't worry about it. A rough estimation is usually more than adequate. If you plan to scale your image to 2 or 3 times the screen size, use an image about 1 and a half times each dimension; if you plan to scale your image to 4 times the screen size, double each dimension, and so on. A little extra resolution doesn't hurt, but a lot extra does. And it's unlikely that you'll ever need an image with more than 2,500 pixels in either dimension.

▶ **TIP**

If you have a 1–4 megapixel still camera, you can generally import an image file from the camera straight into Premiere Elements. Premiere Elements resizes the image as needed, and you should have enough extra resolution to zoom and pan if you chose to do that.

If you need to resize a super-high-resolution image file before importing it into Premiere Elements, you must size it using an outside graphics program such as Photoshop Elements or Paint Shop Pro. After the image is sized to the necessary video dimensions, you'll be able to easily work with it in Premiere Elements.

2 Add Your Still to the Media Panel

Click the **Add Media** button in the shortcuts bar and select **From Files and Folders**. Browse and select the (resized) photo or photos you want to add to your project. (See **14** **Add Media with the Adobe Media Downloader.**) You might find it helpful to create a new folder in your **Media** panel for your still images to better organize your media (see **16** **Create and Use Media Folders**).

3 Place Your Still on the Timeline

When you add the still to the project **Timeline**, it becomes a clip at the default duration, initially 5 seconds (see **24** **Set Still Image Duration** for information on how to change this default setting) and, by default, is sized to the video frame (see **23** **Scale and Position a Still** for information on how to change this default setting).

▶ **NOTE**

Although Premiere Elements accepts most major graphics formats, including TIFs, it does not accept 16-bit TIFs or images in any format saved in CMYK color mode.

---

23 **Scale and Position a Still**	
✔ **BEFORE YOU BEGIN**	→ **SEE ALSO**
22 Prepare a Still for Video	**24** Set Still Image Duration
68 About the Properties Panel	**69** Add Motion to a Still
	70 Pan and Zoom Still Images a la Ken Burns

23

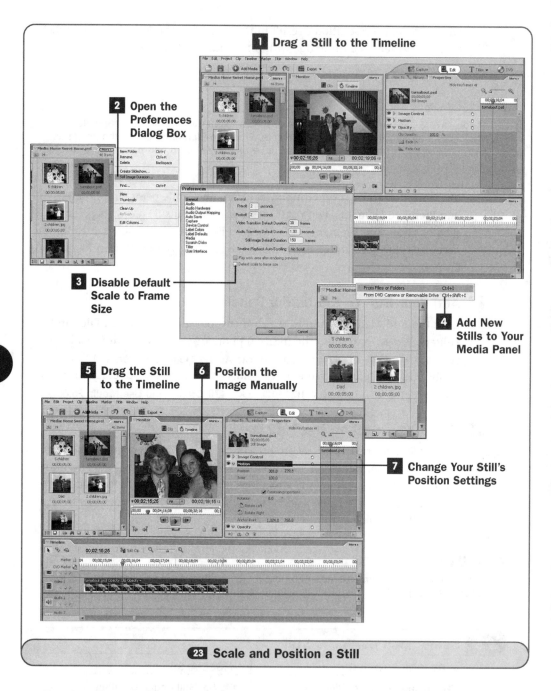

1 Drag a Still to the Timeline

2 Open the Preferences Dialog Box

3 Disable Default Scale to Frame Size

4 Add New Stills to Your Media Panel

5 Drag the Still to the Timeline

6 Position the Image Manually

7 Change Your Still's Position Settings

23 Scale and Position a Still

Premiere Elements has a number of settings that determine how your still images will behave by default when placed on the **Timeline**. Depending on your needs and preferences, you might decide to position your stills manually or change the default settings so your image lands in your preferred position automatically.

1 Drag a Still to the Timeline

By default, Premiere Elements automatically scales the image you drop on the **Timeline** to the size of the video frame.

▶ **NOTE**

Although Premiere Elements automatically scales your image to the size of the video frame when you place it on the **Timeline**, this scaling does not affect the aspect ratio of your image. In other words, if your graphic is not the same shape as your video frame, Premiere Elements does not stretch it in either dimension to fill the frame (which is preferable, of course) and the video frame might be wider or taller than your image, resulting in black bars along the sides of the image.

2 Open the Preferences Dialog Box

Click the **More** button in the **Media** panel. From the drop-down menu, select **Still Image Duration** to open the **Preferences** dialog box to the **General** category page. Alternatively, open the **Preferences** dialog box to this page by choosing **Edit**, **Preferences**, **General**.

If you want, you can change the default duration of your stills (see **24** **Set Still Image Duration**).

3 Disable Default Scale to Frame Size

Uncheck the **Default scale to frame size** option to disable Premiere Elements's automatic scaling feature. With this feature disabled, new stills or graphics placed on the **Timeline** appear at their actual size rather than automatically being scaled to the video frame size.

Click **OK** to close the **Preferences** dialog box.

▶ **NOTE**

If you change the default settings for still duration or scale, this does not affect stills already in the **Media** panel. Only stills added to the **Media** panel after the settings have been changed are affected by the changes (see **24** **Set Still Image Duration**).

4 Add New Stills to Your Media Panel

Click the **Add Media** button, select **From Files or Folders**, and browse to select the images you want to add to the **Timeline** at this new setting.

If you already have a photo in your **Media** panel with which you want to use the new default settings you just established, you must re-import the image to the **Media** panel: Right-click the image in the **Media** panel and select **Clear** to remove it from the panel. (This action does not erase the file from your

23

hard drive.) Then click the **Add Media** button, select **From Files or Folders**, and browse to add the image to your **Media** panel again. The new default setting is applied to this still image.

▶ TIP

You can also change the **Scale to Frame** option for a clip on the fly. Right-click on the clip on the **Timeline** and uncheck **Scale to Frame**. The clip reverts to its actual pixel dimensions in the video frame.

5 Drag the Still to the Timeline

Drag the still (with its new scale settings) to the **Timeline**. The still is added at its actual size rather than at the enforced size of the video frame. In the case of my example, the image is now much larger than the video frame, and only a portion of the image is displayed in the **Monitor**.

If you plan to add motion to your stills by panning and zooming around them (see ❼⓿ **Pan and Zoom Still Images a la Ken Burns**), you might find it easier to work with your still at its actual size as it appears in the example, rather than automatically scaling it to the video frame size. When it is displayed at its actual size, you'll have a much better idea of how much scaling the still's size and resolution will allow for. But this is purely a matter of personal preference. Choose the default setting that best fits your personal workflow.

6 Position the Image Manually

You can reposition your still in this frame of the video by clicking the image in the **Monitor** panel and dragging it into whatever position you'd like.

7 Change Your Still's Position Settings

Alternatively, you can position your still using the **Position** settings in the **Properties** panel. With your still selected on the **Timeline**, click the triangle to the left of **Motion** in the **Properties** panel to reveal the **Motion** property's details, including **Position** and **Scale**. The first number represents the horizontal position (in pixels) *of the center of your image* in the video frame. The second number represents its vertical position. By changing one or both of these numbers, you can adjust the still's placement in the video frame. You can also change these numbers more fluidly by moving your mouse over numbers until the settings icon appears, and then dragging across the numbers to raise or lower the settings.

You can also resize the image in the video frame by changing the **Scale** settings in the **Motion** panel.

24 Set Still Image Duration

✔ BEFORE YOU BEGIN	→ SEE ALSO
22 Prepare a Still for Video	**14** Add Media with the Adobe Media Downloader
29 About the Timeline and Video Layers	**23** Scale and Position a Still
68 About the Properties Panel	**27** Change Slides to the Beat of Music

By default, any still image or graphic you add to the Premiere Elements **Timeline** comes in with a duration of 5 seconds. (The exception is when you create a slideshow set to unnumbered timeline markers, as described in **27** **Change Slides to the Beat of Music**.) However, this default setting can be changed very easily.

1 Open General Preferences

Click the **More** button in the **Media** panel and select **Still Image Duration**. The **Preferences** dialog box opens to the **General** page.

Among the **General Preferences** are options for setting stills to default to the video frame size when imported into your project (See **23** **Scale and Position a Still**.)

▶ NOTE

You can also access the **Preferences** dialog box from the **Edit** drop-down menu. The **Preferences** dialog box offers several pages of settings that can be helpful in troubleshooting functional and hardware problems.

2 Change the Still Image Default Duration

Time, in terms of duration in video, can be set in seconds or in frames. In the NTSC system, video has approximately 30 frames per second. The NTSC factory default of a 5-second duration for stills is therefore listed as 150 frames. In the PAL system, video runs at 25 frames per second, and therefore 5 seconds is represented as 125 frames.

▶ NOTE

In reality, NTSC video runs at 29.97 frames per second rather than 30. However, because the drop-frame system employed by Premiere Elements makes that fractional difference invisible, we can safely use the more manageable rate of 30 frames per second for any calculations.

Type the number of frames you'd like to be the default for your still image duration. Click **OK**.

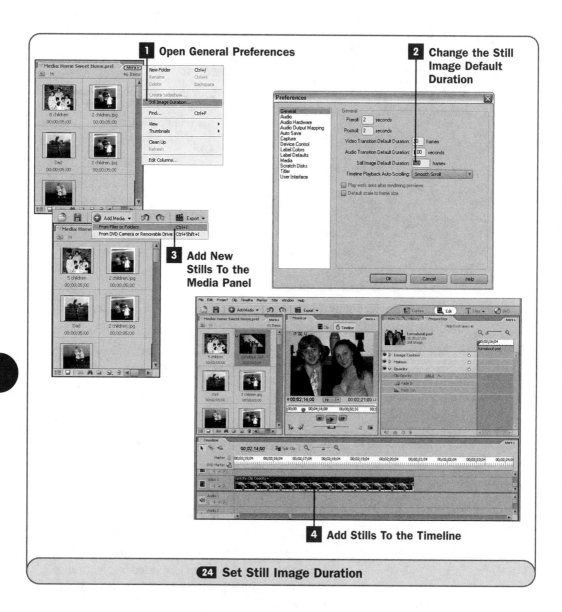

1 Open General Preferences

2 Change the Still Image Default Duration

3 Add New Stills To the Media Panel

4 Add Stills To the Timeline

24 Set Still Image Duration

▶ **NOTE**

Changed default settings for still duration or still size do not affect stills already in the **Media** panel. Only stills added *after* the settings have been changed are affected by the changes. (See also **23** Scale and Position a Still.)

3 Add New Stills To the Media Panel

Click the **Add Media** button, select **From Files or Folders**, and browse to select the pictures you want to add to the **Timeline** at this new setting. (See also **14** **Add Media with the Adobe Media Downloader.**)

If you already have a photo in your **Media** panel with which you want to use the new default settings you just established, you must re-import the image to the **Media** panel: Right-click the image in the **Media** panel and select **Clear** to remove it from the panel. (This action does not erase the file from your hard drive.) Then click the **Add Media** button, select **From Files or Folders**, and browse to add the image to your **Media** panel again. The new default setting is applied to this still image.

4 Add Your Stills To the Timeline

Drag the still image from the **Media** panel to the location you want it to occupy in the **Timeline**. The still has a default duration equal to the new setting.

After you've place the still on the **Timeline**, you can increase or decrease the clip's duration by dragging the ends of the clip out or in as described in **34** **Trim a Clip on the Timeline.**

25

---

25 **Remove Shimmer from a Photo**

✔ BEFORE YOU BEGIN	→ SEE ALSO
22 Prepare a Still for Video	**104** Output to an AVI Movie
23 Scale and Position a Still	**105** Output to DV Hardware or Export to Tape
29 About the Timeline and Video Tracks	**108** Output an MPEG File
	111 About Burning to DVDs
	112 Create an Auto-Play DVD

When you add stills to the video project **Timeline**, the resulting video or DVD isn't always what you expected. Some issues, such as resolution problems, are easily remedied. Others are a little more difficult to diagnose.

The shimmer effect falls into the latter category. It manifests itself as a sort of glare in your video in which the image seems to tremble and shake or distort on screen. The biggest challenge—and most frustrating thing—is that you sometimes can't even see the problem until you output your project to tape or DVD!

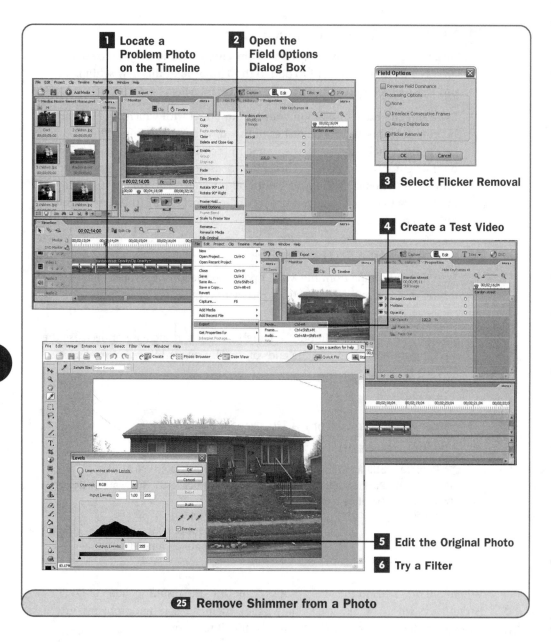

1 Locate a Problem Photo on the Timeline

2 Open the Field Options Dialog Box

3 Select Flicker Removal

4 Create a Test Video

5 Edit the Original Photo

6 Try a Filter

25 Remove Shimmer from a Photo

Fortunately, if you have struggled with this problem in Premiere Elements 1.0, version 2.0 has pretty much resolved this issue. (At least it isn't nearly as chronic a condition as it was in the earlier version of the software.) However, if you are still struggling with flickering images, one or more of the following steps will likely remedy them. Note that the last suggestion requires you to adjust the photo in an outside graphics program such as Photoshop Elements.

1 Locate a Problem Photo on the Timeline

The most frustrating thing about shimmering photos is that you often don't realize that they're going to be problems until after you output your video. If you have a potentially problematic image, you might want to output an AVI of the photo to see how it plays in Windows Media Player, as described in step 4. It's been our experience that if the photo is going to cause problems, you can usually see evidence of it at this level; sometimes doing a test output like this can prevent you from burning a useless DVD later. You might also want to burn a test DVD to a rewriteable DVD-RW disc.

If, after outputting a video or DVD, you find that a photo is exhibiting a shimmer or is trembling, locate that photo on your project **Timeline**.

Recall that video is an interlaced process (as discussed in Chapter 1, "Start Here"). In most cases, interlacing happens too quickly for your mind to perceive, and the two passes of interlacing blend into single frames and the frames blend together into smooth movements. Where interlacing presents potential problems, however, is when a still image is added. Although a still image is displayed as a single frame, when it is converted to video it is interlaced—that is, it is produced in two interlaced steps per frame, as is video.

The occasional problem occurs when a characteristic in the still image—a bright spot, a high-contrast, or a highly-detailed area—exaggerates the interlacing. Hence, a shimmer, tremble, or distortion of the image occurs in the output video.

25

2 Open the Field Options Dialog Box

Fortunately, Premiere Elements offers some automatic options for correcting interlacing-related problems.

Right-click the problem still in the **Timeline** and select **Field Options** from the context menu. The **Field Options** dialog box opens.

3 Select Flicker Removal

Enable the **Flicker Removal** option. In the vast majority of cases, applying **Flicker Removal** to a still remedies or at least reduces the shimmer/flicker problem to an acceptable level.

Alternatively, you can experiment with the **Interlace Consecutive Frames** or **Always Deinterlace** options. These field settings are variations of the basic solution of creating a smoother blend between the interlacing created by Premiere Elements to convert your still image into video frames.

Click **OK** to save the settings and close the **Field Options** dialog box.

4 Create a Test Video

Choose **File, Export, Movie** to create a test video. To save rendering time, you can output only a portion of your video by setting your workspace bar, as discussed in **104** **Output to an AVI Movie**. Open the AVI movie file in Windows Media Player and give it a test drive.

If you're going to create a DVD as your final output, you can test something closer to your final product by exporting an MPEG file instead, as discussed in **108** **Output an MPEG File**.

Unlike television, your computer is a non-interlaced medium and the interlacing problems might not show up on your computer screen. In our experience, these test methods are very effective at predicting potential problems; however, it might be worth your while to actually output a test tape (see **105** **Output to DV Hardware or Export to Tape**) or a test DVD (see **111** **About Burning to DVDs** and **112** **Create an Auto-Play DVD**) and then testing the output on an actual television. (A rewritable DVD or CD-RW is a good investment if you plan to conduct such tests.)

However you conduct your test, if you're still not satisfied with the results, you might have to make some adjustments to the original photo itself.

25

5 Edit the Original Photo

If you decide to edit the original photo to eliminate the shimmer effect, right-click your still in the **Media** panel and select **Edit Original** from the context menu. The photo opens in your default graphics-editing program (this example uses Photoshop Elements).

Generally, the shimmer problem tends to be exaggerated in areas of photos that show a very high contrast and, especially, a very bright or white area. Photoshop Elements allows you to adjust the white point of your image, effectively softening its brightness. In Photoshop Elements 4.0, choose **Enhance, Adjust Lighting, Levels**. In this example, the chart in the **Levels** dialog box in Photoshop Elements indicates that the photo that's been giving me trouble in Premiere Elements has a large number of pixels in the whitest white range. These whitest points are in the sky above the house—not coincidentally the area of the photo where most of my shimmering and trembling is occurring.

Double-click the eyedropper to the farthest right to adjust the white point. In the new dialog box that opens, change the R, G, and B (red, green, and blue) values from 255 to 238. Click **OK** to close this dialog box. Back in the **Levels** dialog box, click **Auto**. The brightest points on your image are softened.

Similar adjustments can be made to the photo's levels in other graphics programs. (As an alternative, you can lower the brightness and contrast.) The goal is to mute some of the whiteness in the still's brightest areas.

Save the photo in the graphics editor; it is automatically updated in Premiere Elements, at which point you can make another test movie.

6 Try a Filter

If these steps do not solve the shimmer problem with the still image, try softening some of the details in the image by applying a subtle Gaussian blur filter to the problematic area or to the entire photo using your graphics editing program.

Although it remains a somewhat elusive problem, chances are one or a combination of these steps will resolve your shimmering issue.

---

26 Make an Instant Slideshow

✔ BEFORE YOU BEGIN	→ SEE ALSO
22 Prepare a Still for Video	**13** About the Media Panel
23 Scale and Position a Still	**16** Create and Use Media Folders
29 About the Timeline and Video Layers	**17** Sort the Media Panel by Different Characteristics
	19 Trim Clips in the Media Panel
	46 Add a Video Transition

26

If you have a selection of still images, Premiere Elements can automatically turn them into a slideshow on your **Timeline**. In addition, this feature gives you the option of customizing several of the slideshow's characteristics.

▶ NOTE

Although we usually think of slides as still images, the **Create Slideshow** feature can also be used to load video clips, which will play at the intervals you designate in the **Still Image Duration** setting.

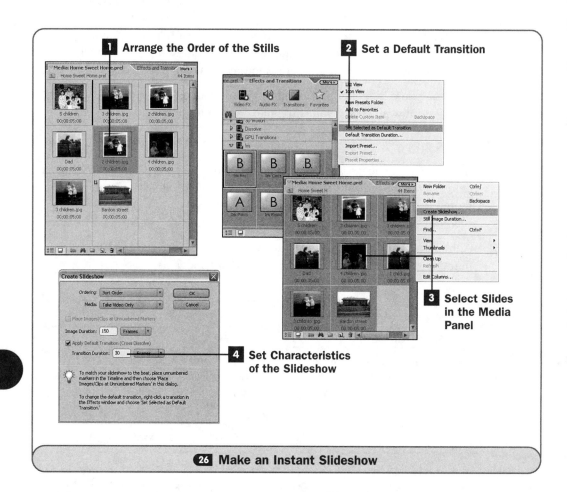

1 Arrange the Order of the Stills

2 Set a Default Transition

3 Select Slides in the Media Panel

4 Set Characteristics of the Slideshow

26 Make an Instant Slideshow

1 Arrange the Order of the Stills

A convenient feature of the **Create Slideshow** tool is that it can add stills to the **Timeline** in the order they appear in the **Media** panel—this is usually much easier than rearranging the order of the slides after the stills have been placed on the **Timeline**. In the **Media** panel, arrange your stills in the order you want them to appear in the final slideshow. To do so, click the **Media** panel's **More** button and select the **Icon View** (see **13** **About the Media Panel**). You can then arrange your clips in any order by simply dragging them around within the panel.

You might find it helpful to create a separate folder in the **Media** panel for the still images, separating your stills from the rest of your project's media (see **16** **Create and Use Media Folders**).

▶ **NOTE**

As an alternative to presorting your stills before creating the slideshow, you can select the slides in the order you want them arranged on the **Timeline**. To do so, hold down the **Ctrl** key and click to select the stills or clips one at a time in the **Media** panel. After you've gathered your slides and chosen **More**, **Create Slideshow**, set the **Ordering** option to **Selection Order**.

An alternative method of arranging your photos in the **Media** panel is to use **List** view (click **More** and choose **View**, **List**) and sort the stills alphanumerically by clicking the word *Name* at the top of the media list. (Click *Name* a second time to reverse the sort order.)

▶ **TIP**

You can easily change the names of your clips or stills so that this sorting method puts them in the order you prefer. To do so, click the name of any clip, pause a moment and then click again (or right-click and select **Rename**). The still or clip's name becomes an editable field. Type the new name and press **Enter**. Changing the name of a clip in the **Media** panel does not change the name of the file on your computer's hard drive. The only thing that changes is how the clip is displayed in Premiere Elements and, ultimately, how that clip is sorted by the **Media** panel.

2 Set a Default Transition

26

Your slideshow can be set to generate with a transition between each slide on the **Timeline**. If you choose this option, the default transition placed between each slide is initially a Cross-Dissolve.

To change the default transition, open the **Effects and Transitions** panel and browse to your preferred transition (see **46** **Add a Video Transition**). Note that clicking any transition starts a thumbnail preview of that transition. The current default transition will be outlined.

When you have selected your preferred transition, click the **More** button in the **Effects and Transitions** panel and select **Set Selected as Default Transition**. A blue box appears around the transition indicating that it is now your program default.

3 Select Slides in the Media Panel

Select the stills or clips you want to use in the slideshow either by holding down the **Shift** key and selecting the first and last of the series (all clips between are automatically selected) or by holding down the **Ctrl** key and clicking to select individual clips in the **Media** panel.

▶ **TIP**

As an alternative to ordering the clips in the **Media** panel as described in step 1, you can hold down the **Ctrl** key and click in the **Media** panel to select the clips or stills in the order you want them to appear.

▶ **NOTE**

The **Create Slideshow** feature loads your clips or stills to the **Timeline** in the order you have arranged them in the **Media** panel or by the order in which you select them.

4 Set Characteristics of the Slideshow

With all your stills or clips selected, click the **More** button in the **Media** panel and choose **Create Slideshow**. The **Create Slideshow** dialog box opens.

If the **Ordering** option is set to **Sort Order**, the slides appear on the **Timeline** in the order they are arranged in the **Media** panel. If, rather than ordering the clips in the **Media** panel, you selected them in the order you want them to appear in your slideshow, choose the **Selection** option to instruct the program to sort your clips in the order you selected them.

Disable the **Place Images/Clips at Unnumbered Markers** option and enable the **Apply Default Transition (Cross Dissolve)** option (which you specified in step 2) if you want to use a transition and set the duration of the transition in frames or seconds. You can also set the **Image Duration** in frames or seconds.

Click **OK**. A slideshow is automatically generated on your **Timeline**, beginning at the position of the current time indicator (CTI).

---

27 Change Slides to the Beat of Music

✔ BEFORE YOU BEGIN	→ SEE ALSO
14 Add Media with the Adobe Media Downloader	**17** Sort the Media Panel by Different Characteristics
22 Prepare a Still for Video	**19** Trim Clips in the Media Panel
23 Scale and Position a Still	**44** About Transitions
26 Make an Instant Slideshow	**70** Pan and Zoom Still Images a la Ken Burns
29 About the Timeline and Video Tracks	**114** Set DVD Chapter Markers

Video is a medium of motion ("movies move"). It is also a medium of both visuals and sound. Ideally, neither should happen independently of the other—rather, both should work together to tell the story you want to tell.

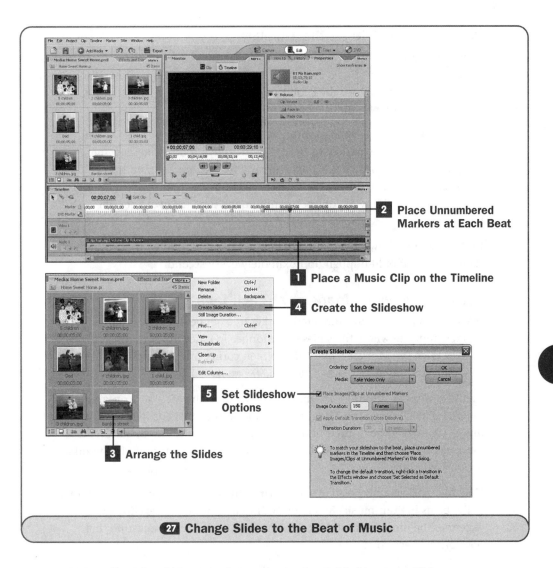

2 Place Unnumbered Markers at Each Beat

1 Place a Music Clip on the Timeline

4 Create the Slideshow

5 Set Slideshow Options

3 Arrange the Slides

27 Change Slides to the Beat of Music

Just as there should be meaning to the motion added to your still images on screen (see **70** Pan and Zoom Still Images a la Ken Burns), any marriage of your visuals to your sound makes the experience of watching your video much more interesting.

One simple way to marry sound and visuals is to synchronize the cuts in your video or your slideshow to the beat or rhythm of a music track. Although this can be and often is done manually on the **Timeline**, Premiere Elements contains tools in its **Create Slideshow** dialog box that enable you to sync the cuts in your slideshow to your music almost automatically.

1 Place a Music Clip on the Timeline

Drag your desired music clip from the **Media** pane to the **Timeline**. The audio track is displayed as a series of sound peaks and valleys. Occasionally, it's possible to actually *see* the beat displayed in these peaks—most likely, though, you'll have to find the beat manually.

Click the **Play** button in the **Monitor** panel or press the **Spacebar** on your keyboard to play the audio clip. As the music plays, watch the movement of the current time indicator (CTI). By listening for a drum beat, guitar riff, or other repeating element, you'll soon get a feel for the rhythm of the music. By watching the CTI, you can soon estimate the time interval between each beat.

In the example shown here, Blind Melon's "No Rain," I noted that rhythmic slide changes should happen approximately every second.

2 Place Unnumbered Markers at Each Beat

You want to place an unnumbered marker at each beat in the audio file. The markers indicate where the slides will change. To place an unnumbered marker, click the **Marker** icon at the top-left corner of the **Timeline**. (The DVD Marker is used in **114** **Set DVD Chapter Markers**.)

Create a series of unnumbered markers by clicking the **Marker** icon and moving the CTI down the **Timeline**. The markers can be easily repositioned and don't have to be in their final positions when you create them. Create markers on the **Timeline** until you have one for every slide you plan to add to your slideshow.

Slide the markers into position on the **Timeline** at the approximate locations of the beats in your music. Reset your CTI and play the music clip again, watching the movement of the CTI over your markers and adjusting their positions as necessary.

You might find it more intuitive to play the music, clicking on the **Marker** icon at each beat. The program will drop an unnumbered marker at the CTI position each time you click the icon.

Spend some time getting these markers positioned as accurately as possible. Doing so will save you a lot of tweaking and trimming of your clips later on.

3 Arrange the Slides

Ordering your slides in the **Media** panel assures that they'll be in the correct order when you create your slideshow. You might want to create a new folder in this panel and move your still images into the folder so you can better manage the image files.

27

Rearrange the order of your slides by dragging and dropping them in the **Media** panel while in the **Icon** view. The order the slides are in the **Media** panel when you select them for your slideshow is the order they will appear on the **Timeline** when you create your instant slideshow.

▶ **NOTE**

Although we usually think of slides as still images, the **Create Slideshow** feature can also load video clips that play at the intervals and duration you designate. You can also set your video clips to change in time with the rhythm of a music clip just as you can still images.

4 **Create the Slideshow**

Select the stills or clips you want to use in the slideshow by either holding down the **Shift** key and clicking the first and last clip (the first, last, and those clips in between are selected) or by holding down the **Ctrl** key and clicking to select one clip or image at a time.

When all the clips are selected, click the **Media** panel's **More** button and select **Create Slideshow**. The **Create Slideshow** dialog box opens.

5 **Set Slideshow Options**

Enable the **Place Images/Clips at Unnumbered Markers** option.

You can also place the default transitions between your clips, although doing so might minimize the effect of cutting the images in rhythm to your music clip.

▶ **NOTE**

You probably don't want to position transitions between your slides if you're setting up your slideshow to change to the beat of music but, if you do use transitions, you can easily change the default transition that is used (see **44** About Transitions).

Click **OK** to close the dialog box; your slideshow is created. Beginning at the first unnumbered marker, each slide changes in rhythm with the beat of the music.

Play your musical slideshow; if you're a little off the beat, you can lengthen or shorten the individual slides accordingly on the **Timeline** by dragging the edge of each slide to make it a bit longer or shorter as needed (see **34** Trim a Clip on the Timeline). You might find it helpful to use the slider at the top of the **Timeline** to zoom in so you can make precise adjustments.

If the whole slideshow is off the beat slightly, adjust its entire position by dragging to lasso the entire range of slides as a group and then dragging to move the group of slides up or down the **Timeline** a frame or two. You might find it helpful to use the + key to zoom into the **Timeline** as close as possible when making very fine adjustments.

---

28   Use and Customize Preset Camera Moves

✔ BEFORE YOU BEGIN	→ SEE ALSO
58 About Preset Effects	29 About the Timeline and Video Layers
67 About Keyframing	65 Create and Save a Preset
	70 Pan and Zoom Still Images a la Ken Burns
	71 Make a Variable-Speed Pan and Zoom

Premiere Elements offers several presets that create motion paths for you. (See 70 **Pan and Zoom Still Images a la Ken Burns** to learn how to add more elaborate, custom motion to your photos.) The good news is that these presets are automatic and easy to use: You just drag them onto your images on the **Timeline**. The bad news is that one size doesn't always fit all, and it's rare that you'll find a preset that works perfectly for your photo right out of the box.

On the other hand, all these motion presets are, in reality, simply motion paths created using Premiere Elements's keyframing feature. In other words, after you've applied them to your clip, you can adjust them, add to them, remove what you don't want, and tweak them until you get exactly the effect for which you're looking.

▶ NOTE

After you've created or customized your keyframed movement or effect, you can save it as a permanent preset, and it will be automatically added to your preset collection. Just select **Save Preset** from the **Properties** panel's **More** menu.

1   Add a Preset Motion Effect to a Still

Before you add motion to your photo (or to any *raster image* for that matter), ensure that you have adequate resolution to allow for any scaling you have planned. See 22 **Prepare a Still for Video** for some important considerations and methods for maintaining your image's quality when scaling.

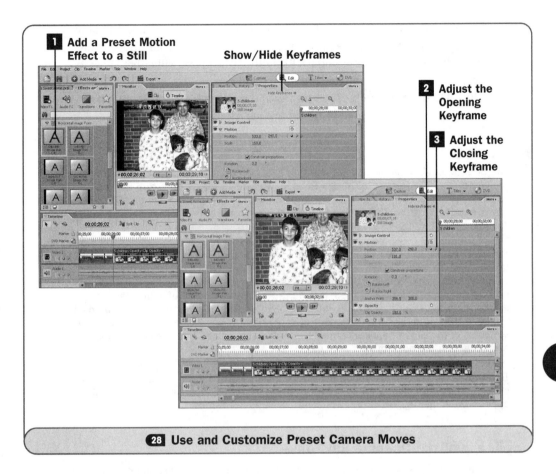

1 Add a Preset Motion Effect to a Still

Show/Hide Keyframes

2 Adjust the Opening Keyframe

3 Adjust the Closing Keyframe

28 Use and Customize Preset Camera Moves

28

▶ KEY TERM

Raster image—Images or graphics composed of pixels, such as photos and other Photoshop images. Usually these pixels are small enough that they aren't perceived as individual blocks of color. However, over-scaling a raster image reveals the pixels, making the image appear jagged or pixilated.

Open the **Effects and Transitions** panel and drag a preset pan (such as the **640×480 L-R Image Pan**) onto a still in the **Timeline**. This effect is located in the **Presets** collection in the group of **Horizontal Image Pans**.

▶ NOTE

The various tools of the **Effects and Transition** panel can be isolated and displayed according to category by clicking the four category icons at the top of the panel. Click **Video FX** to display the presets and video effects; click **Audio FX** to display only the audio effects; click **Transitions** to display only the video and audio transitions; and click **Favorites** to display only the effects and transitions you have designated as favorites.

The selected motion is automatically timed to the duration of the still. Play the clip and watch how the preset affects the clip. Unless your image is the exact dimensions of the preset, it's likely that this preset will either show too little of your image or the motion will extend beyond the edges of it. The **640×480 L-R Image Pan** preset begins and ends off the edges of my photo—but it's easy to customize it to fit my unique needs.

▶ **NOTES**

The **Effects and Transition** panel offers four sets of motion presets, each with several preset options. The **Horizontal Image Pans**, as you might guess, pan from the right to left or from the left to the right of your image, the **Vertical Image Pans** pan up and down, and the **Vertical Zooms** and **Horizontal Zooms** zoom in or out.

The resolution values listed with each preset designate how the pan or zoom will move across, into, or out of your image. In other words, because you're working with a horizontal pan, the 640×480 preset pans as if your image were 640 pixels wide. If you are using an image that is larger than 640 pixels across, this preset pans across only a 640-pixel portion of your image. If the left-to-right pixel measurement of your image is greater than the size of the preset you've applied, you'll pan across only a portion of the image; if the left-to-right measurement of your image is smaller than the size of the preset applied, your image appears smaller than the screen size, and the pan motion might even begin off the edge of your image.

28

To remove a preset or any motion path from a clip, select the clip in the **Timeline** and click the **stopwatch** icon next to the **Motion** effect in the **Properties** panel. A window appears warning that this action will delete existing keyframes. Click **OK**.

2 Adjust the Opening Keyframe

With the clip selected, click **Show Keyframes** in the **Properties** panel to reveal a small timeline to the right of each property, an area where you can set up keyframes for this clip. Click on the triangle to the left of the **Motion** property in the **Properties** panel to reveal the details of the keyframe properties. Notice that, because this preset has been applied to the selected clip, a small diamond, or keyframe point, has been placed at each end of the **Properties Panel Timeline** to the right of the **Position** property. These keyframe points represent the starting and ending positions of the horizontal movement the preset has applied.

▶ **NOTE**

The settings for any **Motion** property apply to the anchor point of the image on the screen, which is by default the image's center. However, in the **Properties** panel, the anchor point can be designated as another point (so that, for instance, you can rotate your image around a corner rather than around the center).

Adjacent to the **Motion** listing in the **Properties** panel, just to the left of the **Properties Timeline**, is a little diamond with an arrow pointing left on one side and an arrow pointing right on the other. This diamond is the keyframe creator. (See **70 Pan and Zoom Still Images a la Ken Burns**.) Click the left arrow, and the CTI jumps back to the position of the opening keyframe point.

With this keyframe point selected, you can change its **Position** and **Scale** settings by typing in new coordinates or percentages, by dragging across the numerical settings so they increase or decrease (the effect is displayed in the **Monitor** panel), or by clicking the image in the **Monitor** panel and dragging it to a new position or resizing it by pulling on the corner handles.

Adjust these settings to create a more accurate opening position for your screen image in the **Monitor** panel.

▶ **NOTE**

When you apply a pan or zoom preset to a clip, the duration of the motion is automatically set to the duration of the clip—beginning the motion at the beginning of your clip and ending it at the end.

3 Adjust the Closing Keyframe

28

Click the arrow to the right of the keyframe point creator; the CTI jumps forward to the position of the closing keyframe point.

Likewise, adjust this point's settings for **Scale** and **Position** to a more accurate closing position for your screen image in the **Monitor** panel.

Keyframes can be added, moved to different positions on the **Timeline**, and even deleted completely.

Finally, you can save the new positions you've created as a custom preset (see **65 Create and Save a Preset**).

▶ **TIP**

You don't have to create a keyframe at the exact position on the **Timeline** you want the effect to occur. After the keyframe is set, you can drag the keyframe point to any desired position on the **Timeline**.

6

Editing on the Timeline

IN THIS CHAPTER:

The **Timeline**: What a concept. Although this is the computer age, the concept of the **Timeline** was taken from the real-life video editing of the past. The best of applications take a manual process and automate it. That is exactly what Adobe has done with Premiere Elements. By using a digital timeline, tasks that weren't possible or even attempted in the past because of their difficulty or the time they took can now be accomplished in a very short and simple fashion. Digital video editing has shortened the amount of time it takes to edit a film, but the overall process has increased because of the unlimited number of things you can do with the video after it is on your computer. There was a time when it was very difficult to get film from several cameras or sources together into one movie. That is no longer the case; and you can do more today with Premiere Elements than the professionals did 20 years ago. Much of this is because of the ability to add many video and audio tracks to your movie.

Many video-editing software applications have some form of Timeline. Some of those even have multiple video and audio tracks. However, very few consumer editing applications can add unlimited numbers of video and audio tracks, like Premiere Elements can do. This is one of the features that helps provide professional results and functions without the cost of professional software.

For you, the video artist, the **Timeline** is your canvas. This is where you do the majority of your editing, add effects and transitions, and perform all of the tasks necessary to produce your movie.

In this chapter, we will cover everything from getting media from the **Media** panel onto the **Timeline** to editing and rendering your clips. We will introduce you to *video tracks* (sometimes called *layers*), and show you how to use them. You will learn how to prepare your clips for transitions, remove unwanted scenes, and do a few things just like they do in Hollywood.

As you begin your video-editing adventure, you will most likely return to this chapter repeatedly. This chapter and Chapter 8, "Advanced Timeline Video and Audio Editing," explain all the features available to you from the **Timeline**. Considering this is where you will spend well over 50% of the your time creating your movie, the information in these two chapters will become second nature to you. Before you know it, you will be creating L-cuts and J-cuts just like the pros.

---

29 **About the Timeline and Video Tracks**

✔ **BEFORE YOU BEGIN**

4 About Video Capture
13 About the Media Panel
14 Add Media with the Adobe Media Downloader

Take a good look at the following figure; you will become very familiar with every feature, every nook and cranny, of this screen. This is the most important area of video editing; it is where you will set your movie apart from the rest.

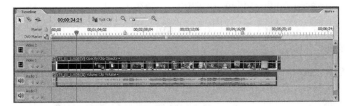

The Premiere Elements **Timeline** *panel.*

▶ **NOTE**

To make viewing the **Timeline** a little easier for the following tasks, resize it to get a larger view. See **2** **Customize Your Workspaces** for details.

For this tour, the **Timeline** is split into three sections. Each section describes a number of features and menus. In the following tasks and chapters, you will use many of these features. The sections start on the left, where the tools and tracks are located; move on to the **More** button; and finish up in the middle work area. This is a brief tour; most of what you see here will be explained in detail in upcoming tasks.

The left side of the **Timeline** contains some basic tools and the labels for the various *tracks* you can incorporate in your movie:

▶ **KEY TERM**

Track—The layers of audio or video clips on the **Timeline**.

- **Select tool**—Use this tool to select from available items—panels, clips, menus, and so on. Some items might not be available if you have not clicked the **Select** tool first.

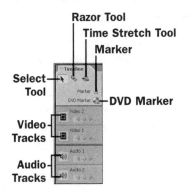

The left side of the **Timeline**.

- **Razor tool**—This tool is used to cut an audio or video clip at any point. See **37** **Remove a Section of a Clip** for additional details.

- **Time Stretch tool**—Select this tool to slow down or speed up your clips. See **40** **Slow/Speed/Reverse Audio/Video** for more information.

- **Marker**—Clicking the **Marker** icon sets an unnumbered Timeline marker at the current CTI position.

- **DVD marker**—Clicking the **DVD Marker** icon brings up the **DVD Marker** dialog box that allows you to set various options, including the type of DVD marker. You can also set the DVD marker at the current CTI position.

- **Video tracks**—Video tracks are located below the **DVD Marker** icon. This is where you place the video clips from the **Media** panel.

- **Audio tracks**—Audio tracks are located below the video tracks. This is where you place audio clips from the **Media** panel.

▶ **NOTE**

29

Right-click in the video or audio track control column area (the left end of the track area) to display a context menu that enables you to rename the current track, add unlimited numbers of new tracks, or delete empty tracks.

The **More** button (in the upper-right corner of the **Timeline** panel) provides additional options for the **Timeline**:

- **Track Size**—This menu option has a submenu that includes a selection for the size of the video and audio track display. Read more about these options in **30** **Add, Delete, and Size Tracks**.

- **Add Tracks**—This menu option performs the same function as the **Add Tracks** item in the track context menu.

- **Delete Empty Tracks**—This menu option performs the same function as the **Delete Empty Tracks** item in the track context menu.

- **Snap**—The **Snap** option is an important aid when moving clips on the **Timeline**. With the **Snap** function checked, you can move a clip on the **Timeline** and it snaps into place next to another clip when you drag it close to the other clip. With the **Snap** function unchecked, you can manually place the clip at any point on the **Timeline**. If you want your clips to automatically snap into position adjacent to another clip, use the **Snap** option. If you want to manually place a clip at a particular spot on the **Timeline**, not adjacent to another clip, uncheck this option.

▶ **TIP**

Having the **Snap** option enabled might cause problems if you are trying to overlay one clip with another. If you are planning to overlay, turn off the **Snap** function.

The main center portion of the **Timeline** is where you will do most of your work:

- **Current CTI Position Indicator**—The time indicated to the left of the **Split Clip** button is the CTI time position on the **Timeline**. The time is listed in **Hours: Minutes: Seconds: Frames** format. The beginning of the **Timeline** is **00:00:00:00** and can extend to a time of **99:59:59:29** (99 hours, 59 minutes, 59 seconds, and 29 frames). That would be one long movie!

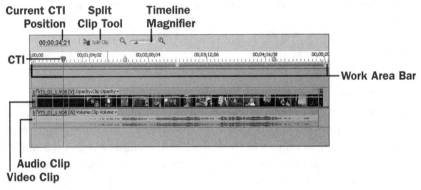

The **Timeline** work area.

- **Split Clip tool**—This tool does just what it says—splits a clip. This tool, unlike the **Razor** tool, splits the clip at the CTI position only. It is represented by an icon of a pair of scissors cutting a piece of film, just like they used to do it in the good old days. For more details on the **Split Clip** tool, see **36** Split a Clip.

- **Timeline Magnifier**—Equipped with a + magnifying glass, a – magnifying glass, and a slider, the magnifier tool can zoom in or out on the **Timeline**. You can go from a view of the entire **Timeline** to a view of just a few frames. As you work, you will do a lot of zooming in and out. Zoom in for fine edits, and zoom out to get a picture of your whole project.

- **CTI**—The Current Time Indicator helps you keep track of where you are on the **Timeline**. When using the **Split Clip** tool, the clip is split at the position of the CTI.

- **Work Area Bar**—The bar above the video and audio clips is known as the *work area bar*. This designates the working area of your project. The work area includes the video and audio tracks—and the clips in them—directly below the work area bar and is defined by the beginning and end of this bar. To learn more about the work area bar and its function, see **32 Define the Beginning and End of Your Project**.

Right-click in the work area or on a clip in the **Timeline** to display the work area context menu. This menu includes additional options for working with clips on the **Timeline** and their properties.

---

30   Add, Delete, and Size Tracks

✔ BEFORE YOU BEGIN	→ SEE ALSO
4 About Video Capture	**77** Create a Picture-in-Picture Effect
14 Add Media with the Adobe Media Downloader	**87** Create a *Brady Bunch* Effect
29 About the Timeline and Video tracks	**97** Create a Title Overlay for Your Video

---

29

By default, Premiere Elements gives you two video and two audio tracks with which to work. You have the ability to add additional video and audio tracks at any time. You'll need additional tracks for special effects such as picture-in-picture (showing multiple images at the same time), adding background images, titles, and text. Each still image also needs its own track; therefore, the more images you want to display simultaneously, the more tracks you need.

Tracks are prioritized from top to bottom (or layered in visibility); the bottom track being track number 1. The higher the track number, the higher the priority. When adding an image to track 1, with nothing above it, the image on track 1 is clearly visible in the **Monitor**. If you add an image to track 2, directly above the track 1 image, all you see in the **Monitor** is the track 2 image because the higher track has priority.

This all becomes more understandable when you resize and position the images, lower their opacity, or make parts of the tracks transparent. When those effects are applied to higher tracks, parts (or all) of the lower tracks become visible. One of the best examples of this is seen in **87 Create a *Brady Bunch* Effect**. Each image in the famous *Brady Bunch* intro is on a separate track, scaled and positioned so all the images are visible in the same screen. Keep **Track Priority** in mind as you add clips to the **Timeline**. Make sure what you want to see is on the proper track; and that there are no clips on tracks above it that don't belong there.

After adding additional tracks, you might need to delete some empty tracks. That can easily be accomplished with a few keystrokes.

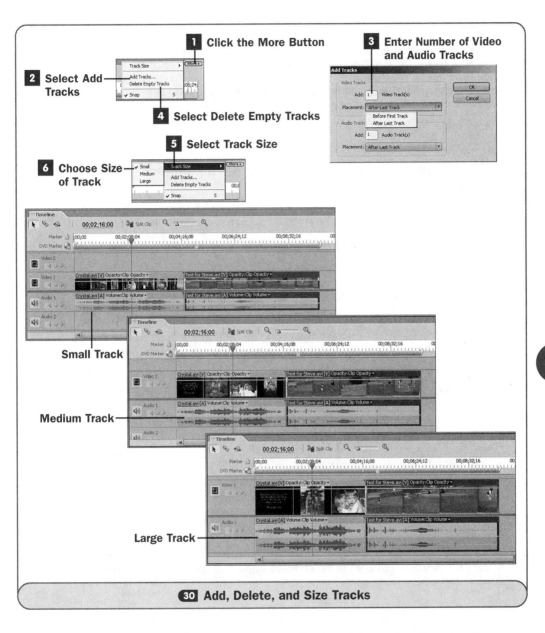

1 Click the More Button

3 Enter Number of Video and Audio Tracks

2 Select Add Tracks

4 Select Delete Empty Tracks

5 Select Track Size

6 Choose Size of Track

Small Track

Medium Track

Large Track

Premiere Elements also enables you to set the size of the tracks. Changing the track size also enlarges the thumbnail images you see on the **Timeline**, making it easier to see the audio and video detail.

▶ **NOTE**

To change the default number of tracks displayed in the **Timeline**, choose **Project**, **Project Settings**, **Default Timeline** from the main menu at the top of your screen. There, you can set the default number of tracks (for both video and audio tracks) for all your future projects. Changing the default does not alter the number of tracks in any projects created before this change.

1 Click the More Button

Click the **More** button in the top-right corner of the **Timeline** to open the **More** menu.

2 Select Add Tracks

To add tracks to the **Timeline**, select the **Add Tracks** option. The **Add Tracks** dialog box opens.

3 Enter Number of Video and Audio Tracks

In the **Add Tracks** dialog box, you see separate entries for **Video Tracks** and **Audio Tracks**. With these settings, you can add only video tracks or only audio tracks if that is what you require. Enter the number of additional tracks in the boxes and select the **Placement** of the new tracks. You can place the new tracks before the first track or after the last track. When you are finished, click the **OK** button to add those tracks to the **Timeline**.

4 Select Delete Empty Tracks

To clean up the **Timeline** and remove unused tracks (audio or video tracks that contain no images or clips), open the **More** menu and choose **Delete Empty Tracks**. All unused audio and video tracks are deleted.

▶ **NOTE**

When deleting empty tracks, Premiere Elements does not show a confirmation dialog box asking, "Are sure you want to delete these tracks?" After you select **Delete Empty Tracks**, the tracks just disappear.

5 Select Track Size

You can change the size of the tracks in the **Timeline**. To do so, open the **More** menu and select **Track Size**. A submenu with three choices opens.

6 Choose Size of Track

For the size of the track, you have the choice of **Small**, **Medium**, or **Large**. Change the setting and notice the difference in the size of the tracks.

Changing the track size also enlarges or reduces the images and clips on the **Timeline**. When you need to see more tracks and less detail, choose **Small** (the default). When you need to see a single track and a lot of detail, choose **Large**. **Medium** is a good setting for average editing tasks.

---

31 | **Set Video and Audio Track Display**

✔ **BEFORE YOU BEGIN**

29 About the Timeline and Video Tracks
30 Add, Delete, and Size Tracks

To the far left of each video track you see a film reel icon; this is the **Video Track Display** toggle. To the far left of each audio track you see a speaker icon; this is the **Audio Track Display** toggle. Depending on your workflow, current task, or personal preference, you can have different display settings for each video and audio track.

1 Set Video Track Display

The video track display can be toggled to different views by clicking the film reel icon at the left end of the video track. Clicking this icon switches between four views; keep clicking the icon until you see the view you want:

- Thumbnails across the entire track

- Thumbnails at the beginning of the clip

- Thumbnails at the beginning and end of the clip

- Hide the thumbnails on the track

▶ **TIP**

To make the keyframe markers more visible, choose the view that hides the thumbnails. The keyframe markers and line will be clearly visible on the **Timeline**.

2 Set Audio Track Display

The audio track display can also be toggled to different views by clicking the speaker icon at the far left of the audio track. Click this icon to switch between two views:

- Audio waveform shown across the entire track

- Hide the audio waveform on the track

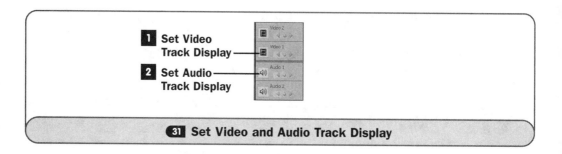

1 Set Video
Track Display

2 Set Audio
Track Display

Video 2

Video 1

Audio 1

Audio 2

31 Set Video and Audio Track Display

32 Define the Beginning and End of Your Project

✔ BEFORE YOU BEGIN

29 About the Timeline and Video Tracks

31

The work area bar is located at the top of the track view, below the **Timeline** where the CTI is located. This bar helps to determine the beginning and end of your project for certain tasks. During the rendering, viewing, playing, and exporting of your project, the work area bar sets the start and end points. You can adjust the start and end points when you are interested in working with only a particular section of your project.

1 Locate the Entire Work Area Bar

Under normal circumstances, the work area bar covers your entire project.

Hover the mouse pointer over the work area bar to display the start timecode, end timecode, and duration of the portion of the movie contained under the work area bar.

2 Lengthen or Shorten the Work Area Bar

When the need arises, you can drag either end of the work area bar to shorten or lengthen it. Simply drag the handles at each end of the bar in or out.

You can click the center of the work area bar and drag the entire bar to another section of the **Timeline**. This action effectively moves the currently active section of the project to encompass a new group of clips in the **Timeline**.

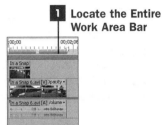

1 Locate the Entire Work Area Bar

2 Lengthen or Shorten the Work Area Bar

32 Define the Beginning and End of Your Project

The ability to move, lengthen, and shorten the work area bar comes in useful when outputting your video (see **104** **Output to an AVI Movie**). When outputting, you will have options to output the entire **Timeline** or what is covered by the work area bar only. Using the work area bar, you can output just portions of your video and create new clips. When adjusting the work area bar, all of your project is still visible on the **Timeline**, and you can play the entire **Timeline** in the **Monitor**. Also, timeline rendering (see **43** **About Rendering the Timeline**) ignores any area not covered by the work area bar: If there is a red line above one of your clips and you want to render only that part of the **Timeline**, make sure that the work area bar is covering that area before you render.

▶ **TIP**

Double-clicking the work area bar stretches or moves it the length of what you see in the **Timeline**. If you see 20 frames, the work area bar will extend over those 20 frames. If you see the entire project, the work area bar will extend over the entire project. Zooming out until your complete project is in view and then double-clicking the work area bar is the best way to ensure that the bar covers your whole project.

You might want to adjust the work area bar before you render a portion of the movie. To render just a portion of the movie in the **Timeline**, position the work area bar over the section of the **Timeline** you want to render and press **Enter**. Even if the whole **Timeline** needs to be rendered, just the portion below the work area bar is rendered at this time. If you're trying to render a section of the **Timeline** but the entire section will not render, double-check the position and length of the work area bar. The work area bar should cover the entire section you want to render. To find out more about rendering, see **43** **About Rendering the Timeline**.

▶ **TIP**

If you cannot render or export your entire movie, double-check the position and length of the work area bar. To render or export the entire movie, the work area bar should extend to contain all the project's clips.

33 | Add or Move a Clip on the Timeline

✔ BEFORE YOU BEGIN

10 Capture to the Timeline or Media Panel

13 About the Media Panel

14 Add Media with the Adobe Media Downloader

29 About the Timeline and Video Tracks

→ SEE ALSO

35 Delete and Close Gaps in the Timeline

41 Move Several Clips at Once

43 About Rendering the Timeline

33

Now it's time to really get down to business: getting clips onto the **Timeline**. Although you can trim clips while they are still in the **Media** panel (as explained in 19 **Trim Clips in the Media Panel**), you can do nothing beyond that without getting those clips onto the **Timeline**, where editing begins (and when you're finished editing, what is on the **Timeline** is what gets burned to DVD). Before we begin this task, you must have a few clips in the **Media** panel that can be added to the **Timeline** (see 13 **About the Media Panel**, 14 **Add Media with the Adobe Media Downloader**, and 4 **About Video Capture**). Of course, if you have captured your clips and used the default **Capture to Timeline** option, your clips are already there. The sooner you get the clips down there, the sooner you can start your editing process and burn that DVD. Note that there are two ways a clip can be added to the **Timeline**: with the **Insert** or **Overlay** option.

The **Insert** option places the new clip on the **Timeline**, splitting an existing clip, or (if positioned at the beginning, end, or *between* video clips), inserting the new clip and moving all clips to the right to make room for the new clip. The **Overlay** option places the new video over existing video, removing any of the existing video it is placed over.

▶ NOTE

You can capture clips directly to the Timeline as explained in 10 Capture to the Timeline or Media Panel.

1 Select a Clip in the Media Panel

Click the clip thumbnail in the **Media** panel that you want to add to the **Timeline** and to your project. The clip is selected and appears highlighted.

2 Drag the Clip to the Timeline

Drag the clip thumbnail to the **Timeline**.

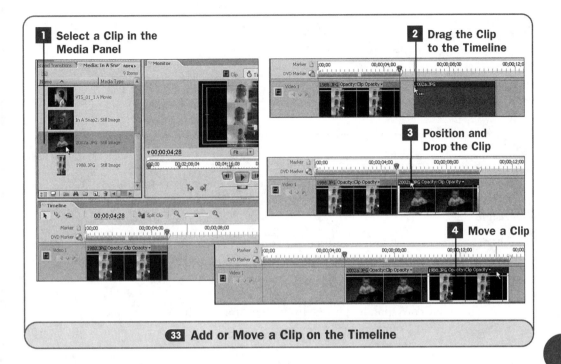

33 Add or Move a Clip on the Timeline

33

▶ **TIP**

Instead of dragging the clip to the **Timeline**, you can right-click the clip in the **Media** panel to open the context menu and choose the **Insert to Timeline** option to insert the selected clip on the **Timeline** at the CTI. If the CTI is positioned in the middle of a clip, the clip on the **Timeline** is split and the new clip is inserted at that point.

3 **Position and Drop the Clip**

Position the clip where you want it to be on the **Timeline** and release the mouse button to drop the clip.

▶ **NOTE**

If you have selected the **Snap** option from the **Timeline**'s **More** menu, the clip snaps to the beginning of the **Timeline** (if there are no other clips present on the **Timeline**). If there are other clips on the **Timeline**, the current clip snaps to an adjacent clip (see **29** About the Timeline and Video Tracks). With the **Snap** option enabled, you don't need to be perfect when you drop your clips, just close. The **Snap** option also prevents you from overlaying or splitting a clip already on the **Timeline** by accident.

4 **Move a Clip**

If, by chance, you don't hit your mark when you drop your clip on the **Timeline**, don't worry. Simply grab the clip on the **Timeline** and drag and drop it to a new position.

34   Trim a Clip on the Timeline

✔ BEFORE YOU BEGIN	→ SEE ALSO
33 Add or Move a Clip on the Timeline	36 Split a Clip 37 Remove a Section of a Clip 39 Remove Audio or Video from a Clip

 As you start your editing experience, you will need to recognize the **Trim** icons. Move the mouse pointer over the edge of a clip and notice that one of these **Trim** icons appears. The only way you can trim your clip is when one of these icons is visible.

There is more than one way to trim a clip, and this is one of them. Later in this chapter you will be instructed in other trimming methods. The trimming method described in this task is not intended for fine, detailed editing, but it *is* a good way to quickly remove unwanted scenes or footage from a clip. As you trim your clip, you can see the corresponding frame in the **Monitor** to help you keep track of where you are and what you are trimming.

34

1 Drag the Right Edge to Extend the Duration of a Still

Drag a still image from the **Media** panel to the beginning of the **Timeline**. If the default **Still Image Duration** has not been changed, the image will have a duration of 5 seconds on the **Timeline**. If you need to extend the duration of a single clip without changing the default setting for still-image duration, you can drag out some additional time for this specific still image.

▶ NOTE

To change the default **Still Image Duration**, select **Edit**, **Preferences**, **General** from the menu at the top of your screen. The default duration for a still image is 150 frames (30 frames per second times 5 seconds). Change this value and click **OK** to change the default duration for still images.

Click the left mouse button over the right edge of the still image clip in the **Timeline**. Make sure that you can see the **Right Trim** icon before clicking. Drag the edge to the right until the CTI gets to the 8-second mark. Release the mouse button; this single still image clip now has an 8-second duration. All other still images maintain the default duration set in the **Preferences** dialog box.

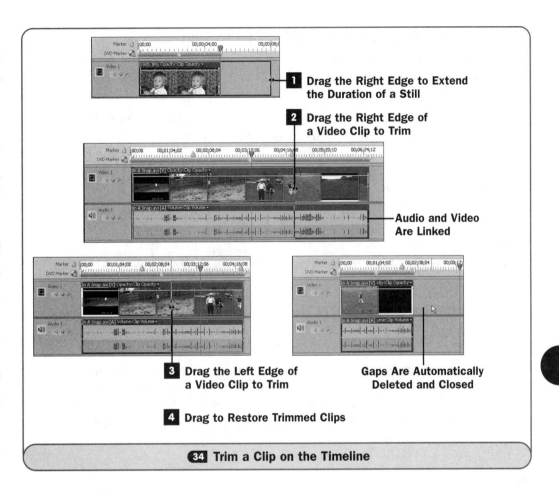

1 Drag the Right Edge to Extend the Duration of a Still

2 Drag the Right Edge of a Video Clip to Trim

—Audio and Video Are Linked

3 Drag the Left Edge of a Video Clip to Trim

Gaps Are Automatically Deleted and Closed

4 Drag to Restore Trimmed Clips

34 Trim a Clip on the Timeline

34

▶ NOTES

If you drag the mouse to the left, you will decrease the duration of the still. When trimming or extending a still image, you are adding or removing identical frames. The only change trimming makes to a still image is to its duration on the **Timeline**.

When you release the mouse button after extending or decreasing the duration of a still image on the **Timeline**, the work area bar adjusts to the new image length. This works as long as you have not manually made adjustments to the position of the bar.

Now right-click the still image in the **Timeline** and select **Clear** from the context menu to delete this practice still from the **Timeline**. Alternatively, select the clip and press the **Delete** key to delete the clip.

2 Drag the Right Edge of a Video Clip to Trim

Drag a video clip from the **Media** panel and drop if at the beginning of the **Timeline**. Click the right edge of the video clip, making sure that you see the **Right Trim** icon before clicking the mouse button.

If you are working with a still image, you can always drag the trimmer to the right; Premiere Elements adds as many additional frames as needed. However, if you are working with video- or audio-only clips, you can only extend to the end of the clip; Premiere Elements will not add or repeat frames in this case. You can grab a still of the last image in the clip and drag that out farther if that is your goal (see 21 **Grab a Still from Video**).

▶ **NOTE**

As you drag the **Right Trim** icon, watch the **Monitor**; it will give you a view of what you are trimming from your clip.

Drag the edge of the clip to the left 10 seconds. As you drag, notice that both the video and audio tracks are being trimmed. Release the mouse button, and your trimmed clip will be 10 seconds shorter than it originally was.

To trim only the video or the audio, right-click the clip and select **Unlink Audio and Video** from the context menu. To trim only the audio, position the mouse pointer over the edge of the audio track and drag without affecting the video track; to trim only the video, position the mouse pointer over the edge of the video track and drag without affecting the audio track.

▶ **TIP**

If you are trimming your clip to be used in an L-cut or a J-cut, see 38 **Create an L-Cut or a J-Cut**.

3 Drag the Left Edge of a Video Clip to Trim

Now move to the beginning of the clip, the left side. Click the left edge of the clip, making sure that you see the **Left Trim** icon before clicking.

Drag the edge to the right 10 seconds and release the mouse button. The clip will now be 20 seconds shorter than the original—you've trimmed 10 seconds off each end of the clip. You can trim as much or as little as necessary; it is totally up to you. Don't be afraid to experiment because the original clip on the hard drive is not altered during the nonlinear editing process.

▶ **NOTE**

As you trim your clips, the clips automatically move to the left on the **Timeline** to close any space or gaps. (see **35** Delete and Close Gaps in the Timeline).

> If your trimming has left gaps in the **Timeline**, Premiere Elements automatically deletes and closes any gaps. In the example you just completed, the clip was moved back to the beginning of the **Timeline**, even though you trimmed 10 seconds from that end.

▶ **TIP**

If you would rather the clip did not move to the left and fill in any gaps in the **Timeline**, hold the **Ctrl** key while you drag the **Trim** icon. Be sure to release the mouse button before releasing the **Ctrl** key. As you hold the mouse pointer over a clip and press the **Ctrl** key or the **Shift** key, notice the messages under the **Timeline**. These messages let you know what will happen when you drag or drop with one of these keys pressed.

4 Drag to Restore Trimmed Clips

If you accidentally trim too much from a clip, move the **Trim** icon in the opposite direction to get the trimmed parts back. The trimmed scenes are never deleted from the actual footage, so the trimmed frames are always available to be added to your project.

35

---

35 Delete and Close Gaps in the Timeline

✔ BEFORE YOU BEGIN	→ SEE ALSO
33 Add or Move a Clip on the Timeline	**36** Split a Clip

If you encounter unwanted gaps in your **Timeline**, there is a quick fix to help you remove them.

1 Right-click a Gap in the Timeline

Right-click a gap in the **Timeline** to display the context menu. If you have more than one gap in the Timeline, you will have to manually close them one at a time.

2 Select Delete and Close Gap

The context menu offers only one option to choose: **Delete and Close Gap**. If the gap cannot be deleted and closed (if there are audio or video clips on other tracks in the same position of the **Timeline**), the context menu option is not available. In this case, you can manually drag the clip to close the gap.

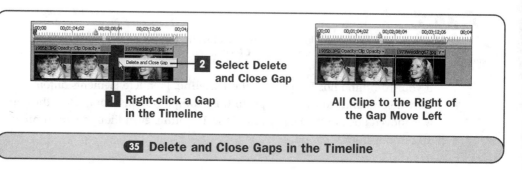

2 Select Delete and Close Gap

1 Right-click a Gap in the Timeline

All Clips to the Right of the Gap Move Left

35 Delete and Close Gaps in the Timeline

After selecting the **Delete and Close Gap** option, the gap is removed from between the clips. All clips to the right of the gap move to the left to fill in the gap.

36   Split a Clip

✔ BEFORE YOU BEGIN	→ SEE ALSO
33 Add or Move a Clip on the Timeline	**37** Remove a Section of a Clip
35 Delete and Close Gaps in the Timeline	**38** Create an L-Cut or a J-Cut
	44 About Transitions
	46 Add a Video Transition

One method of splitting or cutting a clip is by using the **Split Clip** button, located just above the timecode bar in the **Timeline**. You can use this button to do some very detailed trimming of your clips. You can zoom in on the **Timeline** to see individual frames in the video clip, position the CTI on the **Timeline**, and then click the **Split Clip** button to split the clip at the CTI position.

You might use the **Split Clip** feature when you want to add a transition *inside* a clip. As you know, you cannot place a transition in the middle of a clip, only to the beginning, end, or between two clips. You can use the **Split Clip** feature to create two clips so you can place the transition between them. For more details on transitions, see **44** About Transitions. You might want to move a section of a clip to another part of the **Timeline**. By creating two splits in a clip, you create three separate clips, and any of the three can be moved anywhere on the **Timeline**. A clip can be split between every frame, making it possible to have as many as 29 splits in one second of video (creating 30 separate clips of one frame each).

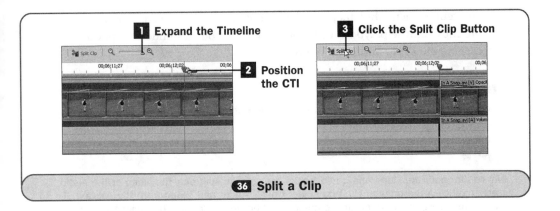

1 Expand the Timeline   **3** Click the Split Clip Button

2 Position the CTI

36 Split a Clip

1 Expand the Timeline

Find the general area of your clip where you would like the split to occur. Move the CTI to that location on the **Timeline**.

Use the **Timeline Magnifier** to expand (or zoom into) the **Timeline** as far as you can to get a view of each individual frame in the video clip. This type of split, or cut, is a very precise and detailed edit. You want to make sure you can see all the detail you can so you are sure you are splitting the clip between the correct frames. When splitting audio clips, you want to split at a precise point in the waveform. Zoom into the **Timeline** to make this possible by providing very clear detail of the audio waveform.

2 Position the CTI

Locate the frames between which you want to create the split, and position the CTI between the two frames.

▶ **TIP**

If the CTI is not visible, click the **Timeline** anywhere above the work area bar. The CTI moves to that position.

3 Click the Split Clip Button

When you have the CTI positioned between the two frames where you want the split created, click the **Split Clip** button. The clip is divided at the CTI location, creating two clips out of the original one. You can now delete, add a transition between, or move either clip—they are totally separate clips now. Notice that the two clips share the same name because they are still parts of the original still on your hard drive as one complete clip. If the clips remain adjacent to each other, there will be no noticeable difference when playing the clips because playback will ignore the split. You can undo the split by clicking the **Undo** button or by pressing **Ctrl+Z**.

▶ TIP

If you select multiple clips on multiple tracks, the **Split Clip** button will split *all* the selected clips at the CTI, not just one.

▶ NOTE

Notice that both the video and audio tracks are split. To split only the video or the audio track, right-click the original clip and select **Unlink Audio and Video** from the context menu. Select either the video or the audio track portion of the clip by clicking it and then click the **Split Clip** button; only the selected track is split.

You can also cut and split clips using the **Razor** tool, as explained in **37** **Remove a Section of a Clip**. When you use the **Razor** tool, the clips are cut at the mouse pointer, not at the CTI position.

36

37	**Remove a Section of a Clip**

✔ BEFORE YOU BEGIN	→ SEE ALSO
29 About the Timeline and Video Tracks	**34** Trim a Clip on the Timeline
33 Add or Move a Clip on the Timeline	**38** Create an L-Cut or a J-Cut
	39 Remove Audio or Video from a Clip

People generally capture way more video than they will use in a movie. Just like in Hollywood, the more footage you have, the better the possibility of creating a great scene. Because you have all this extra footage, you usually need to remove sections from the middle of a clip. Even after trimming a clip in the **Media** panel or on the **Timeline**, you will still have sections you want to remove. This is where the **Razor** tool becomes a valuable feature.

To use the **Razor** tool, you must locate an area of a clip that you want to remove. You make two cuts in the clip, one at the beginning of the section to be removed and one at the end. Selecting the footage to remove requires detailed editing, and you will zoom in and out of your clip, possibly a few times, to get the exact location of each cut. While searching for the section to be removed, look for a place on the clip where two frames meet. One frame is a frame you want to keep, the other is a frame you want to remove. All the frames between the two cuts are turned into a new clip and can be deleted or just moved to another location on the **Timeline**.

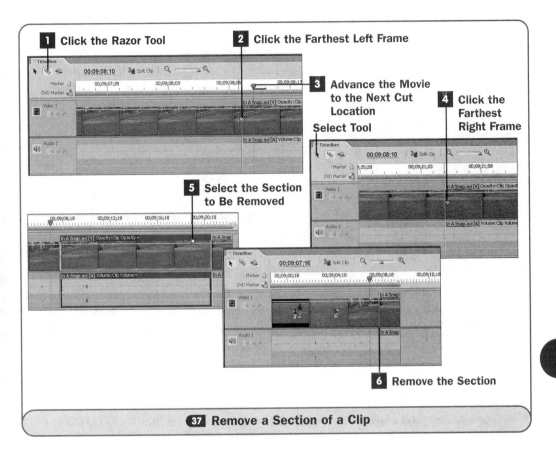

1 Click the Razor Tool

2 Click the Farthest Left Frame

3 Advance the Movie to the Next Cut Location

Select Tool

4 Click the Farthest Right Frame

5 Select the Section to Be Removed

6 Remove the Section

37 Remove a Section of a Clip

37

▶ **NOTE**

When cutting a clip with the **Razor** tool, both the video and audio tracks are cut. If you do not want the audio cut along with the video (or vice-versa), see **39** Remove Audio or Video from a Clip; alternatively, you can unlink the audio and video tracks as explained in **36** Split a Clip.

1 **Click the Razor Tool**

Locate a section of a clip that you want to remove. You can zoom out on the **Timeline** to get a wider view by using the **Timeline Magnifier**. After you have located the section of the clip you want to remove, zoom in on the **Timeline** as far as you can to see individual frames, 30 frames per second. When you have located the first frame of the section you want to remove, click the **Razor** tool.

2 Click the Farthest Left Frame

As you move the mouse pointer to the clip in the **Timeline**, notice that the pointer turns into a razor blade. The line to the left of the **Razor** tool is where the cut occurs. Also notice that the **Razor** position moves along the **Timeline** where the CTI is located. Move the **Razor** tool to the farthest left frame that you want to remove (the first frame of the footage you want to remove) and click. A cut, or split, is placed at the frame where the **Razor** tool was located. If you missed your mark, undo the cut and try again.

▶ NOTE

You cannot cut a clip in the middle of a frame. The **Razor** tool and the **Split Clip** feature always cut the clip between two frames.

3 Advance the Movie to the Next Cut Location

Using the shuttle in the **Monitor** panel or the CTI, find the last frame in the section you want to remove. This is clearly visible when you zoom in to the **Timeline** as far as possible. The tick marks at the top of the **Timeline** show where each frame starts and stops. The current frame is indicated by a marker at the top of the CTI that covers the frame to the right of it.

37

▶ TIP

If you make a mistake and cut the clip at the wrong location, press **Ctrl+Z** to undo the last action. You can then find the correct position and cut again.

4 Click the Farthest Right Frame

When you have identified the last frame of the section you want to cut, click the **Razor** tool on the last frame (the farthest right frame in the section being removed). This action creates another cut at the position of the **Razor** tool.

5 Select the Section to Be Removed

Now you have successfully turned one clip into three, the middle section being the section you want to remove. If you zoom out on the **Timeline**, you will be able to clearly see the two cut points.

Click the **Select** tool and then click the section of clip you want to remove. This action highlights that clip only.

▶ TIP

You can click the **Selection** tool, grab the clip, and drag to move it to another location on the **Timeline**.

6 **Remove the Section**

With the section of the original clip highlighted, press the **Delete** key to remove it from the **Timeline**.

---

38 **Create an L-Cut or a J-Cut**

✔ BEFORE YOU BEGIN	→ SEE ALSO
19 Trim Clips in the Media Panel	**37** Remove a Section of a Clip
33 Add or Move a Clip on the Timeline	**39** Remove Audio or Video from a Clip
34 Trim a Clip on the Timeline	**52** Add Narration to Your Movie
	87 Create a *Brady Bunch* Effect

The two most common and most used transitions in film are the L-Cut and the J-Cut. Both are cutaways and move from one video scene to another, with the same underlying audio track for both.

Here's an example of an L-Cut: Start the scene with a clip showing two people talking. Cut away to a clip of the surrounding area, without the two people in the frame; keeping the audio of the conversation going.

Here's an example of a J-Cut: Start the scene with a clip that shows the surrounding area and the audio of two people talking, without the two people in the frame. Then cut away to the clip showing the two people holding the conversation.

For this task you will need two clips in the **Media** panel, one clip should be longer than the other. You can trim one of the clips in the **Media** panel as explained in **19** **Trim Clips in the Media Panel**, or you can trim the clip after you drop it on the **Timeline** as explained in **34** **Trim a Clip on the Timeline**. The longer clip will be the Track 1 clip, and the shorter clip will be the Track 2 clip in the steps that follow.

38

▶ **TIP**

There are various ways to trim a clip: You can set in and out points in the **Monitor** and drag the trimmed clip to the **Timeline** (see **19** Trim Clips in the Media Panel), you can razor the clip and delete the part you don't need (see **37** Remove a Section of a Clip), you can split the clip and delete the part you don't need (see **36** Split a Clip), or you can drag either end of the clip to trim it (see **34** Trim a Clip on the Timeline).

1 **Add the First Clip to the Timeline, Track 1**

Drag and drop the first (the longer) clip on Track 1, at the beginning of the **Timeline**.

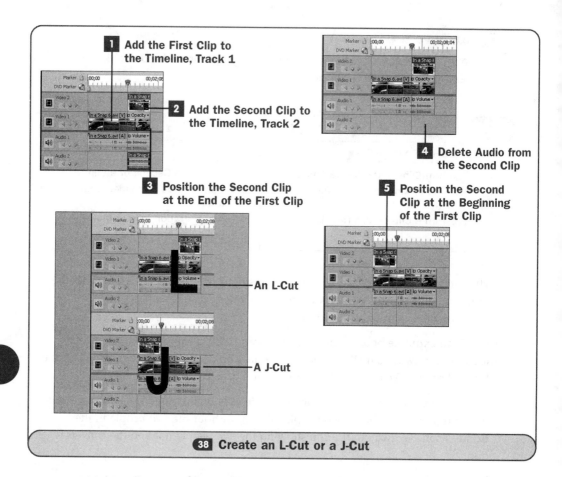

1 Add the First Clip to the Timeline, Track 1

2 Add the Second Clip to the Timeline, Track 2

3 Position the Second Clip at the End of the First Clip

4 Delete Audio from the Second Clip

5 Position the Second Clip at the Beginning of the First Clip

An L-Cut

A J-Cut

38 Create an L-Cut or a J-Cut

2 **Add the Second Clip to the Timeline, Track 2**

Drag and drop the second (the shorter) clip to Track 2 of the **Timeline**.

3 **Position the Second Clip at the End of the First Clip**

Move the second clip—the one on Track 2—so that its right edge lines up with the right edge of the clip on Track 1.

4 **Delete Audio from the Second Clip**

Because this transition effect runs the audio from the first clip over the video of the second clip, you will likely want to remove the audio from the second clip so the audio from the first clip can be heard. Right-click the second clip (the one on Track 2) to open the clip's context menu and select **Delete Audio**.

With the clips as they are currently arranged on the **Timeline**, the scene starts with the video and audio from the Track 1 clip and ends with the video from Track 2. This is the L-Cut.

5 Position the Second Clip at the Beginning of the First Clip

Creating a J-Cut after you've arranged the L-Cut is a simple matter of moving the Track 2 clip. Drag the Track 2 clip from the end of the Track 1 clip to the beginning of the Track 1 clip. Now the scene will start with the video from Track 2 but the audio from Track 1. The scene then cuts away to the video from Track 1, where the audio originates. This is the J-Cut.

---

39 Remove Audio or Video from a Clip

✔ BEFORE YOU BEGIN	→ SEE ALSO
29 About the Timeline and Video Tracks	**38** Create an L-Cut or a J-Cut
33 Add or Move a Clip on the Timeline	**52** Add Narration to Your Movie
35 Delete and Close Gaps in the Timeline	

39

There are two ways to remove audio or video from your clips. Both are important depending on your task and workflow, so we will cover them both here. For purposes of creating an L-Cut, J-Cut, a silent movie, or when adding narration or music, you will need to remove the audio or video portion of a clip.

1 Select a Clip in the Timeline

Add a clip to the **Timeline** that contains both audio and video. When you click the clip's audio or video track, notice that both the audio and video tracks become highlighted. This is because the two tracks are linked together. Before you can delete either the audio or video, you must first unlink the tracks.

2 Select Unlink Audio and Video

Right-click the clip—either the audio or video track will do. The clip's context menu opens. Select **Unlink Audio and Video**.

▶ TIP

You can link audio and video in the same way you unlink them: Select the audio and video clips you want to link and right-click one of them. From the context menu, choose **Link Audio and Video**.

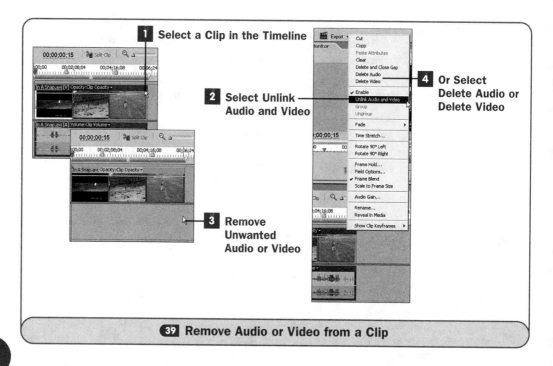

1 Select a Clip in the Timeline

2 Select Unlink
Audio and Video

3 Remove
Unwanted
Audio or Video

4 Or Select
Delete Audio or
Delete Video

39 Remove Audio or Video from a Clip

39

3 Remove the Unwanted Audio or Video Portion

The audio and video tracks are now unlinked. Notice that when you click the video track now, the audio track is not highlighted (and vice-versa). To remove the video portion of the clip, click the clip's video track and press the **Delete** key. To instead delete the audio portion of the clip, click the clip's audio track and press the **Delete** key. Simple isn't it? Well, if all you wanted to do was delete the audio or video there is an easier way to do this.

▶ **TIP**

By unlinking the audio and video tracks, you are now free to move the audio and video clips separately. If your audio is slightly out of sync, unlinking the audio and video gives you the ability to move the audio portion of the clip into sync with the video.

4 Or Select Delete Audio or Delete Video

An alternative approach to deleting the audio or video portion of a video clip saves you the step of unlinking the tracks. To practice this alternative method, add another video clip to the **Timeline**, undo the **Unlink** operation, or relink the audio and video for the current clip. In effect, start this step with a video clip that has both the audio and video tracks present and linked.

Right-click the clip's audio or video track to open the clip's context menu. Select **Delete Audio** or **Delete Video** to delete one or the other track.

40 Slow/Speed/Reverse Audio/Video

✔ BEFORE YOU BEGIN	→ SEE ALSO
29 About the Timeline and Video Tracks	**50** Freeze a Frame

If you've ever thought about doing some slow-motion instant replays, speeding up a clip to look like a silent movie, or playing your clip in reverse, the **Time Stretch** tool is for you. You can use the **Time Stretch** feature two ways: The first is a button on the **Timeline** that enables you to speed up or slow down a clip by simply dragging. The second option is found in the clip context menu and allows you to fine tune the speed, duration, reverse speed, and audio pitch of the select-ed clip. Using the **Time Stretch** tool, you can have multiple copies of a clip on the **Timeline**, play the first copy at normal speed, then show the slow-motion instant replay, then show the clip again in reverse, and finally play it in fast motion—all in the same movie.

1 Select the Time Stretch Tool

Make sure you have a video clip on the **Timeline**. At the top-left side of the **Timeline** is the **Time Stretch** button. Click this button and move the mouse pointer over the edge of your video clip. Notice that the pointer changes to the **Time Stretch** icon.

2 Drag the Outer Edge of a Clip

Click the outer edge (either the left or the right edge) of the video clip and drag the edge. Drag to the right to produce a slow-speed effect; drag to the left to produce a fast-speed effect. What you are actually doing is shortening or lengthening the duration of the clip. Slowing the clip down requires Premiere Elements to repeat frames, speeding it up requires Premiere Elements to remove frames.

3 Or Set Time Stretch Options

If you want finer control over the speed of your video clip, you can get it using the **Time Stretch** dialog box. Undo the drag-and-drop changes you made to the video in steps 1 and 2, and then right-click the clip to open the clip context menu. Select the **Time Stretch** option to open the **Time Stretch** dialog box.

40

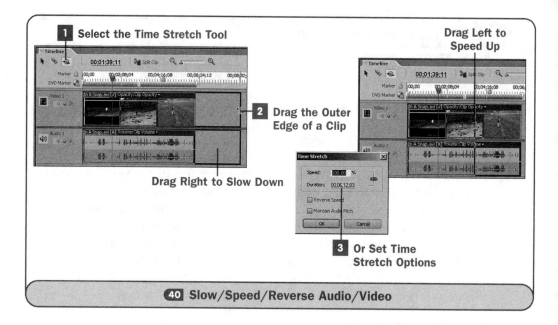

1 **Select the Time Stretch Tool**

Drag Left to Speed Up

2 **Drag the Outer Edge of a Clip**

Drag Right to Slow Down

3 **Or Set Time Stretch Options**

40 **Slow/Speed/Reverse Audio/Video**

40

Here you have a bit more control over what happens to your clip. You can set the precise percent of increase or decrease in speed (a value less than 100% slows down the clip, a value over 100% speeds up the clip), change the speed by setting the duration of the clip (a shorter duration than the original speeds up the clip, a longer duration slows down the clip), choose to play the clip in reverse, and maintain the audio pitch (keeping the pitch of the audio portion of the clip unchanged).

▶ **TIP**

The **Duration** setting in the **Time Stretch** dialog box comes in very handy for music tracks. If your music is a little too short or a little too long, you can set the duration of the audio clip to match the duration of the video on the **Timeline**. A small difference in the duration audio clip is not noticed when you're watching the movie. This happens in television quite often, to fit a 32-minute program into 30 minutes or a 2-hour movie into 1 hour and 55 minutes. That is what makes room for all of those commercials.

After you have made the necessary modifications, click **OK**. These settings are applied to your clip.

▶ **TIP**

You can apply the **Time Stretch** feature to clips not yet on the **Timeline**; just right-click the clip in the **Media** panel and choose **Time Stretch** from the context menu.

41 Move Several Clips at Once

✔ BEFORE YOU BEGIN	→ SEE ALSO
33 Add or Move a Clip on the Timeline	**42** Group Clips

Sometimes it becomes necessary to move a number of clips all at the same time to the same area of the **Timeline**. In this and the following task, **42** **Group Clips**, we will show you how to work with multiple clips as if they were a single entity.

1 Click to the Right of the Clips to Be Moved

Move the mouse pointer just to the right of the clips you want to move. Click and hold the left mouse button.

2 Drag to Lasso the Desired Clips

While holding down the left mouse button, drag across the clips you want to move. When you have lassoed them all, release the mouse button. All the clips you dragged across are now selected, effectively making them one neat little selected package.

▶ TIP

You can also select multiple clips by holding the **Shift** key while clicking the clips. With this approach, the clips do not have to be in consecutive order on the **Timeline**—you can select multiple clips from any location on the **Timeline**.

3 Drag Any One of the Selected Clips

Click any one of the selected clips and drag to move them all together. Drag the group of clips to a new location on the **Timeline**. Notice that even though you are dragging only one of the clips, all the other selected clips go along for the ride.

4 Drop the Selected Clips in the New Position

When you find the new location for your clips, release the mouse button. The clips drop in their newly selected location.

41

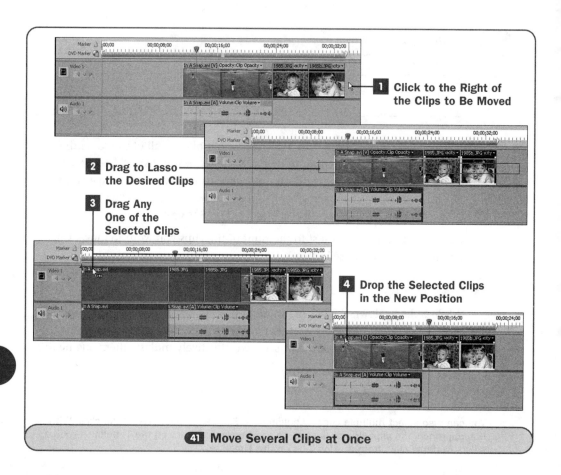

1 Click to the Right of the Clips to Be Moved

2 Drag to Lasso the Desired Clips

3 Drag Any One of the Selected Clips

4 Drop the Selected Clips in the New Position

41

41 Move Several Clips at Once

---

42 | **Group Clips**

✔ **BEFORE YOU BEGIN**

29 About the Timeline and Video Tracks

33 Add or Move a Clip on the Timeline

→ **SEE ALSO**

41 Move Several Clips at Once

64 Copy Effect Attributes from One Clip to Another

Another means of manipulating or moving multiple clips is by grouping them. Unlike the temporary group you created in **41** Move Several Clips at Once, officially grouped clips stay together. In the previous task, lassoing or selecting multiple clips groups the clips only until you click something else. When you group clips, they stay grouped—at least until you ungroup them. If you know you will be moving or copying several clips together on a consistent basis, consider grouping them.

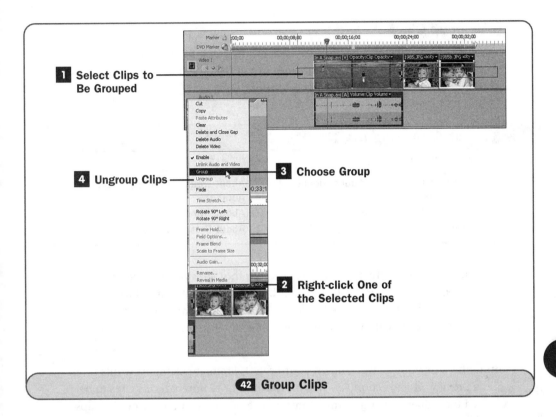

1 Select Clips to Be Grouped

4 Ungroup Clips

3 Choose Group

2 Right-click One of the Selected Clips

42 Group Clips

1 Select Clips to Be Grouped

Drag across multiple clips to lasso the adjacent clips you want to group together. Alternatively, hold the **Shift** key and click to select multiple disparate clips.

2 Right-click One of the Selected Clips

Right-click any one of the selected clips to open the clip context menu.

3 Choose Group

From the context menu, choose **Group**. From that point on, whenever you click one of the grouped clips, all the clips in the group are selected.

▶ TIP

If you rotate one clip in a group, all the clips in the group rotate. Basically, anything you do to one of the clips in the group is applied to all the clips—with the exception of transitions or effects.

4 **Ungroup Clips**

You ungroup clips in the same way you group them: Right-click any one of the grouped clips and choose **Ungroup** from the context menu. All the clips in that group return to being separate clips.

---

43 **About Rendering the Timeline**

✔ BEFORE YOU BEGIN	→ SEE ALSO
14 Add Media with the Adobe Media Downloader	**18** About Troubleshooting Media Additions
33 Add or Move a Clip on the Timeline	**44** About Transitions
	58 About Preset Effects

In digital video editing, there arise various times that clips need rendering. This especially occurs at the time your movie is burned to a DVD, burned to a folder, or exported as one of the various file types. Rendering prepares the video to be written to file or disk with all its transitions, effects, edits, titles, and menus included.

42

During the time you are working on your project, Premiere Elements wants to build a preview of your changes. This preview might require various clips to be rendered for proper viewing in the **Monitor**. The necessity of rendering the clips depends on your computer system and the type of file or effect you are creating. Computers with faster processors, more RAM, and additional video memory do not have to render at all (or at least not as often). Even with a fast processor, lots of RAM, and lots of video memory, you might still have to render after adding certain video-intensive effects or saving to various file types, such as some MPEG files. Although Premiere Elements does a pseudo (or soft) render continuously, you might have to perform a final render to see a smooth video in the **Monitor**. This final render is called the *hard render*.

Premiere Elements wants to hard render under the following conditions:

- After adding a video file not captured by Premiere Elements. These file types include MPEG, MOV, AVI, and WMV files.

- After adding a still image.

- After adding a transition or effect to a clip or clips.

- After using the **Time Stretch** feature on a clip.

- After rotating a clip.

- After changing field options.

▶ **TIP**

Premiere Elements does not request to render a clip it has captured until changes are made to the clip. That rule also applies to anything added with the Adobe Media Downloader.

If your computer has a slower processor or minimal RAM and video memory, the failure to hard render might result in one of the following: a jerky display in the **Monitor**, an inability to see the effect added to the clip, and possible audio or speed issues.

To keep things running smoothly, render the **Timeline** often. By doing so, you will always be aware of any potential problems with clips or the effects you add to them.

When Premiere Elements wants to render a file, it lets you know by placing a red line above the clip that should be rendered in the **Timeline**. The line covers only the section of the **Timeline** where rendering is needed (only the changed areas of the **Timeline**). If you undo the change, the red line goes away and the file reverts back to its condition before the change was made—effectively to its already rendered state. To render the **Timeline**, simply press the **Enter** key.

43

▶ **TIP**

After rendering the **Timeline**, the default action is to play the entire work area in the **Monitor**. This can get rather annoying after awhile, especially if the movie is more than a few minutes long. You can stop the video from playing by pressing the space bar or you can change the Preferences. Choose **Edit**, **Preferences**, **General** from the menu at the top of your screen. When the **Preferences** dialog box opens, disable the **Play work area after rendering previews** check box. Click **OK** to finish.

7

Using Transitions

IN THIS CHAPTER:

One thing that can really make your video appealing is the way you transition, or move, from one clip to the next. If you haven't already done so, start paying attention to your favorite movies and TV shows. They will not only give you some ideas on how to transition from scene to scene, but what kinds of transitions to use where. I love to watch documentaries (this was not the case before I embarked on the video-editing trail) and see how professionals such as Ken Burns do their thing. When you think about it, a home movie is very much like a documentary.

In this chapter, you will be using two basic types of transitions: single-sided and double-sided. A single-sided transition is used when there is no clip to transition from or to or when the clips are on different tracks. A double-sided transition is used between two clips. In both cases, the transition helps create a smooth flow into or out of a clip.

Premiere Elements comes with more than 70 transitions. You can customize each one and add effects, making the effective list of transitions virtually infinite. Transitions, much like the right soundtrack, are a great way to keep the audience interested in your movie. They can be a lot of fun to play with, and they add a real professional touch. But let me warn you: Too many transitions will make your viewers' heads spin and ruin even the best production, so use them sparingly.

44

44 | About Transitions

✔ BEFORE YOU BEGIN	→ SEE ALSO
14 Add Media with the Adobe Media Downloader	**3** Nest Your Panel to Save Desktop Space
34 Trim a Clip on the Timeline	**45** Fade In or Out of a Video Clip
	68 About the Properties Panel

Transitions are easy to find in the **Edit** workspace. They are located in the **Effects and Transitions** panel, by default, in the bottom-left panel above the **Timeline**. For this task, I have moved two of the panels above so we have a much larger view of the transitions and their properties.

▶ KEY TERM

Transition—Controls the way one image or clip in your project leads into the next. Transitions include wipes, dissolves, and page peels.

Thumbnail View Button
List View Button

*The **Effects and Transitions** panel is where you look to find audio and video transitions for your movie.*

In the **Effects and Transitions** panel is a list of categories; click the right-facing arrow next to a category name to open the category and view the effects and transitions in that category. To select an effect or category, open the appropriate category and click the name of the effect or transition.

You can view effects and transitions in the panel in either List view or in Thumbnail view. Click the appropriate button at the bottom-left corner of the **Effects and Transitions** panel to put the panel in that particular view.

44

 ──**List View**

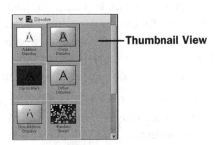 ──**Thumbnail View**

*The **Effects and Transitions** panel in List view and in Thumbnail view.*

Both of these views give you a picture of how the transition will look and what it will actually do. Click the transition thumbnail to see an animation of what it will look like. Use these visual clues to visualize how the transition will appear between your clips, before actually applying it. Take a moment to look through the audio and video transitions to see which ones might interest you.

When you find a transition you like, drag the transition from the panel and drop it on the clip(s) on the **Timeline**. Notice that you must drop the transition at the beginning or end of a single clip or between two clips (see **46** **Add a Video Transition**). Your clips become highlighted when the mouse pointer is over a spot where the transition can be applied. After applying the transition, you can view its effect by moving the CTI over the transitioned area of the clip.

▶ **NOTE**

After you add a transition to the **Timeline**, Premiere Elements displays a red line above the clip or clips to which you applied the transition. This red line indicates that the clip has not yet been rendered in its changed state. Rendering after adding transitions or effects is not necessary or required. However, depending on your system, rendering after adding transitions or effects might make the video play smoother in the **Monitor**.

44

45	**Fade In or Out of a Video Clip**

✔ BEFORE YOU BEGIN	→ SEE ALSO
29 About the Timeline and Video Tracks	**48** Save a Custom-Designed Transition
31 Set Video and Audio Track Display	**67** About Keyframing
44 About Transitions	**72** Control a Video Track's Opacity over Time
	75 Control a Video Effect with Keyframes

In this task, you will begin by adding a quick and easy transition between two video clips. Premiere Elements enables you to fade in or out of a clip with a few keystrokes. The Fade In and Fade Out effect is a very effective transition and is probably the second most used—next to the straight cut (and you can certainly argue whether the straight cut is actually a transition).

If you have two clips side by side on the **Timeline** with no transition, you have a straight cut. Cutting directly from one clip to the next is the most commonly used method for moving from one clip to the next. No frills or twirls. If you place still images on the **Timeline** and do not add transitions between the stills, you will have room to apply Ken Burns-type effects such as Pan and Zoom.

However, there are many cases where a pan, zoom, or a straight cut just doesn't work. You need something not too flashy or dramatic, just a nice little transition from one image to the next. That is were the **Fade In** and **Fade Out** effect comes in handy.

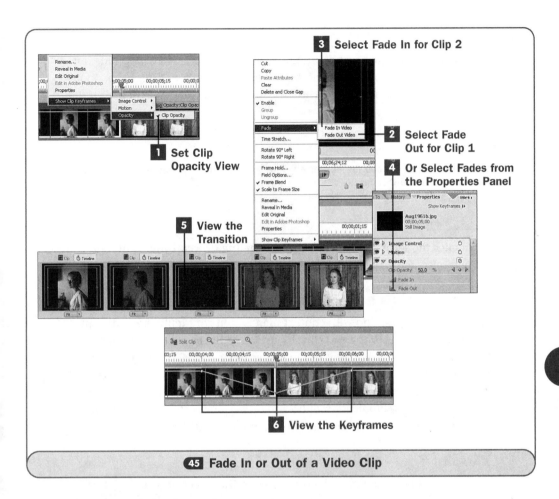

3 Select Fade In for Clip 2

1 Set Clip Opacity View

2 Select Fade Out for Clip 1

4 Or Select Fades from the Properties Panel

5 View the Transition

6 View the Keyframes

45 Fade In or Out of a Video Clip

1 Set Clip Opacity View

Make sure you have two clips side by side on the same track on the **Timeline**. Right-click each of these clips and make sure the **Clip Opacity** option is checked in the clip's context menu. This is the default setting, so if you haven't changed from the default, this option should already be checked. If it is not, select it by simply clicking **Clip Opacity**. In doing this, you can later see the modifications Premiere Elements has made to your clip's opacity. *Opacity* is another word for transparency; if a clip has 0% opacity, it is 100% transparent and therefore is invisible; at 100% opacity, it is 0% transparent.

② Select Fade Out for Clip 1

To create the transition, you want the last frames of the first clip to fade out into black and the first frames of the second clip to fade in from black. Right-click the first video clip on the **Timeline** and select **Fade Out Video** from the context menu.

▶ **NOTE**

If you right-click an audio clip instead of a video clip, you have the option of selecting **Fade In Audio** or **Fade Out Audio**.

③ Select Fade In for Clip 2

Right-click the second video clip on the **Timeline** (the clip you want to fade in to) and select **Fade In Video** from the context menu.

④ Or Select Fades from the Properties Panel

If you don't like working with context menus, you can apply the **Fade Out** and **Fade In** effects to the two clips by using the **Properties** panel. Click to select the first clip and open it in the **Properties** panel. Click the triangle to the left of the **Opacity** section to open the **Opacity** properties for the selected clip. Notice the two options: **Fade In** and **Fade Out** (each has a triangle icon to give you a visual indication of how the effect works). Click to apply the appropriate **Fade In** or **Fade Out** effect to the selected clip.

⑤ View the Transition

Move the CTI back to a point before the **Fade Out** effect starts for the first clip. Click the **Play** button on the **Monitor** panel to start the movie rolling. Observe how clip 1 fades out into black and clip 2 fades in from black.

⑥ View the Keyframes

Looking at the **Timeline**, you can see that applying a fade sets a keyframe marker at the Fade In and Fade Out points. The small diamond shape along the line over the frames of the clip is a keyframe marker, or keyframe point. You can adjust the start, duration, and end of the fade by dragging the markers with your mouse. As your mouse pointer is over a keyframe marker, notice that the mouse pointer changes: It has a small dot at the bottom of the arrow. The markers can be moved anywhere along your clip and allow you to customize the length of your fades. For additional information on keyframes, see **67** About Keyframing. If you're pleased with the resultant fade effect, you can save this customized transition as discussed in **48** Save a Custom-Designed Transition. For information on how to transition audio clips, see **47** Add an Audio Transition.

45

46 Add a Video Transition

✔ BEFORE YOU BEGIN	→ SEE ALSO
29 About the Timeline and Video Tracks	**68** About the Properties Panel
31 Set Video and Audio Track Display	
44 About Transitions	

Adding a transition to the start of a clip, the end of a clip, or between two clips is easy. Simply drag the desired transition from the **Effects and Transitions** panel to the clip in the **Timeline**. When the transition is over an area where it can be placed, the clip becomes highlighted. Drop the transition by releasing the mouse button.

1 Select the Transition

Make sure you have two clips side by side on the same track on the **Timeline**. For this task, you will be using the **Cross Dissolve** transition, located in the **Dissolve** category of the **Video Transitions**. To apply this transition, drag from the **Effects and Transitions** panel to the appropriate clip(s) in the **Timeline**.

46

2 Drop the Transition at the Beginning of a Clip, at the End of a Clip, or Between Two Clips

As you drag the transition over the clips in the Timeline, notice that different parts of the clips are highlighted. Also look for a small icon next to the mouse pointer that shows you the direction in which the transition will be applied (right, left, or middle). You can apply the transition to the end of a clip, between two clips, or at the beginning of a clip. For this example, drop the **Cross Dissolve** transition between the two clips.

After dropping the transition on the desired clip, notice a rectangle at the top of the clip with the transition name inside. This rectangle shows where the transition starts and stops.

▶ NOTES

Right-click the transition rectangle and choose **Clear** from the context menu to remove the transition from the clip.

Drag the beginning or end of the transition rectangle to make the duration of the transition longer or shorter.

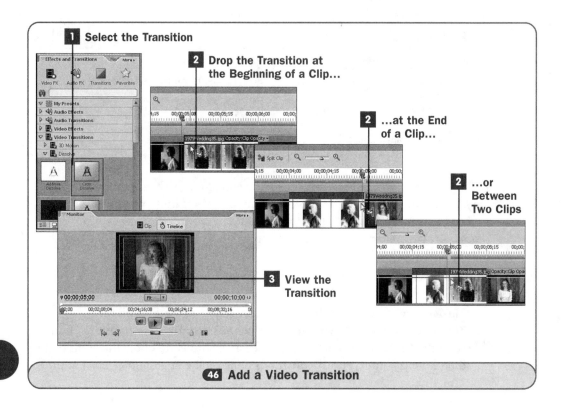

1 Select the Transition

2 Drop the Transition at the Beginning of a Clip...

2 ...at the End of a Clip...

2 ...or Between Two Clips

3 View the Transition

46 Add a Video Transition

46

3 **View the Transition**

View the transition by moving the CTI to a point before the transition begins and clicking the **Play** button in the **Monitor** panel. Alternatively, scrub the CTI over the transition on the **Timeline**.

▶ **TIP**

If, after viewing the transition, you change your mind about its appropriateness, don't worry. Just choose another transition and drop it over the old one to replace the old transition with your new selection. There is no need to undo the first transition, unless you decide not to transition at all.

After the transition is placed on the **Timeline**, a number of controls become available in the **Properties** panel. For most transitions, you can use these controls to set the duration and the center of the transition, and to reverse the motion of the transition. Simply click the transition rectangle, located above the clip on the **Timeline**, and the transition opens in the **Properties** panel. Make adjustments there as appropriate.

47 Add an Audio Transition

✔ BEFORE YOU BEGIN	→ SEE ALSO
29 About the Timeline and Video Tracks	**54** Raise, Lower, and Normalize Sound Volume
31 Set Video and Audio Track Display	**66** Enhance Audio with Advanced Effects
44 About Transitions	**68** About the Properties Panel
46 Add a Video Transition	

In addition to the video transitions on the **Effects and Transitions** panel, you also find audio transitions. Audio transitions have the same purpose as their video counterparts: to move smoothly between clips. Audio transitions are applied the same way as video transitions and have many of the same options available.

1 Select an Audio Transition

Located in the **Effects and Transitions** panel in the **Audio Transitions, Crossfade** category, the two audio transitions can be added to clips on the audio tracks in the **Timeline**. Both transition effects similarly dissolve sound between two clips. The **Constant Gain** transition, however, fades sound out on one clip and in on the other in a linear pattern; the result sometimes sounds rather abrupt. The **Constant Power** transition, on the other hand, curves the sound transitions, offering a smoother dissolve. **Constant Power** is probably the preferred audio transition of the two.

2 Drop the Transition on the Audio Clips

Drag and drop the transition from the **Effects and Transitions** panel on the audio clips in the audio tracks in the **Timeline**, just as you would a video transition. The **Constant Gain** transition can be dropped at the beginning or end of a clip; the **Constant Power** transition can be dropped at the beginning of a clip, between two clips, or at the end of a clip.

3 Listen to the Transition

Scrub the CTI over the audio transition area of the **Timeline**. Alternatively, place the CTI in front of the transition on the **Timeline** and click the **Play** button on the **Monitor**. If you don't like what you hear, continue on.

47

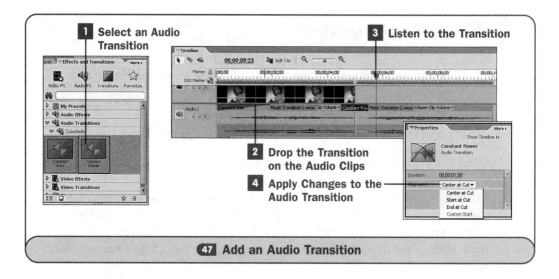

1 **Select an Audio Transition**

3 **Listen to the Transition**

2 **Drop the Transition on the Audio Clips**

4 **Apply Changes to the Audio Transition**

47 **Add an Audio Transition**

4 **Apply Changes to the Audio Transition**

Both transitions can be manipulated to some extent in the **Properties** panel. You play with audio transitions in the same way you do video transitions: Click the transition rectangle above the audio clip to open the transition in the **Properties** panel. You can also drag the left edge of the transition rectangle to lengthen the transition. For the **Constant Gain** transition, the adjustments are limited to changing the **Duration**. For the **Constant Power** transition, you can also choose to place the transition at the beginning, end, or between two audio clips.

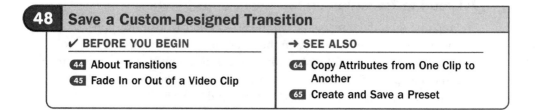

48 **Save a Custom-Designed Transition**

✔ BEFORE YOU BEGIN	→ SEE ALSO
44 About Transitions 45 Fade In or Out of a Video Clip	64 Copy Attributes from One Clip to Another 65 Create and Save a Preset

Any of the transitions that allow you to customize its motion (that is, where you can specify **Scale** and **Position** values), opacity, or Image Control can be saved for later use. Because there is no preset transition that fades in and out on a clip, you will save that customized transition effect for reuse later. If you worked through 45 **Fade In or Out of a Video Clip**, you can create it once, save it, and use it over and over.

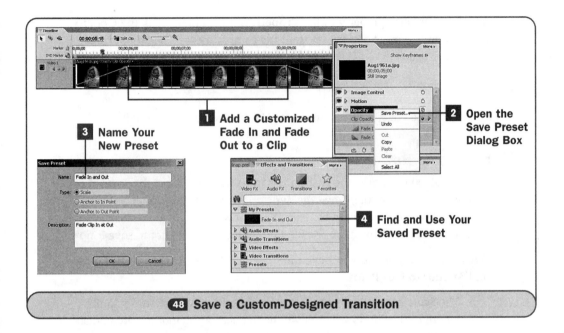

3 Name Your New Preset

1 Add a Customized Fade In and Fade Out to a Clip

2 Open the Save Preset Dialog Box

4 Find and Use Your Saved Preset

48 Save a Custom-Designed Transition

■ Add a Customized Fade In and Fade Out to a Clip

Make sure you have one clip that's 5 seconds long or 150 frames (NTSC), with no effects or transitions applied, on the **Timeline**. Follow the instructions in **45** Fade In or Out of a Video Clip. Apply the **Fade In** effect to the beginning of the clip and the **Fade Out** effect to the end of the clip. As you can see by the keyframe markers on the **Timeline**, the default duration of each effect is 30 frames or 1 second. The first second of the clip shows the Opacity line going up (the **Fade In** effect) and the last second of the clip going down (the **Fade Out** effect). You can change the duration of these effects by moving the keyframe markers until you get the effect for which you are looking.

▶ **NOTE**

After this transition is saved, whenever you apply it to a 5-second clip, the transition will fade the clip in for 1 second, show 3 seconds of the clip, and end with a 1-second fade out.

■ Open the Save Preset Dialog Box

To save your new, customized transition, click the clip to which you've applied the **Fade In** and **Fade Out** effects. This action highlights the clip and opens it in the **Properties** panel. In this case, you have created a transition that affects the **Opacity** of a clip; therefore, the settings and keyframes are

48

under the **Opacity** property in the **Properties** panel. Right-click the **Opacity** heading and choose **Save Preset** from the context menu. The **Save Preset** dialog box opens.

▶ TIP

Saving a customized effect is discussed in detail in **65** Create and Save a Preset.

3 Name Your New Preset

In this dialog box, name the customized transition and select the **Type** of preset it is. For this example, leave the **Type** option set at the default setting **Scale**, and type a description to remind you of what the preset does. Click **OK** to save the custom transition or click **Cancel** if you decide not to save it now.

When creating a preset, you have three options: **Scale**, **Anchor to In Point**, and **Anchor to Out Point**:

- The **Scale** option scales the keyframes markers proportionally to the length of the clip to which it will be applied. Applying this preset also deletes any existing keyframes on the applied clip.

- The **Anchor to In Point** option places the first keyframe marker the same distance from the first frame in the applied clip as it was from the original clip's first frame. This option does not do any scaling.

- The **Anchor to Out Point** option places the last keyframe marker at the same distance from the last frame in the applied clip as it was from the original clip's last frame. This option does not do any scaling.

▶ TIP

Use preset names that will easily remind you, at a glance, what that saved preset does.

4 Find and Use Your Saved Preset

The new transition is added to the **My Presets** category in the **Effects and Transitions** panel. You can now drag and drop your customized transition onto any clip on the **Timeline**.

8

Advanced Timeline Video and Audio Editing

IN THIS CHAPTER:

This chapter continues where Chapter 6, "Editing on the Timeline," left off. Advanced editing gives you the ability to change video field properties, freeze a frame and change clip opacity, add narration, enhance and control audio, add interactive content for Web use, and combine multiple projects into one.

This chapter is considered advanced because it takes you beyond the simple cutting of clips. As you work with analog video, you will probably hear the terms *interlaced* and *deinterlaced*. You will learn how to deal with issues that arise from these two video display methods. You will also look at the opacity, or the transparency, of a clip, and see how simple it can be to make your clip semi-transparent. When you are ready to create your first major documentary, narration will be important, so you will learn how to add that to your movie project. Audio is a major part of most projects and can sometimes need a little tweaking. You will see where the options are that allow you to control how your audio sounds, and make sure that the audio you use is of the best possible quality and balance.

Video is widely used on the Internet these days. Many websites have video introductions that start when you enter the site. You will learn how to create an interactive video that you can use on a website and that will allow your video to interact with other sites, pages, or images on the Internet.

Lastly, you will discover the ease of copying your **Timeline**, or parts of it, from one project to another. This might not seem like a big deal right now, but you will probably need to do this at some time.

49   Control Interlacing and Field Options

✔ BEFORE YOU BEGIN	→ SEE ALSO
29 About the Timeline and Video Tracks	**50** Freeze a Frame
40 Slow/Speed/Reverse Audio/Video	**124** About Troubleshooting DVD Output

Considering that most people use video from various sources (not just digital video), a number of issues might arise when you combine these various video sources in a movie project. One of these issues is related to *interlaced* and *deinterlaced* video. Basically, each frame of video has two fields that are woven or laced together with another frame to form a single frame of video. For more information on interlacing, deinterlacing, progressive scans, and fields, see **18** About Troubleshooting Media Additions.

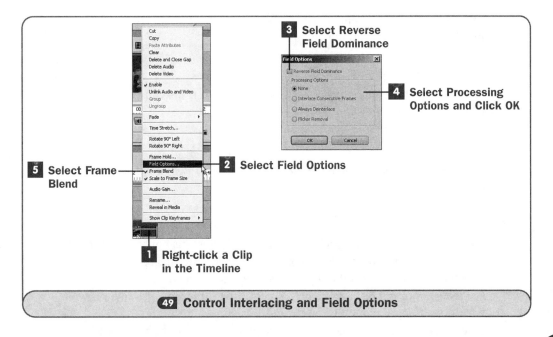

3 Select Reverse Field Dominance

4 Select Processing Options and Click OK

2 Select Field Options

5 Select Frame Blend

1 Right-click a Clip in the Timeline

49 Control Interlacing and Field Options

▶ KEY TERMS

Interlaced—Two video frames merged into one using each frame's odd or even fields. Interlaced video draws only half of the lines on the screen for each frame, taking advantage of the time it takes for a image to fade on a TV and giving the impression of double the actual refresh rate, helping to prevent flicker.

Deinterlaced—The process of converting interlaced images into non-interlaced form by creating two frames out of one interlaced frame.

Under most circumstances, you will probably not have to be concerned about these two types of displays. There is, however, a growing need to be able to interlace or deinterlace video for use in your movie projects. Video that comes from television—either NTSC or PAL—is interlaced and will be fine if the final product will also be viewed on a television. However, the interlaced video will not look so good when viewed on your computer (such as if you post the interlaced video on your web page for viewing in a browser window). On the other hand, video designed for the Internet and computer display will not look so good when played on a television.

▶ TIP

By connecting your camcorder or digital converter's out ports to a television set's in ports, you can view your video while it is still on the **Timeline**. Your television will give you the exact image as it will appear when viewed on a DVD. See the user's manual that came with your converter or camcorder for instructions on how to set up your television as a monitor.

To deal with these issues, Premiere Elements provides various field options you can manipulate for each clip individually.

1 Right-click a Clip in the Timeline

Right-click a clip in the **Timeline** to select it and open the clip's context menu.

2 Select Field Options

From the context menu, select **Field Options** to open the **Field Options** dialog box.

3 Select Reverse Field Dominance

The first option is **Reverse Field Dominance**. Enable this option to reverse the display order of the fields for the clip. If the capture was performed in another application or if the clip comes from an unknown source, Premiere Elements might not display the field order in the same way. Usually this will be noticed as jerky motion when the video is played. Reversing the field dominance resolves some problems with jerky video. You might also have to enable the **Reverse Field Dominance** option if you are going to play a clip in reverse, as explained in **40** **Slow/Speed/Reverse Audio/Video**.

4 Select Processing Options and Click OK

You can also set **Processing Options** for the selected clip (the default setting is **None**). The three additional options are **Interlace Consecutive Frames**, **Always Deinterlace**, and **Flicker Removal**:

- Choose **None** if you do not want to process the clip's fields.

- Choose **Interlace Consecutive Frames** to convert progressive scan frames to interlaced fields.

- Choose **Always Deinterlace** to convert interlaced fields into progressive scan frames. The fields are determined by the **Fields Setting** option, accessed from the **Project**, **Project Settings**, **General** menu command.

- Choose **Flicker Removal** to keep the image from flickering by blurring the two interlaced fields together. (In interlaced clips, some parts of images appear only in every other field, resulting in flickering. This is most prevalent with very thin horizontal details in still images.)

▶ NOTE

For more details on flicker removal, see **25** Remove Shimmer from a Photo.

49

After you have made the appropriate selections for your video clip, click the **OK** button. You might have to apply various combinations and test each one before getting the results for which you are looking.

5 Select Frame Blend

To further minimize interlacing problems, right-click the clip in the **Timeline** and choose **Frame Blend** from the clip context menu. This option is just a check on the menu itself, but it blends speed changes to improve the appearance of your clip. It blends frames together to provide a smoother-looking video if the speed of the clip is not set to 100%.

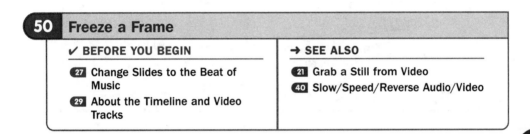

50 Freeze a Frame

✔ **BEFORE YOU BEGIN**	→ **SEE ALSO**
27 Change Slides to the Beat of Music	**21** Grab a Still from Video
29 About the Timeline and Video Tracks	**40** Slow/Speed/Reverse Audio/Video

50

Frame Hold, or freeze frame, is one of the fun video tricks you can use in your movies. This option allows the audio to continue rolling while the video stays put on a single frame. I imagine that at some time during the editing of your movies that you will come up with that one frame in a clip that just needs to be frozen in time.

The frame you choose as the freeze frame will appear and freeze from the beginning (the In Point) to the end (the Out Point) of the clip. Take this into consideration to determine whether your clip needs to be split to better isolate the freeze frame; that way you are not freezing a frame for an entire 45-minute movie.

1 Right-click a Clip in the Timeline

Right-click the clip in the **Timeline** that contains the frame you want to freeze. The clip is selected and the clip's context menu opens.

2 Select Frame Hold

Select **Frame Hold** to open the **Frame Hold Options** dialog box.

3 Select Hold On

Enable the check box in front of the **Hold On** option. This option selects and applies the freeze frame option to the selected clip.

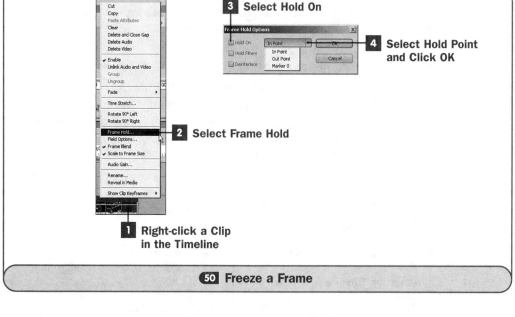

50 Freeze a Frame

▶ **NOTES**

The **Hold Filters** option, also in the **Frame Hold Options** dialog box, prevents any keyframed effects that were applied to the clip from taking place.

The **Deinterlace** option removes one field from an interlaced clip and doubles the remaining field. This option removes interlace artifacts from the freeze frame, if they exist.

4 Select Hold Point and Click OK

You must identify the frame in the clip you want to freeze. The frame you want to freeze is called the *hold point*, and Premiere Elements offers three options for the identifying the hold point in your clip: **In Point**, **Out Point**, and **Marker 0**:

- **In Point**—The hold point is the very first frame of your clip as it appears on the **Timeline**. When you choose this option, the very first frame of the clip is frozen for the entire clip.

- **Out Point**—The hold point is the very last frame in your clip. When you choose this option, the very last frame of the clip is frozen for the entire clip.

- **Marker 0**—This option requires that you set an other numbered clip marker and specify 0 (zero). The marker indicates the frame you want to freeze; that frame is frozen for the entire clip. For details about numbered markers, see **57** **Add an Interactive Marker**.

▶ **TIP**

To set an other numbered clip marker, zoom in on the clip so you can see the individual frames and position the CTI so the frame you want to freeze is selected. From the menu at the top of the screen, choose **Marker, Set Clip Marker, Other Numbered**. A dialog box opens with the option to enter a number; be sure that the marker's number is 0 (zero), and then press OK. The marker is applied to the current frame marked by the CTI.

When selecting the hold point option, remember that when you choose **In Point** or **Out Point**, later changing the In or Out point (as described in **19** **Trim Clips in the Media Panel**) does not change the freeze frame. When you choose the **Marker 0** option, however, changing the position of the marker *does* change the freeze frame.

When you are finished setting your options, click the **OK** button. You can then view the results of your freeze frame by scrubbing over the clip in the **Timeline**. The audio from the clip plays as usual, but the video freezes on the frame you selected as your hold point.

51 Make a Clip Semi-Transparent

✔ BEFORE YOU BEGIN	→ SEE ALSO
30 Add, Delete, and Size Tracks	**72** Control a Video Track's Opacity over Time
31 Set Video and Audio Track Display	**97** Create a Title Overlay for Your Video
33 Add or Move a Clip on the Timeline	
43 About Rendering the Timeline	

51

Opacity is the opposite of *transparency*. So when we talk about a clip's opacity, we are talking about how transparent it is. There are many reasons for making a clip semi-transparent: You can lower the opacity of a clip to create a ghost-type effect or to allow clips on tracks below the current track to become visible. This task explains the quick and easy way to change the opacity of an entire clip.

1 Select a Clip in the Timeline

Make sure you have one clip on video track 1 and another clip on video track 2, directly above the track 1 clip. Click any clip in the **Timeline** to select it. Zoom in to the clip so you can see the individual frames in the clip.

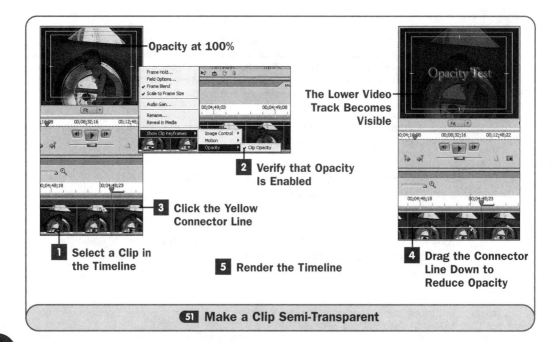

Opacity at 100%

The Lower Video Track Becomes Visible

2 Verify that Opacity Is Enabled

3 Click the Yellow Connector Line

1 Select a Clip in the Timeline

5 Render the Timeline

4 Drag the Connector Line Down to Reduce Opacity

51 Make a Clip Semi-Transparent

51

2 Verify that Opacity Is Enabled

At the top of the selected clip you will see a yellow line; this line is the **Keyframe Connector**. Use this line to adjust the opacity of the clip. To ensure that the **Opacity** feature of the **Keyframe Connector** is enabled, right-click the clip to open the context menu. Select **Show Clip Keyframes**, **Opacity** and make sure that there is a check mark in front of the **Clip Opacity** option. This option specifies that the yellow connector will be used to control the opacity of the clip.

3 Click the Yellow Connector Line

When the yellow connector line is at the top of the frame, the frame is show-ing at 100% opacity (that is, it has no transparency). To adjust the clip's opacity, click and hold the mouse pointer on the yellow connector line.

4 Drag the Connector Line Down to Reduce Opacity

Drag the line down about half way, decreasing the opacity of the selected clip to 50%. You can set the opacity at whatever percent you desire. Notice that you do not see the opacity of the clip change in the **Monitor** panel until you release the mouse button. By lowering the opacity, you are making the lower clip (in this case, a title) visible. The lower the opacity of the track 2 clip, the more visible the clip on the lower track becomes.

5 **Render the Timeline**

After changing the opacity of a clip, you should render that area of your **Timeline**. To do so, press **Enter**.

---

52 Add Narration to Your Movie

✔ BEFORE YOU BEGIN	→ SEE ALSO
9 Capture Video or Audio Only	**54** Raise, Lower, and Normalize Sound Volume
14 Add Media with the Adobe Media Downloader	**55** Filter Audio with Dynamic Effects
	121 Add Audio to a Menu

Normally, we would not add a task for something that Premiere Elements doesn't do. This case, however, is an exception. *Narration* is a very important part of many home movies and independent films, especially documentaries. Even though Premiere Elements cannot *record* your narration, it can capture the audio narration file and sync it to the video on the **Timeline**. You can do this by recording audio onto your camcorder and using Premiere Elements to capture just the audio narration you recorded. Then move the audio clip to the **Timeline** and sync it with your video. This approach to narration is particularly useful for slideshows and documentary-type movies.

1 **Record Your Narration**

The first step in adding narration to a movie project is to record the narration on tape. You can do this by simply talking into your camcorder while you watch the video on your computer. It is best to have some sort of script to refer to or read from, otherwise you might be doing more takes than necessary.

2 **Capture Your Narration**

After you have your narration on tape, capture the audio in Premiere Elements just like you would any other clip from your camcorder. To capture just the audio track from the camcorder, open the **More** menu in the **Capture** workspace and select the **Capture Audio** option. You might also want to make sure that the **Capture to Timeline** option is selected in the **More** menu so the audio track is added to both the **Media** panel *and* the **Timeline**.

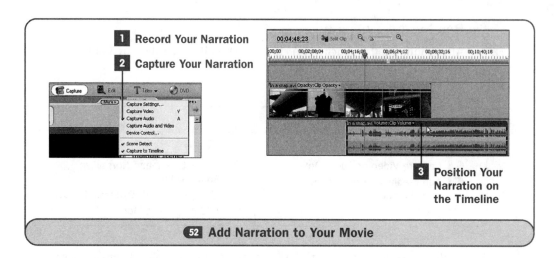

1 Record Your Narration

2 Capture Your Narration

3 Position Your Narration on the Timeline

52 Add Narration to Your Movie

52

▶ **TIP**

When recording your narration, record a loud noise, such as a hand clap, at the beginning of every scene change. This makes it much easier to line up the audio with the video later on. You can edit out the clap (use the **Razor** tool to do this) after you have the narration in sync with the video.

3 **Position Your Narration on the Timeline**

If you started your narration with a noise to reference the start of the first scene, line that noise up with the first frame of the scene. The noise is displayed by a high, sharp peak in the audio waveform and can be clearly heard through the speakers. Play the **Timeline** to determine whether the narration is in sync with the video. If not, make minor adjustments by dragging the narration clip on the **Timeline**, a little at a time, until the narration comes into sync with the video.

53 **Track Audio Volume**

✔ BEFORE YOU BEGIN	→ SEE ALSO
20 Navigate the Monitor Panel	**54** Raise, Lower, and Normalize Sound Volume
29 About the Timeline and Video Tracks	**55** Filter Audio with Dynamic Effects
33 Add or Move a Clip on the Timeline	**56** Balance Sound over Left and Right Channels

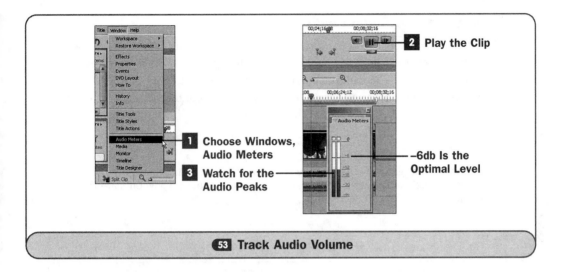

53 Track Audio Volume

If you don't keep an eye on the audio levels in your movie project, you might have a surprise after you view the DVD on a television. Even though the audio might sound okay on your computer speakers, it might not sound that way after putting it onto a DVD or exporting the movie project. One of the ways to avoid audio volume issues in a pro-active way is by using the **Audio Meters** feature.

The **Audio Meters** window helps you determine whether any portions, or possibly all, of your audio clips are over (or under) the recommended levels. To monitor your audio levels, open the **Audio Meters** window and play your clip while watching what the meters do.

1 Choose Windows, Audio Meters

From the menu at the top of your screen, choose **Windows**, **Audio Meters** to open the **Audio Meters** window.

2 Play the Clip

With the **Audio Meters** window open on your screen, click the **Play** button in the **Monitor** panel to play your clip. If you have the time, you can play the entire movie.

▶ NOTE

It is not necessary to view the **Audio Meters** for the entire clip unless you have good reason to do so. You can spot check the clip by scrubbing through the clip, primarily checking the louder portions. You just want to make sure that the audio is not off the scale anywhere. At some point, however, you are going to have to listen to the entire movie, making sure that the audio is at reasonable levels. You wouldn't want your viewers to get a big surprise when they watch your movie.

53

3 Watch for the Audio Peaks

Watch to see where the peaks are in the audio track of the clip. Peaks of –6db or above (between –6 and 0) should be adjusted; peaks of 0 or more (constant red in the audio monitor) must be adjusted or the output will be poor. The tasks that follow show you how to adjust the volume and other audio properties.

▶ **TIP**

Watch for levels that get above –6db (between –6 and 0) and adjust the volume accordingly. Constant levels of between –12db and –6db, with the peaks below 0db, are the best. An average level of –6db is optimal.

---

54 | **Raise, Lower, and Normalize Sound Volume**

✔ **BEFORE YOU BEGIN**

29 About the Timeline and Video Tracks

53 Track Audio Volume

→ **SEE ALSO**

55 Filter Audio with Dynamic Effects

56 Balance Sound over Left and Right Channels

53

Volume levels are important to the overall quality of your production. There is nothing worse that having the volume increase by 20db just as a cannon is being shot off in the video clip. Poor audio levels can really put a damper on the whole video experience. With Premiere Elements, you can control the volume level for each clip individually. You can even split a clip and then control the volume for each piece individually, if you need that kind of control. You can also normalize the sound over an entire clip, making the audio volume levels more consistent over the length of the clip and the project.

1 Right-click an Audio Clip in the Timeline

Right-click an audio clip in the **Timeline** to select it and open the clip's context menu.

2 Choose Audio Gain

From the context menu, select **Audio Gain** to open the **Clip Gain** dialog box.

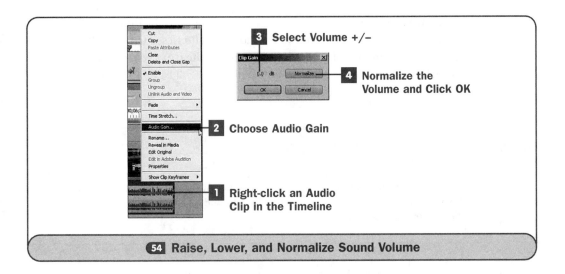

3 Select Volume +/−

4 Normalize the
Volume and Click OK

2 Choose Audio Gain

1 Right-click an Audio
Clip in the Timeline

54 Raise, Lower, and Normalize Sound Volume

3 Select Volume +/−

To change the clip's volume, position the mouse pointer over the **0.0** area. Click and drag to the right or left: Drag left to decrease the number and the volume; drag right to increase the number and the volume. Alternatively, click the **0.0** value and type a specific number, rather than dragging. The **0.0** value is the clip's volume at the point before you make any changes. Entering a positive number increases the volume by that many decibels; entering a negative number lowers the volume by that many decibels.

▶ **NOTE**

When adjusting the volume, remember that **0.0db** is the clip's original volume level. Any positive value is an increase in the original volume, and any negative value is a decrease in the original volume.

4 Normalize the Volume and Click OK

After you have made any volume changes necessary, you can normalize the audio levels. By selecting this option, the audio levels of the clip are automatically adjusted. Levels that are too high are reduced and levels that are too low are increased to create a more even volume across the entire clip. If there are certain places in the audio clip where you want the levels higher or lower on purpose, normalizing might do more harm than good. Listen to the normalized clip to ensure you get the desired result.

After you have made any volume changes and normalized the audio levels for the clip, click the **OK** button. Play your adjusted clip to see whether the changes made accomplished your goal of adjusting the clip's volume. If not, open the **Clip Gain** dialog box again and make finer adjustments. Don't forget you can always undo your changes!

---

55 | **Filter Audio with Dynamic Effects**

✔ BEFORE YOU BEGIN	→ SEE ALSO
29 About the Timeline and Video Tracks	**74** About Advanced Effects
33 Add or Move a Clip on the Timeline	**121** Add Audio to a Menu

---

54

Just as in a real recording studio, Premiere Elements gives you access to some high-quality audio gear. The **Dynamics** audio effect in Premiere Elements provides you with **Expander**, **Compressor**, **Limiter**, and **Gate** options that you can apply to an audio clip and then adjust just like you would in a recording studio, knobs and all. You can apply many audio filters to your clips, each with a special purpose. The Premiere Elements help system provides detailed descriptions of each of these effects. In this task, we use the **Dynamics** effect.

1 Open the Effects and Transitions Panel

To gain access to the audio tools included with the **Dynamics** effect, we must add that effect to the audio clip. First, open the **Effects and Transitions** panel by choosing **Window**, **Effects**. When the panel opens, click the **Audio FX** button at the top of the panel to view the audio effects.

2 Expand the Audio Effects Group

Open the **Audio Effects** group by clicking the arrow to the left of the group's name and locate the **Dynamics** effect.

3 Drag the Dynamics Effect to an Audio Clip in the Timeline

After locating the **Dynamics** effect in the **Audio Effects** group, drag it to the audio clip you want to modify on the **Timeline** and drop it on the clip.

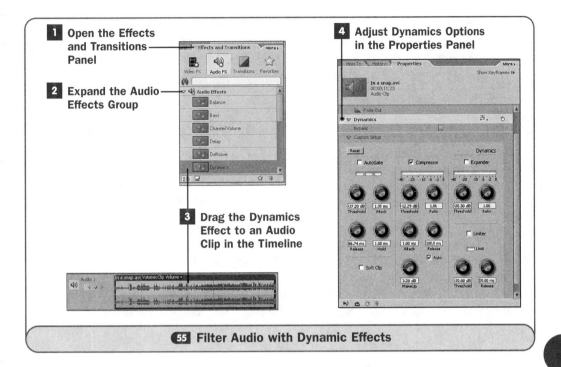

1 Open the Effects and Transitions Panel

2 Expand the Audio Effects Group

3 Drag the Dynamics Effect to an Audio Clip in the Timeline

4 Adjust Dynamics Options in the Properties Panel

55 Filter Audio with Dynamic Effects

55

4 Adjust Dynamics Options in the Properties Panel

Open the **Properties** panel for the targeted audio clip and click the **Dynamics** effect to access all the tools offered by this effect. The options offered by the **Dynamics** effect help eliminate unwanted background signals, balance the dynamic range, and reduce clipping:

- **Gate**—So called because it acts as an audio gate. When the volume reaches a particular point, the gate opens and audio is heard. When volume drops below a particular level, the gate closes and there is no audio output. This option is very useful when you're working with analog audio with hiss or static in the background. There is also an **AutoGate** check box; enable this option to automatically set the gate.

- **Compressor**—These settings compress the audio output at varying levels. You set the point where the compression takes place.

- **Expander**—This control reduces all signals below the specified threshold. The result is similar to the **Gate** control, but subtler. The **Expander** settings work well for audio clips that have very quiet segments and help make them equal to the louder segments.

- **Limiter**—Use this control to set the maximum level for signals, between –12 and 0dB. Signals that exceed the threshold are reduced to the threshold level. This control is similar to the **Normalize** feature described in 🔲54 **Raise, Lower, and Normalize Sound Volume**.

---

56 Balance Sound over Left and Right Channels

✔ BEFORE YOU BEGIN	→ SEE ALSO
🔲29 About the Timeline and Video Tracks	🔲52 Add Narration to Your Movie
🔲33 Add or Move a Clip on the Timeline	🔲54 Raise, Lower, and Normalize Sound Volume

---

The **Balance** audio effect lets you control the volumes of the left and right channels in the audio track for a particular clip. If your audio clip is in stereo, you will see two audio waveforms for each clip—the left stereo channel (on top) and right stereo channel (on the bottom); a mono clip shows only one waveform.

55

1 Open the Effects and Transitions Panel

To gain access to the **Balance** audio effect, you must add that effect to an audio clip. First, open the **Effects and Transitions** panel by choosing **Window, Effects**. When the panel opens, click the **Audio FX** button at the top of the panel to view the audio effects.

2 Expand the Audio Effects Group

Open the **Audio Effects** group by clicking the arrow to the left of the group's name and locate the **Balance** effect in the list.

3 Drag the Balance Effect to an Audio Clip in the Timeline

After locating the **Balance** effect in the **Audio Effects** group, drag it to the audio clip you want to modify on the **Timeline** and drop it on the clip.

4 Open the Balance Properties

Open the **Properties** panel for the targeted audio clip and click the **Balance** effect. The effect provides options to adjust the audio balance between the left and right channels.

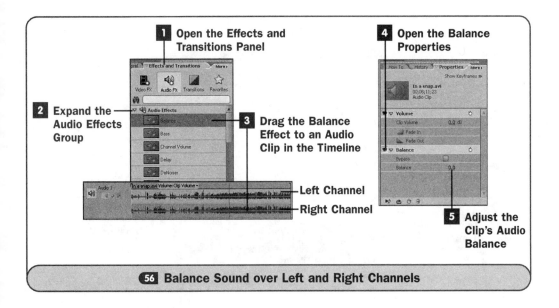

1 Open the Effects and Transitions Panel

2 Expand the Audio Effects Group

3 Drag the Balance Effect to an Audio Clip in the Timeline

Left Channel

Right Channel

4 Open the Balance Properties

5 Adjust the Clip's Audio Balance

56 Balance Sound over Left and Right Channels

5 Adjust the Clip's Audio Balance

Click the **Balance** number indicator and type positive or negative values. Positive values increase the proportion of volume for the right channel; negative values increase the proportion of volume for the left channel. Alternatively, drag the indicator to the left to adjust the volume for the left channel; drag to the right to adjust the volume for the right channel. Play back the audio clip to test your results. You can use the **Bypass** check box to hear the sound before and after. Checking the box ignores the effect, unchecking the box applies the effect.

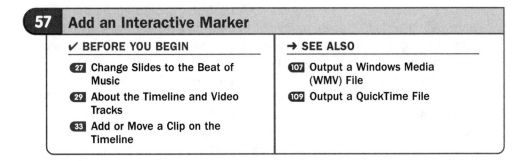

57 Add an Interactive Marker

✔ BEFORE YOU BEGIN

27 Change Slides to the Beat of Music

29 About the Timeline and Video Tracks

33 Add or Move a Clip on the Timeline

→ SEE ALSO

107 Output a Windows Media (WMV) File

109 Output a QuickTime File

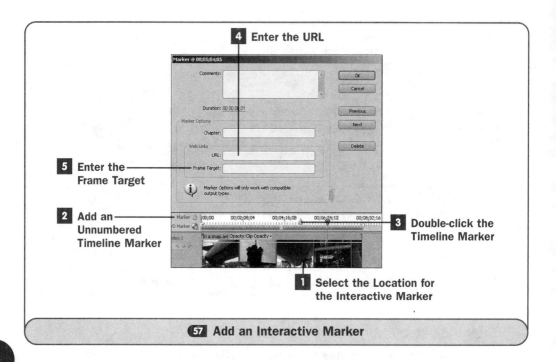

4 Enter the URL

5 Enter the Frame Target

2 Add an Unnumbered Timeline Marker

3 Double-click the Timeline Marker

1 Select the Location for the Interactive Marker

57 Add an Interactive Marker

57

If you are a web master or just want to make your own website a little more interesting, the *interactive markers* might be just the thing. You can place markers in your video that, when displayed on a web page, will trigger various other events, such as opening a web page.

▶ **KEY TERM**

Interactive marker—Marks a point in a video where an event should take place, such as opening a specified web page.

If the website includes frames, your video can play in one frame while the events it triggers play in other frames. Suppose that you are selling various digital products; your main video is an introduction to your store. At points in the video where you mention particular products, you can open the manufacturers' websites in another frame. You could also have images of the equipment open, in different frames, at preselected points in the video. If the website does not include frames, the marker causes the viewer to jump from the site where the video is being viewed to the site defined by the marker. Markers can work well for a website intro that, when it finishes playing, automatically sends the user to the site's home page. You can also have a link to **Skip Intro** for the viewer's convenience.

1 Select the Location for the Interactive Marker

Choose the clip, and frames in that clip, where your interactive markers will be located.

▶ **NOTE**

Interactive markers work only with Windows Media Files (WMV) or QuickTime Files (MOV).

2 Add an Unnumbered Timeline Marker

Position the CTI at the location where the first event should be triggered and click the **Marker Creator** button on the left end of the Timeline. An unnumbered Timeline marker is placed at the location of the CTI. Repeat this step to place all of your markers.

3 Double-click the Timeline Marker

Double-click the first marker in the **Timeline** to open the **Marker** dialog box.

4 Enter the URL

You can enter comments if you like to remind you why the marker is there. In the **URL** text box, type the URL you want to go to when the marker is reached.

5 Enter the Frame Target

If your web page has frames, enter the **Frame Target** (the frame in which you want the specified URL to open, such as '**left_frame**'). When you are finished defining this marker, click **Next** to move to the next marker in the clip. Repeats steps 4 and 5 to define that marker, and continue until you have entered the URL and frame target for all your markers.

When all the markers have been defined, it's time to export your movie and upload it to your website.

57

9

Adding Spice to Your Video

IN THIS CHAPTER:

One of the most interesting aspects of Premiere Elements is that it is accessible by editors with many levels of technical skill and experience. For the hobbyist or the novice user, it offers many automatic and preset features. Yet most experienced users are pleasantly surprised to find how deep this program goes and how customizable nearly all its features are.

In this chapter, we'll look at some of the tools Premiere Elements offers to affect your video and audio qualities. Many of these are automatic or preset effects—but even the more advanced tools are remarkably intuitive and easy to use, and it's likely you'll quickly become very comfortable using them on a regular basis.

---

58 About Preset Effects

→ SEE ALSO

28 Use and Customize Preset Camera Moves
60 Enhance Video with Advanced Image Controls
61 Add and Customize an Effect
67 About Keyframing
68 About the Properties Panel

58

Premiere Elements offers a wide variety of powerful preset effects for changing the qualities of your images or sound. These presets can be applied in one move, and most work effectively right out of the box.

▶ **TIP**

The **Effects and Transitions** panel offers a number of ways to quickly locate any effect, preset, or transition. You can isolate **Video FX**, **Audio FX**, **Transitions**, or **Favorites** by clicking the appropriate category button at the top of the panel. You can also type the name of the effect or transition you're looking for in the space to the right of the binoculars, and Premiere Elements will automatically locate it for you.

There are two categories of effects that are classified as presets. The first category includes keyframed effects, or standard effects from the Premiere Elements **Video FX** collection in which keyframes have been added to produce prescaled or precreated motion paths. These kinds of presets appear in the presets folder in the **Mosaics, PIPs, Solarize, Twirls, Pan,** and **Zoom** categories. When applied to your clips, these presets automatically scale and position the clips in your video frame, create a motion path, or create a transitional effect at the beginning or end of your clip.

A second category of presets is the automatic adjustment effects found in the **Adjust** category in the **Video FX** collection. This category includes effects that automatically balance color and contrast settings for your clips.

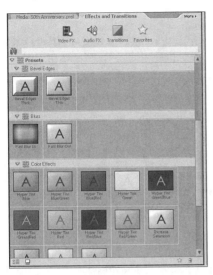

*Video and audio effects and presets, as well as transitions, are displayed in the **Effects and Transitions** panel as thumbnail previews.*

It's important to note, however, that these presets are based on math, not magic, so a little adjustment is often in order. The **Auto Color** effect, for instance, does a fairly effective job of automatically correcting color in a video clip. (See **60** **Enhance Video with Advanced Image Controls**.) However, this automatic adjustment merely works by taking into consideration the whitest point and the blackest point in your screen image and then mathematically estimating the correct values for the rest of the color settings based on those two points. Unfortunately, a perfectly color-corrected screen image is not always the result.

Fortunately, once applied to a clip, every effect opens a control panel that allows you to tweak its settings—correcting with your eye what no computer program can do with its best math.

Apply the **Auto Color** effect to a clip on your **Timeline**, for instance, and then, with the clip selected, look in the **Properties** panel. You'll see that the **Auto Color** effect has been added to the list of auto properties. Toggle open the details by clicking the triangle to the left of the effect, and you'll see, in addition to tools for setting the ranges for the black-and-white points in the screen image (essentially affecting the contrast), controls for adjusting **Temporal Smoothing**, which averages color values of pixels for a smoother color blend; for **Scene Detect**, which overrides **Temporal Smoothing** when the composition of the image on your clip changes drastically (such as a change in scenery); and for **Blending** any changes you make with the original image.

58

Preset Video Effects

The following is a list of the **Video FX** in the **Presets** collection in the **Effects and Transitions** panel. (For information on keyframed motion or transitional effects and how to adjust or create them, see 🞂67 **About Keyframing.**)

The **Horizontal Image Pans, Horizontal Image Zooms, Vertical Image Pans,** and **Vertical Image Zooms** presets are detailed in 🞂28 **Use and Customize Preset Camera Moves.**

🞂 **NOTE**

Every preset effect has been created from a standard Premiere Elements video or audio effect. In fact, after they are applied to a clip, the basic controls of the original effect become available so even preset effects can be tweaked and customized.

The **Bevel Edges** effect tints the edges of your image frame to create the illusion of it being a three-dimensional box. The **Bevel Edges Thick** preset sets the default width of the edge at 15% of the size of the image frame. The **Bevel Edges Thin** preset sets the default width at 2%. Customizable controls include **Width of Edge, Light Angle, Tint Color,** and **Intensity.**

The keyframed **Blurs** presets offer in and out **Transitional** effects from or to a 100% blur (**Fast Blur In, Fast Blur Out**), each with a one-second default duration. Customizable features include keyframe settings, dimensions of the blur, and variable **Speed** controls.

In the **Color Effects** preset category, the **Tint** effects (**Tint Blue, Tint Green, Tint Red, Tint Blue/Green, Tint Blue/Red, Tint Green/Blue, Tint Green/Red, Tint Red/Blue, Tint Red/Green**) tint or replace black or white points on your image with variations of color. Customizable controls include **Selectable Tint, Selectable Tint from White, Selectable Tint from Black,** and **Amount** of tint. The **Increase Saturation** control automatically sets **Brightness, Contrast, Saturation,** and **Hue** to levels designed to enrich color or bring color back to a faded image.

The **Drop Shadow** effect is one in which your clip (presumably reduced in size or moved) leaves the illusion of a shadow on the clip on the video track below it; this effect offers several presets for shadows off the **Lower Left, Lower Right, Upper Left,** and **Upper Right.** Also included are presets for keyframed drop shadows moving from **Lower Left to Lower Right, Lower Right to Lower Left, Upper Left to Upper Right,** and **Upper Right to Upper Left.** In addition to keyframe controls, these effects and presets also offer controls for **Shadow Color, Opacity, Direction of Shadow, Distance from Object, Softness,** and the option to **Hide the Object** and reveal only the shadow.

58

In the **Picture-In-Picture (PIP)** collection, you will find more than 180 **Picture-in-Picture** presets, some stationary and some animated, that reduce your video frame to either 25% or 40% of the standard frame size, creating a picture-in-picture effect when the clip is placed on a video track above another clip.

In addition to the effects found in the **Presets** collection, the following "automatic" color corrections are located in **Video FX**, in the **Adjust** collection:

- **Auto Color** can instantly correct color on your screen image. However, this preset uses math (based on the whitest white point, the blackest black point, and an averaged midrange), not magic, so the results are probably better assumed to be a starting point for adjustments. Additional tweaks can also be made using the controls for setting the ranges of black and white points, **Temporal Smoothing** (which averages adjacent pixels for a smoother color blend), **Scene Detect** (which overrides the **Temporal Smoothing** settings when the scene content changes), the option to **Snap Neutral Midtones** (which matches your midtone color to your black point and white point settings), and **Blend with Original** (which controls the percentage of change from the original clip). We demonstrate how to maximize this effect in **60 Enhance Video with Advanced Image Controls**.

- **Auto Contrast** uses math similar that used in **Auto Color** to correct color range and contrast. Controls for this effect include **Temporal Smoothing**, the **Scene Detect** option, **Black and White Clipping**, and percentage of **Blend** with the original screen image.

- **Auto Levels** works similarly to **Auto Color** and **Auto Contrast** but affects the red, green, and blue values separately. Controls for this effect include **Temporal Smoothing**, the **Scene Detect** option, **Black and White Clipping**, and percentage of **Blend** with the original screen image.

59 | **Adjust Color and Brightness**

✔ BEFORE YOU BEGIN	→ SEE ALSO
58 About Preset Effects	**60** Enhance Video with Advanced Image Controls
68 About the Properties Panel	**67** About Keyframing
	75 Control a Video Effect with Keyframes

Because you often need to correct the color, brightness, or contrast for a clip or still, Premiere Elements places controls for these settings conveniently in the **Properties** panel by default. You can also access these settings directly from the clip in the **Timeline**.

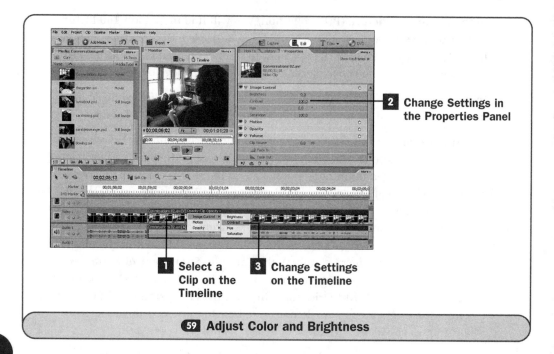

2 Change Settings in the Properties Panel

1 Select a Clip on the Timeline

3 Change Settings on the Timeline

59 Adjust Color and Brightness

59

1 Select a Clip on the Timeline

Click a clip on the **Timeline** to select it. By default, four categories of properties for the selected clip appear in the **Properties** panel: **Image Control**, **Motion**, **Opacity**, and **Volume**. Naturally, these properties appear only if they're applicable to the clip. Stills, for instance, do not have **Volume** properties, and audio clips do not have image properties. (See **68** **About the Properties Panel**.)

2 Change Settings in the Properties Panel

Click the triangle to the left of **Image Control** to expand this property's details. A control panel for setting **Brightness**, **Contrast**, **Hue**, and **Saturation** becomes available.

- The **Brightness** setting, which controls the tonal values of the image, defaults at 0% and can be adjusted from –100% to 100%.

- The **Contrast** setting, which sharpens the image's tonal qualities by emphasizing the difference between dark and light areas, defaults at 100% and can be adjusted from 0% to 200%.

- The **Hue** option is set in degrees as on a color wheel, with different degree settings changing the color tone of the image. It defaults at **0.0** (which is the basic color tone of the original image). Changing this setting 180° sets color tone to the opposite, or complementary, color; other settings move the image's color tone through variations of red, green, and blue.

- The **Saturation** setting defaults to 100%. Change this value to 0% to remove all color, leaving you with a black-and-white image. Change it to 200% to double the amount of all color applied to your image. Values in between produce variations on these results.

These values can either be set numerically by typing in new values, or by sliding the values across settings. To slide the values, mouse over the settings until the mouse pointer changes to a hand with an arrow on either side, and then click and drag. The numbers increase or decrease fluidly, and the results of the new settings are displayed in the **Monitor** panel.

▶ NOTE

Hue, Saturation, and Brightness form the three dimensions of color. The range of hues is usually illustrated as a wheel of color ranging from red through green through blue and back to red. Saturation is the density of hue in a given color, whereas brightness is the amount of lightness or whiteness in the color.

59

3 Change Settings on the Timeline

An alternative way to change these settings is to right-click the clip on the **Timeline** and, from the context menu that appears, choose **Show Clip Keyframe** and then choose one of the submenus for **Hue**, **Saturation**, or **Brightness**.

Select a property detail. This detail now appears on the clip's title bar where the words **Motion: Position** initially were. Raise or lower the horizontal yellow line that appears in the clip to adjust the settings for that property detail.

▶ NOTE

Properties, as well as nearly all effects, when applied to a clip can also be set to change or move over time with keyframes. See **67** About Keyframing and **75** Control a Video Effect with Keyframes.

60 | Enhance Video with Advanced Image Controls

✔ BEFORE YOU BEGIN	→ SEE ALSO
58 About Preset Effects	59 Adjust Color and Brightness
68 About the Properties Panel	67 About Keyframing
	75 Control a Video Effect with Keyframes

In addition to basic **Image Controls** such as **Brightness**, **Contrast**, **Hue**, and **Saturation** (described in 59 **Adjust Color and Brightness**), Premiere Elements offers a variety of more advanced effects for correcting or controlling the color, sharpness, and tone of your image.

1 Select the Clip to Be Affected

Click the clip in need of color correction on the **Timeline**. A default list of the clip's properties appears in the **Properties** panel, including **Image Control**, **Motion**, **Opacity**, and **Volume** (as applicable to the clip).

60

▶ **TIP**

Another excellent tool for image correction is **Shadow/Highlight** (located in the **Adjust** category of the **Video FX** collection). This effect automatically softens the contrast between the brightest and darkest areas in an image while bringing up the midtones— very effective on an image in which, for instance, the brightness of the sky washes out the details of a shaded area.

2 Apply Auto Color to the Clip

Note that, as you browse each collection in the **Effects and Transitions** panel, the effects and transitions are displayed as thumbnails. If an effect involves action, click that effect or transition's thumbnail to see a thumbnail preview of that action.

In the **Adjust** collection on the **Video FX** page, select the **Auto Color** effect and drag it onto your clip. The **Auto Color** effect is added to the **Properties** panel for this clip.

3 Adjust Effect Controls

The **Auto Color** effect works by automatically setting the brightest pixel in your screen image to pure white and the darkest pixel in your screen image to pure black, balancing the midtones based on those settings.

2 Apply Auto Color to the Clip

3 Adjust Effect Controls

1 Select the Clip to Be Affected

60 Enhance Video with Advanced Image Controls

60

But, as discussed in **58 About Preset Effects**, automatic color correction doesn't always work like magic. The effect, after all, merely makes an approximation of the correct image settings.

▶ NOTE

A challenge for the **Auto Color** effect is that it is applied to each frame in a clip. However, because video is a moving image, the composition of your screen image can change over the course of the clip, challenging the **Auto Color** effect to keep up. You can sometimes generate more accurate **Auto Color** results by splitting the clip with the **Razor** tool (see **36 Split a Clip**) at points in which the picture composition changes radically.

In the **Properties** panel, click the triangle to the left of **Auto Color** to open the effect's control panel. Here you'll find settings for **Temporal Smoothing** (which averages the pixels for a smoother color blend), **Scene Detect** (which overrides the **Temporal Smoothing** settings when the scene content changes) and **Blend With Original** (which averages the corrected color of your screen image with the color settings of the original clip).

Experiment with these settings and see how your clip is affected. You can also supplement these changes by making changes to the settings in the **Image Control** property.

The **White Clip** and **Black Clip** percentages limit the range of black and white pixels. **Auto Color**, by default, limits these ranges to .1%. By raising these clip ranges, you can further affect the image by increasing the image's contrast. Each of these settings can go as high as 10%.

Selecting the option to **Snap Neutral Midtones** can also often make a very effective change to your image's color quality by automatically finding and setting the image's midtones based on the darkest and lightest points.

---

61 | Add and Customize an Effect

✔ BEFORE YOU BEGIN	→ SEE ALSO
58 About Preset Effects	**65** Create and Save a Preset
68 About the Properties Panel	**67** About Keyframing
	75 Control a Video Effect with Keyframes

60

Every one of Premiere Elements's effects, whether it's a preset, a motion effect, or a transition, can be tweaked and customized until you achieve precisely the effect for which you're looking. (And after you've changed the settings for an effect, you can save the modified effect as your own personal preset; see **65** **Create and Save a Preset**.)

In fact, it's often more effective, and more fun, to think of preset effects as merely starting points for more elaborate effects.

1 Select the Clip to Be Affected

Click the clip you want to modify on your **Timeline**. A default list of the clip's properties appears in the **Properties** panel, including **Image Control**, **Motion**, **Opacity**, and **Volume** (as applicable to the clip).

2 Apply the Effect

Locate an effect in the **Effects and Transitions** panel and drag and drop it on the clip in the **Timeline**.

For this example, I used the **Spherize** effect, which can be found in the **Video FX** collection in the **Distort** category. The **Spherize** effect, which ultimately produces a fish-eye distortion, is one of many effects that doesn't display an immediate change when applied to the clip. Adding the effect gives you access to a control panel for the effect rather than producing an immediate change. After you change a few settings, you'll see the effect at work.

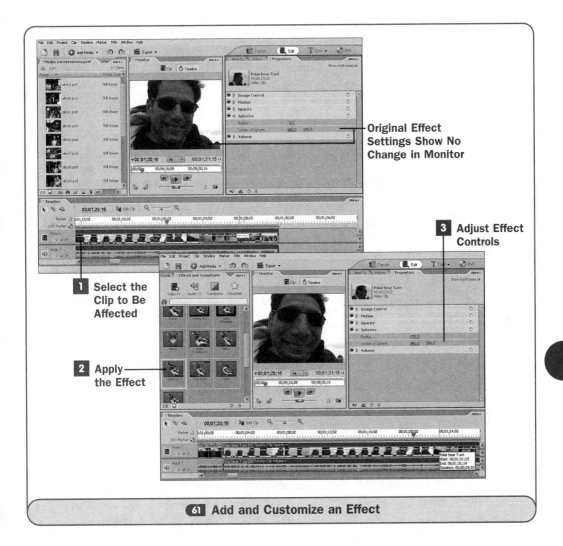

Original Effect Settings Show No Change in Monitor

3 Adjust Effect Controls

1 Select the Clip to Be Affected

2 Apply the Effect

61

61 Add and Customize an Effect

▶ **NOTE**

The center of your video frame is presented as a measurement in pixels, half the width and half the height of a video frame. In other words, in the NTSC system, the center point of your screen image is 360/240. In the PAL system, the center of the frame is 393/288.

3 Adjust Effect Controls

Click the triangle next to your effect in the **Properties** panel to reveal the control panel for that effect's details. The **Spherize** effect offers controls for designating the radius of the sphere (in pixels) and the sphere's center point.

Type new numbers into these settings and view the results in the **Monitor** panel. As an alternative, you can mouse over either setting's numbers until your mouse pointer looks like a hand with a double-headed arrow, and then click and drag left or right to increase or decrease the numbers more fluidly. The results are displayed in your **Monitor** panel.

▶ **TIP**

After you begin applying effects to your clip, you'll notice that the quality of the image played back in the **Monitor** has apparently deteriorated. On slower computers, playback might even seem jumpy or irregular. This is because you are looking at a soft render of your clip—drawn on the fly by your computer as you play the affected clip. (A clip that should be hard rendered is indicated by a red line above the clip on the **Timeline**.) To see a better example of what your clip will look like on final output, press **Enter** to render the **Timeline**. The red line above the clip turns green when rendering is complete, and the quality of your playback will be an accurate representation of what your final output will look like.

61

62 **Rotate or Flip a Clip**	
✔ **BEFORE YOU BEGIN**	→ **SEE ALSO**
68 About the Properties Panel	**58** About Preset Effects
	65 Create and Save a Preset
	67 About Keyframing
	75 Control a Video Effect with Keyframes

Premiere Elements offers a variety of effects for distorting your screen image—both in two-dimensional and three-dimensional space (see **81** **Rotate a Clip in 3D**). What's more, by adding keyframes (see **67** **About Keyframing**), you can even animate these distortions, saving your result as your own, custom preset (see **65** **Create and Save a Preset**).

1 Select the Clip to Be Affected

Click the clip you want to modify on your **Timeline**. A default list of the clip's properties appears in the **Properties** panel, including **Image Control**, **Motion**, **Opacity**, and **Volume** (as applicable to the clip).

Click the triangle to the left of the **Image Control** property to reveal the detail settings.

3 Rotate the Clip Precisely

2 Flip the Clip 90 Degrees

1 Select the Clip to Be Affected

4 Drag to Rotate

5 Change Your Anchor Point

62

62 Rotate or Flip a Clip

▶ **NOTE**

As you can do with all the effects that change the screen image's scale, dimensions, or shape, you can rotate your screen image by clicking the image in the **Monitor** panel and manipulate it by dragging the control handles that appear on the image's corners.

2 Flip the Clip 90 Degrees

The **Properties** panel has two one-click **Rotate** settings that flip your clip 90° to the right or left. Click the **Rotate Left** or **Rotate Right** button to change the orientation of the image.

3 Rotate the Clip Precisely

You can rotate your clip by an arbitrary amount by typing the number of degrees you want to turn your clip in the numerical settings area. You can also change the settings more fluidly by mousing over the numbers until the mouse pointer turns into a little hand with a two-headed arrow. Click and drag left or right over the settings to roll the numbers up or down. The changes are displayed in the **Monitor** panel. You can also rotate your clip in 3D or make it appear to tumble through space (see **81** **Rotate a Clip in 3D**).

▶ NOTES

You can easily flip your clip, horizontally or vertically, in a single move by dragging it onto the **Horizontal Flip** or **Vertical Flip** effects found in the **Transform** collection in the **Effects and Transitions** panel.

When many of the effects are applied to a clip, the clip's position on the **Timeline** can affect what the resulting video will look like. Many distortions, for instance, pull the image in from the sides of the video frame, resulting in the clip appearing against a black background (if the clip is on an upper video track, the background reveals the clip on the video track below it (see **29** **About the Timeline and Video Tracks**).

62

4 Drag to Rotate

Alternatively, you can change your image's position, scale, rotation, and other settings by clicking the screen image in the **Monitor** panel and dragging the clip around by the center and corner handles that appear.

5 Change the Anchor Point

The anchor point is the point around which the clip pivots when you rotate it. By default, this point is the center of the clip.

Change the **Anchor Point** settings in the **Properties** panel and click the screen image in the **Monitor** panel. Note that the image has shifted to one side and that the circled cross, representing the anchor point, is no longer in the center. Even if you drag the screen image back into the center of the frame, the anchor point remains in this new position.

Now type a new **Rotate** value. The image seems to hook around the point rather than spin around its center.

If you'd like, you can use keyframing to set waypoints for the **Rotate** positions, creating an animated spin effect for your clip (see **75** **Control a Video Effect with Keyframes**).

► **NOTE**

If your image is smaller than your video frame—as can be the case with a logo or other graphic—you can set the anchor point for your rotation outside the image, using negative numbers if necessary. By using keyframes to create a motion path, you can animate your graphic to move around a circular path.

---

63 Reset or Remove an Effect

✔ BEFORE YOU BEGIN	→ SEE ALSO
58 About Preset Effects	**62** Rotate or Flip a Clip
61 Add and Customize an Effect	**65** Create and Save a Preset
68 About the Properties Panel	**67** About Keyframing
	75 Control a Video Effect with Keyframes

No change is permanent in nonlinear editing. This is why computer-based, non-linear editing is often referred to as a nondestructive editing process. Everything, short of overwriting your original files, can be undone.

So feel free to experiment with effects on your clips. And if you want to compare how the clip looked before and after you applied the effect, you can do so with a single click of the mouse.

63

1 Apply an Effect to a Clip

Browse the **Effects and Transitions** panel for an effect. As you open each collection, look at the thumbnails to see a sample of each effect. If you click to select a **Motion** or **Transitional** effect, the thumbnail displays an animated preview.

When you've found an effect you want to use, drag it onto a clip on the **Timeline**.

► **NOTE**

You can apply as many effects as you want to a single clip. As you do, the effects are added to the clip's properties in the **Properties** panel. Premiere Elements applies these effects in the order they appear in the **Properties** panel, so rearranging their order can often produce significantly different results.

2 Adjust the Effect

When an effect is applied to a clip and the clip is selected on the **Timeline**, the effect is listed in the clip's **Properties** panel. Click the triangle to the left of the effect name to open the detail controls.

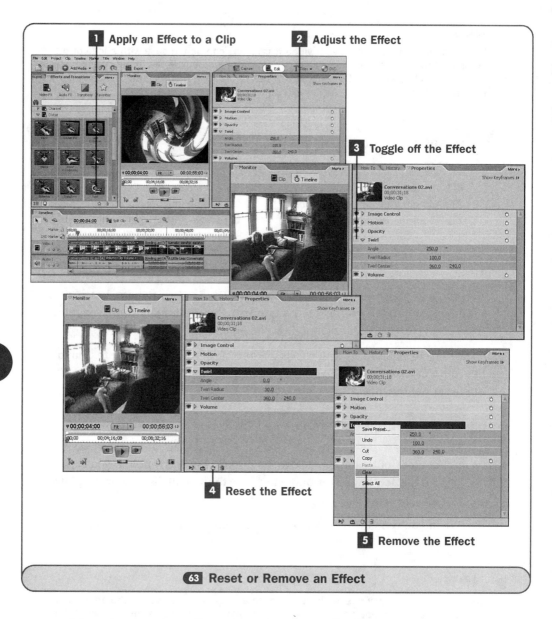

1 Apply an Effect to a Clip   **2** Adjust the Effect

3 Toggle off the Effect

4 Reset the Effect

5 Remove the Effect

63 Reset or Remove an Effect

Adjust the controls to affect your screen image (see **61** **Add and Customize an Effect** and **62** **Rotate or Flip a Clip**). Your changes are displayed in the **Monitor** panel.

3 **Toggle off the Effect**

To compare the before and after of your applied effect, click the eye icon to the left of the effect's name in the **Properties** panel. This action turns on and off the effect and all its current settings.

If you have more than one effect applied to your clip, you can toggle each effect individually.

4 Reset the Effect

Occasionally, especially with preset or automatic effects, you might find that your adjustments to the settings have taken your image some place you really didn't want to go. If so, you can easily reset the effect to its initial settings—without affecting any other changes you've made to other effects for the clip.

With the name of the effect you want to reset selected in the **Properties** panel, click the little stopwatch icon at the bottom of the panel. The effect reverts to its default settings.

5 Remove the Effect

If you decide you don't want any or all of your effects, you can easily remove them from the clip.

To remove an effect, right-click the name of the effect in the **Properties** panel and, from the context menu that appears, select **Clear**.

▶ **NOTE**

To remove all the effects you added to a clip in one move, click the **Properties** panel's **More** button and select **Delete All Effects from Clip**.

---

64 Copy Attributes from One Clip to Another

✔ **BEFORE YOU BEGIN**

58 About Preset Effects
61 Add and Customize an Effect
68 About the Properties Panel

→ **SEE ALSO**

65 Create and Save a Preset
67 About Keyframing
75 Control a Video Effect with Keyframes

After you've added an effect to a clip, whether by color correcting the screen image or by adding and customizing video or audio effects, you can easily transfer those effects and all their settings to another clip (see also **65** **Create and Save a Preset**). This feature can be extremely helpful for applying color adjustments created for one clip across a series of clips or for applying the keyframes for a motion path created for one clip to another clip or series of clips.

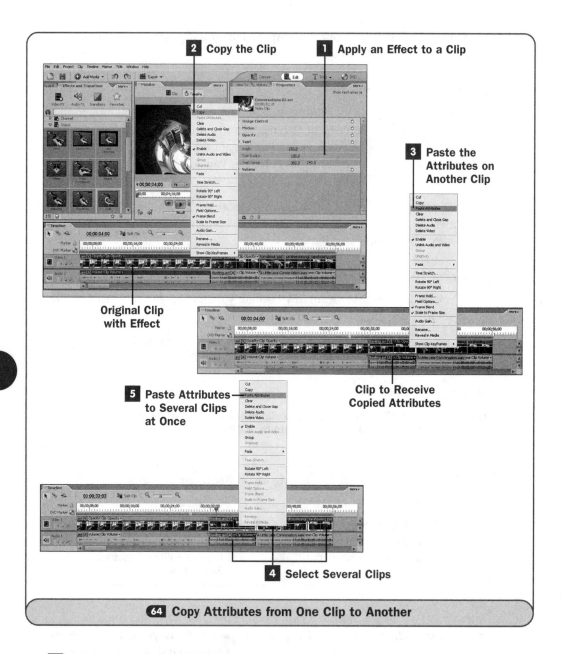

2 Copy the Clip

1 Apply an Effect to a Clip

3 Paste the Attributes on Another Clip

Original Clip with Effect

5 Paste Attributes to Several Clips at Once

Clip to Receive Copied Attributes

4 Select Several Clips

64 Copy Attributes from One Clip to Another

64

1 Apply an Effect to a Clip

Browse the **Effects and Transitions** panel for an effect. As you open each collection, look at the thumbnails to see a sample of each effect. If you click to select a **Motion** or **Transitional** effect, the thumbnail displays an animated preview.

When you've found an effect you want to use, drag it onto a clip on the **Timeline**, as I have done with the **Twirl** effect.

▶ **NOTE**

You can apply as many effects as you want to a single clip. As you do, the clips are added to the clip's properties in the **Properties** panel. Premiere Elements applies these effects in the order they appear in the **Properties** panel, so rearranging their order can often produce significantly different results.

After you've applied the effect, customize it as described in **61** **Add and Customize an Effect**.

2 **Copy the Clip**

Right-click the affected clip on the **Timeline** and, when the context menu appears, select **Copy**.

3 **Paste the Attributes on Another Clip**

Right-click another clip on your **Timeline** (one to which you want to apply the same effect, with the same settings, as you applied to the first clip in step 1) and, from the context menu that appears, select **Paste Attributes**.

All effects and settings you applied to the first clip are applied to the second clip.

64

4 **Select Several Clips**

If you want to apply the copied effect to multiple clips in the **Timeline**, drag your mouse from an empty area on the **Timeline** and across a series of clips to select them all.

5 **Paste Attributes to Several Clips at Once**

As you did in step 3, right-click the selected group of clips and, from the context menu that appears, select **Paste Attributes**.

All effects and settings you copied from the first clip are applied to all the selected clips.

65 Create and Save a Preset

✔ BEFORE YOU BEGIN	→ SEE ALSO
58 About Preset Effects	**67** About Keyframing
61 Add and Customize an Effect	**69** Add Motion to a Still
68 About the Properties Panel	**70** Pan and Zoom Still Images a la Ken Burns
	75 Control a Video Effect with Keyframes

If you like the effects and motions you've applied to a clip, you can save each effect as your own, custom preset, so you can easily recall it in this and future projects.

1 Customize an Effect's Settings on a Clip

Browse the **Effects and Transitions** panel for an effect. As you open each collection, look at the thumbnails to see a sample of each effect. If you click to select a **Motion** or **Transitional** effect, the thumbnail displays an animated preview.

When you've found an effect you want to use, drag it onto a clip on the **Timeline**.

▶ NOTE

Although you can add as many effects as you'd like to any clip, you can save a preset for only one effect or motion at a time.

With the clip selected on the **Timeline**, customize the effect you've applied in the **Properties** panel as described in **61** **Add and Customize an Effect**.

For this example, I applied the **Camera View** effect (from the **Video FX Transform** collection). I set the **Focal Length** to **500**, the **Distance** to **500**, and **Latitude** to **100**—essentially making my initial screen image appear to be rotated facing down in three-dimensional space, a long distance from the camera.

2 Add Motion

If you'd like, you can add keyframed motion to your effect either by starting from a preset motion effect or by creating custom movement from scratch (as described in **69** **Add Motion to a Still** and **70** **Pan and Zoom Still Images a la Ken Burns**).

65 Create and Save a Preset

In my example, I clicked the **Show Keyframes** button at the top of the **Properties** panel and then clicked the stopwatch icon to the right of the **Camera View** listing in the **Properties** panel, which set my first set of keyframes. Then I moved the current time indicator (CTI) in the **Properties** panel one second to the right and changed my effect's **Longitude**, **Latitude**, **Distance**, and **Zoom** settings so the image filled the screen—automatically creating a new set of keyframe points in which my screen image is now a normal, full-screen clip.

Move the CTI back to the beginning of your clip and render the affected clip by pressing the **Enter** key.

▶ **NOTE**

After you apply an effect to a clip, press the **Enter** key to render it. Rendering creates a clean-looking, final version of the modified clip and motion path, improving your playback quality immensely and saving your computer the taxing work of having to re-create a preview of your affected clip on the fly.

In my example, the image zooms into full screen as it appears to rotate up in three-dimensional space toward the camera.

3 **Save the Preset**

Click the effect in the **Properties** panel whose settings or motion path you'd like to save (in this case, the **Camera View** effect) and then click the **More** button. From the menu, select **Save Preset**. The **Save Preset** dialog box opens.

You'll be asked to name your preset. You'll also have the option of beginning any change in the effect or motion path at the clip's In or Out point.

Your new preset is added to the **My Presets** collection in the **Effects and Transitions** panel. You can apply it to any other clips in the current project— or to clips in any other project—by dragging it from the **Effects and Transitions** panel and dropping it on the desired clip, just as you would any of Premiere Elements' standard presets.

If you later decide you want to remove this custom preset from your collection, right-click it in the **Effects and Transitions** panel and select the **Clear** option from the context menu.

65

---

66 | **Enhance Audio with Advanced Effects**

✔ BEFORE YOU BEGIN	→ SEE ALSO
61 Add and Customize an Effect	**58** About Preset Effects
68 About the Properties Panel	**67** About Keyframing
	70 Pan and Zoom Still Images a la Ken Burns
	73 Control Volume at Specific Points
	75 Control a Video Effect with Keyframes

In addition to offering a whole library of video effects and presets, Premiere Elements offers 17 audio effects. Open the **Effects and Transitions** panel and click the **Audio FX** button to view the categories of audio effects. Click a category name to view the thumbnails of the audio effects in that category.

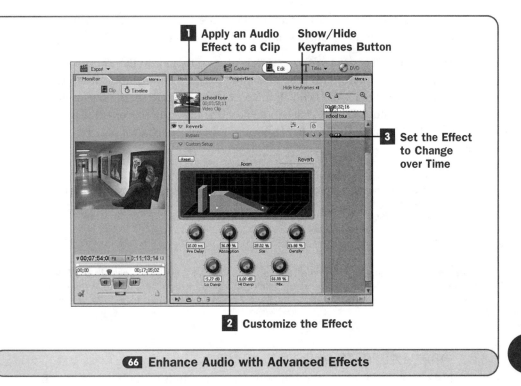

1 Apply an Audio   Show/Hide
Effect to a Clip   Keyframes Button

3 Set the Effect
to Change
over Time

2 Customize the Effect

66 Enhance Audio with Advanced Effects

66

Like video effects, audio effects can be customized, piled on to a clip, keyframed to vary over the course of a clip, and even saved as custom presets.

1 Apply an Audio Effect to a Clip

Browse the **Audio FX** collection in the **Effects and Transitions** panel. (For your reference, we've included descriptions of all 17 audio effects at the end of this task.)

Drag the audio effect from the **Effects and Transitions** panel onto a clip on the **Timeline**. You can apply an audio effect to any clip that contains audio, whether or not the clip also includes video.

For this example, I dragged the **Reverb** effect onto my clip.

2 Customize the Effect

When you click to select a clip on the **Timeline**, the clip's properties are displayed in the **Properties** panel including, as applicable, the default properties of **Image Control**, **Motion**, **Opacity**, and **Volume**.

The effect or effects you've added to the clip are also displayed in this panel. Click the triangle to the left of the effect's name to open the detail controls.

In most cases, the controls for audio effects are a list of numerical settings that often designate frequency, tone, and/or audio levels.

The **Reverb** effect used in this example offers a more intuitive control panel. Because **Reverb** causes an echo effect, the controls show graphical representations of the area of an echo chamber, with controls to set the size of the room, the distance to the reflecting object, the absorption properties, and so on. (The **Dynamics** effect offers a similarly graphical control panel.)

▶ NOTE

As you can with video effects, you can copy any customized audio effect and apply the attributes, including all custom audio effect settings, to one or more other audio or audio/video clips (see **64** Copy Effects Attributes from One Clip to Another).

▶ TIP

Every customized and keyframed effect can be saved as a custom preset in the **My Presets** collection. To save your preset, click the name of the effect in the **Properties** panel, click the **More** button, and select **Save Preset** as described in **65** Create and Save a Preset.

66

③ Set the Effect to Change over Time

Just as you can create a motion path for your visuals using keyframes in the **Properties** panel, you can also use keyframes to set up an audio effect to vary over the course of the clip (see **67** About Keyframing).

If the **Timeline** isn't visible in your **Properties** panel, click the **Show Keyframes** button at the top of the panel. Set the current time indicator (CTI) to the beginning of your clip and click the stopwatch icon to the right of your effect's name. A column of little diamonds appears on the **Properties Timeline**, adjacent to each detail setting for the current effect.

Move the CTI a little to the right and change the settings for the effect. New keyframe diamonds are created, and Premiere Elements automatically creates a transition between the sets of keyframe points. As you can do with video effect keyframes, you can add, reset, reposition, and delete these keyframe points as needed.

In my example, the addition of keyframes allowed me to add an echo effect to one portion of the clip and turn it off for another portion of the clip—as if the person in the clip walked into and then out of an echoey tunnel.

▶ TIP

You can use keyframing to control your audio levels at precise points on the **Timeline** (see **73** Control Volume at Specific Points).

Premiere Elements Audio Effects

The following is a list of the effects in the **Audio FX** collection in the **Effects and Transitions** panel.

Note that audio effects can be applied to a single clip; if you drag the effect to the name of the audio track, you can apply that effect to an entire audio track at once. If you apply an effect to an entire track at once, you can disable the effect for a particular clip by selecting the clip on your **Timeline** and enabling the **Bypass** option in the **Properties** panel.

▶ **NOTE**

In addition to applying the effects and filters in the **Audio FX** collection, you can monitor your audio levels using the **Audio Meters** panel. Open the panel by selecting it from the **Window** drop-down menu.

- **Balance** offers slider controls for balancing the audio level between the left and right channels.

- **Bass** is a slider control that boosts or lowers bass.

- **Channel Volume** offers controls for adding or reducing the audio levels for individual channels; it offers more control of each channel's level than the **Balance** effect does.

- **Delay**, similar to **Reverb**, feeds back or repeats the audio on a clip. The effect offers controls for **Amount of Delay**, **Feedback** (the number of repetitions of sound), and **Mix** (a ratio of the repeated sound's volume to the original sound's volume).

- The **Denoiser** is a powerful tool for removing unwanted or extraneous sound. Controls include settings for the **Noise Floor** (threshold), **Amount of Reduction**, and **Offset**, plus additional high-end controls for the effect.

- **Dynamics** is a powerful audio processor with a host of controls for an **Autogate**, **Compressor**, and **Expander**.

- **Fill Left/Right** is an automatic tool for spreading the sound from either the left channel or the right channel across both channels—effective for filling both channels of stereo when only monaural or one channel of sound is available.

- The **Highpass** and **Lowpass** effects filter, or remove, sound from above or below certain audio frequencies. Settings control the **Cut-Off Frequencies** for each.

- **Invert** switches the phase of audio channels. It is a high-end adjustment that can improve the quality of some recorded audio.

66

- The **Notch** tool can remove sound at a given frequency. It is similar to a **Highpass** or **Lowpass** effect except that it can be set to a middle frequency. For instance, **Notch** can be set to remove a hum or buzz in a clip's audio. Controls include a setting to eliminate a **Central Frequency** and the **Range** of frequencies to eliminate around that center point.

- The **Pitch Shifter** raises or lowers the pitch of an audio clip—for instance, eliminating the higher pitch of a clip that has been sped up. Controls include **Pitch Settings**, **Tincture** (to tweak the half-tones), and **Formant Preserve** (for producing a more natural sound).

- **Reverb** is an echo effect similar to **Delay**, but much more powerful and customizable. Controls include **Predelay** (the time between the original signal and its echo), **Absorption** (softens the echo's sound), **Size** (of the imaginary room in which the echo is occurring), **Density** (sets the density of the "tail" or lingering sound following the initial echo), **LoDamp** (to dampen lower frequencies), **HiDamp** (to dampen higher frequencies), and **Mix** (controls the mix of the original sound and the echo).

- **Swap Channels** switches the left and right channel audio on a stereo clip.

- **Treble** is a slider control that boosts or lowers treble.

- **Volume** boosts the audio level of clip. For very low-level audio, you can add several instances of the **Volume** effect to a clip, setting the levels for each instance of the **Volume** effect to high until you've increased the clip's volume to the necessary level.

66

10

The Power of Keyframing

IN THIS CHAPTER:

Keyframing is one of the most powerful tools in Premiere Elements. Its methodology might seem a bit challenging at first. But, when you master it, you'll find the true power of this program unleashed.

The principle is simple: For any effect, you designate points on your still's, your audio clip's, or your video clip's **Timeline** where you want the effect to occur or change—then Premiere Elements automatically creates the motion path or transition between those points.

The beauty of this system is that these points, or keyframes, can be easily added, moved, changed, and rearranged indefinitely until your video project produces exactly the effect you're trying to achieve. Again, this system might seem a bit challenging at first. However, when you see what's happening, you'll find keyframes a very natural and intuitive way to create movement and effects.

It's also worth noting that many of the movements and presets built into Premiere Elements's video and audio effects are, in reality, composed of or created with keyframes. And, in fact, after you apply these effects to your clips, you can easily manipulate the keyframe points and customize the effects to whatever degree you see fit.

67

67 About Keyframing

✔ BEFORE YOU BEGIN	→ SEE ALSO
68 About the Properties Panel	**47** Add an Audio Transition
	69 Add Motion to a Still
	70 Pan and Zoom Still Images a la Ken Burns
	73 Control Volume at Specific Points

Although audio and video effects can also be controlled right on the **Timeline**, most of the time you will be doing your keyframing on the clip timeline in the **Properties** panel.

▶ KEY TERM

Keyframing—The method used by Premiere Elements (as well as Premiere Pro and After Effects) for creating motion paths and transitioning effects. Points representing precise settings for effects or positions are placed on the **Timeline**, and the program automatically creates a movement or transition between those points.

Whenever you select a clip on the main **Timeline**, all the applied audio and video effects, as well as any keyframing, are revealed in the **Properties** panel. (In fact, there is a wealth of tools, adjustments, and settings available in this panel, and they're discussed in even greater detail in **68** About the Properties Panel.)

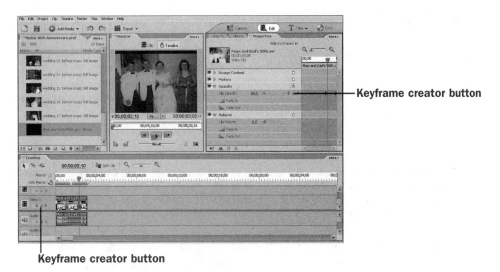

Keyframe creator button

Keyframe creator button

*Keyframe points are set on the **Properties** timeline.*

Select a clip on the main **Timeline** and look at the **Properties** panel. A list of properties appears in this panel by default for every clip or graphic. And, as you add effects, they are also added to the list.

You'll also notice a stopwatch icon to the right of each property. This is the button you use to begin keyframing a movement or effect.

▶ **NOTE**

After you add keyframes to any property or effect, the stopwatch icon to the right of that property or effect shows a second hand. This indicates that specific, changing settings to the clip or still are linked to various keyframe points. Until keyframes are activated for a property or effect by clicking this stopwatch icon, any change in these settings applies to the entire clip or for the duration of a graphic.

After you begin keyframing, keyframe points are added automatically to the **Properties** timeline whenever you reposition the CTI and change a setting. See **69** Add Motion to a Still for more information.

On either side of the keyframe creator buttons (the little diamonds to the right of each property detail such as **Scale**, **Position**, and **Rotation** to which keyframes can be applied) on both the main **Timeline** and the **Properties** timeline are arrows pointing left and right. Click these arrows to jump to the previous or next keyframe point. After you jump to a keyframe point, you can tweak or adjust that point's settings.

Also note the **Properties** panel timeline area to the right of the properties. (If you don't see it, click the **Show Keyframes** button at the top of the panel.) Like the

67

main **Timeline** panel, this keyframe area contains a **Properties** timeline and a current time indicator, or CTI, that tracks along the clip as it plays, just as the main CTI tracks along your video project as it plays. In fact, if you move one CTI, the other also moves.

Now click the triangles to the left of each property in the **Properties** panel to view the details for each of these settings.

▶ **NOTE**

All clips and graphics, by default, show the **Image Control**, **Motion**, **Opacity**, and **Volume** properties, as applicable. (An audio clip, of course, shows only audio properties, and a still photo does not show any audio properties.) As you add effects to your clip, these effects and their controls are also added to the **Properties** panel for that clip.

Under the **Opacity** property, click the automatic **Fade In** button. Two small, diamond-shaped points appear on the **Properties** timeline to the right of this control. These are keyframes, and, as a result of your clicking the **Fade In** button, they appear one second apart on the **Properties** timeline at the beginning of the clip. Drag your CTI from the first to the second of these keyframe points and watch the **Monitor**: The clip's opacity goes from 0% at the first keyframe to 100% at the second keyframe—a fade in from black. The **Fade In** effect is therefore a keyframed effect—the length of the effect is controlled by the keyframe points on the **Properties** timeline.

67

▶ **NOTE**

Because the **Fade In** and **Fade Out Opacity** effects affect the clip's transparency, the effect is a fade in from or fade out to black only if there is no clip on a video layer below the affected clip. Otherwise, the **Fade In** or **Fade Out** effect appears to dissolve in or out of the clip on the layer below.

Suppose that you've previewed your project and, for whatever reason, you don't feel your clip is fading in fast enough. How might you speed up the effect? If you slide the second keyframe point to the left, closer to the first point, the transition happens more quickly. Move it half the distance, and the clip fades in at twice the speed. Drag the second keyframe point to the right to lengthen the transition time.

And that's basically all there is to keyframing.

Just think in terms of time and effects settings. Keyframe points closer together result in faster transitions or motions; keyframe points farther apart result in slower transitions. By clicking the arrows to the right or left of the keyframe creator button (the little diamond), you can jump back or forward to a keyframe point and change the settings of the property to which it applies. If you don't like the results and you want to remove the setting completely, you can right-click the keyframe point and select **Clear** from the context menu to delete the point completely.

Keyframing is used extensively throughout this book because it is the principle system Premiere Elements uses for coordinating movement and effects. You'll also find a simple demonstration of its use in creating movement in **69** **Add Motion to a Still** and an even more detailed explanation of a very popular use in **70** **Pan and Zoom Still Images a la Ken Burns**.

Keyframes can be used with all but a few effects to control virtually any transition or movement. When you become comfortable with the interface, it will be hard to imagine a simpler or more intuitive tool for customizing and revising effects.

68 About the Properties Panel

✔ BEFORE YOU BEGIN	→ SEE ALSO
67 About Keyframing	**2** Customize Your Workspaces
	59 Adjust Color or Brightness
	69 Add Motion to a Still
	70 Pan and Zoom Still Images a la Ken Burns
	73 Control Volume at Specific Points

68

If the **Media** panel is the artist's paint, the **Properties** panel is the artist's brushes. The **Properties** panel adds shape and movement and even dimension to your clips and graphics. It's here that you'll find controls for a wealth of tools to adjust and affect your audio and video; controls for setting keyframing of motion and speed; and tools for manipulating, repairing, and processing your video or audio clips.

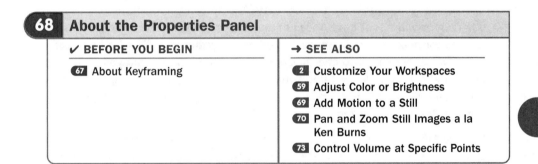

The properties of a clip as well as any keyframing of its effects are displayed in the ***Properties*** *panel.*

The panel toggles between two positions: **Show Keyframes** and **Hide Keyframes**. Click the button at the top of the panel to show or hide the keyframes timeline.

You'll also find information on the clip you've selected on the main **Timeline**, including the name of the clip, the type of medium, and its running time (which might not be the same as the actual running time of the entire original clip).

▶ **NOTE**

In any list of properties for a clip, time is always represented as **00;00;00;00**. The first three sets of numbers indicate the time in hours, minutes, and seconds. The set of numbers to the right of the last semicolon indicates frame count—approximately 30 frames for every second in the NTSC system, 25 frames for every second in the PAL system.

Click the triangles to the left of each property to see the property details for, by default, **Image Control**, **Motion**, **Opacity**, and **Volume**, as applicable, plus any other effects you might have added to the clip. The panel provides easy access to features for making simple image and audio correction (see **59** **Adjust Color or Brightness**). There are also one-click buttons for fading in and out your clip's audio and video and for rotating your clip or still by 90° increments. (You can also rotate the clip by more precise increments by changing the numerical rotation settings as described in **62** **Rotate or Flip a Clip**).

68

Note that each property detail can be set numerically. These settings can be changed a number of ways. The simplest method of changing these settings is, of course, by typing different numerical values. Alternatively, position the mouse pointer over any of the numerical settings; the pointer becomes a settings icon. Click and drag across these settings to increase or decrease the numbers. Watch the **Monitor** panel to see the effect of your changed settings. In many cases, this drag-to-adjust-settings approach is the most natural method for changing settings, as well as being the easiest to control.

You can also click the image in the **Monitor** panel and, by dragging it or manipulating it by its center or corner points, you can change the position, scale, and rotation of the clip. The numeric settings in the **Properties** panel update automatically.

Drag any video effect from the **Effects and Transitions** panel onto your selected clip. Note that the effect also appears in the **Properties** panel. As you can with the default properties, you can click the triangle to the left of the added effect to reveal its details and additional settings and controls. (Note that many effects, such as **Basic 3D**, might not produce a visible change in your clip until you've changed the effect's settings.)

▶ **TIP**

To the left of each property or effect in the **Properties** panel is an eye icon. This icon is a quick switch for turning the effect on and off—a simple way to compare the before and after of any effect or changed setting.

If you haven't already done so, click the **Show Keyframes** button at the top of the **Properties** panel to reveal the keyframing area in the **Properties** timeline. Note that, with few exceptions, a stopwatch icon appears to the right of each property or effect. This button activates the keyframing tool for the property.

After you have activated keyframes for a particular property or effect, the stopwatch icon for that property shows a second hand (see **67** **About Keyframing**).

Keyframe points can be easily moved or deleted. By clicking the stopwatch icon again, you can completely remove them so the effect is applied to your entire clip rather than parts of it.

Likewise, you can remove an entire effect simply by clicking on the name of the effect in the **Properties** panel and clicking the trashcan icon at the bottom of the panel. Alternatively (and more efficiently), right-click the name of the effect and selecting **Clear** from the context menu.

The **Properties** panel also serves as a control panel for transitions. Drag a transition onto the main **Timeline**, select it, and the **Properties** panel takes on a very different look as explained in **44** **About Transitions**. In addition to having the option to preview the transition with the actual clips, the **Properties** panel provides controls for setting the duration of the transition, for setting whether the transition is centered between two clips or over one or the other, and (with the **Properties** timeline revealed) for setting exactly how the transition occurs. Depending on the qualities of the transition itself, you'll also find options for controlling which direction it moves, how the details behave, and how distinct the line is between the clip that is being transitioned out and the one that is being transitioned in. For more information on adding and customizing transitions, see **46** **Add a Video Transition**.

69

69 Add Motion to a Still

✔ BEFORE YOU BEGIN	→ SEE ALSO
22 Prepare a Still for Video	**28** Use and Customize Preset Camera Moves
67 About Keyframing	**65** Create and Save a Preset
68 About the Properties Panel	**70** Pan and Zoom Still Images a la Ken Burns
	71 Make a Variable-Speed Pan and Zoom

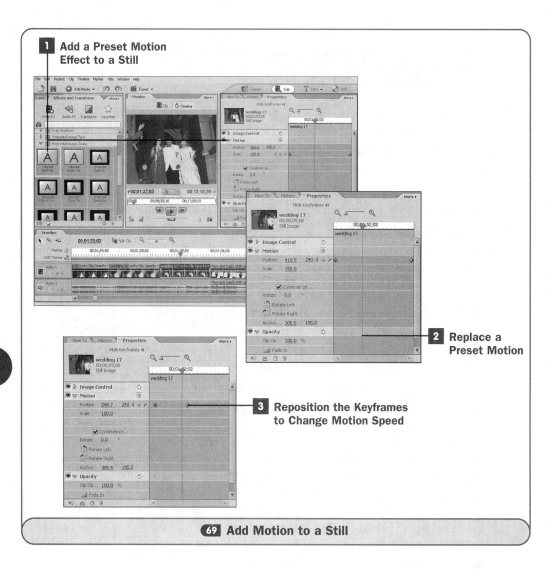

1 Add a Preset Motion Effect to a Still

2 Replace a Preset Motion

3 Reposition the Keyframes to Change Motion Speed

69 Add Motion to a Still

It's the first principle of great movie making: Movies move.

Adding motion to a still photo or graphic in your video gives the still image life. It's the difference between merely running a slideshow and telling a story with pictures. Motion directs your audience's attention to certain elements of your image. It isolates an area and then reveals its context. Motion makes the static dynamic.

Premiere Elements offers a variety of presets that allow you to simply drag and drop horizontal and vertical pans and in and out zooms onto your clips. These presets add the motion you want, and offer you some control over the way the motion works. As you know, creating and customizing such motion is easy using the keyframing tool in Premiere Elements. After you establish the points at which you want your scale and position to change, Premiere Elements fills in the movement between those points, creating a smooth motion from one keyframe point to the next.

▶ **NOTE**

After you've created or customized your keyframed movement or effect, you can save it as a permanent preset, and it will be automatically added to your preset collection. Just select **Save Preset** from the **Properties** panel's **More** menu.

1 Add a Preset Motion Effect to a Still

The preset motions you can add to a still image are limited to panning over the still or zooming in or away from the image. Open the **Effects and Transitions** panel and click the **Video FX** button at the top of the panel. Scroll through the list of preset effects and look for the **Horizontal** or **Vertical Image Pans** or the **Horizontal** or **Vertical Image Zooms**.

Drag a preset pan or zoom onto a still on the **Timeline**. The motion of the selected pan or zoom is automatically timed to the duration of the still. Play the clip and watch how the preset affects the clip.

Unless the size of your image has the same dimensions as those listed in the name of the preset (for example, 640×480 pixels), it's possible that the preset you selected will either show too little of your image or the motion will extend beyond the edges of the clip. If so, you can customize the motion as described in **28** **Use and Customize Preset Camera Moves**.

2 Replace a Preset Motion

Because all preset motions are based on the **Motion** property, dragging another motion or zoom preset onto your clip will overwrite the previous effect.

3 Reposition the Keyframes to Change Motion Speed

The motion path is set to the keyframe points on the **Properties** timeline. By moving these points, you can control the speed of the transition or motion path between the points.

If you lengthen the duration of the clip, the keyframes remain in their original places, ending the motion path at the final keyframe point and holding that position until the end of the clip. Repositioning the keyframe point to the end of the clip results in a steady motion from beginning to end.

Finally, you can save the new positions you've created as a custom preset as explained in **65** **Create and Save a Preset**.

69

70 Pan and Zoom Still Images a la Ken Burns

✔ BEFORE YOU BEGIN	→ SEE ALSO
22 Prepare a Still for Video	**65** Create and Save a Preset
67 About Keyframing	**71** Make a Variable-Speed Pan and Zoom
68 About the Properties Panel	
69 Add Motion to a Still	**73** Control Volume at Specific Points

Although filmmaker Ken Burns (notable for such epic PBS documentaries as *Jazz*, *Baseball*, and *The Civil War*) didn't invent the technique of slowly moving in and around a photo to make it seem to come to life, he has used it so extensively and so effectively that it has become forever linked to his name—the Ken Burns Effect. By carefully and creatively isolating areas of photos and then revealing a wider context by moving across them, Burns has managed to bring action, suspense, and drama to stills and paintings, giving them a dynamic, intriguing, almost movie-like quality.

By controlling the **Scale** and **Position** settings for your stills over time, Premiere Elements's keyframing tool gives you the ability to produce the very same effects. But, even greater, the nature of the keyframing tool is that it also allows for easy revision and customization, making it simple for you to match the motions you create to music, sound effects, and narration.

By controlling motion, you decide how your audience experiences a photo. You show them what to focus on. You decide how the photo is revealed to them; you control their eye movement through the scene. In doing so, you give your audience not merely a picture to look at but a story to experience.

Before you begin, remember that whenever you change the scale of a still or any raster image, there are resolution issues to consider. **22** **Prepare a Still for Video** discusses how best to ensure that your image quality is maintained throughout this effect.

1 Drag to Set the Photo's Duration

Stretch the photo or clip you want to pan and zoom down the main **Timeline** until it's your desired duration.

You can extend or trim the clip later, and it won't affect the positions of the keyframes.

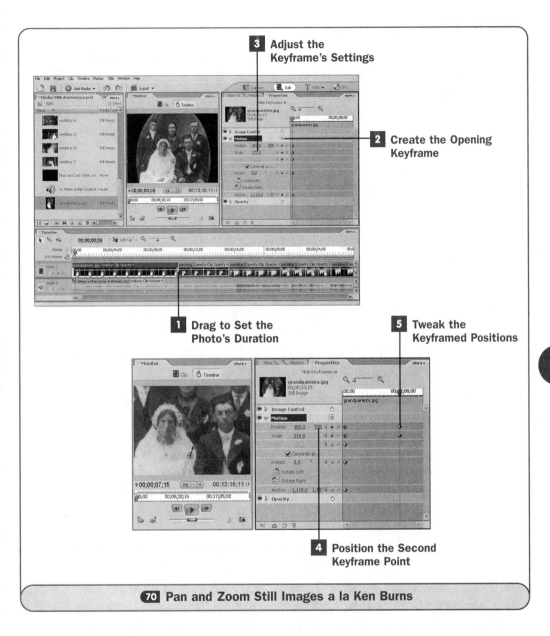

3 Adjust the Keyframe's Settings

2 Create the Opening Keyframe

1 Drag to Set the Photo's Duration

5 Tweak the Keyframed Positions

70

4 Position the Second Keyframe Point

70 Pan and Zoom Still Images a la Ken Burns

▶ **TIP**

When you start changing the positions and scale of your clips and adding effects, you'll find that the playback becomes irregular or that the video image seems degraded. This is because you're actually looking at a *preview* of the affected clip, which the program is creating on-the-fly. (You'll also notice that a red line has appeared on the **Timeline** above the clip.) To see a more true representation of what your final clip will look like, render the clip by pressing the **Enter** key. (When your clip is rendered, the red line above it becomes a green line.)

2 Create the Opening Keyframes

Make sure that the photo to which you want to apply the Ken Burns effect is selected on the **Timeline**. If the **Properties** panel timeline is not already visible, click the **Show Keyframes** button at the top of the panel. Also click the triangle to the left of the **Motion** property to reveal the motion details control panel. Move the current time indicator (CTI) on the **Properties** timeline to approximately the point you want your motion path to begin.

Click the stopwatch icon to the right of the **Motion** property title. A column of small diamonds appears on the timeline to the right of the **Motion** details. These are the opening keyframes for your motion path.

3 Adjust the Keyframe's Settings

As long as the CTI remains at the position of the newly created keyframe points, you can continue to tweak their settings.

You can change the **Position** and **Scale** settings several ways:

- Type new coordinates or percentages
- Drag across the numerical settings so they increase or decrease; watch the effect in the **Monitor** panel
- Click the image in the **Monitor** panel and drag it to a new position or resize it by pulling the corner handles

In this example, I began with a wider shot of the wedding photo, using **Position** settings of **367×330** and a **Scale** of **177%**. (Naturally, I made sure that my photo had enough resolution to allow for this much scaling.)

4 Position the Second Keyframe Points

Move the CTI to the approximate position where you'd like your motion path to change directions.

Change the **Position** and/or **Scale** settings. As you do, new keyframe points are automatically created for those settings at the CTI's current position.

In this example, I set the second set of keyframes to a **Position** of **350×378** and a **Scale** of **318%**—a close-up of the bride and groom's faces.

Premiere Elements will create a smooth path between these two keyframe points. In this example, the clip begins with a wide shot of the entire wedding party and then slowly zooms into a tight shot of just the bride and groom.

70

▶ **NOTE**

As long as the current time indicator (CTI) remains in position, you can tweak your newly created keyframe point's settings. It's only after the CTI is repositioned that the settings become permanently locked to that keyframe point. To change the settings for the keyframe point after moving the CTI, click the left or right arrows to the right of the property in the **Properties** panel. The CTI jumps to the next or previous keyframe point, at which point you can tweak the point's settings.

Just as you can set **Position** values either by changing the property's numerical settings or manipulating the image in the **Monitor** panel, you can set **Scale** and **Rotation** numerically or by clicking the image in the **Monitor** panel and resize or rotate it by dragging the corner handles.

▶ **TIP**

Keyframe points are added only as settings for each individual property changes. It's quite possible for a motion to be created in which one property has several keyframe points while another has one or no keyframe points at all.

5 Tweak the Keyframed Positions

There's no need to create your keyframes in the exact timeline positions you ultimately want them. Positioning them farther apart slows the transition between them. Positioning them closer together speeds the transition. (Also see 71 **Make a Variable-Speed Pan and Zoom**.)

Using the same process you used to create the second keyframe, continue to add a virtually unlimited number of keyframes to a clip, creating custom motion paths or controlling effects as precisely as you desire.

Remember, nothing is permanent in keyframing. And changing a transition or motion path's speed, keyframe points, or even eliminating the keyframe points completely is as simple as moving, revising, or deleting a keyframe point.

71

71	Make a Variable-Speed Pan and Zoom
✔ **BEFORE YOU BEGIN**	→ **SEE ALSO**
22 Prepare a Still for Video	69 Add Motion to a Still
67 About Keyframing	70 Pan and Zoom Still Images a la Ken Burns
68 About the Properties Panel	73 Control Volume at Specific Points

1 Right-click a Keyframe Point

2 Select Bézier Speed Variation

3 Access the Timeline's Keyframe Controls

4 Adjust the Bézier Curves

71 Make a Variable-Speed Pan and Zoom

The basic tools of keyframing allow you to create a simple path of motion around your still photos and graphics. However, there are times when you also want to vary the speed of that motion. Premiere Elements provides several options for varying speed of motion along a path.

You'll find instructions for creating a simple motion using presets in **69** **Add Motion to a Still** or a more complicated motion path using your own keyframe points in **70** **Pan and Zoom Still Images a la Ken Burns**.

After you've clicked to select the clip in the main **Timeline**, open the **Properties** panel and, if the **Properties** timeline is hidden, click the **Show Keyframes** button at the top of the panel. Now you're ready to create a panning or zooming motion that varies its speed across the duration of the clip.

1 Right-click a Keyframe Point

Right-click a keyframe point to open the keyframe general context menu.

By default, the speed of motion from one keyframe point to the next is **Linear**, or constant. In other words, if you were move the CTI to a point halfway between two **Linear** keyframes, you would find that the effect at this point is 50% completed.

2 Select Bézier Speed Variation

The **Spatial Interpolation** options affect the motion of the effect on your image through space. The **Temporal Interpolation** options affect the motion of the effect on your image through time. To change the pan or zoom effect so it varies over time, select the **Temporal Interpolation** option from the context menu you opened in step 1. A submenu of time-based options appears.

The **Linear** option makes the speed of the motion constant; **Ease In** is a *Bézier* preset in which the motion begins slowly and speeds up as it approaches the next keyframe; **Ease Out** is a Bézier preset that begins quickly but slows as it approaches the next keyframe; the **Hold** option holds the keyframe's position until the next keyframe; the **Auto Bézier**, **Bézier**, and **Continuous Bézier** options allow you to manipulate curves to control speed throughout the path or transition.

Choose the **Bézier** motion option and notice that the shape of the keyframe in the main **Timeline** changes from a straight line into a curved figure.

▶ KEY TERM

Bézier—A system for controlling a curve's shape by manipulating handles at the end points of the curve.

3 Access the Timeline's Keyframe Controls

Click the **More** button in the **Timeline** panel and select **Track Size/Large** to give yourself better access to the keyframe controls.

Right-click the clip on the **Timeline** and, from the context menu that appears, choose **Show Clip Keyframes** and then choose the effect whose keyframes you want to control (in this case, **Motion: Position**).

4 Adjust the Bézier Curves

By manipulating the control handles on the Bézier curve in the **Timeline**, adjust the curve of motion or transition to your preference. The shape of the curve represents the variations of the speed of the motion between the

71

keyframes, with the lowest portions of the curve representing slowest motion and the highest portions of the curve representing the fastest motion.

The **Bézier** curve in this example produces a movement between my **Position** settings that is slow in movement to about the three-second point, then increases in speed as it approached the second keyframe. (**Bézier** settings are a rather high-level concept, so you might want to experiment to develop a feel for how the various settings affect the results.)

72   Control a Video Track's Opacity over Time

✔ BEFORE YOU BEGIN	→ SEE ALSO
67 About Keyframing	69 Add Motion to a Still
68 About the Properties Panel	70 Pan and Zoom Still Images a la Ken Burns
	73 Control Volume at Specific Points

71

Just as you can map motion to specific points in a clip using keyframing, you can map other effects and properties (such as **Image Control** and **Opacity**) to specific points in a clip.

In 67 **About Keyframing,** we demonstrate that the automatic video **Fade In** and **Fade Out** effects are actually keyframed effects. Creating such an effect from scratch is also easy, the result being the video equivalent of the audio fade effect created in 73 **Control Volume at Specific Points.**

1 Select a Clip on the Timeline

Click to select a video clip on the main **Timeline.** If you have clips on more than one track and you want to adjust the opacity for one clip so another clip shows through the first clip, arrange the clips in the tracks so the clip to adjust is on an upper track and the clip you want to show through is on a lower track.

The **Properties** panel shows the standard properties of **Image Control, Motion,** and **Opacity** (see 68 **About the Properties Panel**). If the **Properties** panel timeline isn't visible, click the **Show Keyframes** button at the top of the panel to reveal the timeline. Also click the triangle to the left of the **Opacity** property to reveal its detail settings.

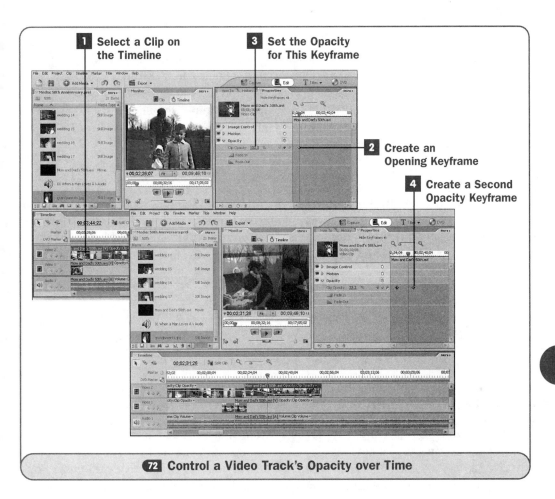

72 Control a Video Track's Opacity over Time

▶ NOTE

The **Opacity** settings affect the transparency of a clip in your **Timeline**. If nothing is on the video track below the affected clip, making your clip transparent reveals the black background. If a clip does exist on the video track below the clip you're affecting, reducing the clip's **Opacity** reveals the clip on the track below.

2 Create an Opening Keyframe

Move the current time indicator (CTI) on the **Properties** timeline to the beginning of the timeline and click the stopwatch icon to the right of the **Opacity** label. A second hand appears on the stopwatch icon, indicating that the property is keyframed, and a keyframe point for the **Opacity** setting appears at the CTI on the timeline.

3 Set the Opacity for This Keyframe

As long as the CTI remains in position, you can adjust the settings for the current keyframe points. (Move the CTI to apply the current settings and create another set of keyframe points.) Set the **Opacity** value for the first keyframe point to 100%. The selected clip (for example, the clip on the Video 2 track), is displayed in the **Monitor** panel and the clip on the Video 1 track (the lower track) is not visible.

4 Create a Second Opacity Keyframe

Move the CTI to the right some distance and set the **Opacity** value for this point to **0%**. A keyframe point is automatically added at the CTI as you change the **Opacity** settings for this clip. (You can reposition the keyframe point on the **Properties** panel timeline if you later decide to do so.)

In the **Monitor** panel, you'll see that the clip has become transparent, revealing the clip on the Video 1 track. (If there is no clip on a lower track, the black background shows through the selected clip.) As you scrub between the two points or play the clip, notice that Premiere Elements has filled in the transitional frames, creating essentially a dissolve from the clip on Video 2 to the clip on Video 1.

72

Creating additional keyframe points, you can continue to control the opacity of the clip at various points.

Any audio or video property can be keyframed to transition in this way. And, just as you can add motion to a still image by setting keyframe points (see **70** Pan and Zoom Still Images a la Ken Burns), you can morph nearly all the effects and image adjustments by modifying the effect's keyframe settings.

---

73 Control Volume at Specific Points

✔ BEFORE YOU BEGIN	→ SEE ALSO
47 Add an Audio Transition	**70** Pan and Zoom Still Images a la Ken Burns
67 About Keyframing	
68 About the Properties Panel	

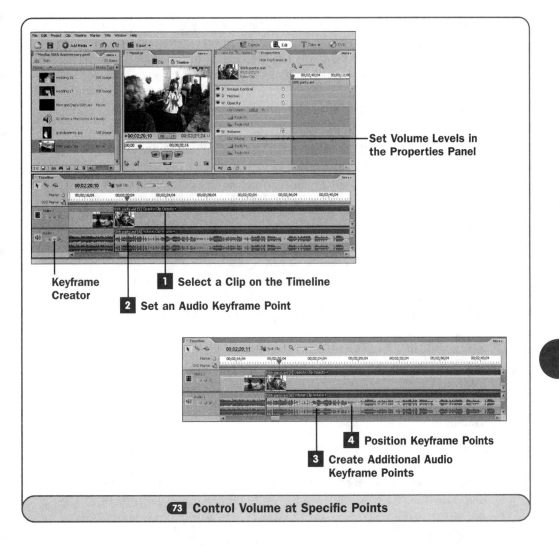

Set Volume Levels in the Properties Panel

Keyframe Creator

1 Select a Clip on the Timeline

2 Set an Audio Keyframe Point

73

4 Position Keyframe Points

3 Create Additional Audio Keyframe Points

73 Control Volume at Specific Points

Unfortunately, some people speak too quietly on camera, and you need to bring up the audio on your video so you can hear them. Others speak louder than anyone else in the scene, and you need to bring down their audio to make the sound levels more even. And sometimes you just want to lower or completely mute the volume on a clip so an alternate track of music or narration can dominate.

Fortunately, Premiere Elements's keyframing tool allows you to easily set the audio levels at specific points on your **Timeline**—points you can also easily revise, move, or remove. (Note that the effect described in **47** **Add an Audio Transition** is essentially a keyframed preset that fades the audio in or out.)

1 Select a Clip on the Timeline

Click an audio or a video clip on the main **Timeline**. In the **Properties** panel, you'll see the standard properties of **Image Control**, **Motion**, **Opacity**, and **Volume** if you selected a video clip; if you selected an audio clip, the only property in the **Properties** panel is **Volume**. For this task, we will be concerned with only the **Volume** property of the clip you've selected.

When using keyframing in audio, it's worth noting that the same principles apply to audio keyframing as apply to video keyframing—namely that you set specific points on the timeline at which you want certain effects to occur. (See **67** **About Keyframing**.) With audio levels, however, your main concern is not so much setting up keyframes for effects (although that is also possible) but with setting your audio volume to raise or lower at specific points.

73

2 Set an Audio Keyframe Point

Although you can set your keyframe points in the **Properties** panel, as you would with a video effect or movement, it is usually easier, and more intuitive, to set audio keyframe points right in the audio track on the main **Timeline**.

After you've selected a video clip with an audio track, the keyframe creator (the little diamond next to the audio track's name on the left end of the **Timeline**) becomes activated. Click the little diamond in this control panel and a keyframe point appears on the yellow line that runs horizontally through the audio track of your clip at the position of the current time indicator (CTI).

This yellow line represents the clip's audio level. By raising and lowering it, you can raise or lower the audio level of the clip. By placing keyframe points on this line, you can raise or lower the levels of *specific points* on the clip.

For this example, I wanted the audio for the clip to start at its default level (the level I recorded when I shot the video with my camcorder) and then increase slightly for about three seconds to compensate for some dialog recorded at a low volume before tapering off again for another four seconds when the sound level on my audio track gets louder than I'd prefer. About 9 seconds into the video clip, I want the volume level to again return to the default level. I'll set keyframe points at roughly the 3-second, 7-second, and 9-second positions on the **Timeline**.

▶ **NOTE**

The yellow, horizontal line that runs through every audio clip is, by default, a volume level control. Without a keyframe point, you can raise or lower the volume of an entire clip by raising or lowering this line in the track.

3 Create Additional Audio Keyframe Points

To create another audio keyframe point, move the CTI on the main **Timeline** to the right and click the audio keyframe creator (the little diamond on the left end of the audio track) again.

You need not create your keyframe points at the exact positions you want them. You can move them around and adjust their levels later as needed.

▶ **NOTE**

Although most people find it easier to set audio keyframe points right in the **Timeline** panel, you can also do so on the **Properties** panel timeline, where volume levels for each keyframe point can be set numerically or by using the slider control.

4 Position Keyframe Points

Drag the CTI back to the beginning of your clip and click the Play button on the **Monitor** panel. Listen to your clip or, better yet, open the **Audio Meters** panel (choose **Window, Audio Meters** to display it) and watch the audio levels. Pause your playback when you reach a spot where you want to raise or lower the audio level for the clip.

The higher you drag the keyframe point, the louder the track plays. The lower you drag the keyframe point, the lower the track plays. To sustain an increased or decreased level, position a keyframe at the beginning and end of the section you want to affect and make sure that the keyframe points are exactly opposite each other on the yellow volume control line (at the level you want to sustain).

Continue to add and position keyframes as necessary to vary the clip's volume as desired.

▶ **NOTES**

You might find it easier to position the keyframed audio levels if you expand the height of the audio track. To do this, mouse over the seam between two audio tracks on the left side of the **Timeline** panel until the mouse pointer becomes a double-horizontal line. Click and drag the audio track to whatever height with which you find it easiest to work.

You can also set the height of the tracks on the **Timeline** by clicking the **Timeline** panel's **More** button and choosing the track size from the menu.

73

11

Special Effects

IN THIS CHAPTER:

Adding special effects to your video project is both fun and easy using Premiere Elements. Premiere Elements offers a variety of professional-level effects for adjusting your image and sound as well as a variety of cool, instant effects for adding lightning bolts, strobes, and picture-in-picture effects, each one infinitely customizable.

---

74   About Advanced Effects

✔ SEE ALSO

33 Add or Move a Clip on the Timeline
61 Add and Customize an Effect
63 Reset or Remove an Effect
65 Create and Save a Preset
67 About Keyframing

74

Premiere Elements offers dozens of professional-level, customizable, and easy-to-use video effects. They're all located in the **Effects and Transitions** panel in the **Video FX** collection (click the **Video FX** button at the top of the panel to open the collection). Within the collection are several categories that help organize the effects. Click the arrow next to a category name to see thumbnails of the effects contained within that category.

Another quick way to find any effect in the **Effects and Transitions** panel is to type its name in the blank space next to the binocular icon. As you type, Premiere Elements automatically locates all effects that match the characters you're typing.

In the **Video FX** collection, you'll find tools for creating a picture-in-picture effect; a **Chroma Key** tool for replacing the background of one video clip with that of another; many color and surreal video effects, controls for manipulating your screen image in 3D; and special tools for creating lightning bolts, a strobe light effect, and a lens flare.

▶ **NOTE**

With few exceptions, you can pile multiple effects onto a single clip. However, the effects are applied in the order they are listed in the **Properties** panel; rearranging the order of the effects in the list can produce very different results.

Premiere Elements's keyframing tool makes these effects even more powerful, giving you the ability to control the intensity of these effects over the duration of the clips and even isolate the effect to one portion of your video, tracking with the action.

*The **Effects and Transitions** panel offers thumbnail previews of all the effects and transitions.*

In addition to the **Video FX** collection, Premiere Elements offers a host of **Audio FX**, which are detailed in **66** **Enhance Audio with Advanced Effects**.

Not all effects immediately change your clip when you drag them from the **Effects and Transitions** panel and drop them on the clip. Many effects simply provide you with a control panel you can use to create the effect, as explained in **61** **Add and Customize an Effect**.

The following categories of effects are located in the **Video FX** collection; many of the individual effects contained in these categories are also represented as presets:

- **Adjust**—This category of effects can be used to adjust or correct the color, brightness, and contrast of your clip.

- **Blur & Sharpen**—Most of the effects in this category sharpen the color breaks in your clips, giving the appearance of clarifying or sharpening focus—sometimes to an exaggerated degree. Additionally, a special effect called **Ghosting** in this collection can be used to create repeated frames in your video, something back in the 1970s was called "making trails."

- **Channel**—The **Invert** effect in this collection creates a negative of your screen image, with several variations available.

- **Distort**—This category of effects can be used to distort, reshape, or swirl your screen image to create a mirror effect or to turn your video into waves of color. The **Polar Coordinates** effect can be used to create some strange and difficult-to-predict color effects.

74

- **Image Control**—Effects in this collection can be used to control or filter the color tone, saturation, or brightness of your clip.

- **Keying**—Keying an effect designates a portion of your clip as transparent based on color values or alpha, revealing through this area the clip(s) on the track(s) below. We put the **Chromakey** effect to work in **76** **Make an Area of a Clip Transparent**, **88** **Make a Person Appear with a Different Background**, and **90** **Make a Person Appear to Fly**. The **Track Matte** effect appears in **92** **Blur an Isolated Spot on a Video Clip a la** *Cops*.

- **Perspective**—This category of effects can be used to manipulate your screen image as if it existed in three-dimensional space.

- **Pixelate**—The **Facet** effect groups the pixels that make up your image into various levels of block patterns. You use this effect to distort a portion of a screen image in **92** **Blur an Isolated Spot on a Video Clip a la** *Cops*.

- **Render**—This powerful collection of effects actually draws on or adds elements to your clips, including a **Lens Flare** and very cool **Lightning** bolts. (See **80** **Add a Lightning Bolt Effect**.)

- **Stylize**—Many of the special effects in this category can be used to produce somewhat surreal results, including a **Strobe Light** effect (which is used in **79** **Add a Strobe Effect**).

- **Time**—The effects in this category change your clip, as the category name implies, over time. The **Posterize Time** effect, for instance, allows you to change the frame rate of your video.

- **Transform**—The **Transform** category contains effects that allow you to **Crop** your clip, produce an **Edge Feather**, as well as repeat your screen image several times and roll these images across the screen. The **Camera View** effect is used in **65** **Create and Save a Preset**.

74

75 Control a Video Effect with Keyframes

✔ BEFORE YOU BEGIN	→ SEE ALSO
33 Add or Move a Clip on the Timeline	**43** About Rendering the Timeline
61 Add and Customize an Effect	**63** Reset or Remove an Effect
67 About Keyframing	**65** Create and Save a Preset
68 About the Properties Panel	**71** Make a Variable-Speed Pan and Zoom
74 About Advanced Effects	

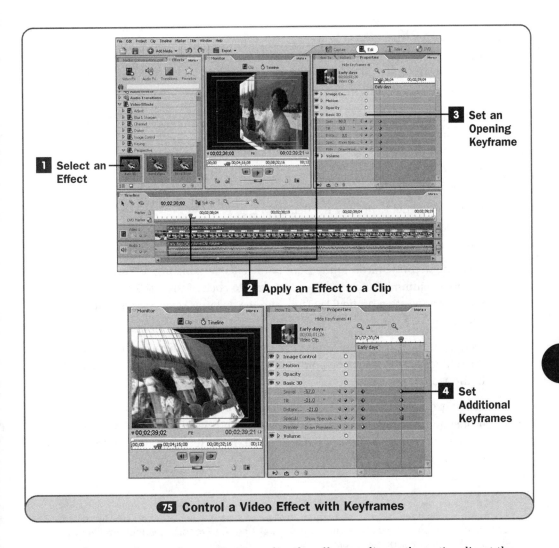

1 Select an Effect

3 Set an Opening Keyframe

2 Apply an Effect to a Clip

4 Set Additional Keyframes

75

75 Control a Video Effect with Keyframes

When you first apply an effect to a clip, the effect applies to the entire clip at the same level. By using keyframing, however, you can control how the effect is applied and when it is applied at what level. With keyframing, you lock the effect's settings to various points on the **Timeline**, and Premiere Elements creates the transition between the points.

1 Select an Effect

Select an effect from the **Effects and Transitions** panel. As you browse each collection (**Video FX, Audio FX,** and **Transitions**) and the categories within each collection, notice that each effect is displayed as a thumbnail preview.

2 Apply an Effect to a Clip

Drag the effect you want to apply from the **Effects and Transitions** panel onto a clip on the **Timeline**. The effect also appears in the **Properties** panel, where you can control the settings for the effect.

With many effects, a change in the clip is not immediately apparent until you adjust the effect's properties.

3 Set an Opening Keyframe

With the clip selected, click the triangle to the left of the effect name in the **Properties** panel to display the details of that effect. If the **Properties** panel timeline is not visible, click the **Show Keyframes** button at the top of the panel.

Click the stopwatch icon to the right of the effect's name in the **Properties** panel. A column of diamonds appears next to each of the effect's controls at the current position of the CTI. These are the opening keyframes of your effect.

As long as the CTI remains in its current position, you can adjust and tweak the settings for the keyframe points. The results of your settings are displayed in the **Monitor** panel.

In this example of the **Basic 3D** effect, I adjusted the **Swivel** setting to **60** degrees to make my clip appear as if it were being viewed in three-dimensional space from the side. I also could have tilted it, made it appear to be farther away, or even added a **Specular Highlight** to it.

▶ NOTE

Keyframe points don't have to be created in their final positions. After you set them, you can slide the keyframe points to different positions on the **Properties** panel timeline to achieve the effect you're going for.

4 Set Additional Keyframes

Move the CTI down the **Properties** panel timeline and adjust the settings for this new position. Keyframe points are automatically created along the CTI when you change any of the settings.

For this example, I made changes to virtually every **Basic 3D** setting including **Swivel**, **Tilt**, and **Distance**, and I even added a **Specular Highlight** to make it appear that a light source was passing over the clip. The result, after Premiere Elements generates the frames between these keyframes, will be as though my screen image is floating and turning through space.

75

Continue creating keyframe points as needed to continue the movement or transition. Adjusting the position of the keyframe points on the **Properties** timeline controls the speed of the transition between keyframes. You can also *vary* the speed of the transition between the keyframes using Bézier curves, as explained in **71** **Make a Variable-Speed Pan and Zoom**.

As you add effects to a clip, you might notice that playback seems stilted or the quality of the image seems to have deteriorated. Also notice that a red bar appears on the **Timeline** above the affected clip. This lower-quality playback happens because your computer performs a soft render of the effect, created on-the-fly as you play your clip. To see a better representation of what your clip will ultimately look like, render it by pressing the **Enter** key. After your clip is rendered, the red bar above the clip turns green.

---

76 Make an Area of a Clip Transparent

✔ BEFORE YOU BEGIN	→ SEE ALSO
22 Prepare a Still for Video	**63** Reset or Remove an Effect
29 About the Timeline and Video Tracks	**85** Move a Car Across a Map
68 About the Properties Panel	**88** Make a Person Appear with a Different Background
74 About Advanced Effects	**89** Make a Person Appear to Be Miniaturized
	90 Make a Person Appear to Fly

76

Keying means making an area of a clip transparent based on its color values. **Chroma Key** is a more general version of the same effect that appears as the **Blue Screen Key**, the **Green Screen Key**, and the **Non-Red Key** effects (the latter effects are preset to certain commonly used key colors, while the **Chroma Key** effect can be set to *any* color).

The **Chroma Key** effect tells Premiere Elements to treat a color or a range of colors in your clip as transparent, revealing a clip or clips on the tracks below through the transparent area.

▶ **NOTE**

The **Chroma Key** effect is the most general of several Key effects, all of which accomplish the task of designating a color or range of colors on a clip as transparent. The **Green Screen Key**, **Blue Screen Key**, and **Non-Red Screen Key** effects are basically the same as the **Chroma Key** effect, although the former effects are prekeyed to certain commonly used color ranges. Green and blue are the most commonly used Key colors—they are used in virtually all television and feature film effects shots—because they are not found in human flesh tones and therefore their effect can be isolated to certain intentionally colored areas of the screen image.

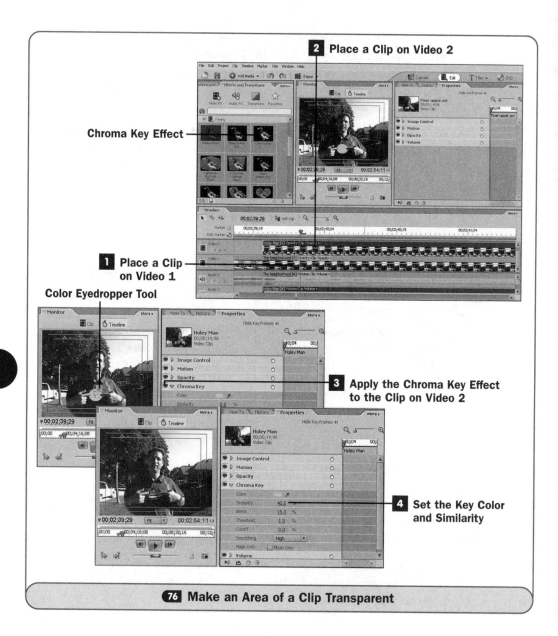

2 Place a Clip on Video 2

Chroma Key Effect

1 Place a Clip on Video 1

Color Eyedropper Tool

3 Apply the Chroma Key Effect to the Clip on Video 2

4 Set the Key Color and Similarity

76 Make an Area of a Clip Transparent

1 Place a Clip on Video 1

Place a clip on the Video 1 track. Because this clip appears on the lower track, it is the clip that will be revealed through the transparent areas of the clip on Video 2. The clip you place on Video 2 should include the background you want to show through your keyed clip.

2 Place a Clip on Video 2

Because of the way the **Chroma Key** effect works, it's best to select as your foreground video a clip that has an area of flat color—such as a blue or green screen or the purple side of a barn, or a red velvet curtain—and this color should appear only in the area you want to make transparent.

In this example, I posed the man in my video clip holding a bright-green circle against his chest. I was careful to choose the material for this circle (a smoothly-colored piece of paper) in a shade of green that did not appear anywhere else in the shot. My intent is to key the green circle so a video clip on a lower track can show through it, making it look as though the man is holding a moving picture between his fingers.

Place this clip on the Video 2 track, directly above the clip you placed on the Timeline in step 1.

3 Apply the Chroma Key Effect to the Clip on Video 2

Open the **Effects and Transitions** panel and click the **Video FX** button. Scroll to find the **Keying** category and look for the **Chroma Key** effect.

Drag this effect to the clip on Video 2. The **Chroma Key** effect is added to the list in the clip's **Properties** panel. Click the triangle to the left of the **Chroma Key** name in the **Properties** panel to open the effect's control panel.

4 Set the Key Color and Similarity

Although you can set the Key color using the color panel, it's usually easier to use your screen image to designate the Key color. Click the **Color** eyedropper icon in the Properties panel; the mouse pointer becomes an eyedropper. Now click the color in the image in the **Monitor** panel that you want to designate as transparent. In this example, I clicked the green circle held against the man's chest.

You'll see an effect immediately: The clip on Video 1 is revealed through the area of the clip on Video 2 that you just keyed. Unless your clip has an absolutely flat area of color with no color variations (as was the case in this example), you'll probably have to adjust the **Similarity** setting (which widens the range of color to be affected) to get a good, clean, transparent area. For example, if you have a video of a man wearing a yellow shirt, and want to make the shirt transparent to reveal a video of a woman and child (so that it looks as if the shirt is made of a moving video), adjust the **Similarity** setting in the **Properties** panel to select all of the varieties of yellow in the man's shirt. The higher the **Similarity** setting, the more shades of yellow will be selected.

76

The **Blend**, **Threshold**, **Cutoff**, and **Smoothing** settings in the Properties panel also help you control transparency and the softness of the transparent area's edge.

When adjusting your key settings, you might find it helpful to turn on the **Mask Only** option. This option temporarily masks the areas that will *not* be keyed out, revealing only the transparent portions of your screen image. When you have a good, clean **Chroma Key** set up, uncheck the **Mask Only** option to return to normal view.

The end result, in my example, is that you can now see the clip which was on a lower video track through this keyed, or transparent, area. And because the clip on the lower track was of the scenery behind the man in my shot, the illusion is that you can actually see through a round hole in the man's chest!

▶ **TIP**

For some illusions, you might want to resize or reposition the clip on the lower track so that it "fits" in the keyed area of the top track. See **23** Scale and Position a Still for more information.

76

77 | **Create a Picture-in-Picture Effect**

✔ **BEFORE YOU BEGIN**	→ **SEE ALSO**
29 About the Timeline and Video Tracks	**63** Reset or Remove an Effect
33 Add or Move a Clip on the Timeline	**65** Create and Save a Preset
58 About Preset Effects	**67** About Keyframing
61 Add and Customize an Effect	**71** Make a Variable-Speed Pan and Zoom
74 About Advanced Effects	**75** Control a Video Effect with Keyframes

Although you can manually create a picture-in-picture effect by scaling one clip to a portion of your video frame to reveal a second clip on the video track below it, Premiere Elements offers a large variety of Picture-in-Picture (or **PiP**) presets that you can easily apply and adjust as needed.

Technically, PiPs are not effects unto themselves. That's why they show up in the **Presets** collection rather than among the **Video FX**. They are, in fact, presets for **Scale** and **Position** (sometimes the effect applies itself to more than one video track at the same time). If you select a clip that has had a **PiP** preset applied to it, you will not see **PiP** listed in the **Properties** panel. To see the settings for the PiP, open the control panel for the **Motion** property.

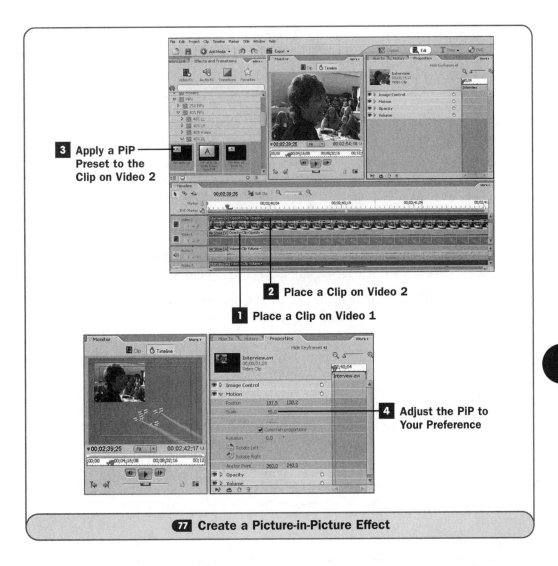

3 Apply a PiP Preset to the Clip on Video 2

2 Place a Clip on Video 2

1 Place a Clip on Video 1

4 Adjust the PiP to Your Preference

77 Create a Picture-in-Picture Effect

77

1 Place a Clip on Video 1

Video 1 is the bottom video track, so the clip you place on this track should be the clip you plan to use as your full-screen, background video.

2 Place a Clip on Video 2

Place a second clip—the one that will serve as your picture-in-picture—on the Video 2 track, directly above the clip you've placed on Video 1.

③ Apply a PiP Preset to the Clip on Video 2

The **PiP** category is located in the **Effects and Transitions** panel in the **Video FX** collection. The **PiP** category contains 180 picture-in-picture variations, divided into two subcategories: **25% PiPs** (in which the picture-in-picture is 25% of the size of the video frame), and **40% PiPs**, in which the picture-in-picture is 40% of the size of the video frame. Each of these subcategories is further divided into groupings based on the quadrant in which the effect appears in the video frame: upper-left (**UL**), lower-left (**LL**), upper-right (**UR**), and lower-right (**LR**). Also included is a **Motion** group, in which the picture-in-picture migrates around the video frame. Each of these quadrant groupings offers both a stationary position and several transitional or moving versions.

The **PiPs**, like all effects and transitions in the panel, are displayed as thumbnails. Click any effect to see an animated preview of its movement.

Drag the PiP you want to apply—or one that is close to what you'd like—onto the clip on Video 2. Immediately, you'll see the result displayed in the **Monitor** panel.

77

④ Adjust the PiP to Your Preference

If the PiP preset isn't quite what you'd like, you can easily tweak it. With the affected clip selected, click the triangle to the left of the **Motion** property in the **Properties** panel to reveal the detail settings for that property. Adjust the **Scale** and **Position** settings as needed (see **68** **About the Properties Panel**).

For best results, turn on your **Safe Margins** (click the **More** button in the **Monitor** panel), to ensure that you don't position your picture-in-picture too close to the edge of the TV screen. (See **20** **About the Monitor Panel**.)

▶ TIP

After you begin applying effects to your clip, you'll find that the quality of the image in your playback has apparently deteriorated. On slower computers, playback might even seem jumpy or irregular. This is because your computer is creating a soft render of the clip on the fly. Also notice that the affected clip is marked by a red line above the clip on the **Timeline**. To see a better example of what your clip will look like on final output, press **Enter** to render the **Timeline**. The red line above the clip turns green when rendering is complete, and the quality of your playback will be an accurate representation of what your final output will look like.

78   Add a Lens Flare

✔ BEFORE YOU BEGIN	→ SEE ALSO
33 Add or Move a Clip on the Timeline **61** Add and Customize an Effect **68** About the Properties Panel **74** About Advanced Effects	**63** Reset or Remove an Effect

The **Lens Flare** effect can add interest to a video clip, particularly when used in conjunction with another effect. Keyframing a lens flare can add excitement to a 3D movement, such as the **Camera View** effect—the flare can appear as a brief highlight on a rotating graphic or can track with another effect's motion. The **Lens Flare** effect can also be used to highlight, or draw attention to, an area of your clip, like the sparkle of a shiny object or the flash of a knife blade.

▶ **TIP**

To make the **Lens Flare** effect appear for only a moment, zoom into the **Timeline** (press the + key) and use the **Split Clip** tool described in **36** Split a Clip to slice your clip. Nudge the CTI about five frames to the right and slice the clip again, creating a tiny, isolated segment of the original clip. Apply the **Lens Flare** effect to this segment. Your clip will still play seamless over the slices, but the flash of light will appear for only those few, isolated frames. (Unfortunately, although you can use keyframes to move or temporarily brighten a **Lens Flare** effect, you can't use them to make the **Lens Flare** suddenly appear and then disappear; for that, you must split the clip.)

The **Lens Flare** effect is one of three effects categorized as **Render** effects. This means that, rather than merely affecting the screen image, they actually render, or add, something to the screen image that wasn't there before (see **80** Add a Lightning Bolt Effect).

You can add several copies of the **Lens Flare** effect to a clip, by the way, with the result being as if many lights or stars were shining into the camera lens while you were filming.

1   Drag the Lens Flare Effect on to a Clip

The **Lens Flare** effect is located on the **Effects and Transitions** panel in the **Render** category of the **Video FX** collection. The flare appears in a default position on the screen image in the **Monitor** panel. Drag the effect from the **Effects and Transitions** panel to the clip in the **Timeline**.

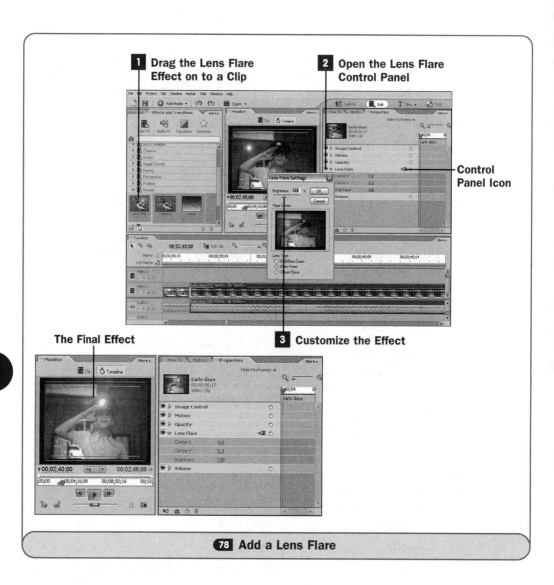

1 Drag the Lens Flare Effect on to a Clip

2 Open the Lens Flare Control Panel

Control Panel Icon

The Final Effect

3 Customize the Effect

78 Add a Lens Flare

2 Open the Lens Flare Control Panel

With the clip selected, click the triangle to the left of the **Lens Flare** listing in the **Properties** panel to access the control panel for the effect.

Click the control panel icon to the right of the effect's name to open a dialog box that offers several settings and a preview of your affected screen image.

3 Customize the Effect

Different lens settings create a wider and softer or smaller and more intense flare. Experiment with the settings to see which combination provides the best visual effect for your clip. To position the lens flare where you want it in the clip, click in the preview pane in the **Lens Flare Settings** dialog box and drag the flare to whatever position you'd prefer.

You can also keyframe the lens flare effect to track with an image, as explained in **75** **Control a Video Effect with Keyframes**.

▶ **TIP**

After you begin applying effects to your clip, you'll find that the quality of the image in your playback has apparently deteriorated. On slower computers, playback might even seem jumpy or irregular. This is because your computer is creating a soft render of the clip on-the-fly. Also notice that the affected clip is marked by a red line above the clip on the **Timeline**. To see a better example of what your clip will look like on final output, press **Enter** to render the **Timeline**. The red line above the clip turns green when rendering is complete, and the quality of your playback will be an accurate representation of what your final output will look like.

---

79 **Add a Strobe Effect**

✔ BEFORE YOU BEGIN	→ SEE ALSO
33 Add or Move a Clip on the Timeline	**63** Reset or Remove an Effect
61 Add and Customize an Effect	**65** Create and Save a Preset
68 About the Properties Panel	**67** About Keyframing
74 About Advanced Effects	**71** Make a Variable-Speed Pan and Zoom
	75 Control a Video Effect with Keyframes

79

Premiere Elements makes it easy to add and customize a strobe effect to your video clip. The **Strobe Light** effect adds a flash of white (or whatever color you designate) at regular intervals to your clip.

1 **Drag the Strobe Light Effect on to a Clip**

The **Strobe Light** effect is found on-the-**Effects and Transitions** panel, in the **Stylize** category of the **Video FX** collection. Drag this effect from the **Effects and Transitions** panel and drop it on a clip in the **Timeline**.

Applying this effect to a clip gives you a flashing strobe effect at the default settings.

2 **Open the Strobe Light Control Panel**

With the clip selected, click the triangle to the left of the **Strobe Light** listing in the **Properties** panel to reveal the effect's control panel.

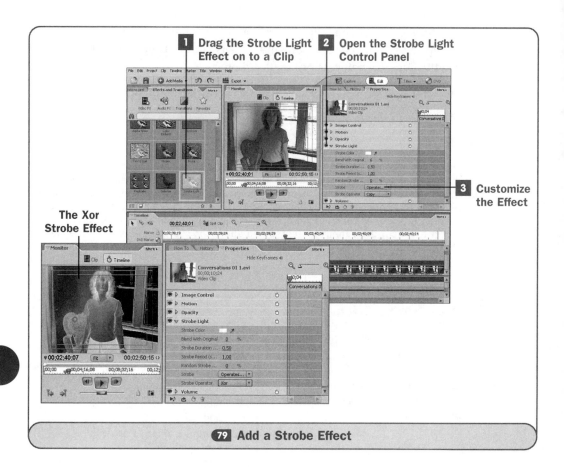

1 Drag the Strobe Light Effect on to a Clip

2 Open the Strobe Light Control Panel

3 Customize the Effect

The Xor Strobe Effect

79 Add a Strobe Effect

3 Customize the Effect

The control panel enables you to set the color of the flash, its duration, its period (rate), an option for blending it with the original image, and an option to randomize the timing of the flashes.

You will also find an additional **Strobe** option for making the clip transparent rather than introducing a flash of color at regular intervals (a particularly interesting effect if you have another clip on the video track below the strobe-affected clip). You set this effect by choosing **Strobe Makes Layer Transparent** from the **Strobe** drop-down list.

You might also want to experiment with the **Strobe Operator** settings, which perform calculations on the colors in the clip to create different effects. The **Xor** option pops in a negative of the screen image rather than a white or colored flash at regular intervals.

▶ **TIP**

After you begin applying effects to your clip, you'll find that the quality of the image in your playback has apparently deteriorated. On slower computers, playback might even seem jumpy or irregular. This is because your computer is creating a soft render of the clip on-the-fly. Also notice that the affected clip is marked by a red line above the clip on the **Timeline**. To see a better example of what your clip will look like on final output, press **Enter** to render the **Timeline**. The red line above the clip turns green when rendering is complete, and the quality of your playback will be an accurate representation of what your final output will look like.

80 Add a Lightning Bolt Effect

✔ BEFORE YOU BEGIN	→ SEE ALSO
33 Add or Move a Clip on the Timeline	**63** Reset or Remove an Effect
61 Add and Customize an Effect	**65** Create and Save a Preset
68 About the Properties Panel	**67** About Keyframing
74 About Advanced Effects	**71** Make a Variable-Speed Pan and Zoom
	75 Control a Video Effect with Keyframes

80

The infinitely customizable **Lightning** effect is one of the coolest in the Premiere Elements **Video FX** collection. By adjusting its settings, you can make the effect appear as anything from a single bolt to an elaborate plasma array of Tesla lightning.

You can also use the effect with keyframing to track the endpoints of the lightning with a moving object on screen. For example, you can follow an object as the camera angle changes, show one end of a lightning bolt following a path (as if it were "writing" text in wood, for instance), or even creating the illusion that a person or object is actually carrying the lightning bolts.

The only downside is that it's definitely a resource-intensive effect, and even state-of-the-art computers might have trouble rendering previews on-the-fly. But be patient. The results are well worth it. In fact, it's worth your time to render the clip as you experiment with its settings (press **Enter** to render) so you can see this effect in all its glory as you work.

▶ **TIP**

To make a lightning bolt appear briefly, as if it were a lightning strike, zoom into the **Timeline** (press the + key) and use the **Split Clip** tool as described in **36** Split a Clip to slice your clip at the point at which you want the lightning bolt to begin. Nudge the CTI about half a second to the right and slice the clip again, creating a tiny, isolated segment of the original clip. Apply the **Lightning** effect to this short segment. The clips will still play seamlessly over the slices, but the dancing bolt of lightning will appear for only those few, isolated frames. Add a sound from your own collection to complete the effect!

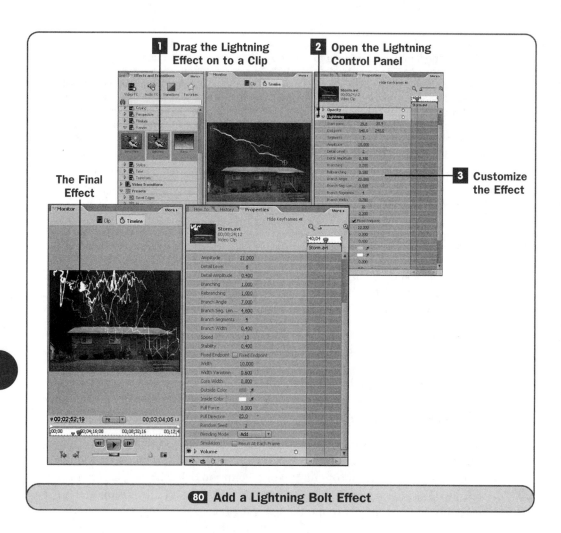

The Final Effect

1 Drag the Lightning Effect on to a Clip

2 Open the Lightning Control Panel

3 Customize the Effect

80 Add a Lightning Bolt Effect

1 Drag the Lightning Effect on to a Clip

The **Lightning** effect is found on the **Effects and Transitions** panel, in the **Render** category of the **Video FX** collection.

Drag the clip from the **Effects and Transitions** panel and drop it on a clip in the **Timeline**. Applying the effect to a clip generates a default lightning array, as you can see in the **Monitor** panel.

2 Open the Lightning Control Panel

With the clip selected, click the triangle to the left of the **Lightning** listing in the **Properties** panel to reveal one of the most powerful control panels in the **Video FX** library.

3 Customize the Effect

The **Lightning** control panel allows you to set the locations of the beginning and end points of the lightning bolt; the number of branches and rebranches; the angle of the branches; the length, width, and flickering speed of the branches; plus options to set a free form (random) endpoint, choose the colors of the lightning branches, specify the pull direction, and choose to have the flickering branches repeat their movements or randomize them.

Experiment with these options to get the lightning effect you're after—or discover an effect you didn't know existed!

You can apply keyframes to the effect to vary the locations of the **Start** and **End Points** over the course of your clip.

▶ TIP

After you begin applying effects to your clip, you'll find that the quality of the image in your playback has apparently deteriorated. On slower computers, playback might even seem jumpy or irregular. This is because your computer is creating a soft render of the clip on-the-fly. Also notice that the affected clip is marked by a red line above the clip on the **Timeline**. To see a better example of what your clip will look like on final output, press **Enter** to render the **Timeline**. The red line above the clip turns green when rendering is complete, and the quality of your playback will be an accurate representation of what your final output will look like.

81

81 Rotate a Clip in 3D

✔ BEFORE YOU BEGIN	→ SEE ALSO
33 Add or Move a Clip on the Timeline	**63** Reset or Remove an Effect
61 Add and Customize an Effect	**67** About Keyframing
68 About the Properties Panel	**71** Make a Variable-Speed Pan and Zoom
74 About Advanced Effects	**75** Control a Video Effect with Keyframes

The **Camera View** effect enables you to treat your screen image as if it were on a flat screen; by controlling its longitude, latitude, and distance, you can make this flat screen appear to rotate in three-dimensional space.

1 Drag the Camera View Effect on to a Clip

The **Camera View** effect is found on the **Effects and Transitions** panel, in the **Transform** category of the **Video FX** collection. Drag the effect from the **Effects and Transitions** panel and drop it on a clip in the **Timeline**. You will not see an immediate change in your clip.

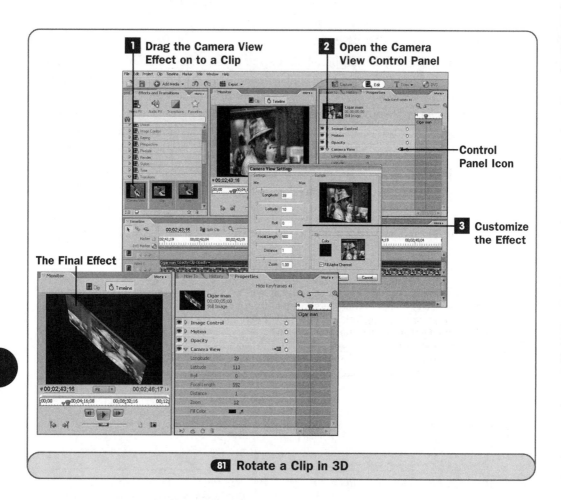

1 Drag the Camera View Effect on to a Clip

2 Open the Camera View Control Panel

Control Panel Icon

3 Customize the Effect

The Final Effect

81 Rotate a Clip in 3D

2 Open the Camera View Control Panel

With the clip selected, click the triangle to the left of the **Camera View** listing in the **Properties** panel to reveal the effect's control panel.

You can also access this effect's controls by clicking the control panel icon to the right of the **Camera View** listing in this panel. The **Camera View Settings** dialog box opens. The controls are exactly the same in the dialog box and the **Properties** panel; only the interface is different. The **Properties** panel settings change numerically while the dialog box settings change with sliders.

▶ **TIP**

Using the **Camera View Settings** dialog box has one advantage over changing the settings in the **Properties** panel—the dialog box allows for the option of filling the alpha channel. With the alpha channel filled, you can designate a color for the background that's revealed as the image rotates. Leaving the alpha channel unfilled makes the background area transparent, revealing whatever clip is on the video track below the effected clip.

3 Customize the Effect

Changing the **Longitude** and **Latitude** settings turns the screen image to the left or right or leans the image forward or backward in space while **Roll** rotates the clip from side to side. The **Focal Length** and **Distance** settings add to the illusion of 3D space by exaggerating the distance between the near and far areas of the screen image; the **Zoom** setting scales your screen image to make it appear nearer or farther away.

In the **Fill** area of the **Camera View Settings** dialog box, enable the **Fill Alpha Channel** check box and click the **Color** swatch to designate a color for the background that's revealed as the image rotates. If you want to make the background transparent so a clip on the video track below is revealed as the image changes shape, disable the **Fill Alpha Channel** check box.

The **Camera View** effect lends itself particularly well to keyframing; setting various positions with keyframes can make your clip appear to tumble through space, as demonstrated in **65 Create and Save a Preset**. A version of it shows up as the **Tumble Away** transition in the **Effects and Transitions** panel, in the **Transitions** collection.

82

▶ **TIP**

Similar to the **Camera View** effect is the **Basic 3D** effect in the **Perspective** category. Although both effects allow you to spin or rotate your clip completely, you might find that the simpler **Basic 3D** effect is much easier to control than the **Camera View** effect.

82 Replace a Color

✔ BEFORE YOU BEGIN	→ SEE ALSO
33 Add or Move a Clip on the Timeline	**63** Reset or Remove an Effect
61 Add and Customize an Effect	**65** Create and Save a Preset
67 About Keyframing	**71** Make a Variable-Speed Pan and Zoom
68 About the Properties Panel	**75** Control a Video Effect with Keyframes
74 About Advanced Effects	

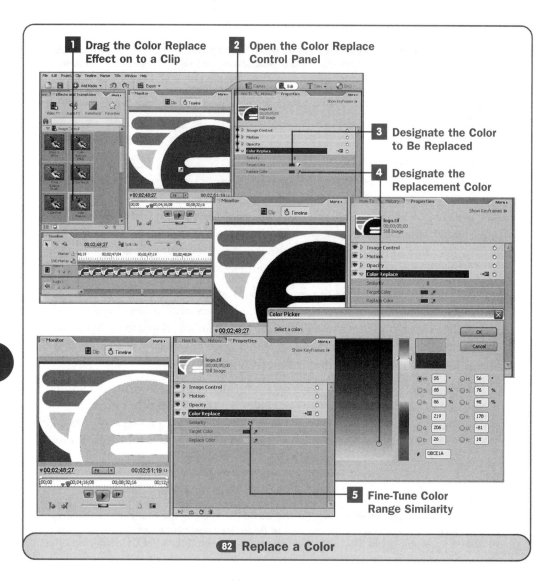

1 Drag the Color Replace Effect on to a Clip

2 Open the Color Replace Control Panel

3 Designate the Color to Be Replaced

4 Designate the Replacement Color

5 Fine-Tune Color Range Similarity

82 Replace a Color

The **Color Replace** effect allows you to select a color or range of colors in your screen image and replace it with a new color you designate—replacing, for instance, a blue area with a red area.

The results of the **Color Replace** effect, however, tend to look rather flat and artificial. For this reason, it is more effective on flat-colored graphics such as company logos and less effective on continuous gradations of color, such as video or photos. If you applied **Color Replace** to a person's shirt, for instance, the result would be that the shirt, with its depth, wrinkles, and shadows, would be replaced with a flat block of color that would look nothing like a shirt.

▶ **TIP**

You can use keyframing, setting points for various replacement colors, to create an interesting effect by having an object's color dissolve into several replacement colors over the course of a clip.

1 Drag the Color Replace Effect on to a Clip

The **Color Replace** effect is located on the **Effects and Transitions** panel, in the **Image Control** category of the **Video FX** collection. Drag the effect from the **Effects and Transitions** panel and drop it on a clip in the **Timeline**. You will not see any immediate change to the clip in the **Monitor** panel.

2 Open the Color Replace Control Panel

With the clip selected, click the triangle to the left of the **Color Replace** listing in the **Properties** panel to reveal the effect's control panel.

3 Designate the Color to Be Replaced

The **Target Color** setting designates which color is to be replaced. Click the eyedropper next to this control; the mouse pointer becomes an eyedropper. Use this eyedropper to click a sample of the color you want to replace in the screen image in the **Monitor** panel.

83

4 Designate the Replacement Color

Click the eyedropper next to the **Replace Color** setting and click in the image in the **Monitor** to select the replacement color. Alternatively, click the white swatch next to the **Replace Color** setting to open the **Color Picker**; select a color from those displayed and click **OK** to designate your replacement color.

5 Fine-Tune Color Range Similarity

By tweaking the **Similarity** setting, you can widen or narrow the **Target Color**'s range of similar colors until you achieve your desired results.

---

83 Morph a Clip into a Painting

✔ BEFORE YOU BEGIN	→ SEE ALSO
21 Grab a Still from Video	**43** About Rendering the Timeline
61 Add and Customize an Effect	**63** Reset or Remove an Effect
67 About Keyframing	**65** Create and Save a Preset
75 Control a Video Effect with Keyframes	**71** Make a Variable-Speed Pan and Zoom

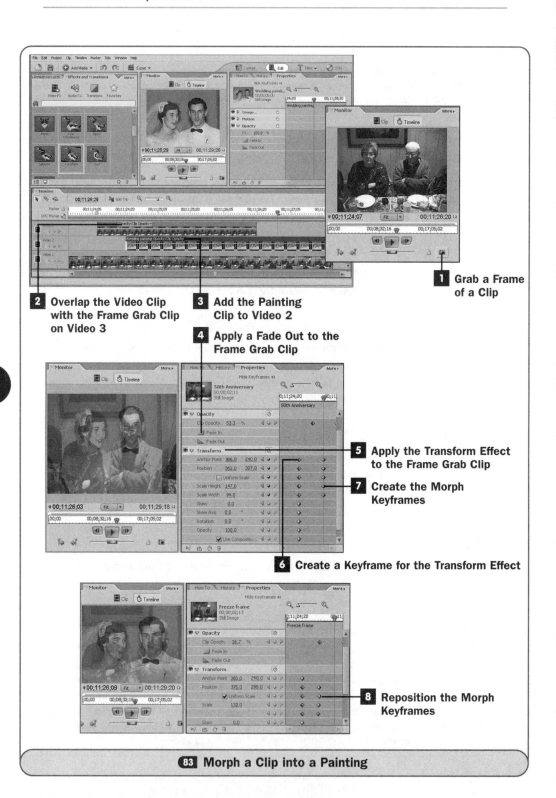

1 Grab a Frame of a Clip

2 Overlap the Video Clip with the Frame Grab Clip on Video 3

3 Add the Painting Clip to Video 2

4 Apply a Fade Out to the Frame Grab Clip

5 Apply the Transform Effect to the Frame Grab Clip

7 Create the Morph Keyframes

6 Create a Keyframe for the Transform Effect

8 Reposition the Morph Keyframes

83 Morph a Clip into a Painting

Morphing live video into a painting or a still using keyframing is a fairly simple effect, but the results can make an interesting statement about the relationship between the clip and the final still image.

There are a number of ways to produce this effect, many of which involve readily available third-party software. This task presents a method that uses effects available in Premiere Elements's **Video FX** collection.

In this version, the resulting sequence will go from a video clip to a freeze frame, which will morph and melt into a painting.

1 Grab a Frame of a Clip

Position the CTI at the point in the clip where you'd like to begin the freeze frame. Click the **Frame Grab** button in the **Monitor** panel as explained in **21** **Grab a Still from Video**. You'll use this frame grab to create a freeze-frame effect for the video clip, and you'll then morph this freeze frame into your painting clip.

Save the still as a JPEG or BMP image file. The still image is automatically added to the **Media** panel.

2 Overlap the Video Clip with the Frame Grab Clip on Video 3

Place the frame grab you created in step 1 on the Video 3 track, partially overlapping the original video clip on Video 1, beginning at the point at which you grabbed the frame. (If you don't move the CTI after you perform the frame grab in step 1, you can use the CTI as a marker to exactly position the frame grab clip.)

▶ **TIP**

Should you need to add more video or audio tracks, do so by dragging a clip into the blank area above or below the existing tracks on the **Timeline** or by selecting **Add Tracks** from the **Timeline** panel's **More** button menu.

Trim the frame-grab clip to about two and one-half seconds by dragging the right end of the clip to the left. (As you drag the end of the clip and then release it, its duration is displayed in the **Properties** panel.) This arrangement will make it appear as though the video has suddenly halted and become a freeze frame.

You might want to continue the audio from the original video clip under this morphing so the freeze frame effect doesn't seem an abrupt halt. Or you can use audio keyframes to slowly fade the audio from the clip, beginning at the point at which the frame grab appears. (See **73** **Control Volume at Specific Points**.)

In this example, I'll be transitioning, by way of the frame grab, out of the video clip showing the couple celebrating their fiftieth anniversary and into a painting of them on their wedding day. Rather than having the audio end abruptly when the frame grab appears, I chose to continue the audio from the anniversary party under the freeze frame, slowly fading out the sound as the painting appears. This arrangement of clips created a more natural transition between the different visual elements.

3   Add the Painting Clip to Video 2

Use a graphics editing program to create a painterly image you can use at the end of the movie. In this example, I took a scan of an old wedding photograph and applied some Photoshop Elements filters to create an image that looked like an oil paining. I saved the image as a JPEG and captured it to the **Media** panel as explained in **14** **Add Media with the Adobe Media Downloader**.

Drag the clip of the painting from the **Media** panel to the Video 2 track, overlapping it with the last two seconds of the frame grab clip on the Video 3 track.

83

▶ NOTE

Photoshop and Photoshop Elements offer some great tools for creating a simulated painting from a photo. In the **Filters** menu in these programs, you'll find a variety of effective artistic effects.

4   Apply a Fade Out to the Frame Grab Clip

With the frame grab clip on Video 3 selected, click the triangle to the left of **Opacity** in the **Properties** panel and then click the **Fade Out** setting.

Note that, because **Fade Out** is an **Opacity** effect, rather than fade to black, the frame grab clip will appear to dissolve, revealing the painting clip on the Video 2 track under it.

5   Apply the Transform Effect to the Frame Grab Clip

Actually, you can use any of a number of effects to warp the frame grab clip to transition into the painting clip. The **Twirl** and **Blur** effects (found in the **Effects and Transitions** panel in the **Distort** category of the **Video FX** collection) both distort the picture; couple one of these effects with the **Fade Out** **Opacity** effect described in step 4 to create interesting transitions.

For this example, I used the **Transform** effect because it enabled me to reshape the frame grab clip so the people or objects on it can be made to shape themselves into positions similar to those of the people or objects in the painting clip.

The **Transform** effect is located on the **Effects and Transitions** panel, in the **Distort** category of the **Video FX** collection. Drag this effect onto the frame grab clip. The **Transform** property appears in the **Properties** panel.

6 Create a Keyframe for the Transform Effect

If the timeline isn't visible on the **Properties** panel, click the **Show Keyframes** button. Position the CTI to a point on the **Properties** timeline about a half-second before the **Fade Out** begins.

Click the triangle to the left of the **Transform** listing on the **Properties** panel to reveal the effect's control panel. Without changing any settings, click the stopwatch icon to the right of the **Transform** listing. A column of keyframe diamonds is created next to the **Transform** controls at the CTI's position on the **Properties** timeline. At this point, the settings for these keyframe points show no effect from the **Transform** effect.

7 Create the Morph Keyframes

Position the CTI about halfway through the **Fade Out** effect you created in step 4 (watch the **Monitor** to judge the position at which the **Fade Out** effect is about midway). This should allow you to see a double exposure of both the painting and the frame grab clips.

Change the **Transform** settings for **Scale Height** and **Scale Width**—and the settings for **Position**, if necessary—to transform the frame grab clip so the images in it line up as much as possible with the related images in the painting clip. Change the **Transform** settings either by typing in new coordinates or by mousing over each coordinate until the scroll icon appears and then clicking and dragging over the numbers to raise or lower them.

As you change each of these settings, new keyframes are automatically created at the CTI's current position.

In my example, I'm lining up the couple celebrating their fiftieth anniversary with the painting of them on their wedding day.

8 Reposition the Morph Keyframes

When you finish creating the morph keyframes in the **Transform** effect, position the keyframe points in the **Properties** panel timeline almost directly under the first **Fade Out** keyframe.

83

Render the sequence by pressing **Enter** to preview the movie's final appearance. Premiere Elements automatically animates the transformation of the frame grab screen image between the two sets of **Transform** keyframes to make it appear that the frame grab clip is changing shape to morph into the painting clip.

When the sequence is played back, the original video clip gives way to a freeze frame taken from the original clip, which morphs and then dissolves into the painting clip.

83

12

Cool Tricks

IN THIS CHAPTER:

Premiere Elements offers many easy-to-use effects that do a host of cool tricks right out of the box. But sometimes the most obvious use for an effect is only the beginning. With a little creativity, you'll be amazed at what you can do!

This chapter offers some not-quite-so-obvious but oft-requested tricks you can perform with the Premiere Elements's **Video FX** collection.

How *do* you make a line move across a map anyway?

---

84 Create a Split-Screen Effect

✔ BEFORE YOU BEGIN	→ SEE ALSO
20 About the Monitor Panel	**43** About Rendering the Timeline
33 Add or Move a Clip on the Timeline	**63** Reset or Remove an Effect
61 Add and Customize an Effect	**67** About Keyframing
68 About the Properties Panel	**71** Make a Variable-Speed Pan and Zoom
74 About Advanced Effects	**77** Create a Picture-In-Picture Effect
	87 Create a *Brady Bunch* Effect

84

It's easy to create a Picture-In-Picture effect, as explained in **77 Create a Picture-in-Picture Effect**. But what happens when you want to balance the images in your video frame more evenly—or you want two or more clips to share the screen at once?

With a combination of Premiere Elements's **Crop** and **Motion** effects, it's easy to shape and position any number of clips on your screen.

1 Place Clip A on Video 1

Drag one clip from the **Media** panel to the **Video 1** track on the **Timeline**. (See **33 Add or Move a Clip on the Timeline**.)

2 Place Clip B on Video 2

Drag another clip from the **Media** panel to the **Video 2** track, directly above clip A.

▶ TIP

When positioning your clips on the **Timeline**, view them in the **Monitor**. Be sure you have the safe margins turned on (click the **More** button in the **Monitor** panel to access the margin guides). The safe margins indicate both the possible and likely edges of your video frame that will be cut off by a typical television. Stay within these margins to ensure that you don't position the clip offscreen! (See **20 About the Monitor Panel**.)

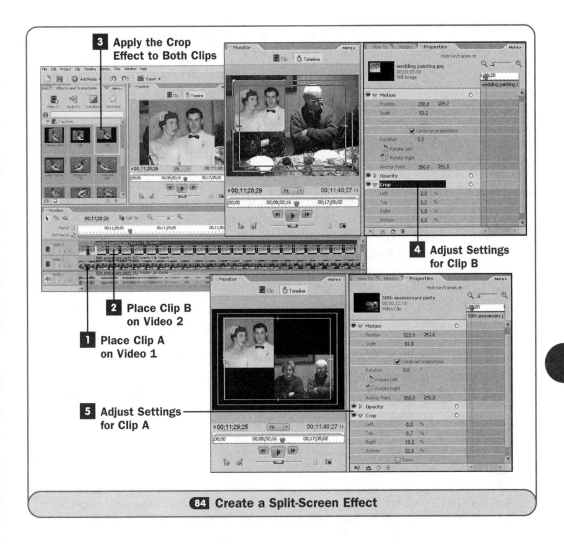

3 Apply the Crop Effect to Both Clips

4 Adjust Settings for Clip B

2 Place Clip B on Video 2

1 Place Clip A on Video 1

5 Adjust Settings for Clip A

84 Create a Split-Screen Effect

3 Apply the Crop Effect to Both Clips

The **Crop** effect is located on the **Effects and Transitions** panel, in the **Video FX** collection, in the **Transform** category. (See **74** **About Advanced Effects**.)

Drag this effect to the clip on **Video 1** and drag it again to the clip on **Video 2**. The effect initially shows no change to either clip.

4 Adjust Settings for Clip B

With clip B selected, click the triangle to the left of the **Crop** listing in the **Properties** panel as well as the triangle to the left of the **Motion** listing to open each effect's control panel.

Use the **Position**, **Scale**, and **Crop** settings in the **Motion** control panel to position, size, and shape your clip. (See ⑥ **Add and Customize an Effect**.)

To change the settings for either effect, you can type in new coordinates or percentages for each setting; you can drag across the numerical settings so they increase or decrease, watching the results of the changes in the **Monitor** panel; or you can click the image in the **Monitor** panel and drag the sides in or position the image manually. Use the method that makes the most sense for you.

When you make adjustments by dragging the clip in the **Monitor**, make sure that the effect you want to adjust at the time is selected in the **Properties** panel. In other words, by clicking the **Motion** listing, you can change your clip's **Position** and **Scale** in the **Monitor** by dragging it and manipulating its corner handles. When you have the **Crop** effect selected, however, dragging the corner handles will crop your image instead of resizing it.

⑤ Adjust Settings for Clip A

As you did with clip B, crop and position the image on **Video 1**.

Repeats steps 2–4 with as many clips on as many separate video tracks as you'd like. (See ⑧⑦ **Create a *Brady Bunch* Effect**.)

You can even use keyframing for either or both effects so your clips keep moving and changing shape throughout the sequence. (See ⑥⑦ **About Keyframing**.)

▶ **TIP**

As you know, virtually any time you apply an effect, the clip does not have to remain in one position, at one **Crop** setting, throughout its duration. Using the keyframing feature, you can keep the clips in your split screen in constantly changing shape and position (see ⑥⑦ **About Keyframing**.)

84

---

85 Make a Car Move Across a Map

✔ BEFORE YOU BEGIN	→ SEE ALSO
⑬ About the Media Panel	㊸ About Rendering the Timeline
㉒ Prepare a Still for Video	㉛ Make a Variable-Speed Pan and Zoom
㉝ Add or Move a Clip on the Timeline	㊱ Make a Line Move Across a Map
⑥⑦ About Keyframing	㊴ Frame Your Video with an Image
⑥⑧ About the Properties Panel	
⑦⓪ Pan and Zoom Still Images a la Ken Burns	

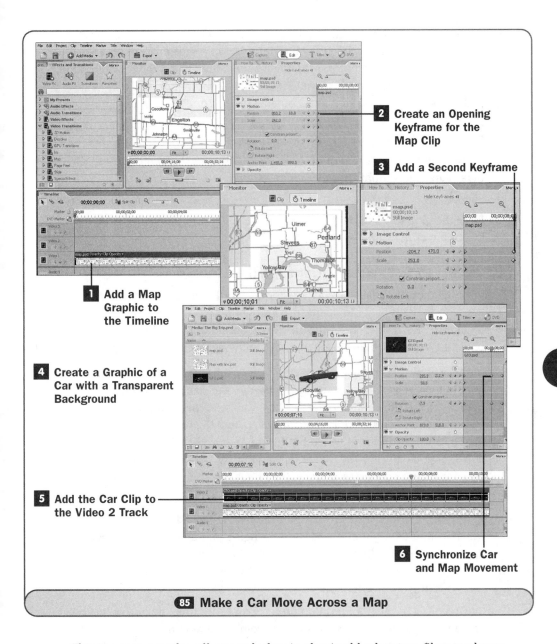

2 Create an Opening Keyframe for the Map Clip

3 Add a Second Keyframe

1 Add a Map Graphic to the Timeline

4 Create a Graphic of a Car with a Transparent Background

5 Add the Car Clip to the Video 2 Track

6 Synchronize Car and Map Movement

85

85 Make a Car Move Across a Map

This is a very popular effect, used often in classic old adventure films, and parodied in movies such as *Raiders of the Lost Ark*: To show the path of a long voyage, a car, boat, or plane is shown moving across a map.

It's a very simple effect to create, and yet it can be very effective in orienting your audience to a scene's location by demonstrating how far your subject had to travel to get there.

To add interest to this effect, rather than simply showing the car moving across the stationary map graphic, begin with a tight shot of a specific location on the map and then create a motion path so the clip actually follows the car along the route of travel. Like many such special effects, there's more than one way to do this trick. This method uses Premiere Elements's effects and keyframing tool.

1 Add a Map Graphic to the Timeline

You'll want to be able to pan and zoom along the map graphic you use, so make sure your graphic has enough resolution. (See **22** **Prepare a Still for Video**.)

Place the map clip/still on the **Video 1** track and position the CTI at the beginning of the clip.

2 Create an Opening Keyframe for the Map Clip

With the map clip selected, click the triangle to the right of the **Motion** listing in the **Properties** panel to open the control panel. Also, if the **Properties** timeline is not visible, click the **Show Keyframes** button at the top of the panel. Move the **Properties** timeline CTI to the beginning of the clip.

In the **Motion** listing, adjust the **Scale** and **Position** values for the map clip to reflect where you want the map to be when the clip starts. There are a number of ways to change these settings: You can type in new coordinates or percentages for each setting; you can drag across the numerical settings so they increase or decrease, watching the changes in the effect in the **Monitor** panel; or you can click the image in the **Monitor** panel and scale it by dragging the corner handles or position the image by dragging it. Use the method that makes the most sense for you.

When you've established the first position for the map clip, click the stopwatch icon to the right of the **Motion** listing. A column of little diamonds appears on this timeline, adjacent to each **Motion** setting.

3 Add a Second Keyframe

Move the CTI to the final position on the **Properties** timeline and adjust the **Position** and **Scale** settings for the final point of motion across the map. New keyframes are automatically added as you change settings. (See **70** **Pan and Zoom Still Images a la Ken Burns**.)

Continue to add additional keyframes between the beginning and end motion. Slide the keyframe points into positions on the timeline to create the motion path and speed of motion you think best depict the travel route.

4 Create a Graphic of a Car with a Transparent Background

You can create your car graphic by deleting the background from a photo of an actual car or, if you'd prefer, you can draw the graphic from scratch in a graphics program. The most important thing, though, is that the graphic of the car has a transparent background. A Photoshop file with no background layer, for instance, is an excellent choice (see **94** **Frame Your Video with an Image**).

To maintain the transparency in your car graphic, save the file as a Photoshop (PSD), PDF, or TIF file with the layers intact.

5 Add the Car Clip to the Video 2 Track

Import the car graphic as explained in **13** **About the Media Panel**) and drag the still/clip into position to the **Video 2** track on the **Timeline**, above the map clip. Trim or stretch the clip as necessary so it is the same duration as the map clip.

6 Synchronize Car and Map Movement

With the car clip selected, use the **Timeline** in the **Properties** panel to set **Position** keyframes (as you did when you created the motion path for the map in steps 2 and 3) to create a similar, synchronized motion path so the car follows the necessary roads along the route.

In my example, I added keyframes for **Rotation** to the motion path so my car not only tracked along the route of travel, but also rotated at certain points to simulate changes in direction of travel.

86

86 | Make a Line Move Across a Map

✔ BEFORE YOU BEGIN	→ SEE ALSO
22 Prepare a Still for Video	**64** Copy Effect Attributes from One Clip to Another
29 About the Timeline and Video Tracks	**71** Make a Variable-Speed Pan and Zoom
67 About Keyframing	**85** Make a Car Move Across a Map
70 Pan and Zoom Still Images a la Ken Burns	**94** Frame Your Video with an Image

A similar effect to **85** **Make a Car Move Across a Map**, making a line move across a map is, in fact, a very good companion to it (just add the car graphic on Video 3 and you can combine both effects). Making a line move across a map is a great way to show your audience where your travels have taken you.

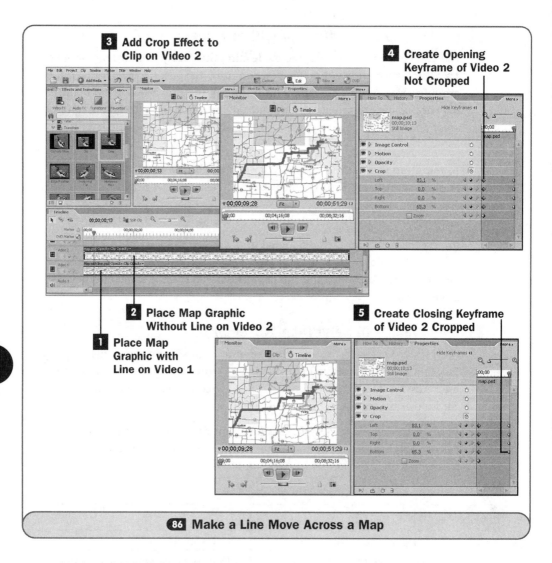

3 Add Crop Effect to Clip on Video 2

4 Create Opening Keyframe of Video 2 Not Cropped

2 Place Map Graphic Without Line on Video 2

1 Place Map Graphic with Line on Video 1

5 Create Closing Keyframe of Video 2 Cropped

86 Make a Line Move Across a Map

As with many of these types of effects, there is more than one way to create it. The method shown in this task is one of the simplest; when combined with keyframing, it's also one of the most effective.

1 Place Map Graphic with Line on Video 1

You'll want two otherwise identical map clips—one plain and one with your route drawn as a dark line (using a graphics program such as Photoshop Elements or Paint Shop Pro).

Drag the map clip with the line onto the **Video 1** track.

2 Place Map Graphic Without Line on Video 2

Drag the plain map clip to the **Video 2** track, directly above the clip showing the map with the line. Set the two clips to exactly the same duration.

You can see only the plain map clip in the **Monitor**; the map with the line is hidden underneath the plain map clip.

3 Add Crop Effect to Clip on Video 2

The **Crop** effect is found on the **Effects and Transitions** panel, in the **Video FX** collection, in the **Transform** category. Drag this effect onto the plain map clip on **Video 2** (see **74 About Advanced Effects.**)

4 Create Opening Keyframe of Video 2 Not Cropped

With the clip on **Video 2** selected, click the triangle to the left of the **Crop** listing in the **Properties** panel to open the effect's control panel. If the **Properties** panel timeline is not visible, click the **Show Keyframes** button at the top of the panel. Move the **Properties** panel timeline's CTI to the beginning of the clip.

With all the controls at their default settings (no crop is applied to the clip), click the stopwatch icon to the right of the **Motion** listing. A column of little keyframe diamonds appears on the timeline adjacent to each **Crop** setting.

▶ **TIP**

For added effect, add synchronized motion to your two map clips. Before you apply the **Crop** effect, create a motion path by increasing the plain map's scale to zoom in to one area and then panning across the route of travel as described in **85 Make a Car Move Across a Map.** Right-click the plain map clip in **Video 2**, select **Copy**, and then right-click the map clip with the line on **Video 1** and select **Paste Attributes.** The motion path from the clip in **Video 2** is copied to the clip in **Video 1.**

5 Create Closing Keyframe of Video 2 Cropped

Move the CTI to the end of the **Properties** timeline for the plain map clip and adjust the **Crop** settings for two adjacent sides so the map with a line clip is completely revealed. (See **84 Create a Split-Screen Effect.**) Your changed settings should crop the sides of the plain map clip to reveal the map with the line as you'd like it to be revealed in the final animation.

There are a number of ways to change the settings for the plain map clip: You can type new coordinates for each corner point; you can drag across the numerical settings so they increase or decrease, watching the effect as it changes in the **Monitor** panel; or you can click the image in the **Monitor** panel and crop it by dragging the side handles. Use the method that makes the most sense for you.

After you have the opening and closing keyframes in place, Premiere Elements creates the motion frames in between.

When you play this segment, you'll see the side of the plain map clip on **Video 2** crop back to reveal the map with a line on **Video 1**—but the effect is as if the line were being drawn on the screen as the sequence plays.

If you'd like to control the movement of the **Crop** effect throughout the movie segment—such as to reveal the line moving as it changes directions from east to north—add additional keyframes.

▶ **TIP**

By creating additional keyframe points, you can vary the direction and speed of the line's movement across the map—even stopping its motion completely if you'd like. Because you can add an indefinite number of keyframes, you can precisely control how and how fast the map, or any object, moves.

86

87 Create a *Brady Bunch* Effect

✔ BEFORE YOU BEGIN	→ SEE ALSO
20 About the Monitor Panel	22 Prepare a Still for Video
29 About the Timeline and Video Tracks	64 Copy Effect Attributes from One Clip to Another
30 Add, Delete, and Size Tracks	70 Pan and Zoom Still Images a la Ken Burns
33 Add or Move a Clip on the Timeline	71 Make a Variable-Speed Pan and Zoom
84 Create a Split-Screen Effect	104 Output to an AVI Movie

Why is it impossible to see a tic-tac-toe pattern of headshots without thinking of the opening to the 1970s television show *The Brady Bunch*?

No matter. This same effect can be used to have several clips running at once in the same video frame, no matter what arrangement you place them in.

▶ **TIP**

When arranging my clips in a video frame, I've often found it helpful to create a template—in this case, a tic-tac-toe-style grid—in Photoshop Elements as a guide for positioning my clips. I place this template on the **Video 1** track and use it as a guide until my clips have all been arranged; then I delete the grid graphic from the **Timeline**.

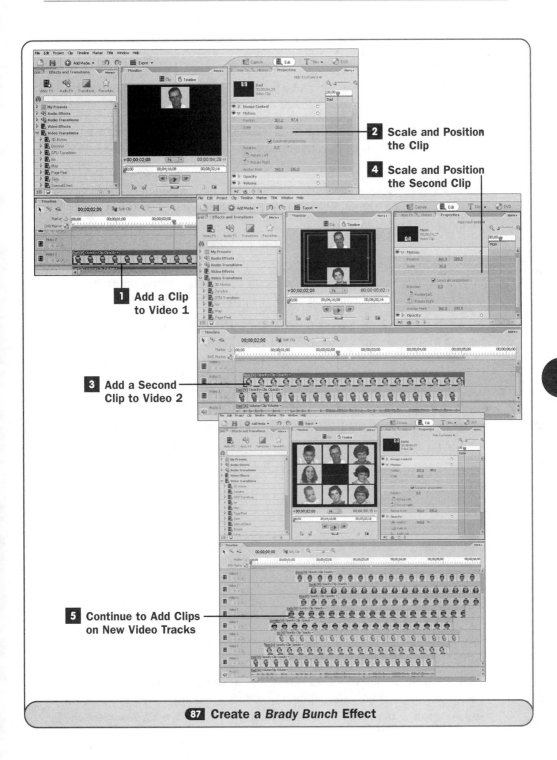

1 Add a Clip to Video 1

Drag your first clip from the **Media** panel to the **Video 1** track. For a true *Brady Bunch* effect, the clips you'll be using will be headshots, although other limited-motion clips can also be used to great effect.

You can create in advance as many video tracks as you'll ultimately need. Click the **More** button in the **Timeline** panel and select **Add Tracks** to create more video tracks.

Because you are ultimately going to be using eight or nine video tracks, you might want to reposition the panels in your workspace to allow plenty of room for the **Timeline** panel.

2 Scale and Position the Clip

With the clip selected in the **Timeline**, click the triangle to the left of the **Motion** listing in the **Properties** panel to open the control panel.

Adjust the values for the **Scale** and **Position** settings for the clip to position the clip in its opening location on the screen. You can change these settings in a number of ways: You can type new coordinates or percentages for each setting; you can drag across the numerical settings so they increase or decrease, watching the changes to the effect in the **Monitor** panel; or you can click the image in the **Monitor** panel and scale it by dragging the corner handles or position the image by dragging it. Use the method that makes the most sense for you to place a scaled-down image in position on the screen.

If necessary, you can apply a **Crop** effect to shape the clip, as explained in **84 Create a Split-Screen Effect**.)

▶ **NOTE**

Remember, nothing has to stay in one place or at one setting. With keyframing, your clips can be moving around and changing shape throughout the video sequence (see **67 About Keyframing**).

3 Add a Second Clip to Video 2

Drag a second clip from the **Media** panel to the **Video 2** track, partially overlapping the first clip on the **Timeline**.

Positioning the second and subsequent clips at staggered positions on the **Timeline** will have the clips popping in pseudo-randomly when you play the sequence rather than the entire set coming in at once. (See **29 About the Timeline and Video Tracks**.)

4 Scale and Position the Second Clip

Repeat step 2 to adjust the **Scale** and **Position** settings for the second clip, moving it into position in the **Monitor**.

When positioning clips in the **Monitor** panel, make sure you have the safe margins turned on (click the **More** button in the **Monitor** panel to access the margin guides) to ensure that you don't position your clips off the edges of a typical TV screen. (See **20** **About the Monitor Panel**.)

5 Continue to Add Clips on New Video Tracks

Continue to position new clips on new video tracks until you've assembled your pattern of clips in the video frame.

▶ **TIP**

Although Premiere Elements allows you to add a virtually unlimited number of video and audio tracks, you might find that running 8 or 10 tracks of video at once is a bit taxing on your system. If so, after you've built your multi-track, multi-clip segment, you might want to export it as an AVI, which is automatically added to your **Media** panel. You can then use this AVI clip to replace the multi-track segment of video in your final movie project. See **104** **Output to an AVI Movie**.

88

88	**Make a Person Appear with a Different Background**

✔ BEFORE YOU BEGIN	→ SEE ALSO
13 About the Media Panel	**22** Prepare a Still for Video
29 About the Timeline and Video Tracks	**30** Add, Delete, and Size Tracks
33 Add or Move a Clip on the Timeline	**71** Make a Variable-Speed Pan and Zoom
76 Make an Area of a Clip Transparent	**89** Make a Person Appear to Be Miniaturized

Here's a very simple and very commonly used application of the **Chroma Key** effect. It's so commonly used, in fact, that you can see it every night on the local news—as the weatherperson, standing in front of a green screen, appears to actually be standing in front of a moving weather map. We have even more fun with this effect in **89** **Make a Person Appear to Be Miniaturized** and **90** **Make a Person Appear to Fly**.

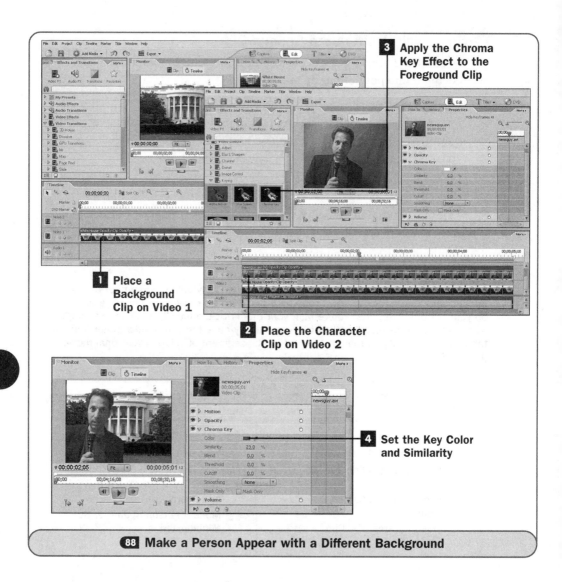

3 Apply the Chroma Key Effect to the Foreground Clip

1 Place a Background Clip on Video 1

2 Place the Character Clip on Video 2

4 Set the Key Color and Similarity

88 **Make a Person Appear with a Different Background**

1 Place a Background Clip on Video 1

Drag the background clip onto the **Timeline**. The background clip need not be animated. You can use a still or even a drawing. But video, with action and movement, can make the effect seem even more realistic.

2 Place the Character Clip on Video 2

Preparation means everything for the character clip. Shoot your character against a flat-colored background—ideally blue, green, or some color not likely to be in the person's flesh tones or clothing. Lighting the background evenly is very important, too. The smoother the color of the background, the easier it is to key out.

▶ **TIP**

You can key out the background behind the person or character much more easily if the background is a smooth, consistent color. For this reason, it's much better to use a drape made of a soft fabric or cloth than a shiny surface such as plastic.

Place the character clip on the **Timeline**, directly above the background clip.

3 Apply the Chroma Key Effect to the Foreground Clip

The **Chroma Key** effect is located on the **Effects and Transitions** panel, in the **Video FX** collection, in the **Keying** category. Drag the effect to the clip on **Video 2**. When the clip in **Video 2** is selected, you will see the **Chroma Key** effect listed in the **Properties** panel.

▶ **NOTE**

If your background moves or if you're using a background video clip that pans, you can use keyframing to synchronize the movement of your foreground clip to match the motion of the background (see **67** About Keyframing).

4 Set the Key Color and Similarity

Click the triangle to the left of the **Chroma Key** listing in the **Properties** panel to open the effect's control panel. Although you can set the color manually using the color panel, it's usually easier to use the screen image to designate the **Key** color. Click the eyedropper icon to the right of the color swatch in the **Chroma Key** control panel. The mouse pointer becomes an eyedropper. Click the color in the screen image in **Video 2** (the background behind the person or character) that you want to designate as transparent.

You'll see an effect immediately, as the clip on **Video 1** replaces the plain-color background of the character clip on **Video 2**. You'll probably have to adjust the **Similarity** setting in the **Properties** panel, widening the range of color to be affected, to get a good, clean transparent area. The **Blend**, **Threshold**, **Cutoff**, and **Smoothing** settings can also help control the transparency and the softness of the transparent area's edge.

▶ **NOTE**

Occasionally, when you scale a clip that has been modified with the **Chroma Key** effect, an edge line shows. You can remove this easily by adding and adjusting the **Crop** effect to the clip. (As you know, you can apply multiple effects to a clip.)

88

89   Make a Person Appear to Be Miniaturized

✔ BEFORE YOU BEGIN	→ SEE ALSO
33 Add or Move a Clip on the Timeline	**22** Prepare a Still for Video
76 Make an Area of a Clip Transparent	**30** Add, Delete, and Size Tracks
88 Make a Person Appear with a Different Background	**67** About Keyframing
	90 Make a Person Appear to Fly

Although this trick uses the same basic principles described in **88** Make a Person Appear with a Different Background, this effect adds another level of complexity to the illusion, and the results can be even more fun!

Naturally, the key here is to shoot all of the elements of this composite—the background, the character, and the foreground—in a similar style. For example, use similar lighting conditions, similar color tones, and similar camera angles. Also, you'll add to the illusion of miniaturization if you shoot your character clip from a slightly higher-than-eye-level angle.

1 Add the Background Clip to Video 1

Because we're creating the illusion of looking at the world of a miniaturized person, shoot your background full of recognizable objects, such as the leg of a table or a desk telephone, but much closer and from a much lower angle than you usually see them. Drag this background clip onto the **Video 1** track.

2 Add the Character Clip to Video 2

Try to shoot your character under lighting conditions that are similar to what you used when shooting your background clip. As explained in **88** Make a Person Appear with a Different Background, shoot your character in front of a blue, green, or other flatly colored background—a background whose color does not appear in the person's clothes, skin tones, or hair.

▶ TIP

You'll be able to key out the background behind the character much more easily if the background is a smooth, consistent color. For this reason, it's much better to use a drape made of a soft fabric or cloth than a shiny surface such as plastic.

Position the character clip on **Video 2**, directly above the clip on **Video 1**.

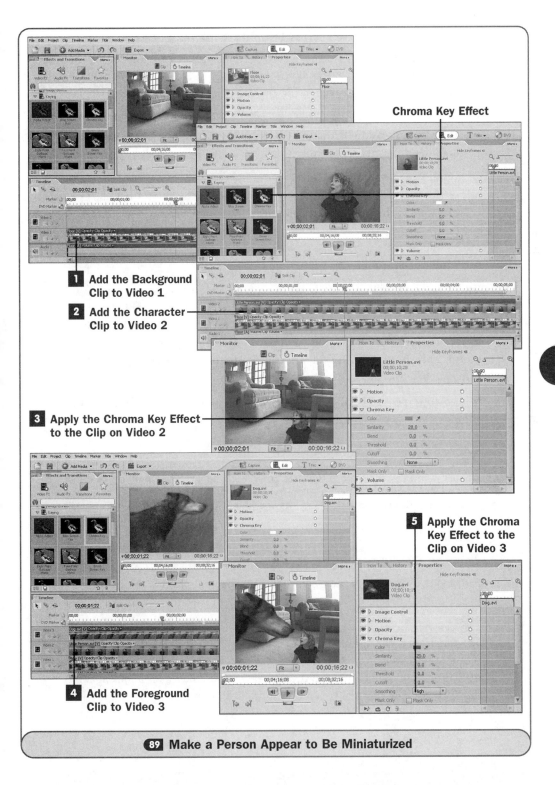

Chroma Key Effect

1 Add the Background Clip to Video 1

2 Add the Character Clip to Video 2

3 Apply the Chroma Key Effect to the Clip on Video 2

5 Apply the Chroma Key Effect to the Clip on Video 3

4 Add the Foreground Clip to Video 3

3 Apply the Chroma Key Effect to the Clip on Video 2

The **Chroma Key** effect is located on the **Effects and Transitions** panel, in the **Video FX** collection, in the **Keying** category. Drag the effect onto the character clip on **Video 2**. When the clip on **Video 2** is selected, you will see the **Chroma Key** effect listed in the **Properties** panel.

Click the triangle to the left of the **Chroma Key** listing in the **Properties** panel to open the effect's control panel.

Although you can set the key color manually using the color panel, it's usually easier to use the screen image to designate the **Key** color. Click the eyedropper icon to the right of the **Color** swatch in the **Chroma Key** control panel. The mouse pointer becomes an eyedropper. Click the color in the screen image that you want to designate as transparent (the background behind the character in the **Video 2** clip).

You'll see an effect immediately, as the clip on **Video 1** replaces the plaincolor background of the character clip on **Video 2**. You'll probably have to adjust the **Similarity** setting for the **Chroma Key** effect, which widens the range of color to be affected, to get a good, clean transparent area. The **Blend**, **Threshold**, **Cutoff**, and **Smoothing** settings can also help control transparency and the softness of the transparent area's edge.

In the **Motion** control panel, change the **Scale** and **Position** settings for the character clip to place him or her in the scene.

▶ NOTE

Occasionally, when you scale a clip that has been modified with the **Chroma Key** effect, an edge line shows around the clip's video frame. You can remove this easily by adding and adjusting the **Crop** effect to the clip. (As you know, you can apply multiple effects to a clip.)

4 Add the Foreground Clip to Video 3

Although you'll already have a nice miniaturization effect going at this point, this third, foreground clip is what really makes the illusion come to life!

The foreground clip should be of a person, animal, or object shot in a way that emphasizes its size. Another alternative is to use a clip of a person's relatively huge hand reaching into the scene. Or (think *Incredible Shrinking Man*) maybe a cat who believes he's found some fresh meat.

89

The purpose of the foreground clip is to give perspective to your miniaturization effect. It gives a point of reference, an "actual size" object to compare to the miniaturized person.

As with the character clip on **Video 2**, this person or thing should be shot against a plain, solid-colored background.

Position the foreground clip on **Video 3**, directly above the other two clips.

5 Apply the Chroma Key Effect to the Clip on Video 3

Apply the **Chroma Key** effect to the foreground clip, as you did to the character clip in step 3. Remember, you can adjust the settings for **Position**, **Scale**, and **Rotate** in the **Motion** control panel to modify the clips any way you like to add to the sequence's drama!

---

90 Make a Person Appear to Fly

✔ BEFORE YOU BEGIN	→ SEE ALSO
29 About the Timeline and Video Tracks	**22** Prepare a Still for Video
33 Add or Move a Clip on the Timeline	**67** About Keyframing
76 Make an Area of a Clip Transparent	**71** Make a Variable-Speed Pan and Zoom
88 Make a Person Appear with a Different Background	**89** Make a Person Appear to Be Miniaturized
	104 Output to an AVI Movie

90

Although this task uses the same basic principles as **88** **Make a Person Appear with a Different Background**, this effect uses keyframing to add motion to the mix. Dress your character in a cape and blow a fan in her face when you film her, and you'll have made your friend or child into a full-blown super-hero!

1 Place a Background Clip on Video 1

What you use for a background clip depends on what you're trying to accomplish. Video clips with lots of sky work great, as do tall buildings to be leapt in a single bound and footage of clouds shot from an airplane. Just make sure that the background clip has plenty of room for your character to zip around.

Of course, you can opt to use a still photo or even a drawing for the background—there is no wrong answer to the question of what background to use.

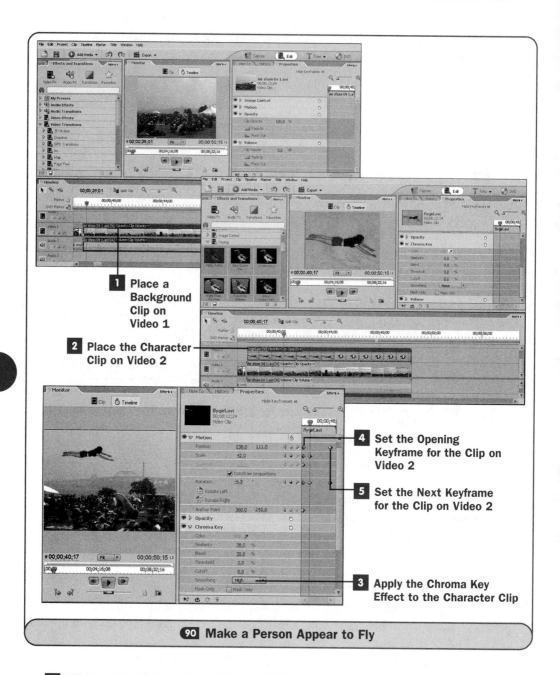

1 **Place a Background Clip on Video 1**

2 **Place the Character Clip on Video 2**

4 **Set the Opening Keyframe for the Clip on Video 2**

5 **Set the Next Keyframe for the Clip on Video 2**

3 **Apply the Chroma Key Effect to the Character Clip**

90 Make a Person Appear to Fly

2 **Place the Character Clip on Video 2**

Preparation means everything when shooting the character clip. Shoot your character against a flat-colored background—ideally blue, green, or some color not likely to be in the person's flesh tones or clothing. Lighting the backdrop evenly is very important, too. The smoother the color, the easier it will be to key out.

If you position your character on her stomach, drape the area the person is lying on with backdrop material as evenly as possible. Place the character clip on the **Video 2** track, above the background clip.

▶ **TIP**

To add dimension to your character's flight, move the camera around her during the green-screen shoot to capture your character from more than one angle—and then keyframe the motion path to coincide with those angles.

3 Apply the Chroma Key Effect to the Character Clip

The **Chroma Key** effect is located on the **Effects and Transitions** panel, in the **Video FX** collection, in the **Keying** category. Drag the effect onto the character clip on **Video 2**. When the character clip is selected, the **Chroma Key** effect is now listed in the **Properties** panel.

Click the triangle to the left of the **Chroma Key** listing in the **Properties** panel to open the effect's control panel. Although you can set the key color manually using the color panel, it's usually easier to use the screen image to designate the key color. Click the eyedropper icon to the right of the **Color** swatch in the **Chroma Key** control panel. The mouse pointer becomes an eyedropper. Click the color in your screen image that you want to designate as transparent (the backdrop behind the person in the character clip on **Video 2**).

You'll see an effect immediately, as the background clip on **Video 1** replaces the plain-color background of the character clip on **Video 2**. You'll probably have to adjust the **Similarity** setting in the **Chroma Key** control panel, which widens the range of color to be affected, to get a good, clean transparent area. The **Blend**, **Threshold**, **Cutoff**, and **Smoothing** settings can also help control transparency and the softness of the transparent area's edge.

90

4 Set the Opening Keyframe for the Clip on Video 2

With the character clip on **Video 2** still selected, click the triangle to the left of the **Motion** listing in the **Properties** panel. Change the values for the **Position** and **Scale** settings to place the character at a starting point (even offscreen, if you'd prefer) in your background. (See **67** About Keyframing and **70** Pan and Zoom Still Images a la Ken Burns.)

There are a number of ways to change the settings for **Position** and **Scale**: You can type new coordinates or percentages for each setting; you can drag across the numerical settings so they increase or decrease, watching the changes in the effect in the **Monitor** panel; or you can click the image in the **Monitor** panel and drag the sides in or position the image manually. Use the method that makes the most sense for you.

If the **Timeline** in the **Properties** panel isn't visible, click the **Show Keyframes** button at the top of the panel. When you have positioned the character in her opening position, click the stopwatch icon to the right of the **Motion** listing in the **Properties** panel. A column of keyframe diamonds appears on the timeline adjacent to each of the **Motion** settings. These are the opening keyframes of your clip. Slide them all to the very beginning of the clip's timeline in the **Properties** panel.

5 Set the Next Keyframe for the Clip on Video 2

Position the CTI at the point on the **Properties** timeline at which you want your character to change directions. Adjust the **Scale** and **Position** settings in the **Motion** control panel for the next waypoint for the motion. As you do, keyframe points are automatically created.

Set as many keyframes as you need to complete your sequence and adjust their positions or delete them as necessary. Premiere Elements creates the motion path between these keyframes, making your character appear to zip magically from rooftop to rooftop!

90

91	Make Your Clip Appear on an Object

✔ BEFORE YOU BEGIN	→ SEE ALSO
29 About the Timeline and Video Tracks	**22** Prepare a Still for Video
61 Add and Customize an Effect	**30** Add, Delete, and Size Tracks
74 About Advanced Effects	**67** About Keyframing
	71 Make a Variable-Speed Pan and Zoom

Although you can pin your clip onto any object, large or small, it's especially impressive to make your clip appear to be projected onto the side of a tall building above a crowded street—sort of the Big Brother effect. In this task, you learn to "project" a video clip onto an object in another clip or a still image. Using the **Corner Pin** effect, you can distort your video clip so it truly looks as if it is part of the background clip or still.

1 Place a Background Clip on Video 1

A background clip with recognizable scenery, such as the Times Square Jumbotron or the side of a well-known building, can be particularly effective. Other objects that can be fun to project a clip onto are a drive-in movie screen (if you can still find one!) or a billboard.

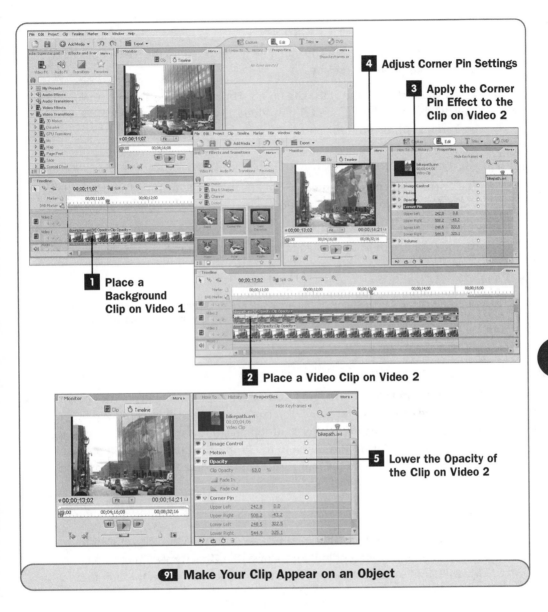

4 Adjust Corner Pin Settings

3 Apply the Corner Pin Effect to the Clip on Video 2

1 Place a Background Clip on Video 1

2 Place a Video Clip on Video 2

5 Lower the Opacity of the Clip on Video 2

91

91 Make Your Clip Appear on an Object

Although you can use keyframing to track the motion of an object (see **67 About Keyframing**), it's often easier—and just as effective—to use a stable, tripod-steady shot of a scene or object as the background clip for this effect. Drag the background clip from the **Media** panel to the **Video 1** track on the **Timeline**.

2 Place a Video Clip on Video 2

The second clip is the video clip you'll be projecting onto the scenery or object in the background clip on **Video 1**.

When you first place the video clip on the **Timeline** on the **Video 2** track, directly above the background clip in **Video 1**, you won't be able to see the background in the **Monitor** panel.

3 Apply the Corner Pin Effect to the Clip on Video 2

The **Corner Pin** effect is located on the **Effects and Transitions** panel, in the **Video FX** collection, in the **Distort** category.

Drag the effect onto the video clip on **Video 2**. When the video clip is selected, the **Corner Pin** effect is listed in the **Properties** panel.

▶ **TIP**

To shape your clip to fit the shape of the area you are projecting it onto, you can also combine the **Corner Pin** effect with the **Crop** effect or even with one of the **Garbage Mattes**. You can combine as many effects as you'd like on a single clip.

91

4 Adjust the Corner Pin Settings

Click the triangle to the left of the **Corner Pin** listing in the **Properties** panel to open the effect's control panel. You can adjust the corners of the clip by changing the coordinates in this control panel, but you might find it easier to simply click the **Corner Pin** listing in the **Properties** panel and then manipulate the clip by dragging the four corner control handles that appear as encircled crosses in the **Monitor**.

5 Lower the Opacity of the Clip on Video 2

To blend your clip into the background—to make the video clip appear to be projected onto an object or building—lower the **Opacity** setting of the clip on **Video 2** until some of the object's or building's texture shows through the video clip.

---

92   Blur an Isolated Spot on a Video Clip a la *Cops*

✔ BEFORE YOU BEGIN	→ SEE ALSO
33 Add or Move a Clip on the Timeline	**71** Make a Variable-Speed Pan and Zoom
61 Add and Customize an Effect	**94** Frame Your Video with an Image
74 About Advanced Effects	**104** Output to an AVI Movie

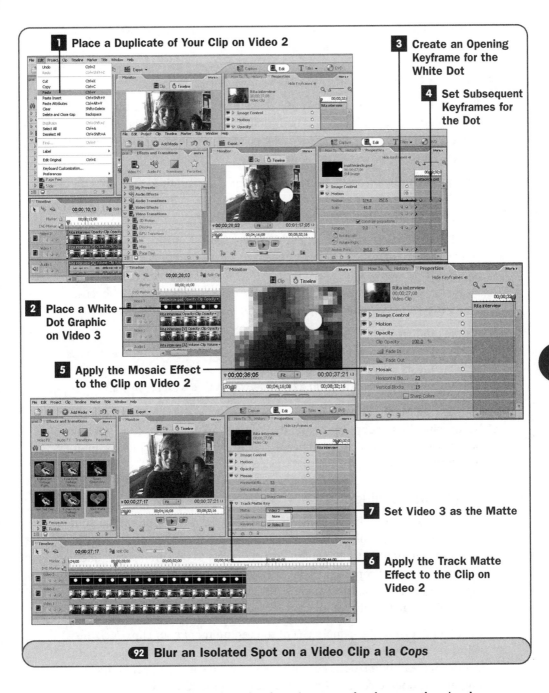

1 Place a Duplicate of Your Clip on Video 2

3 Create an Opening Keyframe for the White Dot

4 Set Subsequent Keyframes for the Dot

2 Place a White Dot Graphic on Video 3

5 Apply the Mosaic Effect to the Clip on Video 2

7 Set Video 3 as the Matte

6 Apply the Track Matte Effect to the Clip on Video 2

92 Blur an Isolated Spot on a Video Clip a la *Cops*

There's someone in your video who doesn't want to be there, or there's a logo or text in the background that you don't want to show. Or, heaven forbid, you've accidentally taped nudity!

Here's how to blur out the unwanted area in your video and then, using keyframing, track with its movement across the screen.

1 Place a Duplicate of Your Clip on Video 2

Because Premiere Elements can paste a clip only to the **Video 1** track, drag the original clip to **Video 2**, and then right-click the clip and choose **Copy**. From the menu at the top of the screen, choose **Edit, Paste**. A duplicate of the clip on **Video 2** will appear on **Video 1**.

Ensure that both clips are perfectly aligned on the **Timeline**.

2 Place a White Dot Graphic on Video 3

You'll need a graphic of a white circle (or whatever shape best fits the area you want to blur) with no background. This graphic can be created in Photoshop Elements, Paint Shop Pro, or whatever graphics program you are using. If you are using Photoshop Elements, delete the background layer so that, aside from the white circle, the graphic is completely transparent.

Graphic shapes without background layers travel only with Photoshop (PSD), TIF, and PDF files, so you'll have to save the graphic to one of those formats with the layers intact in order to maintain the graphic's transparency. (See **22** Prepare a Still for Video and **94** Frame Your Video with an Image.)

Use the **Add Media** button (described in **13** About the Media Panel) to add the graphic file to your project and then place the graphic on the **Timeline** on the **Video 3** track, directly above the other two clips. Adjust its duration to match that of the other two clips, if necessary.

3 Create an Opening Keyframe for the White Dot

The object you are trying to blur will most likely be moving around in your video frame, so you will have to set up a motion path for the white dot (so that it continues to block the object you are trying to obscure). If the timeline isn't visible in the **Properties** panel, click the **Show Keyframes** button at the top of the panel. Click the triangle to the left of the **Motion** listing to reveal the control panel for this property.

Position the **Properties** panel's CTI at the beginning of your clip. Click the white dot in the **Monitor** and drag it so it covers the area you want to blur. Use the **Scale** and **Position** settings in the **Motion** control panel on the **Properties** panel to cover the spot you want to blur. (See **23** Scale And Position A Still.)

When the dot is in position and scaled, click the stopwatch icon to the right of the **Motion** listing in the **Properties** panel. A column of little keyframe diamonds appears on the **Properties** timeline at the position of the CTI. These are the opening keyframes for your motion path.

4 Set Subsequent Keyframes for the Dot

Move the CTI to the end of the clip and reposition the dot so it again covers the area you want to blur. As you do, new keyframe points are automatically added.

Move the CTI along the clip to check that the dot is tracking with the person or object you are trying to blur. Set up additional keyframes as needed to track with these positions (so the dot continues to obscure the portion of the image you want to blur). The goal is that the motion path of the white dot will follow the area you want to blur for the clip's entire duration.

5 Apply the Mosaic Effect to the Clip on Video 2

The **Mosaic** effect is located on the **Effects and Transitions** panel, in the **Video FX** collection, in the **Stylize** category. (As an alternative, you can use the **Blur** effect from the **Blur/Sharpen** category.) Drag the effect onto the clip on **Video 2**.

Click the triangle to the left of the effect listing in the **Properties** panel to reveal the control panel, and adjust the settings until your screen image is distorted beyond recognition.

6 Apply the Track Matte Effect to the Clip on Video 2

The **Track Matte** effect is located on the **Effects and Transitions** panel, in the **Video FX** collection, in the **Keying** category. Drag this effect onto the **Mosaic**-modified clip on **Video 2**.

7 Set Video 3 as the Matte

A *matte* is an area of a clip you designate to be transparent. In this case, you are using the white dot to define the area you want to be transparent (the dot is the matte). True to its name, the **Track Matte** effect tracks this white dot around the video frame, applying transparency wherever the white dot appears.

▶ KEY TERM

Matte—An area of a clip designated as transparent. The shape and position of a matte can be defined using vector points (as with Premiere Elements's **Garbage Matte**) or by linking it to the size and position of an image on another video track (as with Premiere Elements's **Track Matte**).

With the clip on **Video 2** selected, click the triangle to the left of the **Track Matte** listing in the **Properties** panel to reveal the effect's control panel. From the **Matte** drop-down menu, select **Video 3**.

The Track Matte creates a mask for the clip on **Video 2** around the white dot. In other words, only the spot where the white dot is positioned will show the **Mosaic**-effected clip—the rest of the video frame displays the clear clip on **Video 1**. As the dot moves along the motion path you've created for it, only that area appears with the **Mosaic** effect.

▶ NOTES

Note that, in Premiere Elements version 1.0, the **Track Matte** effect does not follow a keyframed graphic. To make this effect work in version 1.0, you must export the keyframed clip of the white circle as a movie (see 104 **Output to an AVI Movie**) and then use that new clip as your matte.

As an alternative to using the **Track Matte** effect, you can duplicate your clip as explained in step 1, blur the clip on **Video 2** as explained in step 5 but, rather than using the **Track Matte** effect with a keyframed graphic, apply the **4-Point Garbage Matte** effect (from the **Keying** category in the **Video FX** collection) to the clip on **Video 2**. Positioning the four vector points for the **Garbage Matte**, you can isolate which area of the clip appears blurred. The positions for these vector points can, likewise, be keyframed for motion.

92

93	Show Your Video Through a Shape or Text

✔ BEFORE YOU BEGIN	→ SEE ALSO
61 Add and Customize an Effect	13 About the Media Panel
68 About the Properties Panel	22 Prepare a Still for Video
95 About Titles	33 Add or Move a Clip on the Timeline
99 Create Rolling and Moving Credits	43 About Rendering the Timeline

The **Track Matte** effect uses any black or white image, even text, as a sort of cookie cutter through which you can show a video clip. The effect uses black and white (and even grayscale) to define an *alpha channel*—an invisible channel that masks your clip or controls its transparency. (See 94 **Frame Your Video with an Image**.)

▶ KEY TERM

Alpha channel—The area of a graphic or video clip that Premiere Elements reads as transparent. This transparency can be inherent in the native file, as with a Photoshop file that has no background layer, or the alpha channel can be created in Premiere Elements by using the **Key** effects to define color ranges as transparent.

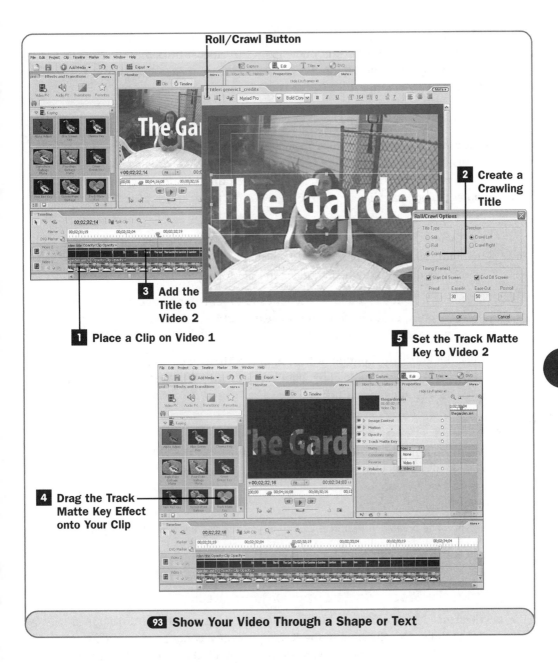

Roll/Crawl Button

2 Create a Crawling Title

3 Add the Title to Video 2

1 Place a Clip on Video 1

5 Set the Track Matte Key to Video 2

4 Drag the Track Matte Key Effect onto Your Clip

93

93 Show Your Video Through a Shape or Text

1 Place a Clip on Video 1

Select the clip you want to play through the cookie-cutter openings of the matte and place it on **Video 1**.

If you want to cookie cutter the clip and have it appear over another background clip, place the background clip on the **Video 1** track and the clip you want to apply the effect to on the video track above it. (See 🔲 29 **About the Timeline and Video Tracks**.)

2 Create a Crawling Title

Click the **Titles** button in the upper-right corner of the workspace to open the **Titles** workspace. Select a title template and click **OK**. As an alternative to using an existing template, you can click the **Cancel** button to close the templates dialog box, allowing you to create a title from scratch. (See 🔲 95 **About Titles**.)

After you leave the title template area, a **New Title** dialog box pops up. Type the name you want to give your title in the text box provided and click **OK**. Your new title is automatically added to the **Media** panel.

Customize the title text and set the font size to something large, around 150 points. (You can use any font, but the text must be white and might work more effectively if it is boldfaced.)

Click the **Roll/Crawl** button at the top of the **Titler** panel and, in the **Roll/Crawl Options** dialog box, enable the **Crawl Left**, **Start off Screen**, and **End Off Screen** options. Click **OK**. (See 🔲 99 **Create Rolling and Moving Credits**.)

3 Add the Title to Video 2

Locate your newly created title and place this clip on the **Video 2** track, directly above the video clip on **Video 1**.

▶ NOTE

In place of a title created in Premiere Elements, you can use any white text or graphic that has a transparent alpha channel rather than a solid background (the graphics file must be in PSD, PDF, or TIF format) for this effect.

4 Drag the Track Matte Effect onto Your Clip

The **Track Matte** effect can be found on the **Effects and Transitions** panel, in the **Video FX** collection, in the **Keying** category. Drag the effect onto the clip on **Video 1** (the clip you want to show through the cookie cutter matte).

▶ **TIP**

You can also use the **Track Matte** effect with a flat, non-transparent graphic—any white shape on a black background. With the **Track Matte** effect applied to the clip you want to modify and the white shape on the **Video** track above it, set the **Matte** drop-down option to the layer where you placed the graphic; from the **Composite** drop-down list, select **Matte Luma**. The matte will use the white shape in the specified graphic clip to define the transparent area.

5 **Set the Track Matte Key to Video 2**

With your video clip selected, click the triangle to the left of the **Track Matte Key** listing in the **Properties** panel to open the control panel for the effect. From the **Matte** drop-down list, select **Video 2** (the title) track. Ensure that the **Composite** drop-down list is set to **Matte Alpha**.

Your clip will appear cookie-cutter style within the shape of the title text. And because the title was created as a crawling title, as the clip plays, this text shape moves left across the screen.

The black background that is revealed behind your shape is actually the Premiere Elements default background. If you have a clip on a video track below this matted clip, the non-matted area instead reveals the clip below. (See **29** **About the Timeline and Video Tracks**.)

Enable the **Reverse** option in the Track Matte Key control panel, and your text or shape will be made transparent with the clip playing around it.

▶ **NOTE**

Keyframing motion to a pattern or text will, strangely, make it immune to the **Track Matte** in Premiere Elements 1.0. To use a moving object or text as a cookie cutter in version 1.0, you must export the clip of the moving object as a movie (see **104** **Output to an AVI Movie**)—a white object against a black background—and then use that newly created clip as your **Track Matte** pattern.

94	**Frame Your Video with an Image**
✔ **BEFORE YOU BEGIN**	→ **SEE ALSO**
22 Prepare a Still for Video **23** Scale and Position a Still	**33** Add or Move a Clip on the Timeline **43** About Rendering the Timeline

94

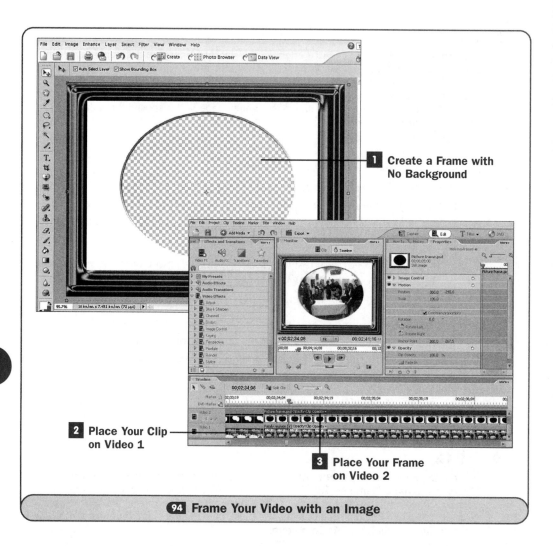

1 Create a Frame with No Background

2 Place Your Clip on Video 1

3 Place Your Frame on Video 2

94 Frame Your Video with an Image

The alpha channel travels, usually invisibly, along with the red, green, and blue color channels in a graphic or video clip. However, unlike the color channels, the alpha channel designates transparency, communicating which areas of a clip are transparent and which areas are opaque.

A layered Photoshop document (PSD), or a PDF or TIF document that has no background layer and in which the graphics do not completely fill the frame, carries its non-filled areas as an alpha channel. When you place these types of graphic files into Premiere Elements, the alpha channel remains intact, and these unfilled areas are read as transparent, revealing the clip or clips on the video tracks below.

▶ **NOTE**

The graphics that make up many of the Title templates and DVD templates and menus are, in fact, layered Photoshop documents with no backgrounds and their transparency areas are carried as alpha channels.

Any graphic or photo with the alpha channel enabled can be used as a frame for your video clips.

1 Create a Frame with No Background

With Photoshop Elements, Paint Shop Pro, or whatever graphics program you are using, create a multi-layered graphic. (In Photoshop Elements, double-click the **Background** layer in the **Layers** panel to turn the background into a layer that can be deleted, leaving you with a transparent canvas.)

Create a graphic with a window cut through it. This window should be completely transparent, showing whatever your graphics program uses to indicate no background behind it (in this example from Photoshop Elements, the transparent background is indicated by a gray-and-white checkerboard pattern).

Save your frame as a Photoshop (PSD), PDF, or a TIF document with layers enabled. The transparent background travels with these file formats as an alpha channel.

2 Place Your Clip on Video 1

Add the video clip you want to frame on a lower video track (such as **Video 1**) on the **Timeline**.

3 Place Your Frame on Video 2

Add your frame graphic to the **Media** panel using the **Add Media** button (as explained in **13** About the Media Panel) and then drag the graphic to the **Timeline** and place it on the video track directly above the clip you want to frame (on **Video 2** in this example). Your clip is visible through the transparent area of the frame graphic.

Depending on how much of your screen your frame graphic covers, you might have to adjust the **Scale** setting in the **Properties** panel for the clip on **Video 1** to keep too much of it from being covered. (See **68** About the Properties Panel.)

94

13

Adding Text, Creating Titles, Making Credits

IN THIS CHAPTER:

If the workspaces you spent the most time in were put on a top-four list, **Titles** would be number two, right behind the **Edit** workspace. *Titles* make your movie unique and give it that professional look. Premiere Elements gives you 10 categories of predesigned title templates; with more than 60 titles and an average of four variations of each title, that's more than 240 title templates.

▶ KEY TERM

Title—An image used to display credits, the name of a movie, identify people or places when they appear in a movie, or to superimpose text.

Some of the uses for titles are rolling credits, movie intros, lists, framing a scene or still, track mattes, and lower thirds. Every time you watch a television show or go to a movie, you see titles. The intro is a title, the credits are a title, breaks before commercials are titles, and any time text or a shape is shown over video (or a video is shown through the text or shape), you're seeing a title. You see lower-third titles whenever you watch the news—they are the titles at the bottom of the screen with the reporters' names. Track mattes are used to make text move across a screen with video behind the text remaining stationary, or to have text remaining stationary with video behind the text moving.

95

With Premiere Elements, titles are easy to create; the program gives you many templates to help you get started. You can use the templates as they are, or you can customize them to suit your particular project. You can even start from scratch with a blank canvas and make your very own creation. It doesn't matter if you use or customize the templates or create titles from scratch—titles are a lot of fun.

95	**About Titles**	
✔ BEFORE YOU BEGIN		**→ SEE ALSO**
29 About the Timeline and Video Tracks		**67** About Keyframing
33 Add or Move a Clip on the Timeline		**117** Customize a DVD Menu Screen Template

The first thing to do is to get familiar with the **Titles** workspace. From the workspace, you can create many types of titles to add to your movie. In the following tasks, you will learn many ways to use titles. In this task, the goal is to let you know where to find all the tools you will need during title creation.

To get to the **Titles** workspace, you have two options: You can click the **Titles** button or use the **Title** menu. Click the **Titles** button at the top-right corner of the screen to open the **Template Selection** dialog box. Hold down the **Titles** button to open a menu with title choices. Alternatively, choose **Title**, **New Title** from the menu bar to open a submenu of title choices.

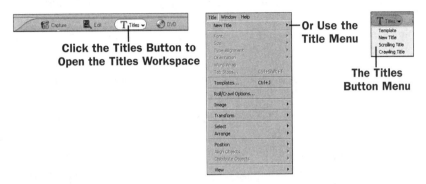

Click the Titles Button to Open the Titles Workspace

Or Use the Title Menu

The Titles Button Menu

*Access the **Titles** workspace using the **Titles** button or the **Title** menu.*

The **Title** menu is still available while you're in the **Titles** workspace. It has many options you will use while you're creating titles. Most of these options are also available to you as buttons on toolbars or in other menus.

Media Panel **The Title Toolbar** **Titler Panel**

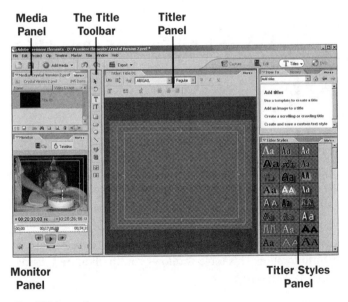

Monitor Panel **Titler Styles Panel**

*The **Titles** workspace.*

When you're working in the **Titles** workspace, you'll use the **Titler** panel, the **Titler Styles** panel, and the **Title** and **Align/Distribute** toolbars.

95

The **Titler** panel provides options that enable you to set the font and its attributes (bold, italic, or underline), create a new title, and experiment with roll/crawl options. Click the **More** button and choose **Safe Title Margin** or **Safe Action Margin** to display the safe margins around the clip (these margin guides are especially useful in ensuring that the whole title is visible when viewed on a television screen).

The **Titler Styles** panel has a large number of predefined fonts in various sizes and shapes. You can create your own fonts or use the predefined ones. Simply click the style you want to use, click the **Type** tool in the **Title** toolbar, and type away.

The **Title** toolbar contains 12 tools to help you create titles: **Selection** tool, **Rotation** tool, **Type** tool, **Vertical Type** tool, **Rectangle** tool, **Rounded Rectangle** tool, **Ellipse** tool, **Line** tool, **Add Image** button, **Color Properties** button, **Vertical Center** button, and **Horizontal Center** button.

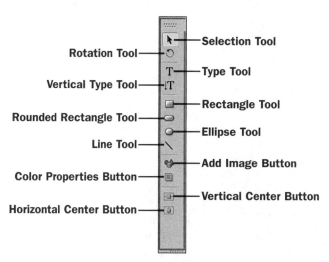

*The **Title** toolbar.*

From the main menu at the top of your screen, select **Window, Title Actions** to open the **Align/Distribute** toolbar. This toolbar allows you to align and distribute your text and images over the title.

The title templates are a great place to start when creating your first title, and even after you have become fluent at creating titles from scratch (see **103 Create a Title from Scratch**). The title templates can be accessed by clicking the **Titles** button or by choosing **Title, New Title, Based on Template** from the menu bar. They include the following types of titles:

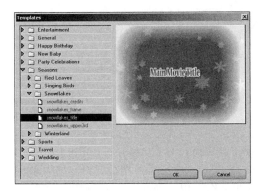

*The title categories and various options from the **Seasons** category.*

- **Title**—Template names in this category end with **_title** and have a full background title with an image and, generally, text. There is no transparent area to this type of title.

- **Credits**—Template names in this category end with **_credits**; they are rolling titles with predefined text boxes, similar to what you find in the **List** category. This type of title usually has a transparent background.

- **Frame**—Template names in this category end with **_frame** and are used to frame an image or a video clip. These templates have a transparent section cut out of the background and can include text.

- **Lower, Upper, and Other Thirds**—Templates in this category are the type of titles you see during television newscasts. The title takes up 1/3 of the viewable area—and the title can appear in the lower third of the viewable area, the upper third of the viewable area, and so on. You also see this type of title at some churches (which show the song lyrics on an overhead screen) and during sportscasts (to show a player's stats while still showing the action). The template names end with text such as **_upper3rd**.

- **Roll**—Templates in this category have a predefined roll. The title will roll from the bottom to the top of the screen.

- **List**—Templates in this category provide a stationary text list. You can customize these titles to turn them into rolling credits.

All the title templates are customizable. If you find a specific type you like, but it is not exactly the type you need, customize it. The following tasks show you how.

95

96 Use and Customize a Title Template

✔ BEFORE YOU BEGIN	→ SEE ALSO
95 About Titles	**94** Frame Your Video with an Image
	103 Create a Title from Scratch

This task guides you through the selection, use, and customization of one of the many title templates available in Premiere Elements. Considering that the titles are already predesigned, all you really have to do is select the proper template and change the text. Doing so gives you a very nice, easily created title. The hardest part is trying to decide which template to use!

1 Click the Titles Button

In the main taskbar at the top of the screen, click the **Titles** button to open the **Title Templates** dialog box.

2 Choose Title Template and Click OK

The **Title Templates** dialog box has a list of title categories, title names, and title types on the left; click a title and view the selected title in the preview screen on the right. Click the arrow to the left of a category name to see a list of title names for that category. The title names also have an arrow in front of them; click that arrow to see a list of title types. For this example, I used a title type from the **General** category, with the title name **Comicbook**, and with the title type **Comicbook_title**. When you click the **Comicbook_title** selection, the title appears in the preview on the right side of the dialog box. You can choose any other category of titles and look for title types that end in _**title** to achieve similar results.

When you're satisfied with the title you've selected, click **OK**. The **Titles** workspace opens with the selected title in the work area.

3 Highlight a Text Box and Change the Text

By default the **Type** tool is selected when you enter the **Titles** workspace. To edit the placeholder text in the title, simply click the main title text (in this example, *Our Hero*) and either press **Delete** or use the **Backspace** key to delete all the existing text. Either action empties the text box and allows you to enter new text into the area. Now just type the main title for your movie.

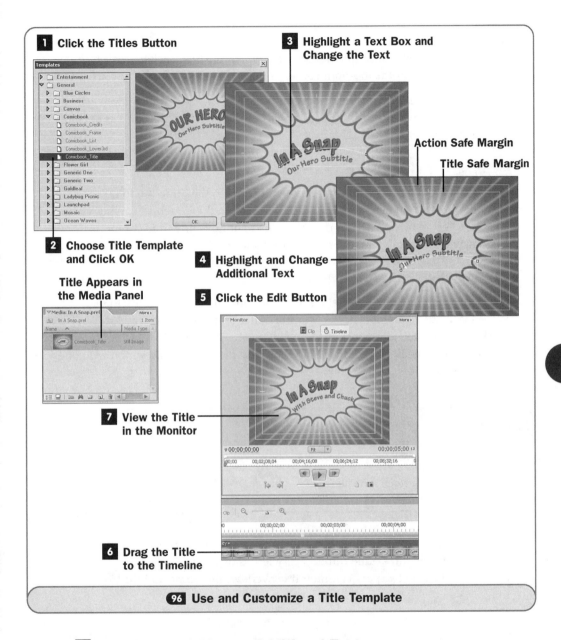

1 Click the Titles Button

2 Choose Title Template and Click OK

Title Appears in the Media Panel

3 Highlight a Text Box and Change the Text

Action Safe Margin

Title Safe Margin

4 Highlight and Change Additional Text

5 Click the Edit Button

7 View the Title in the Monitor

6 Drag the Title to the Timeline

96 Use and Customize a Title Template

4 Highlight and Change Additional Text

Most title templates also have another text area you can edit. For the **Comicbook_title** template, click in the text box that says *Our Hero Subtitle* and clear out the text box; you can leave it blank or enter new text here just as you did in step 3.

5 Click the Edit Button

When you are finished making text changes in the title, click the **Edit** button in the taskbar at the top-right corner of the screen.

Locate the **Media** panel and notice that the title has been added to the list of clips automatically. This happens every time you create a new title or open a title template.

6 Drag the Title to the Timeline

Simply drag the title clip from the **Media** panel to the **Timeline** to use it in your project. You can place the title anywhere on the **Timeline**, on any video track. Just remember that a main title does not have any transparent areas and will cover any images on tracks below it.

7 View the Title in the Monitor

Position the CTI in the **Timeline** over your title clip and click **Play** to see what the title looks like in the **Monitor**. After a title is on the **Timeline**, it behaves just like any other clip of a still image. You can add transitions and effects, change the duration, or anything else that you can do with a regular still-image clip.

96

97	**Create a Title Overlay for Your Video**
✔ **BEFORE YOU BEGIN**	→ **SEE ALSO**
95 About Titles **96** Use and Customize a Title Template	**93** Show Your Video Through a Shape or Text

One of the most used title types is a *title overlay*. You see this often in newscasts, sportscasts, movie intros, and almost every television show imaginable. In this task you will create two very common title overlays: the frame and the lower third.

▶ KEY TERM

Title overlay—The use of a title, containing transparent areas, to overlay a clip so the clip shows through the title. The title can contain text, shapes, or graphics in any combination.

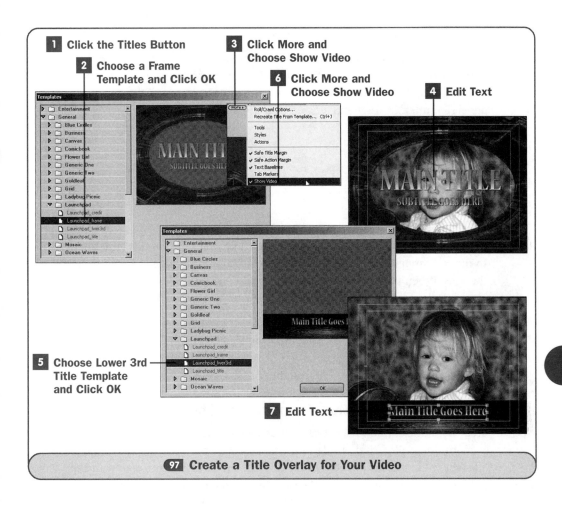

97 Create a Title Overlay for Your Video

◻ Click the Titles Button

From the main taskbar at the top of your screen, click the **Titles** button to open the **Title Template** dialog box.

◻ Choose a Frame Template and Click OK

For this example, I used the title type **Launchpad_frame**, located in the **General**, **Launchpad** selections. Click this frame to select it and look at the frame title in the preview window on the right side of the dialog box. You can choose any other category of titles and look for title types that end in **_frame** to achieve similar results.

When you've selected a frame you like, open it in the **Titles** workspace by clicking the **OK** button.

3 Click More and Choose Show Video

After clicking the **OK** button, the **Titles** workspace opens with your template in the **Titler** panel. Make sure that the CTI is over a video or a still clip on the **Timeline**. Click the **More** button at the top-right corner of the **Titler** panel. From the **More** menu, ensure that the Show Video option is selected.

▶ **TIP**

By moving the CTI over different clips, you can see what will look best behind your new title.

4 Edit Text

You should see the frame overlaying the current video clip on the **Timeline**. To make changes to the title text, click the text area and type to make your changes. When you're satisfied with the text, your frame title is ready and is placed in the **Media** panel, ready to be used in your movie.

Drag the title to the **Timeline** and place it on a track above the clip you want to overlay. Position the title by moving it up and down the **Timeline** and watching the **Monitor**, making sure that you place the title in just the right spot. To save your title for use in another project see **102 Save Your Title**.

97

5 Select a Lower 3rd Title Template and Click OK

Creating a title frame was just as easy as you'd expect it to be in Premiere Elements. A similar kind of title that lets a video clip show is the lower-third title—the title graphic appears in the lower third of the video screen with the video clip playing behind the title. Now let's create a lower-third title.

Without doing anything to your current workspace, click the **Titles** button in the top-right corner of the screen to launch the **Title Template** dialog box. For this example, I chose the **Launchpad_lwer3rd** type and clicked **OK**. You can choose any other category of titles and look for title types that end in **_lwer3rd** to achieve similar results.

When you're satisfied with the title you've selected, click the **OK** button.

6 Click More and Choose Show Video

Click the **OK** button to open the new title template in the **Titler** panel. Again, make sure that you have a video or still clip on the **Timeline** and that the CTI is positioned over that clip. Click the **More** button in the **Titler** panel and make sure that the **Show Video** option is selected.

7 **Edit Text**

Make any changes to the text; the title is automatically added to the **Media** panel, ready to be added to your movie.

Drag the title to the **Timeline** and place it on a track above the clip you want to overlay. Position the title by moving it up and down the **Timeline** and watching the **Monitor**, making sure that you place the title in just the right spot. To save the title for use in another project, see **102** **Save Your Title**.

---

98 Customize a Title Text Font

✔ BEFORE YOU BEGIN	→ SEE ALSO
96 Use and Customize a Title Template	**101** Create a *Star Wars*–Style Credit Roll

---

Not only can you customize a title template and change the text that appears there, you can also customize the attributes for the font you are using. The font attributes can be customized not only in style, size, italics, and underline, but also with various color and drop shadow options. Using the **Color Properties** dialog box to create unique fonts to use in your titles.

1 **Select and Open a Title**

If you have already created a title and it is located in the **Media** panel, double-click it to open the title in the **Titles** workspace. If you have not created a title yet, follow the instructions in **96** **Use and Customize a Title Template** to select and open a title in the **Titles** workspace. In this example, I used a title created from the **Stage_Title** template in the **Entertainment** category.

2 **Right-click the Text and Choose Color Properties**

Right-click the block of text in the title that you want to customize. The context menu opens. Select **Color Properties** to open the **Color Properties** dialog box.

▶ **NOTE**

For instruction on changing the text font; making the font bold, italic, or underlined; and changing the text direction or size, see **103** **Create a Title from Scratch**.

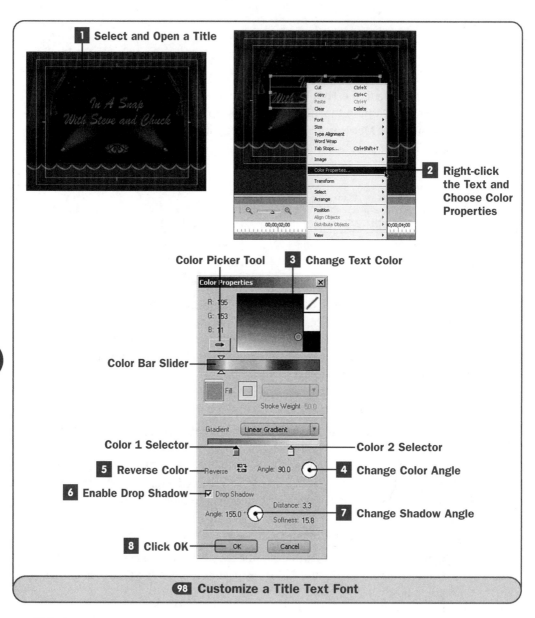

1 Select and Open a Title

2 Right-click the Text and Choose Color Properties

Color Picker Tool   **3** Change Text Color

Color Bar Slider

Color 1 Selector —————— Color 2 Selector

5 Reverse Color —— **4** Change Color Angle

6 Enable Drop Shadow

7 Change Shadow Angle

8 Click OK

98 Customize a Title Text Font

98

3 Change Text Color

Depending on the color format used by the text in the original template, you will have various options for changing the text color. In this example, you are customizing text with a linear gradient color fill. You can change the colors by clicking the **Color 1 Selector** and then clicking in the color picker window or by entering the correct R, G, and B numbers. Then click the **Color 2 Selector** and click to choose another color. You can also use the **Color Bar**

Slider to change the colors in the color picker window. Alternatively, click the **Color Picker** tool and select a color with it. The linear gradient fill provides a two-color gradient; other options provide as many as four colors.

4 Change Color Angle

For the color gradients like the one in the sample, you can change the color angle. Do this by rotating the **Angle** icon or by entering an exact number of degrees.

5 Reverse Color

Click the **Reverse Color** button to reverse the gradient colors.

6 Enable Drop Shadow

Not only does the **Color Properties** dialog box enable you to adjust the text color, it also allows you to add and adjust a drop shadow effect for the text. To add a drop shadow to your text, enable the **Drop Shadow** check box.

7 Change Shadow Angle

To change the angle of the drop shadow, you can rotate the **Angle** icon or enter an exact number of degrees.

99

8 Click OK

When you are finished customizing the text color and effects, click the **OK** button.

---

99 Create Rolling and Moving Credits

✔ BEFORE YOU BEGIN	→ SEE ALSO
96 Use and Customize a Title Template	**98** Customize a Title Text Font **101** Create a *Star Wars*–Style Credit Roll

Just like in Hollywood, you can create rolling credits for your movie. I can't even think of a movie that doesn't have rolling credits—it's an unwritten law that you have to have them!

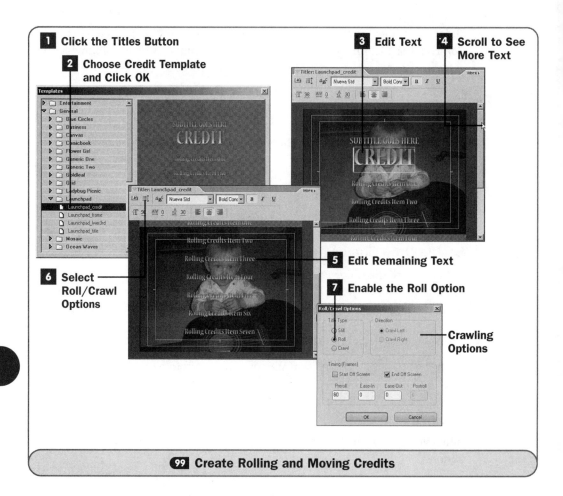

99 Create Rolling and Moving Credits

▶ **NOTE**

Moving panoramas have been in use since the days of Lewis and Clark. The moving panorama, or diorama, consists of a series of paintings on canvas which were then joined together to form one very long canvas sheet. This sheet was wound onto a vertical roller and moved across the stage and wound up on a similar roller on the other side. The canvas could be lighted from behind, front, or both, using oil or gas lamps. Smaller panoramas were placed in a box that someone could look into. If these dioramas had stationary objects inside the box while the canvas moved from behind, the result was a kind of modern video effect. In those days, moving panoramas were used primarily for advertising, but the same principle is still with us today in rolling credits.

Obviously, rolling credits are a good way to display a lot of information in a little space. I say "obviously" because the idea has spanned decades of film and is used constantly by the film industry. Seeing that this type of title has stood the test of time and that no one has seemingly come up with a better idea, I am sure that you will find a need to use rolling credits in your projects at some time.

With Premiere Elements, you can not only roll your title, you can also crawl your title. *Crawling* moves the title across the screen from right to left or from left to right. *Rolling* moves the title from the bottom of the screen to the top. No matter what type of motion you use, rolling or crawling, I am sure that you will find dozens of uses for this type of title. This type of title always has a transparent background so you can view the title over a color matte, a clip, a still image, or just a black background.

▶ **TIP**

To run your title over a color background instead of black, use a color matte. You can add a color matte to a track from the **Media** panel by clicking the **New Item** icon and selecting **Color Matte**. After the matte is created, you can drop it on a track below your title. For more details on color mattes, see **15** Add Special Media Clips.

1 **Click the Titles Button**

In the main taskbar, click the **Titles** button to open the **Title Templates** dialog box.

2 **Choose Credit Template and Click OK**

For this example, I used the title type **Launchpad_credit**, found in the **General**, **Launchpad** category. You can choose any other category of titles and look for title types that end in **_credit** to achieve similar results.

When you have selected the credit title you want to use, click **OK** to open the title in the **Titles** workspace.

▶ **TIP**

You can have your title move over a black background, a color background, a still image or video clip. Click the **More** button and select **Show Video**; the CTI controls what video is visible behind the title. You can view the image behind the title exactly as it will appear if, when finished, you place your title on a video track above the selected image on the **Timeline**.

3 **Edit Text**

This particular credit title template provides you with many lines of text. The text even continues below what you see in the **Titler** window. Click each section of text and make the appropriate changes to create a meaningful credit list for your movie project.

4 Scroll to See More Text

When you have edited all the lines of text you can see in the **Titler** panel, drag the scrollbar on the right side of the **Titler** panel to reveal additional text boxes.

5 Edit Remaining Text

Make changes to the remaining text. If there are more text lines than you need, you can delete the text boxes altogether: Click in the text area and press **Backspace** or **Delete** to clear the existing text. If you don't have enough lines of text, you can add more text by clicking the Type tool (see **95 About Titles**) and then clicking the space in the title where you want the text to be. This action creates a text box into which you can enter your additional text. You can also add additional text to an existing text box. Using the **Type** tool, select the text box you want to add text to and then position the cursor where you want to start typing. When you get to the end of a line, press the **Enter** key to create a new line.

6 Select Roll/Crawl Options

Click the **Roll/Crawl Options** button at the top of the **Titler** panel to open the **Roll/Crawl Options** dialog box.

7 Enable the Roll Option

Considering that in this example we have chosen a credit type title, the **Roll** option should already be selected. If you want your title to crawl horizontally across the screen instead of roll from top to bottom, enable the **Crawl** option.

> **▶ TIP**
>
> If you chose the **Crawl** option in step 7, the **Direction** options become available. Choose **Crawl Left** to make the text move from the right side of the screen and off the left side; choose **Crawl Right** to make the text start on the left side of the screen and move off the right side.

This dialog box also offers options under the **Timing (Frames)** section:

- **Start Off Screen**—The title starts rolling or crawling from off the screen. If it is a rolling title, the title appears first at the very bottom of the screen.

- **End Off Screen**—The title continues moving off the screen until it disappears from view. If it is a rolling title, the title disappears off the top of the screen.

If neither of these options is selected, the title will not roll or crawl. To start a title somewhere other than off screen, position the title where you want it to start and select only the **End Off Screen** option. To end your title somewhere other than off the screen, position your title where you want it to end and select only the **Start Off Screen** option.

- **Preroll**—The number of frames that will play before the roll or crawl begins. Only available if the **Start Off Screen** option is not checked.

- **Ease-In**—The number of frames to move at a slowly increasing speed at the beginning of the roll or crawl, increasing to the normal crawl or roll speed.

- **Ease-Out**—The number of frames to move at a slowly decreasing speed at the end of the roll or crawl, decreasing from the normal crawl or roll speed.

- **Postroll**—The number of frames that will play after the title has finished its roll or crawl. Only available if the **End Off Screen** option is not checked.

Make any changes you want to the settings in the **Roll/Crawl Options** dialog box and click the **OK** button. The rolling title has already been added to the **Media** panel for use in your movie.

100

To use the credit clip as either opening or closing credits in your movie project, drag the credit title clip off the **Media** panel and drop it on an upper video track on the **Timeline**. Position the clip so it aligns with the clip you want to show through the transparent background of the credit title clip.

---

100 **Create Custom Motion for Text**

✔ BEFORE YOU BEGIN	→ SEE ALSO
29 About the Timeline and Video Tracks	**93** Show Your Video Through a Shape or Text
67 About Keyframing	**103** Create a Title from Scratch
69 Add Motion to a Still	
95 About Titles	

Sometimes you want something more than a simple rolling or crawling title. You might want the title to move like an old Pong game, or maybe you want the text to move diagonally. Premiere Elements gives you the tools you need to accomplish this task. Using keyframes, you can make a title change size or direction easily. By adjusting title size and movement, and adding additional effects, the number of title possibilities is unlimited.

100

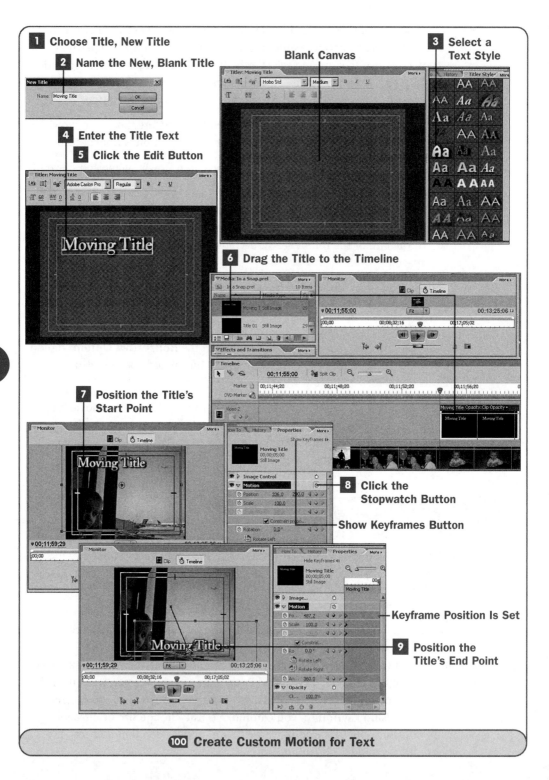

1 Choose Title, New Title

2 Name the New, Blank Title

Blank Canvas

3 Select a Text Style

4 Enter the Title Text

5 Click the Edit Button

Moving Title

6 Drag the Title to the Timeline

7 Position the Title's Start Point

8 Click the Stopwatch Button

Show Keyframes Button

Keyframe Position Is Set

9 Position the Title's End Point

100 Create Custom Motion for Text

1 Choose Title, New Title

From the menu bar at the top of the screen, choose **Title**, **New Title**, and then select your title type (**Default Still**, **Default Roll**, or **Default Crawl**) to open the **New Title** dialog box. For this task, I selected the **Default Still Title**; we will add the motion later.

▶ NOTES

Alternatively, you can access the **New Title** dialog box in a more roundabout fashion: In the main taskbar at the top of your screen, click the **Titles** button to open the **Title Templates** dialog box. Click the **Cancel** button to dismiss the **Templates** dialog box and instead open the **New Title** dialog box.

Alternatively, you can click and hold the **Titles** button to access a submenu with an option for a **New Title**.

2 Name the New, Blank Title

In the **New Title** dialog box, give your title a name. Click the **OK** button; the **Titles** workspace opens with a completely blank title in the **Titler** panel.

3 Select a Text Style

From the **Titler Styles** panel, select the text style you want to use for the title by clicking it.

4 Enter the Title Text

Click the location in the **Titler** panel where you want to add the text. This action opens a text box to hold the text you are typing. For this example, I added text to the upper-left area in the **Titler**. Be sure to keep your text within the safe title margin.

In most cases, you want to limit your text to a single line or even a single word. With the text moving around, you don't want to make it difficult for your audience to read.

5 Click the Edit Button

When are done entering your text, click the **Edit** button on the main taskbar at the top of your screen. The **Edit** workspace opens, where you can start to put motion to your title.

100

▶ **NOTE**

It is possible to complete this task from within the **Titles** workspace. The **Effects and Transitions** panel, along with the **Timeline** and **Monitor**, are visible in the Titles workspace. And the **Properties** panel can be opened as a free-floating window by choosing **Window, Properties** from the main menu. The only problem with working from the **Titles** workspace is that space gets even more limited than normal. With video editing, space is very important, and the **Edit** workspace is designed for just that: editing.

6 Drag the Title to the Timeline

The title you just created has been automatically added to the **Media** panel. To add the title to your current project, just drag the title from the **Media** panel and drop it on the **Timeline**. This particular title, as well as many others, has a transparent background. Video shows through the title when it is placed on a track above an image or clip on the **Timeline**. If the title is placed on **Video 1**, the background is black.

7 Position the Title's Start Point

Position the CTI at the first frame of your title. You might have to zoom way in on the **Timeline** to make sure you get the very first frame; view the title in the **Monitor**. Make sure that the title is still selected on the **Timeline** and look at the **Properties** panel.

8 Click the Stopwatch Button

In the **Properties** panel, click the arrow in front of the **Motion** listing to open up the control panel for that property. For this moving-title effect, you are interested in the title's opening **Position** and **Scale** keyframe options. In the **Monitor**, drag the title to the position where you want it to appear when the title clip starts playing. When the title text is where you want it, click the stopwatch icon next to the **Motion** listing in the **Properties** panel to set the keyframe markers.

▶ **NOTE**

If you don't see the timeline in the **Properties** panel, click the **Show Keyframes** button at the top of the panel to display it.

9 Position the Title's End Point

Position the CTI in the main **Timeline** at the very last frame of the title. You might have to zoom out and back in on the **Timeline** to ensure that you have selected the last frame of the title. You should still be able to see the title in the **Monitor**.

100

Click the title in the **Monitor** and drag it to the position you want it to be at the end of its movement. Because you have already set keyframe markers for this clip in step 8, the markers for this new position are set for you automatically.

The only thing left to do is render the **Timeline** and play the title. If you don't quite like the movement, go back to the first frame of the title clip and make adjustments; then make adjustments to the final frame of the title clip. Continue tweaking the positions of the title until you have the exact movement for which you are looking.

▶ **TIP**

Use the **Scale** option in the **Properties** panel to make your title shrink or grow as it moves. Simply adjust the scale up (more than 100) to make it larger, or down (less than 100) to make it smaller. Try setting it very small on the first frame and very large on the last frame. Not only will the title text move across the screen as you've plotted it, it will grow in size as it does.

---

101 | **Create a *Star Wars*–Style Credit Roll**

✔ BEFORE YOU BEGIN	→ SEE ALSO
68 About the Properties Panel	**87** Create a *Brady Bunch* Effect
74 About Advanced Effects	**93** Show Your Video Through a
103 Create a Title from Scratch	Shape or Text

101

On the Adobe user's forum, one of the most commonly asked questions about titles is how to create *Star Wars*–style rolling credits. This style of credit roll has been used for years, especially in science fiction movies. But the *Star Wars* title is a bit unique in its style and application. It must have been quite a bit of work creating that title in the late 1970s. It took a lot more time and equipment to do then what you can do today in Premiere Elements in about 10 minutes.

1 Open a Blank Title and Enter Text

For this task, start from a blank canvas and only enter text. Choose **Title**, **New Title**, give the title a name, and click **OK** to open a blank title in the **Titles** workspace. Using the default text style, enter all the text for your title. I have yet to find a limit to the lines of text you can enter on a title; just keep pressing **Enter** to start a new line. If, by chance, you should run out of room for text in one title clip, just start a second title. Be sure to keep your text within the safe title margin as you are entering it, and center the text using the **Horizontal** and **Vertical Center** tools in the **Title** toolbar.

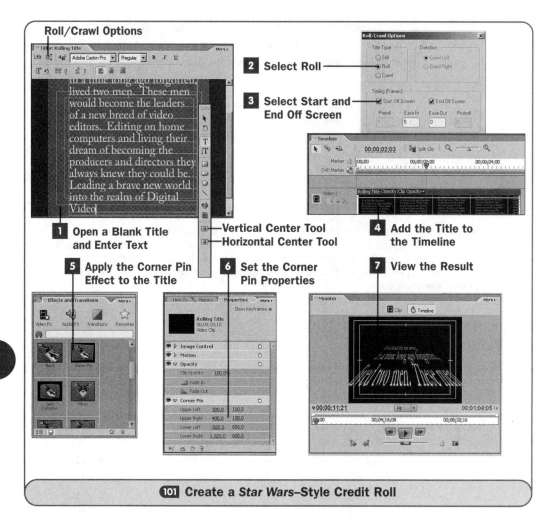

101 Create a *Star Wars*–Style Credit Roll

2 Select Roll

When you have entered all your title text, click the **Roll/Crawl Options** button at the top of the **Titler** panel to open the **Roll/Crawl Options** dialog box. Select **Roll** as the type of title you want to create.

3 Select Start and End Off Screen

Under the Timing (Frames) section of the **Roll/Crawl Options** dialog box, enable both the **Start Off Screen** and **End Off Screen** check boxes. Make sure that the **Ease-In** and **Ease-Out** values are set to **0**.

4 Add the Title to the Timeline

Click the **Edit** button located on the main taskbar to open the **Edit** workspace. Your title has automatically been added to the **Media** panel. Drag the title from the **Media** panel and drop it on a video track on the main **Timeline**. If you drop the title on the **Video 1** track, it will have a black background. Because the title has a transparent background, you can place it on a track above another clip and have the lower track video show through the title.

5 Apply the Corner Pin Effect to the Title

In the **Effects and Transitions** panel, locate the **Corner Pin** effect. It is located in the **Video FX** collection in the **Distort** category. Drag and drop the effect on the title.

6 Set the Corner Pin Properties

Place the CTI in the main **Timeline** over any part of the title and make sure that the title is selected by clicking it. In the **Properties** panel, click the arrow in front of the **Corner Pin** listing to open the control panel for the **Corner Pin** effect. Set the **Corner Pin** properties as follows:

101

Upper Left: 300.0 and 100.0

Upper Right: 400.0 and 100.0

Lower Left: –500.0 and 600.0

Lower Right: 1220.0 and 600.0

Each time you enter or change a value in one of the position fields, you can view the change to the title in the **Monitor**. You can adjust these values over and over again. If you don't quite like the way it looks, try a higher or lower number until you get it just right.

7 View the Result

Render the **Timeline** by pressing **Enter**. Move the CTI in the main timeline to the first frame of the title clip and play your *Star Wars*–style credit roll. Enjoy the fruit of your labors!

102 Save Your Title

✔ BEFORE YOU BEGIN	→ SEE ALSO
95 About Titles	**103** Create a Title from Scratch
96 Use and Customize a Title Template	

As you know, after you create and edit a title, it is automatically added to the **Media** panel. You can use that title again in the project in which it resides. But what if you want to use that same title in another project?

A simple process allows you to save any title for use in any project. After you save a title, it is as easy to add it to a project as it is to add any other media to your project. When you have created a few different titles (as described in the previous tasks), let's learn how to save a title to use again.

102

1 Select the Title to Be Saved

In the **Media** panel, highlight the title you want to save as a template for use in other projects.

2 Choose File, Export, Title

From the main menu bar, select **File**, **Export**, **Title**. The **Save Title** dialog box opens.

3 Select Title/File Location

In the **Save in** text box, select the location where you want to save the title. You can use the default location or browse to another folder or directory.

4 Name the Title

In the **File name** text box, type a name for your title. Be sure to give it a name that will help you remember what type of title it is and what it would be used for.

5 Click Save

Click **Save**, and the title is saved in the selected destination. It will have the filename you entered followed by a **.prtl** extension.

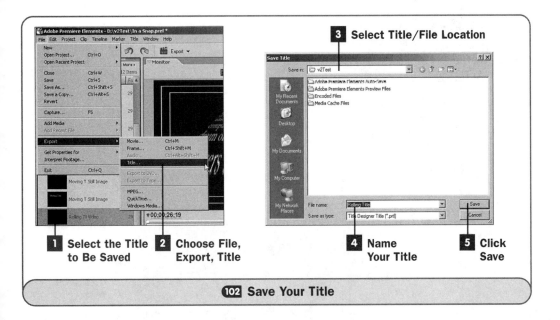

3 Select Title/File Location

1 Select the Title to Be Saved   **2** Choose File, Export, Title   **4** Name Your Title   **5** Click Save

102 Save Your Title

► **TIP**

Titles are saved with a **.prtl** extension. If you want to use this particular title in another project, use the **Add Media** button to add the title file to the **Media** panel, just as you would to add any other type of media to your project (see **14** **Add Media with the Adobe Media Downloader**). When browsing for the file, look for the filename you gave the title and the **.prtl** extension at the end.

103

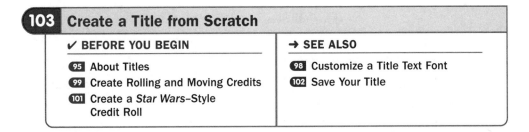

103 | **Create a Title from Scratch**

✔ **BEFORE YOU BEGIN**

95 About Titles
99 Create Rolling and Moving Credits
101 Create a *Star Wars*–Style Credit Roll

→ **SEE ALSO**

98 Customize a Title Text Font
102 Save Your Title

Even though Premiere Elements comes with hundreds of title templates, sometimes you just can't find a template that will accomplish what you want. What do you do then?

That's what this task is all about. Here we will provide the instruction you need to successfully create a title from scratch. With virtually unlimited fonts, styles, colors, backgrounds, and various other options, I doubt there is a limit to what you can do. You can even create your own unique background in Photoshop Elements and use that as your title.

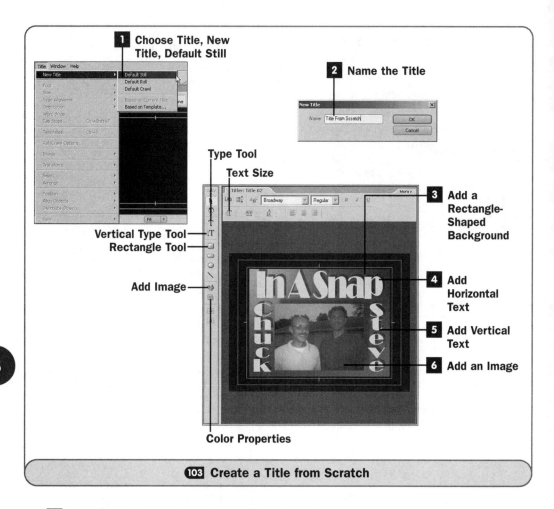

1 Choose Title, New Title, Default Still

2 Name the Title

Type Tool

Text Size

3 Add a Rectangle-Shaped Background

Vertical Type Tool
Rectangle Tool

4 Add Horizontal Text

Add Image

5 Add Vertical Text

6 Add an Image

Color Properties

103 Create a Title from Scratch

103

1 Choose Title, New Title, Default Still

From the main menu, choose **Title, New Title, Default Still**. The **New Title** dialog box opens, where you can name your new title.

2 Name the Title

In the **New Title** dialog box, type a name for your title and click **OK**. The **Titles** workspace opens.

In the **Titles** workspace, you will see a blank canvas to work with. Now it is up to you and your imagination. For this task, you will add a shape, horizontal and vertical text, and an image, just to get your creative juices flowing.

3 Add a Rectangle-Shaped Background

Click the **Rectangle** tool, and then click in a corner of the **Titler** panel. Drag the mouse to create a rectangle to cover the inside margin box (the Title Safe Margin). After you have the rectangle the correct size, open the **Color Properties** dialog box by clicking the **Color Properties** button. Select a four-color gradient, your colors, and a drop shadow. For details on the color properties and how to use them, see **98 Customize a Title Text Font**.

▶ **NOTE**

For details about the tools and menus available in the **Titles** workspace, see **95 About Titles**.

4 Add Horizontal Text

Click the **Type** tool and then click on the area of the **Titler** panel where you want the text to appear. Before you start typing, select the font you want to use by clicking the **Font** selection; a drop-down menu shows all the available fonts. Pick a font. To the right of the **Font** drop-down list are font attributes (bold, italic, and underlined). Use these options the same as you do in most word-processing applications such as Microsoft Word. To change the size of the text, click the **Text Size** button and drag the mouse to the right to make the text larger, or to the left to make the text smaller.

103

▶ **TIP**

To center your text vertically or horizontally, use the centering tools in the **Title** toolbar, located below the **Color Properties**.

5 Add Vertical Text

Add vertical text by clicking the **Vertical Type** tool and then clicking the area of the **Titler** panel where you want the text to be placed. The same options mentioned in step 4 are available to change the font and the text characteristics.

6 Add an Image

Click the **Add Image** button to open a browse dialog box that will allow you to find an image for your title. Select the image you want to use and click **OK** to open that image in the **Titler** panel. To resize the image to fit in the available space, right-click the image and choose **Transform, Scale** from the context menu. In the **Scale** dialog box that opens, enter a number greater than or less than 100%. Entering a number greater than 100% makes the image larger; entering a number less than 100% makes the image smaller.

▶ TIPS

To add an image to your title, use the **Add Image** button or choose **Image**, **Add Image** from the main menu bar or a context menu. You cannot drag an image clip from the **Media** panel to the **Titler** panel.

If you have photo-editing software such as Photoshop Elements, you can use that to create a unique background for your title. The image you create can have transparent areas that video can show through, or you can create transparent cookie-cutter shapes. Premiere Elements works very well with Photoshop Elements; all the images you create in Photoshop Elements can easily be imported into Premiere Elements, retaining all the image characteristics and properties.

▶ NOTE

At any time, you can click the **Selection** tool and then click any item in the **Titler** panel to drag, reposition, or resize the item.

103

14

Exporting Your Video

Not only can you burn your finished movie to a DVD, you can also output your project file in four formats. You can even output your movie back to your camcorder or, with the proper mechanical setup, to a VHS tape. All the tasks in this chapter dealing with outputting your video start in the same place: the **File, Export** submenu on the taskbar at the top of your screen. You can export a clip from the **Media** panel, a portion of the **Timeline**, or the entire **Timeline**. This submenu contains the following output, or export, options:

- The **Movie** option creates your movie as a Microsoft DV-AVI file, or as other formats if you use the **Advanced** features.

- The **Frame** option grabs a still from your video. For details on how to capture a still image from your video clip, see **21 Grab a Still from Video**.

- The **Audio** option exports only the audio from a video clip.

- The **Title** option exports a selected title.

- Selecting the **Export to DVD** option opens the **Burn DVD** dialog box.

- Details about the **Export to Tape** option are covered in **105 Output to DV Hardware or Export to Tape**.

- The **MPEG** option outputs your movie as an MPEG file, as explained in **108 Output a MPEG File**.

- The **QuickTime** option outputs your movie as a QuickTime MOV file, as explained in **109 Output a QuickTime File**.

- The **Windows Media** option outputs your movie as a Windows Media WMV file, as explained in **107 Output a Windows Media (WMV) File**.

These output options are necessary if you would like to put your movie on a CD, send your movie as an email attachment, or upload your movie to be viewed on a website.

The **MPEG, Windows Media (MWV)**, and **QuickTime** file outputs all have settings you can change. These settings control the viewable size, the choice of codec, various audio properties, and the choice of template suitable for web viewing. The templates are based on the viewer's Internet connection speed. For example, the DSL template creates a larger file and viewable image than the mobile phone template does.

▶ **WEB RESOURCES**

www.apple.com/quicktime

www.real.com

MPEG files play in a variety of media players, WMV files play in Windows Media Player, and QuickTime files play in the QuickTime Player. Many of these files can also be played in RealPlayer. QuickTime Player and RealPlayer are available free at their respective websites.

▶ **NOTES**

Make sure you have a clip highlighted in the **Media** panel or on the **Timeline** before you choose an option from the **File, Export** submenu. If not, the **Export** option is not available.

If you do not have your camcorder or DV device connected and online, the **Export to Tape** option is not available.

When outputting to the various formats in this chapter, we will talk briefly about the advanced settings. Although the advanced settings are illustrated in the tasks, I recommend that you leave them at their defaults. If you are already—or when you become—an advanced user, the basic information in these tasks can help you find the advanced settings you need.

104

104 | **Output to an AVI Movie**

✔ BEFORE YOU BEGIN	→ SEE ALSO
4 About Video Capture	**105** Output to DV Hardware or Export to Tape
14 Add Media with the Adobe Media Downloader	**111** About Burning to DVDs

Audio Video Interleaved (AVI) is a container format for video with synchronized audio. An AVI file can contain different compressed video and audio streams. AVI files can be played on most computers using software such as Windows Media Player. The AVI format has less compression than formats such as MPEG2 and therefore creates larger files. Although the lesser-compressed files produce better quality video, they are not very useful for the Internet. The most common use for AVI files with Premiere Elements is for combining projects. You can export multiple projects as AVI files and then add them all to a single project using the **Add Media** feature. The AVI files created can also be opened in many third-party editing and DVD authoring applications.

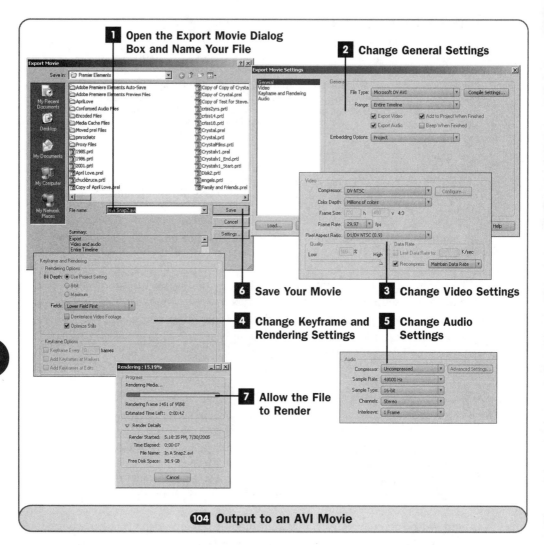

104 Output to an AVI Movie

■ Open the Export Movie Dialog Box and Name Your File

To get started outputting your movie as an AVI file, choose **File**, **Export**, **Movie** from the menu bar at the top of the screen. Choose a name for your AVI file and type it in the **File name** box.

■ Change General Settings

If you want to change the settings for your AVI file, click the **Settings** button; otherwise jump ahead to step 6.

In the **Export Movie Settings** dialog box that appears, click a category name in the left pane to switch between the various kinds of settings (**General**, **Video, Keyframe and Rendering**, and **Audio**). In the **General** settings, you can change the following options:

▶ **TIP**

For more information about all the settings available when exporting to any of the file formats (AVI, WMV, MPEG, or QuickTime), see the Adobe Premiere Elements Help files. Simply enter the setting name in the search box to get a detailed description of what that setting does. You can also search the Internet using your favorite search engine to come up with even more detailed information on various settings.

- **File Type**—Allows you to select from various codecs and file types such as Microsoft AVI, Microsoft DV-AVI, and various image formats, as well as filmstrip. The filmstrip option exports a video as a number of still images. The default is Microsoft DV-AVI.

- **Compile Settings**—These options vary depending on the file type you choose.

- **Range**—Specifies the range to export (**Entire Timeline** or **Work Area Bar**). The **Work Area Bar** option exports the range covered by the work area bar. The default is **Entire Timeline**.

- **Export Video**—When this option is selected, the video tracks are exported. Do not select this option if you do not want to export the video tracks.

- **Export Audio**—When this option is selected, the audio tracks are exported. Do not select this option if you do not want to export the audio tracks.

- **Add to Project When Finished**—Selecting this option adds the resulting file to the **Media** panel.

- **Beep When Finished**—When this option is selected, your computer will beep when it has finished creating the file.

- **Embedding Options**—Includes in the exported file the information needed to use the **Edit Original** command. When this information is available in your file, you will be able to open and edit the original project from any application that supports the **Edit Original** command. This option is on by default.

When you have made the changes you want to these settings, click the **Video** option in the left pane to move to the **Video** settings.

104

3 Change Video Settings

On the **Video** page of the **Export Movie Settings** dialog box, the following options are available:

- **Compressor**—Selections vary depending on the file type. For Microsoft DV-AVI, the options are **DV NTSC** and **DV PAL**.

- **Color Depth**—Selections vary depending on the file type. In most cases, the only choice is **Millions+** of colors.

- **Frame Size**—Enter the horizontal and vertical size in pixels. The default for NTSC is **720×480**. Depending on your use, you might want to make changes to the frame size such as 800×600 or 1024×768.

- **Frame Rate**—Selections vary depending on the file type. For Microsoft DV-AVI, you can choose a frame rate between 1 frame per second and 60 frames per second. The default for NTSC is 29.97 frames per second.

- **Pixel Aspect Ratio**—Selection varies depending on the file type. For Microsoft DV-AVI and NTSC, there are various options such as 2:1 or 16:9 (widescreen). The default is **D1/DV NTSC (.09)**.

- **Quality**—This slider can range from 1% to 100%. This option is not available for all codecs.

- **Data Rate**—Allows you to change the data rate in kb/second and also enables you to choose whether to recompress the video.

104

When you have made the changes you want to these settings, click the **Keyframe and Rendering** option in the left pane to move to the **Keyframe and Rendering** settings.

4 Change Keyframe and Rendering Settings

On the **Keyframe and Rendering** page of the **Export Movie Settings** dialog box, the following **Rendering** options are available:

- **Bit Depth**—Choose from **Use Project Setting**, **8 bit**, or **Maximum**.

- **Fields**—Choose from **Progressive Scan**, **Lower Field First**, or **Upper Field First**. The default is **Lower Field First**. You also have the option to select **Deinterlace Video Footage** and **Optimize Stills**.

- **Keyframe Options**—Select from **Keyframe Every XX frames**, **Add Keyframes at Markers**, or **Add Keyframes at Edits**. These options are not enabled with all file types.

When you have made the changes you want to these settings, click the **Audio** option in the left pane to move to the **Audio** settings.

5 Change Audio Settings

On the **Audio** page of the **Export Movie Settings** dialog box, you can change the following options:

- **Compressor**—Allows you to select the type of codec used for compression of the audio portion of the file. The default is **Uncompressed** and is usually the only option.

- **Sample Rate**—Allows you to select a rate in Hz (32000, 44100, or 48000); the default is 48000Hz. CD quality is 44.1kHz. Resampling (setting a different rate than the original audio) also requires additional processing time; avoid resampling by capturing audio at the final rate.

- **Sample Type**—Choose from 8 bit or 16 bit. In most cases, the only option is the default of 16 bit. Choose a higher bit depth and **Stereo** for better quality, or choose a lower bit depth and **Mono** to reduce processing time and disk-space requirements. CD quality is 16-bit stereo.

- **Channels**—Choose between **Mono** and **Stereo**. **Stereo** provides two channels of audio; **Mono** provides one channel. If you choose to export a stereo track as mono, the audio will be downmixed.

- **Interleave**—This setting deals with audio processing. Higher values store longer audio segments and require less frequent processing. Higher values also require more RAM. The default is 1 Frame.

When you are finished making changes to any of the settings in the **Export Movie Settings** dialog box, click **OK** to go back to the **Export Movie** dialog box.

6 Save Your Movie

When you finish naming the AVI file and changing any necessary settings, click the **Save** button. Premiere Elements starts exporting your movie and opens the **Rendering** dialog box.

7 Allow the File to Render

Before Premiere Elements can save your movie, it must render the current video. How long this takes depends on the size of the video and the speed of your computer. You can watch the progress bar, see the number of frames rendered so far and the total number of frames, as well as the estimated time left. If, for some reason, you change your mind and don't want to save the

104

AVI file with the settings you supplied, click the **Cancel** button to stop the rendering.

▶ NOTE

If you cancel the rendering of your movie, the AVI file is not saved.

If you selected the **Add to Project** option, your new AVI file is now in the **Media** panel. You can also import your AVI file into another project, combining multiple projects together. The resulting file can also be opened in Windows Media Player and other video-editing programs.

---

105 | **Output to DV Hardware or Export to Tape**

✔ BEFORE YOU BEGIN	→ SEE ALSO
4 About Video Capture	**107** Output a Windows Media (MWV) File
14 Add Media with the Adobe Media Downloader	**112** Create an Auto-Play DVD

104

Sometimes you might have a need to put your movie back onto a DV tape or even a VHS tape. Even in the year 2006 and beyond, not everyone has a DVD player, but most people have a VCR. So for those family members and friends who can't seem to jump into the twenty-first century, you can put your movie onto VHS tape or DV tape as easily as you can put it on a DVD.

Another good reason to put your movie projects onto camcorder tape is for archiving purposes. Moving your completed video to one or two tapes will get those huge files off your computer, leaving them only a capture away from being used again.

The hardware setup for this procedure is no different from capturing video (see **4** **About Video Capture**). The only changes might be in the set up of your camcorder or digital converter. See the user's manual for your device for instructions on recording from your computer.

1 Open the Export to Tape Dialog Box and Set Device Control

Choose **File**, **Export**, **Export to Tape** from the menu bar at the top of your screen. The **Export to Tape** dialog box opens. Notice that there are three sections: **Device Control**, **Options**, and **Export Status**.

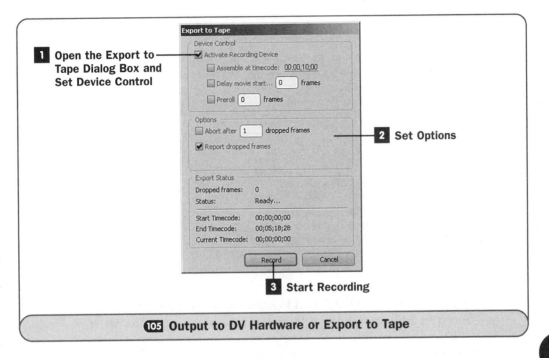

1 Open the Export to Tape Dialog Box and Set Device Control

2 Set Options

3 Start Recording

105 Output to DV Hardware or Export to Tape

In the **Device Control** section are the following options:

- **Activate Recording Device**—If you have a digital camcorder, this option starts the camcorder in record mode automatically.

- **Assemble at timecode**—Indicates the place on your DV tape that you want the recording to begin. You can stripe a tape by first recording only black video. (Record black video by recording any length of tape with the lens cap on.) If your tape is not striped, leave this option disabled. The recording begins at the current tape location.

▶ **NOTE**

Opinions vary as to whether striping a tape is beneficial. Striping the tape places a continuous timecode on your tape, which is good in theory because no spaces on the tape are missing a timecode and your editing is much easier when this information is available. For one thing, it is the way that Premiere Elements determines scene changes when capturing video to your project. Some camcorders might have a problem with striping when footage is recorded over the existing timecode and for some reason the timecodes don't match. It is always best to consult your camcorder manual before deciding to stripe your tapes.

- **Delay movie start**—Specifies the number of quarter frames to delay the movie so it can be synchronized with the DV device's recording start time.

• **Preroll**—Specifies the number of frames to back up on the recording deck before the specified **Assemble at timecode**. Specify enough frames for the deck to reach a constant tape speed. Many decks operate fine with a 5-second or 150-frame preroll.

For most purposes, there is no need to change these settings.

▶ NOTES

If you are exporting to a digital converter such as the ADS A/V Pyro Link, be sure to disable the **Activate Recording Device** check box.

If you are exporting to a digital converter instead of to a camcorder, check your user manual. The device might require additional set up, cables, or another device before being able to perform the digital-to-analog conversion.

▌2 Set Options

The **Options** section of the **Export to Tape** dialog box includes two items: **Abort after (number) dropped frames** and **Report dropped frames**. If you check the **Abort after** box and enter a number into the text box, Premiere Elements stops the recording if it drops that number of frames. If you check only the **Report dropped frames** box, Premiere Elements keeps a running total of all dropped frames. You can see this total in the **Export Status** section.

▶ TIP

Dropping a frame or two is not necessarily a bad thing. Because your eye cannot see each individual frame at 30 frames per second, one or two dropped frames won't likely be noticeable. So don't sweat a few dropped frames. If you encounter *many* dropped frames, however, check all your cables and your setup in general because something is not working properly.

▌3 Start Recording

When all the settings are just the way you want them, click the **Record** button. A **Rendering** dialog box appears for a few seconds to a few minutes, depending on the size of your movie and the speed of your computer. Generally, the audio portion of your video is the only thing that has to be rendered at this point unless you have added transitions or effects to your clips. After the rendering is completed, the recording will start automatically.

If you selected the **Activate Recording Device** option, your camcorder will start recording automatically as well. If not, you will have to activate your recorder manually.

In the **Export Status** section of the **Export to Tape** dialog box, notice whether the export is experiencing any dropped frames (this value should remain at 0 but will grow if frames are being dropped); the status (during export, it should say **Recording**); and the **Start Timecode**, **End Timecode**, and **Current Timecode** (the starting and ending points of your movie on the **Timeline**, and the position on the **Timeline** at which recording is currently taking place; when the current timecode reaches the end timecode, the recording stops).

▶ **TIPS**

It is a good idea to have a television monitor hooked up to view the output from Premiere Elements. That way, you can easily view what is being recorded. If there are any problems, you will be aware of them when it is happening, not when you attempt to watch the tape. Refer to your camcorder or digital converter manual to set up a television monitor for viewing the output.

After you click **Record**, Premiere Elements renders the audio portion of your video. This takes a few seconds; if you are using a digital converter rather than a camcorder, don't be too quick to press the record button on your VCR.

106 **About Different TV Standards**   **106**

✔ BEFORE YOU BEGIN	→ SEE ALSO
4 About Video Capture	**18** About Troubleshooting Add Media
14 Add Media with the Adobe Media Downloader	

There are three primary TV standards in the world: PAL, NTSC, and SECAM. Premiere Elements uses only the PAL or NTSC standard when burning a DVD. Most DVD players can play only one of the standards (PAL or NTSC—the Premiere Elements DVD format does not directly support SECAM because SECAM devices play PAL formats just fine). Additionally, there is the confusion surrounding region specifications. Here we briefly describe the formats and how they affect you and your video editing.

At their heart, DVDs are merely carriers of data files containing compressed audio-visual information. This information can be placed on DVD in one of two resolutions: 720×576 pixels (PAL DVDs) or 720×480 pixels (NTSC DVDs) with various frame rates (24, 25, and 30 frames per second are common). The DVD player itself takes this data file and formats it appropriately for display in either PAL or NTSC.

Here are the three primary television standards used throughout the world:

- **PAL (Phase Alternate Line)**—The television broadcast standard throughout Europe (except in France, where SECAM is the standard). This standard broadcasts 625 lines of resolution, nearly 20% more than the U.S. NTSC standard of 525 lines.

- **NTSC (National Television Systems Committee)**—There was a time when TV was just black and white. Eventually, color TV took over, and the Federal Communications Commission established the NTSC standard of 525 lines of resolution per second for broadcasts in the United States. The NTSC standard combines blue, red, and green signals with an FM frequency for audio.

- **SECAM (Sequential Couleur avec Mémoire)**—The television broadcast standard in France, the Middle East, and most of Eastern Europe, SECAM broadcasts 819 lines of resolution per second.

The DVD world is divided into six regions. To keep it simple, this means that DVD players and DVDs are labeled for operation only within a specific geographical region in the world. For example, the United States is in region 1; all DVD players sold in the United States are made to region 1 specifications. As a result, region 1 players can play only region 1 discs. That's right—the DVDs themselves are encoded for a specific region. On the back of each DVD package, you will a find a region number (1 thru 6).

106

▶ **NOTE**

The DVDs you create with Premiere Elements are region free; you can play them in any of the six regions. Just be careful of the standard you use (PAL or NTSC). NTSC-formatted DVDs play on all NTSC and most PAL DVD players; but PAL-formatted DVDs will not play on NTSC DVD players.

▶ **WEB RESOURCES**

www.dvddemystified.com/dvdfaq.html

www.microcinema.com/index/ntsc

Visit either of these sites to learn more about TV standards and DVD regions.

---

107 | **Output a Windows Media (WMV) File**

✔ **BEFORE YOU BEGIN**	→ **SEE ALSO**
4 About Video Capture	**109** Output a QuickTime File
14 Add Media with the Adobe Media Downloader	**111** About Burning to DVDs

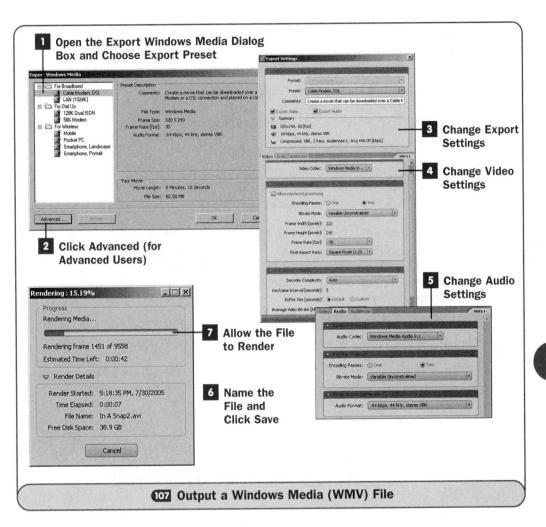

1 Open the Export Windows Media Dialog Box and Choose Export Preset

2 Click Advanced (for Advanced Users)

3 Change Export Settings

4 Change Video Settings

5 Change Audio Settings

6 Name the File and Click Save

7 Allow the File to Render

107 Output a Windows Media (WMV) File

Windows Media Video (WMV) is a popular format primarily because it plays well in Windows Media Player, a free media player that comes with the Microsoft Windows XP operating system. The WMV file format can also be compressed small enough to make it a great choice for email or websites, and the quality can be rather good. If bandwidth is an issue, this is a good option. A WMV file can be scaled to allow streaming over dialup and DSL connections and even for portable devices. If any of these options is your goal, consider outputting your Premiere Elements movie project as a WMV file.

1 Open the Export Windows Media Dialog Box and Choose Export Preset

Choose **File**, **Export**, **Windows Media** from the menu bar at the top of your screen to open the **Export Windows Media** dialog box.

If you want to output an DV-AVI file (as explained in 📺 **Output to an AVI Movie**), you know that DV-AVI files are much too large for email or website use; therefore, the output process does not ask you to make choices to establish the size (or compression and quality) of the output file. WMV, MPEG, and QuickTime formats, however, all provide you the ability to choose how the file will be viewed most often; you make a selection by choosing a preset.

When you choose one of the presets in the **Export Windows Media** dialog box, Premiere Elements automatically sets all the default settings based on that preset. The preset options are, broadly, **For Broadband**, **For Dialup**, and **For Wireless**. Each preset has an additional number of options based on the speed of the viewer's connection.

Select a preset option from the pane on the left side of the **Export Windows Media** dialog box; look at the description of the selection on the left.

After you have selected an output format, continue with step 2 to set more advanced options; if you do not need to make any advanced settings changes, skip ahead to step 6.

2 Click Advanced (for Advanced Users)

If you have a need to change your output settings, click the **Advanced** button at the bottom of the **Export Windows Media** dialog box to open the **Export Settings** dialog box.

3 Change Export Settings

The **Export Settings** dialog box has four sections that allow you to change various properties of your output file. The **Export Settings** section includes the file **Format** (not changeable) to which you are outputting, the **Preset** (which you selected in step 1), and **Comments** (type a brief description of the settings you are creating). Enable the **Export Video** option to export the video tracks; deselect this option to prevent exporting video tracks. Enable the **Export Audio** option to export the audio tracks; deselect this option to prevent exporting audio. The **Summary** section summarizes the current property settings.

107

4 Change Video Settings

The **Video Settings** appear on a tab just below the **Export Settings** in the **Export Settings** dialog box. In this section are three tabs you can navigate between. The changeable properties on the **Video** tab are **Video Codec**, **Allow interlaced processing**, **Encoding Passes**, **Bitrate Mode**, **Frame Width [pixels]**, **Frame Height [pixels]**, **Frame Rate [fps]**, **Pixel Aspect Ratio**, **Decoder Complexity**, **Keyframe Interval [seconds]**, **Buffer Size [seconds]**, and **Average Video Bitrate [Kbps]**. For additional information on most of these settings, see **104** **Output to an AVI Movie**.

5 Change Audio Settings

By clicking on the **Audio** tab, you open a panel of audio settings. The available **Audio** settings are **Audio Codec**, **Encoding Passes**, **Bitrate Mode**, and **Audio Format**. For additional information on these settings, see **104** **Output to an AVI Movie**.

▶ **TIP**

Click the **Audiences** tab to choose between **Compressed** and **Uncompressed**. The audience you are concerned about is mainly related to the Internet connection speed. If the people viewing the file have a dialup connection, you want a compressed file; if your audience uses a DSL connection, an uncompressed file might be best.

107

If you have made changes to the advanced settings that you want to save, click the **Save** button at the bottom of the **Export Settings** dialog box. If you have not made any changes or do not want to save the changes you have made, click **Cancel**.

6 Name the File and Click Save

After clicking **Save** or **Cancel**, you return to the **Export Windows Media** dialog box (back where you selected the preset). Click the **OK** button to open the **Save File** dialog box. Choose the destination location for the file, type the name of the file, and choose the **Export Range**. Here you have the option to export the **Entire Sequence (project)** or just what is under the **Work Area Bar**.

Click the **Save** button to begin saving your movie as a WMV file. After you click the **Save** button, the **Rendering** dialog box opens.

7 Allow the File to Render

The file must be rendered, just as if you were burning it to a DVD. The rendering process varies in time depending on the size of your project and the speed of your computer. The **Rendering** dialog box shows you the progress and estimated time remaining. If you decide not to continue rendering the file and click **Cancel**, the WMV file will not be created.

Now you have a file that can be used on a web page, emailed to a friend, or possibly even put onto a CD (size permitting). The file can also be viewed in Windows Media Player and even imported into Windows Movie Maker.

108 Output an MPEG File

✔ BEFORE YOU BEGIN	→ SEE ALSO
4 About Video Capture	**18** About Troubleshooting Media Additions
14 Add Media with the Adobe Media Downloader	**107** Output a Windows Media (WMV) File
	110 Archive Your Project

107

► **WEB RESOURCE**

www.chiariglione.org/mpeg

This is the homepage for the **Moving Picture Experts Group,** which can provide information about the MPEG file format.

The Moving Picture Experts Group (MPEG) format is available in a number of flavors: MPEG-1, MPEG-2, and MPEG-4. MPEG files are more compressed than DV-AVI files and cannot be edited as easily in Premiere Elements. Depending on the codec used to encode the MPEG, Premiere Elements might not be able to edit these files at all. By default, Premiere Elements uses the MainConcept MPEG codec for encoding and decoding MPEG files.

Premiere Elements can export your movie as either an MPEG-1 or MPEG-2 file. For the best quality, choose the MPEG-2 format. If you want to put your movie onto a CD so people can view it on computers and some DVD players, this is the format you should choose. These CDs are called VCD (Video Compact Disc, MPEG-1) and SVCD (Super Video Compact Disc, MPEG-2).

► **WEB RESOURCES**

www.videohelp.com/vcd

www.videohelp.com/svcd

If you want to learn more about VCDs and SVCDs, check out the resources at www. videohelp.com.

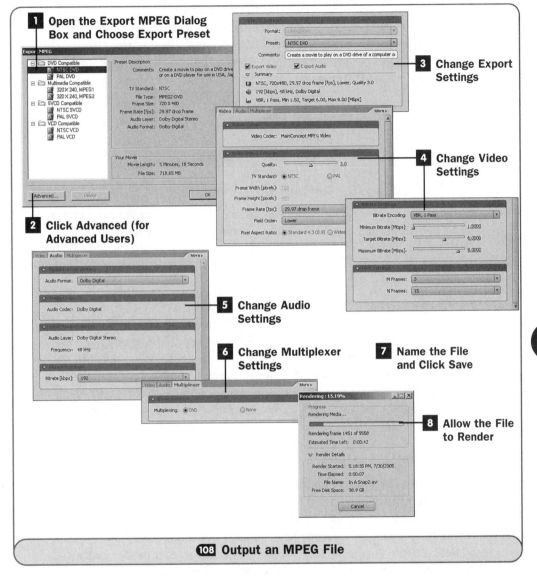

1 Open the Export MPEG Dialog Box and Choose Export Preset

3 Change Export Settings

2 Click Advanced (for Advanced Users)

4 Change Video Settings

5 Change Audio Settings

6 Change Multiplexer Settings

7 Name the File and Click Save

8 Allow the File to Render

108 Output an MPEG File

---

1 Open the Export MPEG Dialog Box and Choose Export Preset

Choose **File, Export, MPEG** from the menu bar at the top of your screen. If you want to output an AVI file (as explained in **104** Output to an AVI Movie), you know that AVI files are much too large for email or website use; therefore, the output process does not ask you to make choices to establish the size (or compression and quality) of the output file. WMV, MPEG, and QuickTime formats, however, all provide you the ability to choose how the file will be viewed most often; you make a selection by choosing a preset.

When you choose one of the presets in the left pane of the **Export MPEG** dialog box, Premiere Elements automatically sets all the defaults based on that preset. The preset options are, broadly, **DVD Compatible**, **Multimedia Compatible**, **SVCD Compatible**, and **VCD Compatible**. Each preset has an additional number of options based on NTSC and PAL or on MPEG1 and MPEG2.

After you choose a preset, continue with step 2 to change the advanced options. If you do not need to make any changes to the advanced settings, skip ahead to step 7.

2 Click Advanced (for Advanced Users)

If you have a need to change your output settings, click the **Advanced** button at the bottom of the **Export MPEG** dialog box to open the **Export MPEG Settings** dialog box.

3 Change Export Settings

MPEGs have the most modifiable settings of all four output file types. The **Export Settings** options include the **Format** (not changeable) of the file you are exporting, the **Preset** (which you chose in step 1), **Comments** (type a note explaining what purpose you plan to use these settings for), **Export Video** (exports the video tracks; deselect this option to prevent exporting video tracks), **Export Audio** (exports the audio tracks; deselect this option to prevent exporting audio tracks), and a summary of the current format settings.

4 Change Video Settings

Under the **Export Settings** area in the dialog box are three tabs, **Video**, **Audio**, and **Multiplexer**. The **Video** options you can change are **Video Codec**, **Quality**, **TV Standard** (NTSC or PAL), **Frame Width in Pixels**, **Frame Height in Pixels**, **Frame Rate**, **Field Order**, **Pixel Aspect Ratio** (**4:3** or **16:9**), **Bitrate Encoding**, **Minimum Bitrate**, **Target Bitrate**, **Maximum Bitrate**, **M Frames**, and **N Frames**. For additional information on most of these settings, see 🔳 **Output to an AVI Movie**.

5 Change Audio Settings

Click the **Audio** tab to change the following options: **Audio Format**, **Audio Codec**, **Audio Layer**, **Frequency**, and **Bitrate in kbps**. For additional information on most of these settings, see 🔳 **Output to an AVI Movie**. The default audio option is **Dolby Digital**. You can take advantage of **Dolby Stereo** and **AC-3** support when importing and exporting video; these options give you

108

full quality sound and leave more space on your DVD for the high-quality video.

6 Change Multiplexer Settings

Click the **Multiplexer** tab to choose either the **DVD** or **None** option. The **DVD** option creates one MPG file that contains both video and audio; such a file is known as a *program stream*. Selecting the **None** option creates separate video (**.m2v**) and audio (**.ac3**) files; such files are known as *elementary streams*. Use the **None** option if you are going to author a DVD from the resulting MPEG files. Some authoring programs prefer program streams while others prefer elementary streams. If you plan to use the MPEG files in a third-party DVD authoring application, consult your DVD authoring software documentation to determine the proper settings.

If you have made changes to the advanced settings that you want to save, click the **Save** button at the bottom of the **Export MPEG Settings** dialog box. If you have not made any changes or do not want to save the changes you have made, click **Cancel**.

7 Name the File and Click Save

108

After clicking **Save** or **Cancel**, you return to the **Export MPEG** dialog box (back where you selected the preset). Click the **OK** button. The **Save File** dialog box opens. Choose the destination location for the file, type the name of your file, and choose the **Export Range**. You can choose to export the **Entire Sequence (project)** or just what is under the **Work Area Bar**.

Click the **Save** button to begin saving your movie as an MPEG file. After you click the **Save** button, the **Rendering** dialog box opens.

8 Allow the File to Render

The file must be rendered, just as if you were burning it to a DVD. The rendering process varies in time depending on the size of your project and the speed of your computer. The **Rendering** dialog box shows you the progress and estimated time remaining. If you decide not to continue rendering the file, click **Cancel**; the MPEG file will not be created.

The resulting MPEG file can be put onto a CD (size permitting), used on a website, or even emailed to friends and family. The MPEG file can also be played in most media players and imported into third-party editing and DVD authoring software.

109   Output a QuickTime File

✔ BEFORE YOU BEGIN	→ SEE ALSO
4 About Video Capture	108 Output an MPEG File
14 Add Media with the Adobe Media Downloader	

When outputting a QuickTime file, the resulting file will have the MOV extension. The QuickTime format was developed by Apple Computer. As are the other formats (AVI, MPEG, and WMV), QuickTime is a method of storing sound, graphics, and movie files. The latest version of QuickTime can be downloaded from Apple's website.

▶ WEB RESOURCE

www.apple.com/quicktime/download/win.html

You can download the latest version of QuickTime Player from Apple's website. The player is free, but a Pro version is available for a fee. The Pro version allows you to convert MOV files to various other formats and also comes with a number of other options not included with the free version.

109

QuickTime files are very prevalent on websites because they can be scaled down to a small size (that is, they can be highly compressed). The QuickTime player is free from Apple, so the files can be played by virtually anyone with a computer—Windows PCs as well as Macintosh computers.

▶ NOTE

The Moving Picture Experts Group chose the QuickTime file format as the foundation for the MPEG-4 standard.

1   Open the Export QuickTime Dialog Box and Choose Export Preset

Choose **File**, **Export**, **QuickTime** from the menu bar at the top of your screen. If you want to output an AVI file (as explained in 104 **Output to an AVI Movie**), you know that AVI files are much too large for email or website use; therefore, the output process does not ask you to make choices to establish the size (or compression and quality) of the output file. WMV, MPEG, and QuickTime formats, however, all provide you the ability to choose how the file will be viewed most often; you make a selection by choosing a preset.

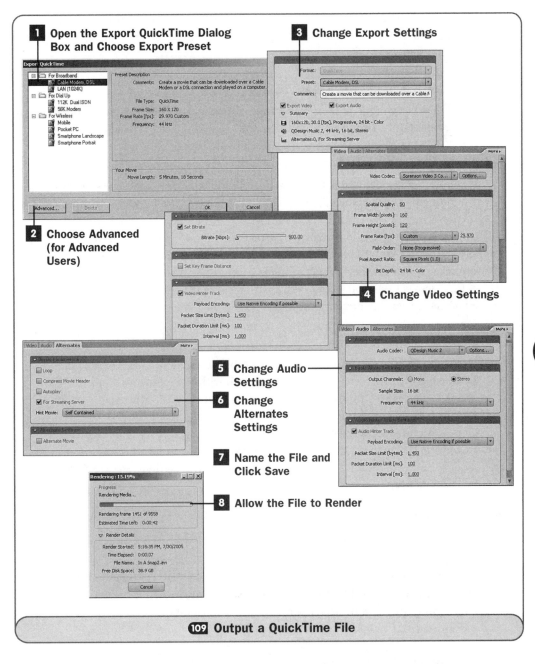

1 Open the Export QuickTime Dialog Box and Choose Export Preset

2 Choose Advanced (for Advanced Users)

3 Change Export Settings

4 Change Video Settings

5 Change Audio Settings

6 Change Alternates Settings

7 Name the File and Click Save

8 Allow the File to Render

109 Output a QuickTime File

When you choose one of the presets in the left pane of the **Export QuickTime** dialog box, Premiere Elements automatically sets all the defaults based on that preset. The preset options are, broadly, **For Broadband**, **For Dialup**, and **For Wireless**. Each preset has an additional number of options based on the speed of the viewer's connection.

Choose a preset and, if you want to set advanced options, continue with step 2. If you do not need to make any changes to the advanced settings, skip ahead to step 7.

2 Click Advanced (for Advanced Users)

If you need to change the output settings, click the **Advanced** button to open the **Export QuickTime Settings** dialog box.

3 Change Export Settings

Opening the **Export QuickTime Settings** dialog box gives you access to various properties of the QuickTime file you are creating. The **Export Settings** section includes the **Format** (not changeable) of the file, the **Preset** (which you chose in step 1), **Comments** (type text to remind yourself what these particular settings do), **Export Video** (exports the video tracks; deselect this option to prevent exporting video tracks), **Export Audio** (exports the audio tracks; deselect this option to prevent exporting audio tracks), and a summary of the current file property settings.

4 Change Video Settings

Under the **Export Settings** area are three tabs; navigate through these tabs by clicking on them. The first is the **Video** tab with the following options: **Video Codec** (and **Options**), **Spatial Quality**, **Frame Width [pixels]**, **Frame Height [pixels]**, **Frame Rate [fps]**, **Field Order**, **Pixel Aspect Ratio**, **Bit Depth**, **Bitrate**, **Set Key Frame Distance**, **Video Hinter Track**, **Payload Encoding**, **Packet Size Limit in bytes**, **Packet Duration Limit**, and **Interval**. For additional information on some of these settings, see **104 Output to an AVI Movie**.

5 Change Audio Settings

To change the audio settings for the QuickTime file you are creating, click the **Audio** tab. You can make changes to the following options: **Audio Codec**, **Output Channels** (choose **Mono** or **Stereo**), **Sample Size**, **Frequency**, **Audio Hinter Track**, **Payload Encoding**, **Packet Size Limit in bytes**, **Packet Duration Limit**, and **Interval**. For additional information on some of these settings, see **104 Output to an AVI Movie**.

6 Change Alternates Settings

Click the **Alternates** tab to modify the following options: **Loop, Compress Movie Header, Autoplay, For Streaming Server, Hint Movie**, and **Alternate Movie**.

109

If you have made changes to the advanced settings that you want to save, click the **Save** button at the bottom of the **Export QuickTime Settings** dialog box. If you have not made any changes or do not want to save the changes that you have made, click **Cancel**.

7 Name the File and Click Save

After clicking **Save** or **Cancel**, you return to the **Export QuickTime** dialog box (back where you selected the preset); click the **OK** button. The **Save File** dialog box opens. Choose the destination location for the file, type the name for the file, and choose the **Export Range**. You can choose to export the **Entire Sequence (project)** or just what is under the **Work Area Bar**.

Click the **Save** button to begin saving your movie as a QuickTime MOV file. After clicking **Save**, the **Rendering** dialog box opens.

8 Allow the File to Render

The file must be rendered, just as if you were burning it to a DVD. The rendering process varies in time depending on the size of your project and the speed of your computer. The **Rendering** dialog box shows you the progress and estimated time remaining. If you decide not to continue rendering the file and press **Cancel**, the QuickTime file is not created.

QuickTime files are great because they can be viewed on a PC or a Mac with the free QuickTime Player. That makes this format an overwhelmingly popular choice for Internet viewing. The files can also be opened and edited in QuickTime Pro as well as converted to another format (such as MPEG4) from there.

110 ►

---

110 Archive Your Project

✔ BEFORE YOU BEGIN	→ SEE ALSO
1 Start a New Project	**105** Output to DV Hardware or Export to Tape
4 About Video Capture	
14 Add Media with the Adobe Media Downloader	

The **Project Archiver** lets you save your project under a separate name and even on a separate hard drive. Archiving a project (making backups) is always a good idea to ensure their safe keeping.

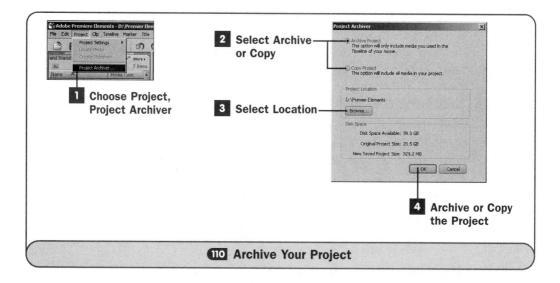

1 Choose Project, Project Archiver

2 Select Archive or Copy

3 Select Location

4 Archive or Copy the Project

110 Archive Your Project

110

The **Project Archiver** gives you two methods of archiving: **Archive** and **Copy**. The **Archive** option saves your project using only the media used on the **Timeline**, taking out all of the edits and anything not used that is still in the **Media** panel. The **Copy** option copies the *entire* project and *all* of the media, resulting in a file as large as the current project. The **Copy** option does not save disk space as the **Archive** option does.

1 Choose Project, Project Archiver

From the taskbar menu at the top of your screen, choose **Project**, **Project Archiver** to open the **Project Archiver** dialog box.

2 Select Archive or Copy

Select the **Archive Project** or **Copy Project** option, whichever you prefer.

3 Select Location

The default location is the same as your project. Alternatively, you can browse to a new location. You can even choose to store the archive or copy onto an external hard drive as a backup. Just make sure that whatever location you archive to has enough space for all the files.

4 Archive or Copy Your Project

After making your selections, click the **OK** button. A dialog box appears, showing you the progress of the archive or copy. When it is finished, you can open the copied or archived project at any time by browsing to the directory location you specified in step 3.

15

DVD Authoring

IN THIS CHAPTER:

Those who've been with Premiere Elements since version 1.0 should be very pleased with the new features in the **DVD** authoring workspace in version 2.0.

Adobe has made several improvements to this workspace, including options for customizing fonts and the placement of navigation controls as well as the ability to add motion, video, and audio backgrounds to DVD menus. In addition, it has added several attractive, new menu templates.

With these improvements, Premiere Elements now has both the advantages of an integrated DVD program and most of the features of a quality, standalone DVD authoring application.

---

111 | **About Burning to DVDs**

→ **SEE ALSO**

112 Create an Auto-Play DVD
117 Customize a DVD Menu Screen Template

111

The first thing to understand about burning your project to a DVD is that, although you might start the process with only a click or two, a whole series of things is actually happening during this process. First, your project is rendered and coded as an MPEG-2 file; then your menus are created and hyperlinked to your video files; and, finally, these files are sent to your DVD burner for output.

This is important to know because, should you run into problems along the way, the best way to diagnose your problem is to break the process down to its individual components and try to isolate the roadblock. We do exactly that in **124** **About Troubleshooting DVD Output.**

Producing a successful DVD does not, unfortunately, guarantee that your disc will play in a DVD player. Although your home-burned DVD will play on virtually any DVD-equipped computer, *not all standalone DVD players are capable of playing them!* This is not an issue related to Premiere Elements (or any other DVD authoring program, for that matter). It's simply the nature of the hardware. Not all DVD players can play home-burned DVDs.

This compatibility problem is, fortunately, becoming much less of an issue. In fact, most newer DVD players will not only play home-burned DVDs, but they will also play music CDs and CDs loaded with MP3s. But, as you burn and distribute your DVD masterpiece to friends, family, and clients, bear in mind that not everyone you send it to will be able to successfully play it on their home theater systems. Most will. But there are no guarantees.

▶ NOTES

In the early years of home DVD burning, there were compatibility advantages to different DVD formats, with DVD-Rs more often playable on standalone DVD players than DVD+Rs. However, most current DVD players are capable of handling both formats equally well.

Can you send your American-burned DVD to your friend in Europe? A little-known fact is that virtually all PAL DVD players are perfectly capable playing NTSC DVDs. In fact, considering the challenges inherent in converting NTSC video to PAL, it's probably the preferred way to send video to your friends across the pond. (Unfortunately, American DVD players are not so capable of reading PAL discs—you probably won't be able to play a disc your European friend sends you.)

This is, in essence, related to the fact that home-burned DVDs are materially different than commercial DVDs. Commercially-produced DVDs have their data physically molded into the surface of the metal disc—a process that not only makes for easier reproduction but also provides some longevity for the disc.

Home-burned DVDs, on the other hand, affect only a chemical change on the disc material. Although the discs are read in a similar manner by the DVD player, this slight physical difference between PC-burned and commercially produced discs can mean the difference between the player being able to read the disc or not. (Rewritable DVDs, also called RWs, use yet another recording process, and even players capable of playing home-burned DVDs might have problems with RW discs.)

Also note that because home-burned DVDs save data with a chemical rather than material process, they unfortunately won't last nearly as long as commercial DVDs. In fact, although no one knows for sure how long home-burned DVDs will last, many people believe that home-burned DVDs won't maintain their integrity any longer than a typical videotape—an important fact to consider if you plan to convert all your videos to DVD in hopes of preserving them better for future generations.

Both kinds of discs will certainly last until the next generation of recording medium is introduced. However, neither will likely last for a lifetime.

Finally, there are the issues of disc capacity. Many people assume that, because commercial DVDs can hold more than two hours' worth of video, a two-hour video project can easily be made to fit onto a single DVD. This is, unfortunately, not the case with most single-layer DVDs.

For the most part, a standard, single-layer DVD can hold about an hour of quality video. Premiere Elements 2.0 also supports dual-layer DVDs, which double that capacity. Regardless, if you are planning to output a 1–2 hour (or longer) video to DVD, it's best to check Premiere Elements's file-size estimate and adjust your quality level as necessary to ensure a good fit. Needless to say, squeezing much more than an hour's worth of video on a single-layer DVD can mean making some significant compromises to your video's quality.

112 Create an Auto-Play DVD

✔ BEFORE YOU BEGIN	→ SEE ALSO
111 About Burning to DVDs **117** Customize a DVD Menu Screen Template	**113** Add Dolby Digital Sound to a DVD **122** Preview and Test Drive a DVD Movie **123** Burn Multiple Copies of a DVD **124** About Troubleshooting DVD Output

An *auto-play DVD* is simply a no-frills, drop-it-in-and-play DVD movie. No menus. No colorful splash screen. Just your video on a shiny, little disc. Naturally, they're the simplest of all DVDs to create.

▶ **KEY TERM**

Auto-play DVD—A DVD in which the video automatically begins to play when it is loaded into a DVD player without first launching a splash screen or menu.

112

1 Open the DVD Templates

Use the instructions in the tasks in the first part of this book to create a movie project that you want to burn to a DVD. Make sure that that project is open and visible on the **Timeline**.

If you aren't already in the **DVD** workspace, click the **DVD** button in the upper-right corner of any workspace.

If you haven't already selected a DVD menu template for your project, simply jumping to this workspace will open the **DVD Template** library. To access the library otherwise, click the **Change Template** button in the **DVD Layout** panel. The **DVD Templates** dialog box opens.

2 Select Auto-Play DVD with No Menus

Select the option to create an **Auto-Play DVD with no Menus** at the top of the **DVD Templates** dialog box. Click **OK**. (For information on menu templates and their themes, see **117** Customize a DVD Menu Screen Template.)

3 Burn Your DVD

Back in the **DVD Layout** panel, click the **Burn DVD** button. In the **Burn DVD** dialog box that opens, you'll have the option of burning directly to a DVD or burning to a folder on your hard drive (See **123** Burn Multiple Copies of a DVD) as well as the option to burn to a different TV format.

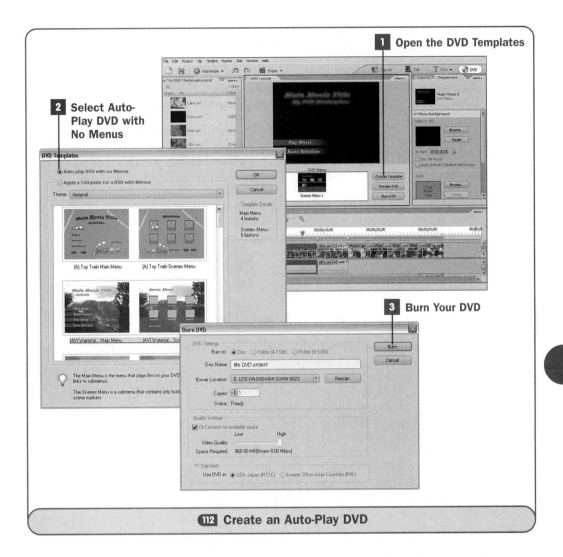

1 Open the DVD Templates

2 Select Auto-Play DVD with No Menus

3 Burn Your DVD

112

112 Create an Auto-Play DVD

If you're trying to fit a long movie onto a DVD, you can adjust the **Video Quality** slider or enable the **Fit Contents to available space** check box. Watch the **Space Required** area to make sure that the movie is small enough to fit onto a single-layer DVD (less than 4.7GB) or a dual-layer DVD (less than 8.5GB).

When you've selected the appropriate options, click the **Burn** button to burn your DVD.

> ## 113 Add Dolby Digital Sound to a DVD
>
> | ✔ BEFORE YOU BEGIN | → SEE ALSO |
> |---|---|
> | 🔘108 Output an MPEG File | 🔘112 Create an Auto-Play DVD |
> | 🔘111 About Burning to DVDs | 🔘117 Customize a DVD Menu Screen Template |
> | | 🔘122 Preview and Test Drive a DVD Movie |
> | | 🔘123 Burn Multiple Copies of a DVD |
> | | 🔘124 About Troubleshooting DVD Output |

Stereo Dolby Digital Sound is an exciting new feature in Premiere Elements's DVD authoring workspace. A compressed but dynamic sound technology, it's turned on in the program by factory default. But, should you want to ensure that the option is selected or to deselect the option, here's how to do it.

1 Open the Export MPEG Dialog Box

With the **Timeline** panel active, choose **File**, **Export**, **MPEG**. The **Export MPEG** dialog box opens.

The default MPEG and DVD settings are selected. Most likely, these options are set to your full television standard (PAL or NTSC) and frame rate, MPEG-2 compression, and the default settings for Audio Layer and Audio Format.

If you're happy with these settings, exit the window by clicking **OK** and then proceed with creating either your auto-play DVD (see 🔘112 **Create an Auto-Play DVD**) or selecting and customizing your DVD menu (see 🔘117 **Customize a DVD Menu Screen Template**). To change these settings, go to step 2.

2 Open Advanced Options

Click the **Advanced** button in the lower-left corner of the **Export MPEG** dialog box to open the **Export Settings** dialog box with settings for your MPEG and DVD output.

Audio settings are under the **Audio** tab in the lower half of this dialog box.

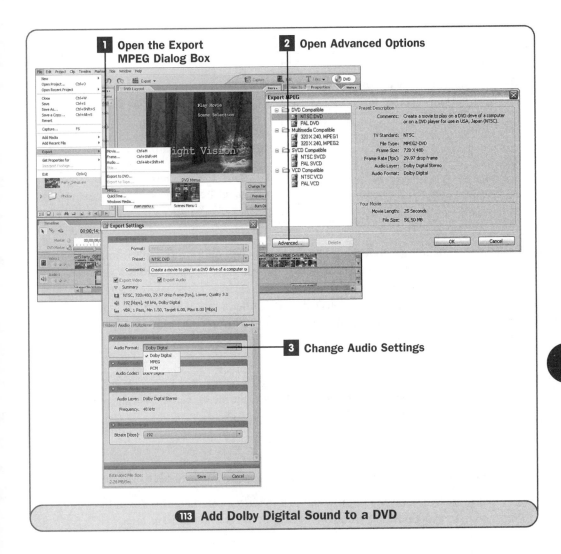

1 Open the Export MPEG Dialog Box

2 Open Advanced Options

3 Change Audio Settings

113

113 Add Dolby Digital Sound to a DVD

3 Change Audio Settings

The **Audio Format** drop-down menu offers you the options of **Dolby Digital** (an advanced digital sound technology, similar to that used in movie theaters), **MPEG** (a compressed, digital sound technology similar to that used in MP3s), or **PCM** (a less compressed and more universal digital sound technology).

Choose the appropriate audio option and click **OK** to close the **Export Settings** dialog box. Click **OK** to close the **Export MPEG** dialog box.

114 Set DVD Chapter Markers

✔ BEFORE YOU BEGIN	→ SEE ALSO
111 About Burning to DVDs **117** Customize a DVD Menu Screen Template	**115** Auto-Generate Scene Markers **116** Customize an Image As a Chapter Marker **119** Create a Motion Menu **122** Preview and Test Drive a DVD Movie **123** Burn Multiple Copies of a DVD **124** About Troubleshooting DVD Output

One of the advantages to having an integrated DVD authoring application such as Premiere Elements is that you can use your standard editing **Timeline** to set your DVD *chapter markers*. Links to these DVD chapter markers are then automatically generated when you select your DVD menu template. With a single click on a link in the DVD menu, your viewer can jump to a point you've specified as a chapter marker in your video.

▶ KEY TERM

Chapter markers—Designated points in a video that the viewer can quickly jumped to by following links from a DVD menu.

1 Locate a Position on Your Timeline

You can access the **Timeline** in either the **Edit** or **DVD** workspace.

Position the CTI at the point you'd like to place a marker. This doesn't have to be an exact position. You can reposition the chapter marker later.

▶ NOTE

Although you can reposition your DVD markers at any point in the editing process, it should be pointed out that the marker positions are relative to the **Timeline** itself, not to your video project. In other words, if you lengthen, shorten, or change the positions of your clips, the markers remain in position relative to the **Timeline** itself, and not the clips, until you manually move the markers.

2 Create a DVD Marker

Click the **DVD Marker** creator button at the top-left corner of the **Timeline**. A green marker appears on the **Timeline** at the point where the CTI is positioned, and the **DVD Marker** dialog box opens.

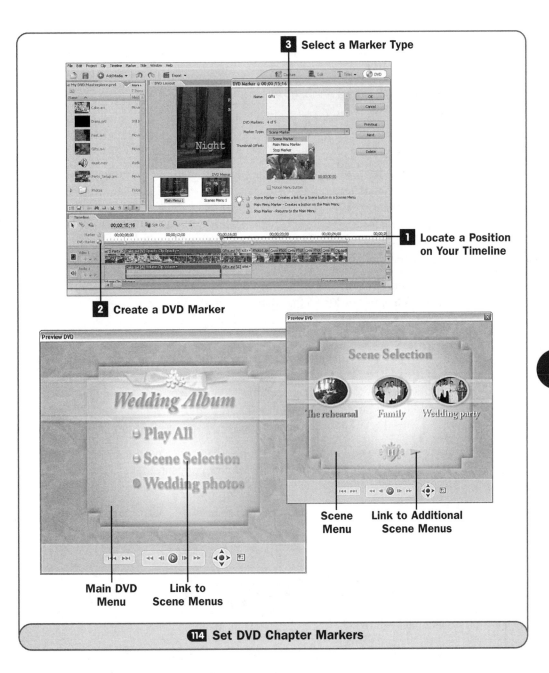

3 Select a Marker Type

1 Locate a Position on Your Timeline

2 Create a DVD Marker

Scene Menu

Link to Additional Scene Menus

Main DVD Menu

Link to Scene Menus

114 Set DVD Chapter Markers

3 Select a Marker Type

The **DVD Marker** dialog box is where you designate your marker type as well as customize the appearance of the chapter marker (see **116** **Customize an Image As a Chapter Marker**.)

Select the type of DVD chapter marker you want to create from the **Marker Type** drop-down menu. A DVD chapter marker can serve one of three purposes:

- A **Main Menu Marker** creates a link to the main (opening) menu on your DVD. This main menu is the menu that appears when the viewer initially launches the DVD.

- A **Scene Marker** creates a link to the secondary (scene) menu on your DVD. (The viewer accesses the scene menu from a link on the main menu.) Links are automatically generated in this menu as you create them on the **Timeline**, and additional pages of scene menus are automatically added as needed to accommodate any number of scene markers; links to those additional scene menu pages are automatically generated.

- A **Stop Marker** stops DVD play and returns the viewer to the main menu. A **Scene Marker** followed by a **Stop Marker** can isolate a sequence for playback from the menus.

114

After you've selected a **Marker Type**, type the name you want to give the marker in the space at the top of the dialog box. Scene markers and main menu markers automatically generate links to your menus after you select a DVD template. The name you've given your DVD marker appears as this link, along with the Thumbnail Offset image, in the menu.

DVD markers can be repositioned at any time; when you move the markers, the links from the appropriate menu to these new points in the movie are automatically updated.

For information on creating an animated thumbnail, see **119 Create a Motion Menu**.

---

115 Auto-Generate Scene Markers

✔ BEFORE YOU BEGIN	→ SEE ALSO
111 About Burning to DVDs	**116** Customize an Image As a Chapter Marker
114 Set DVD Chapter Markers	
117 Customize a DVD Menu Screen Template	**119** Create a Motion Menu
	122 Preview and Test Drive a DVD Movie
	123 Burn Multiple Copies of a DVD
	124 About Troubleshooting DVD Output

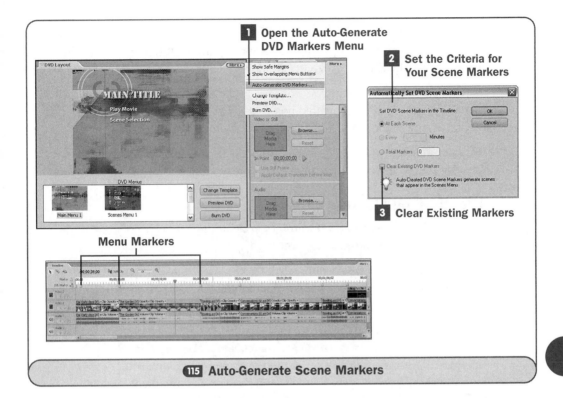

1 Open the Auto-Generate DVD Markers Menu

2 Set the Criteria for Your Scene Markers

3 Clear Existing Markers

Menu Markers

🔢 Auto-Generate Scene Markers

115

Scene markers are DVD chapter markers used to create menu links to give your viewer quick, easy access to scenes in your video. You can set up your own scene markers as explained in 🔢 **Set DVD Chapter Markers**, or you can have Premiere Elements set them up for you, according to your criteria, as explained in this task.

▶ KEY TERM

Scene marker—A type of DVD chapter marker that links from the scenes menu to a designated point in the video.

1 Open the Auto-Generate DVD Markers Menu

Open the movie project for which you want to create scene markers. Make sure that you can see the project in the **Timeline**.

If you aren't already in the **DVD** workspace, click the **DVD** button in the upper-left corner of any workspace.

Click the **More** menu in the **DVD Layout** panel and select **Auto-Generate DVD Markers**. The **Automatically Set DVD Scene Markers** dialog box opens.

2 Set the Criteria for Your Scene Markers

Enable the **At Each Scene** option if you want to place a DVD scene marker at the beginning of each clip on your **Timeline**.

Enable the **Minutes** option if you want to place a scene marker at the time intervals you designate. In the text box that follows the option, type the time interval in **mm:ss** format at which you want to place markers.

The **Total Markers** option places the number of scene markers you indicate at evenly spaced intervals throughout your movie project.

3 Clear Existing Markers

Enable the **Clear Existing DVD Markers** to clear all previously set scene markers as your new markers are generated.

When you've made your selections, click **OK** to close the **Automatically Set DVD Scene Markers** dialog box and generate the markers you've defined.

As with any DVD chapter marker, after the automatically-generated DVD scene markers appear on the **Timeline**, they can be positioned or customized as needed (see **116** **Customize an Image As a Chapter Marker**). Automatically generated DVD scene markers appear in the scenes menu with rather generic names, such as *Scene 1*, *Scene 2*, and so on. You can rename them by double-clicking the text in the menu template itself (see **117** **Customize a DVD Menu Screen Template**) or by double-clicking the DVD chapter marker on the **Timeline**.

115

---

116 | **Customize an Image As a Chapter Marker**

✔ BEFORE YOU BEGIN	→ SEE ALSO
111 About Burning to DVDs	**117** Customize a DVD Menu Screen Template
114 Set DVD Chapter Markers	
115 Auto-Generate Scene Markers	**119** Create a Motion Menu
	122 Preview and Test Drive a DVD Movie
	123 Burn Multiple Copies of a DVD
	124 About Troubleshooting DVD Output

Scene buttons, which are automatically generated by Premiere Elements and linked to your DVD scene markers, appear on your scenes menu as visual indicators of where the links will take the viewer in the DVD movie project. (For information on how to select and create a DVD menu, see **117** **Customize a DVD Menu Screen Template**.)

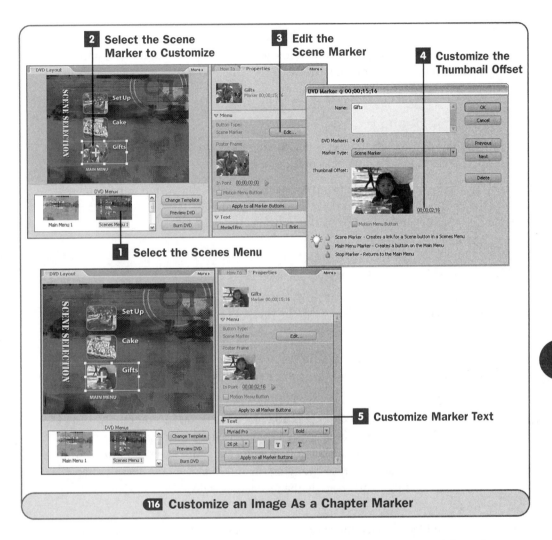

116 Customize an Image As a Chapter Marker

By default, these markers include a thumbnail showing the frame of the video at which you placed your DVD scene marker. You can customize the image that appears as the thumbnail without changing the location of the marker.

■ Select the Scenes Menu

In the **DVD Menus** list box at the bottom of the **DVD Layout** panel, click the **Scenes Menu** that contains the chapter marker you want to customize. The selected menu screen appears in the **DVD Layout** panel.

2 Select the Scene Marker to Customize

In the **DVD Layout** panel's monitor, click the DVD menu button (the scene marker thumbnail) you want to customize. The **Properties** panel displays the picture and text options for this item.

3 Edit the Scene Marker

Double-click the **Edit** button in the **Menus** listing in the **Properties** panel. The **DVD Marker** dialog box for that marker opens.

The space adjacent to the word **Name** at the top of this dialog box is where you name or rename your DVD marker. The text you type in this box is the text that appears with the chapter marker on the scenes menu of your DVD menu.

4 Customize the Thumbnail Offset

The **Thumbnail Offset** is the icon that appears on the scene menu (or the main menu, in the case of a main menu marker) as a visual indicator of the scene to which the menu button links.

To change the image that appears on the DVD menu button, change the timecode counter to the right of the current **Thumbnail Offset** image.

The **00;00;00;00** timecode means that the current thumbnail is the exact frame at which the DVD chapter marker is located. You can manually change these numbers, but it's more intuitive to drag your mouse across them. As you do, the numbers scroll up and down, and the video frames will advance or retreat. Note that changing the thumbnail image doesn't affect the location of the marker—only the frame that is displayed on the menu button.

After you have selected the frame that you want displayed, click **OK** to close the dialog box. To create an animated icon, see **119** **Create a Motion Menu**.

5 Customize Marker Text

The **Text** customization area of the **Properties** panel enables you to select the font, font size, font color, and font style for the text on the menu button. Choose from the drop-down menus to apply these text attributes to the text associated with the currently selected menu button.

Click the **Apply to All Markers** buttons to apply the picture (the frame) or text settings for this button to all the menu buttons in the currently selected menu.

116

117 Customize a DVD Menu Screen Template

✔ BEFORE YOU BEGIN	→ SEE ALSO
111 About Burning to DVDs **114** Set DVD Chapter Markers **115** Auto-Generate Scene Markers	**118** Customize a Menu with Any Background **120** Add Video to a Menu Background **121** Add Audio to a Menu **122** Preview and Test Drive a DVD Movie **124** About Troubleshooting DVD Output

Although you can't create a DVD menu from scratch in Premiere Elements, your ability to customize the existing templates in Premiere Elements 2.0 is light years ahead of where it was in version 1.0.

Premiere Elements 2.0 offers more than 70 DVD menu templates grouped in categories such as **Entertainment**, **General**, **Birthday**, **New Baby**, **Party Celebrations**, **Seasons**, **Sports**, **Travel**, and **Wedding**. Several of these templates include a default video background loop (these templates are marked with a **(V)**), an audio background loop (these templates are marked with an **(A)**) or both, and all can be modified to include a custom still background (see **118** **Customize a Menu with Any Background**), a custom video background (see **120** **Add Video to a Menu Background**), or a custom audio background (see **121** **Add Audio to a Menu**). Fonts, positions, and content of the navigation text can also be customized, and the thumbnail graphics for the scene markers can be customized and even animated.

▶ **NOTE**

Although Premiere Elements 2.0 allows you to customize existing DVD menu templates, it still doesn't allow you to create a template from scratch. Premiere Elements's companion program, Photoshop Elements 4.0, however, *does* include features for creating DVD templates as well as modifying existing ones. The new DVD templates you create in Photoshop Elements are automatically added to Premiere Elements's **DVD Templates** collection.

1 Open the DVD Templates Library

Open the movie project for which you want to modify a DVD menu. If you aren't already in the **DVD** workspace, click the **DVD** button in the upper-right corner of any workspace.

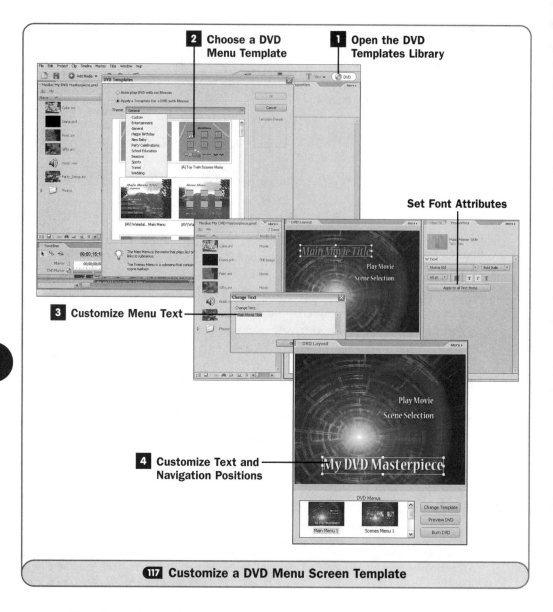

2 Choose a DVD Menu Template

1 Open the DVD Templates Library

Set Font Attributes

3 Customize Menu Text

4 Customize Text and Navigation Positions

117

117 Customize a DVD Menu Screen Template

If you haven't already selected a DVD menu template for the current project, simply jumping to this space opens the **DVD Template** library. Otherwise click on the **Change Template** button in the **DVD Layout** panel.

2 Choose a DVD Menu Template

The **Theme** drop-down list gives you options for several collections of DVD menu templates. The most easily customized templates—and the templates with the least extraneous graphical elements—are the **Generic** and **Standard** templates in the **General** collection. Select a template collection from the **Theme** drop-down list to see a list of DVD menu templates within that collection.

Templates with a (**V**) in front of their names have animated video backgrounds. Templates with an (**A**) have an audio track. Those with an (**AV**) have both video backgrounds and an audio track. All templates can potentially have a still or video background and/or audio track added. (See **118 Customize a Menu with Any Background**, **120 Add Video to a Menu Background**, and **121 Add Audio to a Menu**.)

Note that all DVD menu templates have a main menu that includes a **Play** button; most also have a scenes menu that allows for links up to the number of scenes or chapters indicated. If the number of scene markers included with your project exceeds the number indicated for that menu template, Premiere Elements automatically generates additional scenes menu screens with links between the menus.

When you have selected the DVD menu template you want to use for the current movie project, click **OK**.

117

3 Customize Menu Text

Double-click any text block to open a **Change Text** dialog box where you can replace the generic template text with your custom text.

When a text box is selected, the **Properties** panel indicates the customizable text properties including font, size, and color. You can also adjust the font size and shape by dragging the sides or corner handles of the text box.

Note, however, that some aspects of the text block are inherent in the template and are not customizable—most notably drop-shadows and stroking.

Click the **Apply to All Text Items** button to apply the text styles and colors you've set up for one text block to all text blocks in the current menu.

4 Customize Text and Navigation Positions

Drag the text and navigational graphics to any positions you'd like in the menu screen. To customize the chapter icons, see **116 Customize an Image As a Chapter Marker**.

118   Customize a Menu with Any Background

✔ BEFORE YOU BEGIN

111 About Burning to DVDs
114 Set DVD Chapter Markers
115 Auto-Generate Scene Markers
117 Customize a DVD Menu Screen
Template

→ SEE ALSO

119 Create a Motion Menu
120 Add Video to a Menu Background
121 Add Audio to a Menu
122 Preview and Test Drive a DVD
Movie
124 About Troubleshooting DVD
Output

A nice new feature of the DVD menu templates in Premiere Elements 2.0 is that they all offer the option of replacing or customizing the menu backgrounds. (You can even replace the background with a video clip, as explained in 120 **Add Video to a Menu Background**.) Any graphic, photo, or video clip that can be used in a Premiere Elements project can be used as a DVD menu background.

1 Select a DVD Menu Template

With your movie project open, select a DVD menu template as described in 117 **Customize a DVD Menu Screen Template**.

Note that nearly all DVD menu templates contain foreground graphic elements in addition to the background image. In some cases, these graphics frame the background image. In other cases, the graphics appear over it. (For this example, I have selected a template with no foreground graphics. You can see an example of a template with foreground graphics in 120 **Add Video to a Menu Background**.)

Click the **Change Template** button in the **DVD Layout** panel and choose a template collection. From the list of individual templates that appears, select the one you want to use; it appears in the monitor. If you'd prefer minimal interference from these permanent graphics, choose the **Standard** template or one of the **Generic** templates from the **General** collection, as I have done in my example.

2 Browse for a Background Image

When you have selected a template, the option for changing the background image appears in the **Properties** panel.

118

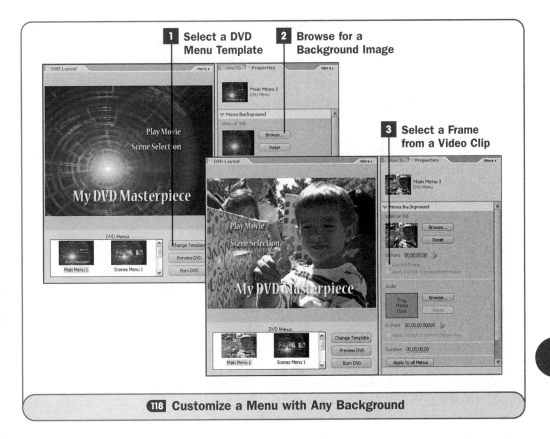

1 Select a DVD Menu Template

2 Browse for a Background Image

3 Select a Frame from a Video Clip

118 Customize a Menu with Any Background

Click on the **Browse** button in the **Menu Background Video or Still** section of the **Properties** panel and browse to the image of your choice. Note that this image does not have to have been imported into your video project. You can select it from anywhere on your hard drive. (For an explanation of how to create a video background for your menu, see **120** **Add Video to a Menu Background**.)

▶ **NOTE**

Photoshop Elements 4.0 has a custom work area, specifically designed for working with Premiere Elements's DVD menu templates. This work area allows for easy revision of existing templates, including removing extraneous graphic elements, as well as the ability to create new DVD menu templates from scratch.

3 Select a Frame from a Video Clip

Although you can use a still image for your menu background, you can also designate that a frame from a video clip be used. Click in the **Timeline** to select an existing clip from which you want to select a frame.

After you have selected a clip, click the green arrow in the **Properties** panel to play the clip, or drag across the timecode to scrub through the clip until you locate the frame you'd like to use as the background image for the DVD menu.

Enable the **Use Still Frame** check box.

---

119 Create a Motion Menu

✔ BEFORE YOU BEGIN	→ SEE ALSO
⑪ About Burning to DVDs	⑪ Customize a DVD Menu Screen Template
⑭ Set DVD Chapter Markers	⑱ Customize a Menu with Any Background
⑮ Auto-Generate Scene Markers	⑳ Add Video to a Menu Background
	㉑ Add Audio to a Menu
	㉒ Preview and Test Drive a DVD Movie

118

Although Premiere Elements 1.0 gave you the ability to use a still frame from your video as a scene marker, Premiere Elements 2.0 gives you the ability to use a portion of a clip from your video project to create an animated, motion menu scene marker.

1 Select the Scenes Menu

Click the **Scenes Menu** thumbnail in the **DVD Layout** panel that contains the scene marker you want to customize. The scenes menu appears in the monitor in the **DVD Layout** panel.

2 Select the Scene Marker to Customize

In the **DVD Layout** panel, click the scene marker you want to customize. The **Properties** panel displays the current video frame being used as this scene's marker as well as the options for customizing the text for this marker.

3 Select the Motion Menu Option

In the **Properties** panel, enable the **Motion Menu Button** check box.

When the scene menu is displayed, the clip will play as a thumbnail, and then loop and repeat indefinitely.

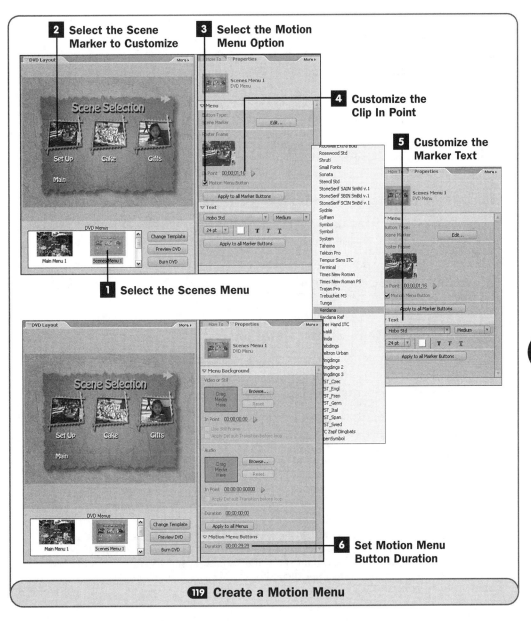

2 Select the Scene Marker to Customize

3 Select the Motion Menu Option

4 Customize the Clip In Point

5 Customize the Marker Text

1 Select the Scenes Menu

6 Set Motion Menu Button Duration

119 Create a Motion Menu

4 Customize the Clip In Point

To change the point in the clip at which the motion menu begins, click the green play button or change the timecode.

You can manually change the timecode numbers, but it's more intuitive to drag the mouse across them. As you do, the numbers scroll up and down and the video advances or retreats. Note that this adjustment doesn't affect the actual location of the scene marker on the **Timeline**. The scene marker still links to the spot in your movie where the marker is positioned. This adjustment only changes the image that is displayed as the scene marker button in your DVD menu.

▶ **TIP**

If you are locating the In Point by playing through the clip, click the yellow pause button when you've reached your desired In Point.

5 Customize the Marker Text

The **Text** customization area of the **Properties** panel enables you to select the font, font size, font color, and font style for the scene marker button text.

Click the **Apply to All Marker Buttons** button to apply the picture and/or text attributes you've just set for this menu button to all the menu buttons in the scene menu.

6 Set Motion Menu Button Duration

In the **DVD Layout** monitor, click the background of the scene menu (anywhere behind the DVD menu buttons). The **Menu Background** options appear in the **Properties** panel.

At the bottom of the **Menu Background** options are settings for the **Motion Menu Buttons Duration**, listed as a timecode.

The time period you designate here will set the duration of the video loops for all motion menu buttons.

▶ **NOTE**

In the timecode listed as **00;00;00;00**, the first set of numbers represents hours and the second set of numbers represents minutes (both pretty unlikely settings for a loop that plays on a menu button). The third set of numbers represents seconds, and the last set represents frames (25 frames per second of time in PAL and approximately 30 frames per second in NTSC).

120 Add Video to a Menu Background

✔ BEFORE YOU BEGIN	→ SEE ALSO
111 About Burning to DVDs **114** Set DVD Chapter Markers **115** Auto-Generate Scene Markers **117** Customize a DVD Menu Screen Template **118** Customize a Menu with Any Background	**121** Add Audio to a Menu **122** Preview and Test Drive a DVD Movie **123** Burn Multiple Copies of a DVD **124** About Troubleshooting DVD Output

A welcome feature in Premiere Elements 2.0 is the ability to use a loop of video as the background for a DVD menu template. (You can also replace the background with a still image, as explained in **118** **Customize a Menu with Any Background**.)

1 Select a DVD Menu Template

Open the movie project for which you want to customize the DVD menu. Select a DVD menu template as described in **117** **Customize a DVD Menu Screen Template**.

Note that nearly all DVD menu templates contain foreground graphic elements in addition to the background image. In some cases, these graphics frame your background image. In other cases, they appear over it. In this example, the stars and streamers across the top of the template are foreground graphics. As you will see, even after you replace the background imagery for this DVD menu, these graphic elements remain. Premiere Elements does not give you the ability to remove these graphics. (They can be easily removed, however, with the Photoshop Elements 4.0 DVD menu tools.)

Click the **Change Template** button in the **DVD Layout** panel and choose a template collection. From the list of individual templates that appears, select the one you want to use; it appears in the monitor. If you'd prefer an easily customizable template that is free from foreground graphics, choose the **Standard** template or one of the **Generic** templates located in the **General** collection.

2 Browse for a Background Video Clip

When a template is selected, the **Menu Background** listing and its options appear in the **Properties** panel.

120

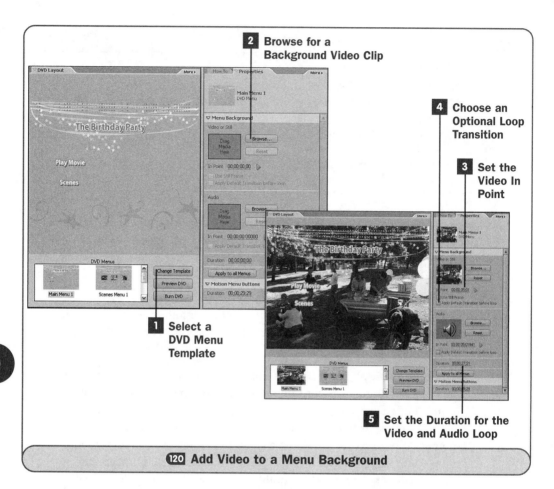

2 Browse for a Background Video Clip

4 Choose an Optional Loop Transition

3 Set the Video In Point

1 Select a DVD Menu Template

5 Set the Duration for the Video and Audio Loop

120 Add Video to a Menu Background

Click the **Browse** button and browse to the video clip you want to use as the background image for this DVD menu. Note that this clip does not actually have to be a part of your current video project and can exist any place on your hard drive.

▶ NOTE

Photoshop Elements 4.0 has a custom work area, specifically designed for working with Premiere Elements's DVD menu templates. This work area allows for easy revision of existing templates, including removing extraneous graphic elements, as well as the ability to create new DVD menu templates from scratch.

3 Set the Video In Point

To change the point in the clip at which the menu background video loop begins, click the green arrow play button or change the timecode for the In Point.

You can manually change these numbers, but it's more intuitive to drag the mouse across them. As you do, the numbers scroll up and down and the video advances or retreats.

If you are locating the In Point by playing the video, click the yellow pause button when you reach the desired In Point.

4 Choose an Optional Loop Transition

Enable the **Apply Default Transition before loop** check box to apply the default transition between the end of the video clip and the frame at which it restarts.

▶ **TIP**

To change the default transition, select any transition from the **Transitions and Effects** panel, click the **More** button at the top of that panel, and select **Set As Default Transition** (see **44** About Transitions).

5 Set the Duration for the Video and Audio Loop

At the bottom of the **Menu Background** options in the **Properties** panel are the settings for the duration of the loop, listed as a timecode. The time you set here determines how long the background video clip plays before it restarts.

In the timecode **00;00;00;00**, the first set of numbers represents hours, and the second set of numbers represents minutes (both pretty unlikely settings for a background video loop). The third set of numbers represents seconds, and the last set represents frames (25 frames per second of time in PAL and approximately 30 frames per second in NTSC). The **Duration** setting you specify applies to both the video and audio tracks in the background video for this menu.

The **Apply to All Menus** button applies these duration settings to all looping menu backgrounds for this project.

---

121 **Add Audio to a Menu**

✔ BEFORE YOU BEGIN	✔ SEE ALSO
111 About Burning to DVDs	**120** Add Video to a Menu Background
114 Set DVD Chapter Markers	**122** Preview and Test Drive a DVD Movie
115 Auto-Generate Scene Markers	**123** Burn Multiple Copies of a DVD
117 Customize a DVD Menu Screen Template	**124** About Troubleshooting DVD Output
118 Customize a Menu with Any Background	

121

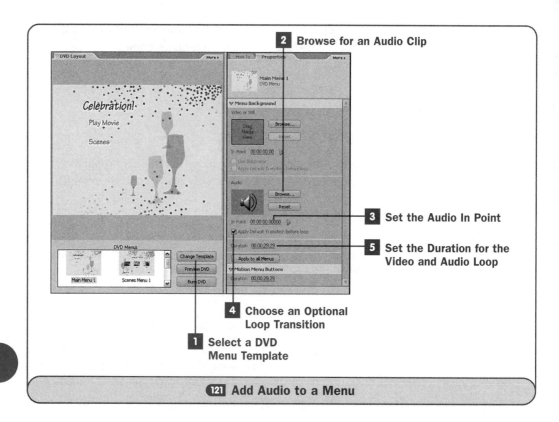

2 Browse for an Audio Clip

3 Set the Audio In Point

5 Set the Duration for the Video and Audio Loop

4 Choose an Optional Loop Transition

1 Select a DVD Menu Template

121 Add Audio to a Menu

In addition to being able to customize the background of your DVD menu template (as explained in **118** Customize a Menu with Any Background and **120** Add Video to a Menu Background), Premiere Elements 2.0 gives you the option of adding your own custom audio loop. (Note that some templates—those marked with an **(A)** or a **(AV)**—have default audio loops. These templates, nonetheless, give you the option of replacing the default audio with a custom audio clip.)

1 Select a DVD Menu Template

Open a movie project that contains a DVD menu you want to customize. Select a DVD menu template for the project as explained in **117** Customize a DVD Menu Screen Template.

▶ **TIP**

The order in which you customize the DVD menu background video and audio affects how the template is ultimately customized. In other words, if you add a video background *after* you add customized audio, the audio from the video clip overwrites the audio selection. To override this effect, select or reselect your audio loop after you've selected your video background.

2 Browse for an Audio Clip

After you select a template, the **Menu Background** listing appears in the **Properties** panel, offering an option for changing or adding an audio clip.

Click the **Browse** button in the **Audio** section of the properties panel and browse to the audio clip of your choice.

3 Set the Audio In Point

To change the point in the audio clip at which the menu background audio begins, click the green arrow (play) button or change the timecode.

You can manually change the timecode numbers, but it's more intuitive to drag the mouse across them. As you do, the numbers scroll up and down and the audio clip advances or retreats.

In the audio timecode **00;00;00;00000**, the first set of numbers represents hours and the second set of numbers represents minutes (both pretty unlikely settings for your audio loop). The third set of numbers represents seconds, and the last set of numbers represents audio samplings—a standard 48,000 per second.

If you are locating the In Point by playing the audio clip, click the yellow pause button when you reach the desired In Point.

4 Choose an Optional Loop Transition

Enable the **Apply Default Transition Before Loop** check box option to apply the audio dissolve transition between your loop's end and its restart.

5 Set the Duration for the Video and Audio Loop

At the bottom of the **Menu Background** options in the **Properties** panel are the settings for the duration of the audio loop, listed as a video timecode. The time you set here determines how long the audio clip plays before it restarts.

In the video timecode **00;00;00;00**, the first set of numbers represents hours, and the second set of numbers represents minutes (both pretty unlikely settings for a background audio loop). The third set of numbers represents seconds, and the last set represents frames (25 frames per second of time in PAL and approximately 30 frames per second in NTSC). This setting applies to *both video and audio background loops* for this menu.

121

122 Preview and Test Drive a DVD Movie

✔ BEFORE YOU BEGIN	→ SEE ALSO
ⓚ About Burning to DVDs ⓚ Create an Auto-Play DVD ⓚ Customize a DVD Menu Screen Template	ⓚ Customize an Image As a Chapter Marker ⓚ Customize a Menu with Any Background ⓚ Add Video to a Menu Background ⓚ Burn Multiple Copies of a DVD ⓚ About Troubleshooting DVD Output

After you've set up and customized your DVD menus, you'll want to give them a good test drive to make sure that everything works as it should before you burn it to DVD or otherwise export the project.

Note, however, that animating menu backgrounds and menu buttons can be taxing on your computer system. Unless you have a very fast computer, the preview video might seem a bit sluggish or jumpy. Don't be concerned. The important thing is that everything appears as it should and that what you want animated is indeed animated.

■ Start the DVD Preview

Click the **DVD Preview** button in the **DVD Layout** panel. This should open a full-sized window **Preview DVD** window displaying your main menu.

② Test the Play Button

Click the **Play** button.

Ensure that the video starts at the point you're expecting it to start. If not, check your work area settings. (See **32** **Define the Beginning and End of Your Project**.)

To return to the main menu from any point in the movie, click the **Menu** icon on the play window's control panel.

③ Test the Scene Buttons

In the main menu, click the link to the scene menu(s). Depending on the template or customizations you've made to the template, this link might be labeled **Scene Selections** or something similar.

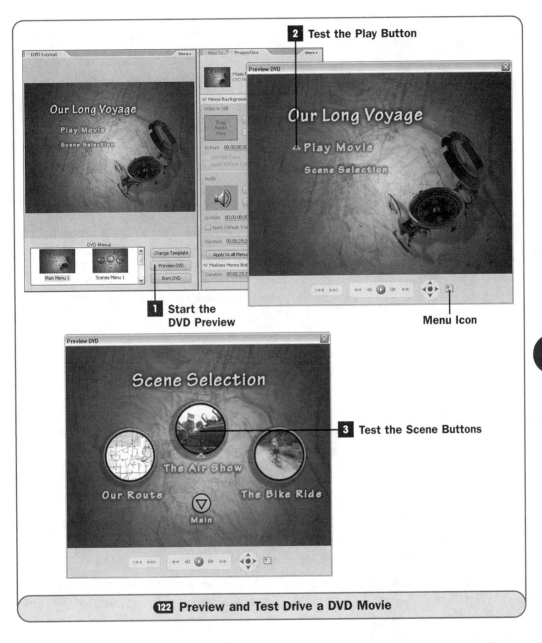

2 Test the Play Button

1 Start the
DVD Preview

Menu Icon

3 Test the Scene Buttons

122 Preview and Test Drive a DVD Movie

Click each chapter marker icon to ensure that each button begins playback at the correct In Point and, if applicable, returns to the main menu at the Out Point you've designated with a stop marker. (For information on setting a chapter marker as a stop marker, see **114** Set DVD Chapter Markers.)

If you're happy with the preview, close the window and click the **Burn DVD** button back in the **DVD Layout** panel.

123 | **Burn Multiple Copies of a DVD**

✔ BEFORE YOU BEGIN	→ SEE ALSO
111 About Burning to DVDs	122 Preview and Test Drive a DVD Movie
112 Create an Auto-Play DVD	
117 Customize a DVD Menu Screen Template	124 About Troubleshooting DVD Output

Although this task creates a set of DVD files on your hard drive that ostensibly you can use and re-use to burn several DVD copies, it's often the preferred way to produce even one copy of a DVD.

DVD burning actually combines several process—rendering and encoding, creating and linking menus, and the actual burning of the disc. Of these, the step most prone to problems is the burning of the DVD itself (an issue related to driver compatibility). Burning to a folder rather than directly to a disc removes one potentially problematic step, increasing the likelihood of producing a successful DVD.

1 Click Burn DVD

If you aren't already in the **DVD** workspace, click the **DVD** button in the upper-right corner of any workspace. Open the project you want to burn to multiple DVDs.

After you've selected and customized your menu screens (see 117 **Customize a DVD Menu Screen Template**) or chosen the option to create an auto-play DVD (see 112 **Create an Auto-Play DVD**), click the **Burn DVD** button in the **DVD Layout** panel. The **Burn DVD** dialog box opens.

2 Select the Burn to Folder Option

In the **Burn DVD** dialog box, you'll have the option to burn directly to a DVD or to burn to a folder. At the bottom of the dialog box, you can choose which TV format you plan to play the disc in—NTSC or PAL.

You have a choice between saving your files for a standard 4.7BG DVD or an 8.5GB dual-layer disc. Select the **Burn to Folder** option that is compatible with your DVD burner and media.

3 Select the Quality Level

The **Burn DVD** dialog box also indicates the approximate size of your final DVD output in the **Space Required** area in the middle of the dialog box.

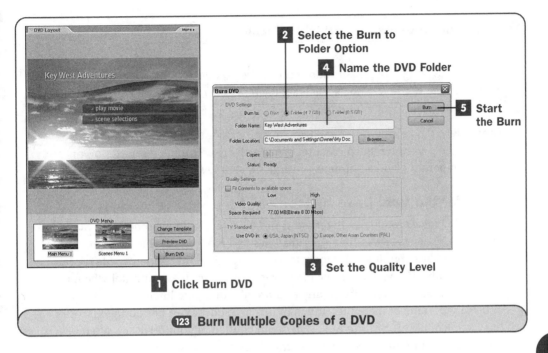

2 **Select the Burn to Folder Option**

4 **Name the DVD Folder**

5 **Start the Burn**

3 **Set the Quality Level**

1 **Click Burn DVD**

123 **Burn Multiple Copies of a DVD**

123

A 4.7GB DVD can hold approximately one hour of standard-quality video (see ⓐ **About Burning to DVDs**). If the estimated output size is greater than your disc capacity, you can reduce the quality level of your video to accommodate the video.

Enable the **Fit Contents to Available Space** check box to force your movie project to fit on the selected media type.

4 Name the DVD Folder

Type a name for your DVD folder and browse to the folder location to which you want to save your video files. If you don't name your folder, the program automatically generates a default name based on the date and time of your burn.

5 Start the Burn

Click the **Burn** button. The program will render and encode your video project and save the menu and video files in two subfolders within the folder you specified in step 4.

To produce a DVD, use the software that came with your DVD burner or your system to burn the two subfolders and all their contents to a disc.

124   About Troubleshooting DVD Output

If there's anything more frustrating than not being able to bring video into your computer (see **12** About Troubleshooting Capture Problems), it's not being able to output your movie when it's done.

Fortunately, diagnosing and remedying output problems is rarely as random a process as doing so for video capture. Usually, the issue can be resolved—or, at worst, temporarily worked around—with a few simple steps.

Consider the Hard Drive Space

The single biggest roadblock to output is inadequate hard drive space. The hard drive not only needs room for your video files and room for the files you are going to produce, but it needs gigabytes of scratch disk and temporary file space. Your hard drive is a very dynamic place, with temporary files continually being written and read—and a great many of those files are quite large. In fact, because of the size of some of these files, much of this free space must be contiguous, or in big, clean chunks. For this reason, a defragmentation of your drive can often be a good first step in remedying your output problems.

124

▶ TIP

A rule of thumb for calculating how much free space you'll need for processing your project is to estimate how much space your project's video files are currently taking up, add to that an estimate of how much your output files will take up, and then multiply that by one-and-a-half.

Although the estimate calculation given in the tip might err just a bit on the liberal side, the principle is right on the money—you really can't have too much free hard drive space. Nothing keeps intensive processes moving smoothly like plenty of RAM and lots of free hard drive space.

If you've added a second hard drive, one dedicated to video, ensure that all of your scratch disk and temporary files are directed to it. (Choose **Edit**, **Preferences** and set all the **Scratch Disks** to point to **Same As Project**.) Doing so keeps your temporary files on the dedicated drive and frees your C drive up to handle the other needs of the operating system.

Make Sure Your Second Drive Is Properly Installed

If you are using a second hard drive, one dedicated to your video files, ensure that it is properly connected to your system and installed. If your drive is installed internally, make sure it is set up not just in your operating system but also in your BIOS. To check your BIOS settings, press the **Esc** or **F1** key (or whatever your manufacturer recommends) when the blue logo screen appears as your computer first boots up.

If your drive is connected using a FireWire or USB connection, ensure that you have a fast enough data flow to allow for the necessary processes.

Burn to a Folder

It's important to note that the **Burn to DVD** process is not one task but several. First, the program renders your effects, transitions, and stills; this video is then encoded as an MPEG-2 file. The program then creates menus and links, generating your DVD. Finally, the program launches your DVD burner. Quite often, when a **Burn to DVD** process fails, it's this final step that stalls the process. Remember, there are dozens of DVD burners on the market, each with sometimes several versions of drivers floating around, and Premiere Elements might simply be unable to make the driver start the hardware.

There's a simple test to see whether that is the case—and, if it *is* the case, this test can also double as a workaround. Rather than burning directly to a DVD, burn to a folder on your hard drive as explained in **123** **Burn Multiple Copies of a DVD**).

If this process works, you'll know where your problem lies. A driver update from your DVD burner's manufacturer's site might solve the problem. Otherwise, you can still create a DVD from the files in this hard drive folder. Simply burn these folders and their contents to a DVD using the software that came with your system or hardware.

124

Output to an AVI

If your **Burn to DVD** process stalls before it even gets to the point of burning to a folder on your hard drive, it could be a sign that there's a problem with the rendering or encoding processes. To test this, output your project as an AVI, as explained in **104** **Output to an AVI Movie**.

If your output to AVI is successful, you now have the option of opening a new video project, dropping this AVI on the **Timeline** and then outputting this new project as a DVD—thus eliminating one more step in the process and eliminating one more place where the process can go wrong.

Look for a Troublesome Clip

Regardless of whether you can output an AVI, but especially if you can't, problems producing DVD files can often come as a result of an incompatible clip or a poorly prepared still. And, quite often, eliminating this clip will allow the rest of the project to burn.

Unnecessarily large photo files (see 22 **Prepare a Still for Video**) can overwhelm the program and will often cause the rendering or encoding process to stall. Keep your photo file sizes to the minimum size necessary, and you'll minimize possible downsampling logjams.

DV-AVI files form the workflow for Premiere Elements. Although Premiere Elements 2.0 has a much-improved tolerance for non-DV-AVI files, it's not unusual to have one of these files stick in its craw. When considering which files might be choking the rendering or encoding process, start by removing the most unusual files first: video and stills from picture phones; video from digital still cameras; MPEGs; AVIs with codecs other than AVI. Eventually, you'll be able to output an AVI that, as described in the preceding section, "Output to an AVI," you should be able to use to produce a successful DVD.

Look for a Troublesome Effect or Transition

As with clips, occasionally one of Premiere Elements's internal effects or transitions can corrupt an output file. Although this is rare, it's worth checking if all other options have been eliminated.

124

A

Premiere Elements Keyboard Shortcuts

Premiere Elements allows you to modify any of these keyboard shortcuts or to add shortcuts for dozens of other tasks. You'll find the option to do so under the **Edit** menu in the main menu bar.

Program Controls

Ctrl+O	Open project
Ctrl+W	Close project
Ctrl+S	Save project
Ctrl+Shift+S	Save project as
Ctrl+Alt+S	Save a copy
Ctrl+Z	Undo
Ctrl+Shift+Z	Redo
Ctrl+X	Cut
Ctrl+C	Copy
Ctrl+V	Paste
Tab	Close floating windows
Ctrl+Q	Quit program
F1	Help

Import/Export

F5	Capture
Ctrl+I	Add media
Ctrl+M	Export movie
Ctrl+Shift+M	Export frame
Ctrl+Alt+Shift+M	Export audio
Ctrl+Shift+H	Get properties for selection

Work Areas

Shift+F7	Capture
Shift+F8	Edit
Shift+F9	Effects
Shift+F10	Advanced effects
Shift+F11	Titles
Shift+F12	DVD

Media and Trimming

I	Set in point
O	Set out point
G	Clear all in/out points
D	Clear selected in point
F	Clear selected out point
Ctrl+E	Edit original
Ctrl+H	Rename

Timeline Views

Enter	Render work area
Ctrl+K	Razor cut at CTI
+	Zoom in
−	Zoom out
\	Zoom to work area

Play/Scrub Controls

Spacebar	Play/stop
J	Shuttle left
L	Shuttle right
Shift+J	Slow shuttle left
Shift+L	Slow shuttle right
K	Shuttle stop
Left arrow	One frame back
Right arrow	One frame forward
Shift+Left arrow	Step back five frames
Shift+Right arrow	Step forward five frames
Home	Go to beginning of clip/Timeline
End	Go to end of clip/Timeline
Q	Go to in point
W	Go to out point
Page Down	Go to next edit point
Page Up	Go to previous edit point
Ctrl+Alt+Spacebar	Play in point to out point with preroll/postroll

Timeline Controls

Ctrl+A	Select all
Ctrl+Shift+A	Deselect all
Ctrl+F	Find
, (comma)	Insert
. (period)	Overlay
Ctrl+Shift+V	Insert clip
Alt+*Video clip*	Unlink audio/video
Ctrl+G	Group
Ctrl+Shift+G	Ungroup
Ctrl+R	Time stretch
Delete	Clear
Backspace	Ripple delete
S	Toggle snap
Ctrl+Alt+C	Copy attributes

Ctrl+Alt+V	Paste attributes
Ctrl+Shift+\	Duplicate
Shift+*	Set next numbered marker (must use the * on the number pad)
*	Set unnumbered marker (must use the * on the number pad)

Title Window Controls

Ctrl+Shift+L	Title type align left
Ctrl+Shift+R	Title type align right
Ctrl+Shift+C	Title type align center
Ctrl+Shift+T	Set title type tab
Ctrl+J	Open title templates
Ctrl+Alt+]	Select object above
Ctrl+Alt+[	Select object below
Ctrl+Shift+]	Bring object to front
Ctrl+[	Bring object forward
Ctrl+Shift+[	Send object to back
Ctrl+[	Send object backward

The following keyboard shortcuts are unique to each panel. For instance, those listed for the **Properties** panel work only when the **Properties** panel is activated. Note that many of these functions are only available as keyboard shortcuts!

Capture Panel

G	Start capture
F	Fast forward
R	Rewind
Left arrow	Step back
Right arrow	Step forward
S	Stop play/capture
V	Capture video only
A	Capture audio only

Properties Panel

Backspace   Delete selected effect

Effects Panel

Backspace   Delete custom item

History Panel

Left arrow   Step back
Right arrow   Step forward
Backspace   Delete
Ctrl+H   Clear History

Media Panel

Ctrl+Del   Delete selected options
Shift+Down arrow   Extend selection down
Shift+Left arrow   Extend selection left
Shift+Up arrow   Extend selection up
Down arrow   Move selection down
End   Move selection to end
Home   Move selection to home
Left arrow   Move selection left
Page down   Move selection page down
Page up   Move selection page up
Right arrow   Move selection right
Up arrow   Move selection up
Shift+]   Thumbnail size next
Shift+[Thumbnail size previous
Shift+\   Toggle panel view

Timeline Panel

Shift+Del	Clear selection
Del	Delete and close gap
Alt+Shift+, (comma)	Nudge clip left five frames
Alt+, (comma)	Nudge clip left one frame
Alt+Shift+. (period)	Nudge clip right five frames
Alt+. (period)	Nudge clip right one frame
C	Activate Razor tool
V	Activate Selection tool
Alt+[	Set work area bar In point
Alt+]	Set work area bar Out point
Alt+Shift+Left	Slide clip left five frames
Alt+Left	Slide clip left one frame
Alt+Shift+Right arrow	Slide clip right five frames
Alt+Right arrow	Slide clip right one frame
Ctrl+Alt+Shift+Left arrow	Slip clip left five frames
Ctrl+Alt+Left arrow	Slip clip left one frame
Ctrl+Alt+Shift+Right arrow	Slip clip right five frames
Ctrl+Alt+Right arrow	Slip clip right one frame
X	Time Stretch options

Titler Panel

Alt+Shift+Left arrow	Decrease kerning five units
Alt+Left arrow	Decrease kerning one unit
Alt+Shift+Down arrow	Decrease leading five units
Alt+Down arrow	Decrease leading one unit
Ctrl+Alt+Shift+Left arrow	Decrease text size five points
Ctrl+Alt+Left arrow	Decrease text size one point
E	Activate Ellipse tool
Alt+Shift+Right arrow	Increase kerning five units
Alt+Right arrow	Increase kerning one unit

Alt+Shift+Up arrow	Increase leading five units
Alt+Up arrow	Increase leading one unit
Ctrl+Alt+Shift+Right arrow	Increase text size five points
Ctrl+Alt+Right arrow	Increase text size one point
Ctrl+Alt+Shift+C	Copyright symbol
Ctrl+Alt+Shift+R	Registered symbol
L	Activate Line tool
Shift+Down arrow	Nudge objects down five units
Down arrow	Nudge objects down one unit
Shift+Left arrow	Nudge objects left five units
Left arrow	Nudge objects left one unit
Shift+Right arrow	Nudge objects right five units
Right arrow	Nudge objects right one unit
Shift+Up arrow	Nudge objects up five units
Up arrow	Nudge objects up one unit
Ctrl+Shift+D	Position objects on bottom safe margin
Ctrl+Shift+F	Position objects on left safe margin
Ctrl+Shift+O	Position objects on top safe margin
R	Activate Rectangle tool
O	Activate Rotation tool
V	Activate Rounded Rectangle tool
T	Activate Type tool
C	Activate Vertical Type tool

DVD Layout Panel

. (period)	Decrement
= (equal sign)	Increment
Down arrow	Move object down
Up arrow	Move object up
Left arrow	Move object left
Right arrow	Move object right

Index

B

E

H

I

N

O

P

Q – R

S

W

X – Y – Z

Key Terms

Don't let unfamiliar terms discourage you from learning all you can about Premiere Elements. If you don't completely understand what one of these words means, flip to the indicated page, read the full definition there, and find techniques related to that term.

Alpha channel   *The area of a graphic or video clip that Premiere Elements reads as transparent. This transparency can be inherent in the native file, as with a Photoshop file that has no background layer, or the alpha channel can be created in Premiere Elements by using the Key effects to define color ranges as transparent.*   **Page 290**

Analog   *Literally meaning a representation of something else, the word refers to the recording of sound or images with traditional, non-computer-based means, such as a vinyl record album or a VHS videotape.*   **35**

Auto-play DVD   *A DVD in which the video automatically begins to play when it is loaded into a DVD player without first launching a splash screen or menu.*   **352**

AV inputs   *The usually red, white, and yellow (white and yellow only on a monaural unit) RCA-style jacks used for connecting an analog camcorder to a television or other playback device.*   **50**

Bézier   *A system for controlling a curve's shape by manipulating handles at the end points of the curve.*   **227**

Capture   *The process by which video is transferred from a camcorder to a computer-based editing program and, if necessary, digitized in the process.*   **34**

Chapter markers   *Designated points in a video that the viewer can quickly jump to by following links from a DVD menu.*   **356**

Clip   *Any graphic, still, audio, or video segment placed on the Timeline in a video project.*   **4**

CTI   *The current time indicator; the vertical hairline that indicates your frame position on the Timeline.*   **4**

Deinterlace   *The process of converting interlaced images into noninterlaced form by creating two frames out of one interlaced frame.*   **169**

Digital   *The recording and processing of any information, including picture and sound, using mathematical measurements, as in the way computers use chains of 1s and 0s to represent all data.*   **Page 35**

Digital video   *Video which records sound and motion as computer data, or chains of 1s and 0s. Also called DV.*   **16**

Digitizing   *The process of converting analog information or video into computer files or digital information.*   **36**

DV bridge   *A hardware device that connects an analog camcorder to a computer for the purpose of converting the analog video stream into digital video files.*   **48**

DV-AVI   *A PC-based video file format, designated by the file extension* .avi, *but distinguished from other kinds of AVI files by its use of the near-lossless DV codec, or file compression system. Because of its perfect balance of size and quality, it is the preferred video format for PC-based video editors as well as being the universal language that all PC-based video-editing software speaks.*   **17**

FireWire   *Initially a brand name for Apple's high-speed data connection, it has become universal shorthand for any OHCI-Compliant IEEE-1394 connection. It is also the current standard for transferring digital video data from a camcorder to a computer and back again.*   **16**

Folders   *A sorting system used in the Media panel in which clips can be stored in collections and subcollections for easy access and categorization.*   **4**

Interactive marker   *Marks a point in a video where an event should take place.*   **184**

Interlaced   *Two video frames merged into one using each frame's odd or even fields. Interlaced video draws only half of the lines on the screen for each frame, taking advantage of the time it takes for a image to fade on a TV and giving the impression of double the actual refresh rate, helping to prevent flicker.*   **169**